MW00615270

COMIC BOOK ARTIST™
COLLECTION VOLUME 1
CELEBRATING THE LIVES & WORK OF THE GREAT CARTOONISTS, WRITERS, & EDITORS

EDITED BY JON B. COOKE • TWOMORROWS PUBLISHING • RALEIGH, NORTH CAROLINA

Dedicated to my one true love

Beth Ann

COMIC BOOK ARTIST Collection, Volume One
Compiling *Comic Book Artist* #1-3, plus new material
©2000 Jon B. Cooke & TwoMorrows Publishing

TwoMorrows Publishing, 1812 Park Drive, Raleigh, NC 27605
(919) 833-8092 • FAX: (919) 833-8023
E-Mail: twomorrow@aol.com • Web: www.twomorrows.com

ISBN 1-893905-03-9

June 2000
First Printing • Printed in Canada

"Woody" mascot illustration by J.D. King
Logo design by Arlen Schumer

The Comic Book Renaissance

Forget Watergate & Disco! Reconsidering Comics of the '70s

If you were alive during those days of the "Me" decade, you gotta admit that a lot about the '70s sucked. Insipid corporate rock dominated the airwaves; disaster movie after disaster movie lived up to their name; America's debacle in Vietnam, along with the tragedy of Watergate, helped foster a crippling national cynicism; mood rings and *Charlie's Angels* came into vogue; and don't get me started on the advent of disco music! Though we generally dismiss those lackluster years as a retreat from the progressive, experimental days of the 1960s, certain aspects of our culture did blossom, including—for a few years—the quality of mainstream comic books. Perhaps it was the "first-generation" comics fan's rise to professional status in the field, giving young creators a chance to play in the DC and Marvel playgrounds. Or maybe it was the influence of the subversive, often sublime underground comix movement rubbing off on the "Big Two" and their competitors, offering a creative challenge to simply try something different. Or could it be this "renaissance" is a sentimental, nostalgic illusion, the books a result of publishers desperately scrambling to salvage a drifting audience, kids losing interest in comics and attracted to the more hedonistic pleasures of the time?

Whatever. Comics in the early '70s were cool. Seasoned vets, perhaps taking a cue from the creative goings-on in Haight-Asbury, came roaring into the new decade, producing often the best work of their careers. Jack "The King" Kirby was creating new universes at DC with his Fourth World. Steve Ditko was exploring the rights and wrongs of our culture with his idiosyncratic, often brilliant Mr. A. Gil Kane, creatively unleashed, found a new dynamic, lively approach to his artistry. Joe Kubert pounced upon his status as editor-artist with vigor, executing a rendition of Tarzan still unsurpassed. Alex Toth, the artist's artist, skipped from publisher to publisher, refining his divine design sense and cinematic approach. Will Eisner discovered a new, more appreciative generation of readers, emboldening him to stretch the barriers of sequential storytelling and to draw the stories he wanted to tell. And, on his good days, nobody could touch the exquisite rendering of Wally Wood.

And then, perhaps most importantly, there was the New Blood, infusing the once-sedate industry with sheer unbridled enthusiasm and exploding talent. With the support of those Young Turks, Neal Adams, Roy Thomas, and Archie Goodwin (themselves only a few years older than their charges) nurturing and inspiring an entire generation of artists and writers—talented comics fans determined to bust wide open the closed-shop mentalities of the industry. And this New Blood, sparked by an appreciation for the "Good Stuff" of the past—the works of Lou Fine, Jack Cole, Harvey Kurtzman, Bernie Kriegstein, and so many others—did it hardly for money (of which there was little) or prestige (of which there was virtually nil), but out of pure love for the art form.

Bernie Wrightson, Barry Windsor-Smith, Michael W. Kaluta, Ralph Reese, Jeffrey Jones, Alan Weiss, Howard Chaykin, Mike Ploog, Jim Starlin, P. Craig Russell, Paul Gulacy, Vaughn Bodé, are only a few of the multitude of young artists whose work grew in leaps and bounds during the decade, embracing the freedom of the comic book format and generally going to town. And *Comic Book Artist*, a magazine devoted to the great artists, writers, editors, and publishers of the past, remembers and celebrates their achievements.

CBA seems to have struck a chord with today's readership as we've quickly grown—in our brief two years of existence—from quarterly, 100-page status to today's bi-monthly issues of varying page count. Featuring predominately interviews with the comic book "players" of yesteryear, we've been nominated for numerous industry awards and we're gratified circulation continues to rise on our retrospectives of the comics of the 1960s, '70s, and '80s. And we are thankful to our loyal following for sticking with us, whether the subject is DC, Marvel, Warren, or independent comics. We promise you the best is yet to come.

But in this, our inaugural collection compiling the first three sold-out issues of *CBA*, we think you'll find some neat stuff: Celebrations of the editor-artist era at DC Comics between 1967-74, Marvel's Second Wave of the early '70s, and an in-depth examination of Neal Adams and his Marvel Age of Comics. Plus we've thrown in some new material to jazz things up: A thorough look at Neal Adams' DC magnum opus, *Superman vs. Muhammad Ali,* an interview with Marvel/DC stalwart Alan Weiss, and pages of unseen work by Jack Kirby, Jeffrey Jones, and Bernie Wrightson. We hope you enjoy the ride.

And just what the heck are my credentials to be editor of *CBA*? Not much except as one who has had a lifelong love for comics. My brothers—Richie and Chris (the two oldest), and especially my younger brother Andy—and I shared an admiration for Marvel, DC, Warren, and the undergrounds so much that we started our own fanzine in the early '70s, *The Omega Comics Magazine Review* (thankfully shortened to *Omegazine* by our seventh—and last—issue). We were lucky to have achieved a circulation of thirty copies, but each issue of the short-lived 'zine was a labor of love, drenched in respect for the great comics of the day, and we did it for each other anyway, psyched to collaborate on a common project. And I never forgot how much fun it was to produce each issue, and that enthusiasm led me to chose art directing and graphic design as my vocation, so I'll always be grateful to my siblings, *OCMR,* and comic books. Honestly, *CBA* is probably my attempt to recapture not only the thrill of reading the comics of the early '70s and their celebration, but also to experience the kindred enthusiasm of doing a job well done together. I just hope I've done my new "brothers," publisher John Morrow, Roy Thomas, Alex Toth, Chris Knowles, David A. Roach, Trina, Jon B. Knutson, Fred Hembeck, Jim Amash, and so many others, justice with the final product. Thank you all.

Enough rhapsodizing. Now, get to it, kind reader: Prepare to re-enter a world when comics were thriving and the creators were challenged to brought to life innovative work. Welcome to *Comic Book Artist.*

— *Jon B. Cooke,* CBA *editor*

Above: *J.D. King, artist of our Woody icon on page two, will probably kill me for this, but here's his 1975 cover to the never-completed first issue of ye ed's* Omegazine.
©2000 J.D. King.

Below: *Ye ed in 1966 at age even er ying his avorite reading material.*

COMIC BOOK ARTIST
COLLECTION VOLUME 1

CBA Staff

Editor/Designer
Jon B. Cooke

Publisher
TwoMorrows
John & Pam Morrow

Contributing Editors
Roy Thomas
John Morrow
Arlen Schumer

Associate Editors
Chris Knowles
David A. Roach

Designer, Adams Section
Arlen Schumer

Proofreading
Richard Howell
John Morrow
Roy Thomas

Logo Design, Title Originator
Arlen Schumer

Cover Art
Neal Adams

Cover Colorist
Cory Adams

Contributors

Neal Adams • Jim Aparo
Sergio Aragonés • Terry Austin
BWS Studios • Nick Cardy
Dave Cockrum• Continuity Assoc.
Gerry Conway • Irwin Donenfeld
Steve Englehart• Wendy Everett
Mike Friedrich• Dick Giordano
Sam Glanzman • Archie Goodwin
Mark Hanerfeld• Carmine Infantino
Jeff Jones • Michael W. Kaluta
Gil Kane • Todd Klein • Joe Kubert
Stan Lee • Paul Levitz
Don McGregor• Dennis O'Neil
Joe Orlando • Tom Palmer
Mike Ploog • John Romita, Sr.
Arlen Schumer • Julius Schwartz
Marie Severin • Joe Simon
Steve Skeates • Walter Simonson
Jim Starlin • Roy Thomas
Alex Toth • Barry Windsor-Smith
James Warren • Marv Wolfman
John Workman • Bernie Wrightson

Cory Adams •Steve Alhquist
Atomic Comics • Sal Amendola
Jim Amash • Mike W. Barr

Alex Bialy • David Berkebile
Bob Brodsky • Garrie Burr
Kevin Eastman • John Fanucchi
Carl Gafford • Shawna Ervin-Gore
James Guthrie • P.C. Hamerlinck
David Hamilton • Fred Hembeck
Tom Horvitz • Richard Howell
The Jack Kirby Estate • Victor Lim
Bruce Lowry • Don Mangus
Richard Martinez • Rich Morrissey
Albert Moy • Amy Kiste Nyberg
Jerry O'Hara • Rick Pinchera
Allan Rosenberg • Fiona Russell
Danny Serafin • Glenn Southwick
Kevin Stawieray • Andrew Stevens
Tom Stewart • Phil Straub
Mike Thibodeaux • W&P Museum
Bob Yeremian • Tom Ziuko

Special Thanks To Those Who Helped Make CBA Possible:

Beth Cooke
Benjamin, Joshua & Daniel Cooke
Ina Cooke & Nick Mook
Andrew D. Cooke & Patty Willett
John & Pam Morrow/TwoMorrows
Arlen Schumer & Sherri Wolfgang
Roy Thomas • Neal Adams
Constance Mussells • Jon B. Knutson
Providence Creative Group, Inc.
Tim McEnerney • James Larkin
Paulo Chaves • Donovan
Graphic Innovations, Inc.
Alex Toth • Kris Stone • JD King
The Staff of Continuity Associates
Bill Schelly • Kevin Eastman
Allan Rosenberg • Steve Leialoha
Jim Amash • Bill Black
Marv Wolfman • Tony Isabella
Mark Evanier • Frank Brunner
Chris Staros • Shel Dorf
Bud Plant • Quebecor Printing
Ed Hatton • Glenn Danzig
Batton Lash & Jackie Estrada
Jerry Bails • DC Comics
Ian Cairns • Les Daniels
Randy Hoppe • Patty Jeres
Mark Chiarello • Richard Kyle
John D. Coates • Mike Gartland
Anne T. Murphy • Rick Pinchera
Fred Hembeck • Sal Amendola

CBA #1 dedicated to Archie Goodwin

CBA #2 dedicated to Wheffy & The Boys

CBA #3 dedicated to Robert H. D. Aherns

1967-74: The Era of Adams
Our thanks to DC's House Artist & the story behind the cover

No history of DC Comics between 1967-74 could be justified without acknowledging the enormous contributions of Neal Adams, an artist of uncanny ability and original vision who took that company—and the entire comics industry—by

storm. His superb artwork was as vibrant, alive and challenging as his convictions to produce the best work possible. He was for those years, the essence of change at DC and his touch permeated nearly every book, from the covers of *Tomahawk* to, of all things, *The Adventures of Jerry Lewis*. For an all-too-brief period, his "Deadman," a comics series rife with innovation and risk, was a bolt of lightning to DC's readers, as it shattered design conventions with glorious experimentation. With his long-time writing partner Dennis O'Neil, Adams redefined the quintessential Batman and made that character *real* for millions of fans, usurping the quaint campy image of only a few years prior. His mere presence in the office invigorated the staff, as dusty cobwebs were shaken off, and the challenge to do daring work was met by such diverse creatives as Giordano, Kubert, and Infantino. In the history of comics, Neal Adams matters.

Neal Adams also gives a damn: When I asked his permission to use an unused Batman sketch as a cover, I also requested his opinion on who was the best inker for the piece. He said, "Me." (Or actually, Kris Adams, Neal's daughter, relayed the message but, regardless, I was floored.) To have possibly the first new Batman image in a decade by one of his greatest artists is a coup and I am indebted by his support. Thank you, Neal.

His overall impact on the House of Superman and the field is staggering and, in celebration, *Comic Book Artist* is proud to feature a portfolio of unpublished Adams work in these pages. The sketch that ended up as our cover was discovered among Neal Adams' thumbnails by Arlen Schumer (my good friend, former Continuity employee, and co-owner of the art studio Dynamic Duo) while Arlen was compiling his seminal piece on Adams' DC years for *Comic Book Marketplace* (recently reprinted and still available—tell Gary I sent ya!). After Neal kindly inked it for us, he told the story behind the drawing: "When I was no longer at DC Comics [circa 1978], I proposed to write stories and do covers for Batman through my old partner, Dick Giordano. I submitted several sketches; one had to do with Batman turning into a vampire, there was this one, and a third one. But I guess that DC didn't want to get into the issue of work-made-for-hire, so they dropped it. It seemed

that DC at that point was being more flexible so I was making a gesture but apparently it was not welcome at that time."

Our gratitude and thanks to Neal, Kris, Continuity, and Cory Adams (who supplied us with the superb cover colors).

Welcome to this first issue DC Special 100-Page Super Spectacular of *Comic Book Artist;* and get ready for more excellence—not only from Neal, but the greatest group of artist/editors to work for a comic book publisher at one time: Infantino, Orlando, Giordano, Kubert, Sekowsky, Kirby, and Goodwin. Just turn the page…

Above:
Note how Neal reposed the fat guy for our cover!
©1998 DC Comics

The Daring & the Different
Celebrating DC Comics, 1967-1974

For me, it was those orange covers. It was *Superman* #233, *Superman's Pal, Jimmy Olsen* #133, and *Wonder Woman* #179 that got me hooked as a youngster to become a *bona fide* DC fan. I was an eclectic reader of comics before those discoveries, reading the spare Marvel of my oldest brother when he wasn't looking, digging *Classics Illustrated*, Gold Keys and *Little Archie.*

But it was DC Comics between 1967 and 1974 which gave me and my younger brother Andy the ride of our lives. I reveled in Kirby's Fourth World, while he grooved to the "teeny" Titans and endlessly traced Curt Swan drawings to do his version of *Superman,* "Mr. X." We were addicts.

And many of those books, to this day, stand as great comics. What recent books have matched the grandeur of any number of DC Comics from that era? (And I'm no Super-hero fanboy either! I'll buy a Chris Ware, R. Crumb, Peter Bagge, David Mazzuchelli, Evan Dorkin, Jason Lutes—to drop some names—and many others over a dumb ol' Super-hero comic nowadays.)

I think that it was the cover blurb on the first issue of Joe Kubert's *Tarzan of the Apes* that made me realize that I was experiencing something special with the comics National Periodicals was coming out with back in the late '60s and early '70s. It said "1st DC Issue" and while it was obviously put there by Carmine or Sol or Joe to differentiate this new series from the post-Manning issues of Gold Key's run, it also acknowledged that DC Comics were indeed daring and different. Along with Kirby's astonishing output, the odd and delightful books by Ditko, *Aquaman* by Skeates and Aparo, and just about anything Adams and O'Neil collaborated on, the comics of that publisher, at that time, resonated of innovation and risk.

It was also a time when nostalgia was in full swing, with access to reprints (thanks to Bridwell's brilliant choices of material, whether Fine's beautiful work in those *100-Page Super Spectaculars* or the priceless collection of Cole's *Plastic Man* in *DC Special* #15), and for whatever reason, some of the greatest creators in the history of the medium excelled at their vocation as never before. Gil Kane's *Captain Action,* Bernie & Len's *Swamp Thing,* Toth's *Hot Wheels* and assorted War shorts, Cardy & Co.'s *Bat Lash,* Adams' "Deadman," Kubert's "Firehair," Sekowsky's *Wonder Woman,* Kaluta & O'Neil's *The Shadow,* C.C. Beck's *Shazam!*… Lord, we could

go on and on, and with help, we will—in the following pages!

So I think we came up with a pretty good snapshot of National Periodicals in them grand old days. We were blessed to get interviews with most every major creative working at the company, from Carmine Infantino—the Editorial Director/Publisher who helmed the company through the Artist/Editor glory years—to Archie Goodwin, cartoonist/ writer/editor who brought a brief (but shining) moment to the War books and *Detective.*

My time with these people over the last few months has been glorious. From yakking across the kitchen table in Dick Giordano's Connecticut home, to chowing down Tex-Mex with Carmine Infantino in a Manhattan eatery, I have discovered why these artists achieved such great work. They are good people and, for the most part, the artist/editors allowed their creators the freedom to do daring and truly *different* work.

There were many, many other creatives whom we interviewed for inclusion in this issue, from Steve Skeates to Bernie Wrightson, and we apologize—but hey, we first announced that this issue was to be a 68-page book and we're delivering a honest-to-goodness DC Special 100-Page Super Spectacular at no extra cost to you! (Never mind the added surprise bonus of the revival of Roy Thomas' *Alter Ego* as our regular "flip-feature." Tell us if you like it!) We promise a special issue devoted to DC's New Blood in *CBA* #5 to give those kind folks their say; our regrets to all.

Doubtless, we left out someone's favorite comic or creator in this retrospective, but try as we did, we could not make the magazine any bigger without heading for a loss.

My sincere apologies to those who went above and beyond to help me and were unfortunately omitted from the magazine, among them: Sam Glanzman, Dennis O'Neil, Steve Skeates, Mark Hanerfeld, Paul Levitz, Michael W. Kaluta, Bernie Wrightson, Mike Friedrich, Roy Thomas, Gerry Conway, Len Wein, Marv Wolfman, Jim Aparo, Nick Cardy, and too many others. Your day *will* come…!

So drag out the funny hats, pop the corks, and let's get this party started right!

— Jon B. Cooke
April, 1998

Left:
Illustration by Carmine Infantino used in The Amazing World of DC Comics *#3. ©1998 DC Comics*

DC Timeline
Our sidebar feature, which runs throughout the issue, is a timeline examining the publishing output of DC between 1967-1974. I've included some arbitrary listings, most which pertain to the contents of this issue.
[c] denotes cancellation.
[r] denotes revival.
Listings are of cover dates (traditionally three months ahead of on-sale date).
—JBC

DC Comics Published Going into 1967:
Action Comics
Adventure Comics
Adventures of Bob Hope
Adventures of Jerry Lewis
Aquaman
The Atom
Batman
Blackhawk
The Brave and the Bold
Challengers of the Unknown
Detective Comics
The Doom Patrol
80-Page Giant
Falling in Love
The Flash

Director Comments

From Art Director to Publisher: The Infantino Interview

Conducted by Jon B. Cooke

This interview was conducted by phone on February 28 and March 1, 1998. It was copy-edited by Carmine Infantino.

Comic Book Artist: *What was your first official position at DC? You started as a freelance artist?*

Carmine Infantino: I was a freelance artist there, and Marvel was really kicking the hell out of DC. There's no big secret about that. Irwin Donenfeld (whose father founded the company with Jack Leibowitz) asked me if I'd like to become Art Director. I was spoiled dealing with Donenfeld and Leibowitz; their word was their bond—no contracts were needed.

CBA: *Did Marvel try to hire you in the '60s?*
Carmine: Before I became Art Director, Stan made me the offer and Martin Goodman backed it. They offered a couple of thousand more than DC was giving me. DC found out about it and offered the Art Director position, so I accepted.

CBA: *You achieved the position on the strength of the covers that you designed?*
Carmine: Julie Schwartz would tell me to go home and design covers which they would write stories around. I would come in with a series of covers starting with *The Flash* and later on *Batman*, Adam Strange, and others. Apparently, every time my covers came out, they connected and sold very well, so Donenfeld suggested that I should become Art Director. I said I wasn't sure at the time but I would give it a try. I took the job, Irwin left, and I was designing most of the covers. That was about the time that Kinney National, later Time Warner, came in and took over.

CBA: *As Art Director you designed all of the covers?*
Carmine: Yes. The editors would come to me and I would create their covers. They would then go off and edit the rest of the books. That's how it began.

CBA: *The stock of National rose during the "Batmania." Did that success attract Kinney to buy it?*
Carmine: That part I don't know. I assume that's what happened. Bob Kane apparently really owned Batman and Kinney didn't have a part of it. Kane came in with his lawyer and Kinney settled a deal with him for a million dollars, payable at $50,000 a year for twenty years, plus a percentage of licensing. I'm sure it was a minute percentage but that threatened to kill the whole arrangement, so Liebowitz took it out and the deal went ahead with Kinney National.

CBA: *Leibowitz took a position upstairs with Kinney and left National?*

Special thanks to Mark Hanerfeld and Joe Orlando for their assistance in getting this interview.

A Note From The Publisher:

Back in 1995, during the early days of our sister publication *The Jack Kirby Collector*, a controversy arose in the letter column of *Comics Buyer's Guide* involving comments made there by former DC Publisher Carmine Infantino about Jack Kirby. I and many others jumped in with our own comments, heated words were exchanged, and feelings were hurt all around. In the process, a lot of people were left with ill feelings toward Mr. Infantino, one of the true greats in the history of comics, and that's something I really regret.

Hopefully, this issue will go a long way toward remedying that. Despite our past differences, Mr. Infantino graciously agreed to be interviewed for this inaugural issue, and I'm pleased to be able to publish what I hope will be seen as a fair, balanced, and heartfelt tribute to all those great books that he, as Publisher, made happen. He has my respect and appreciation—for his willingness to be a part of this issue, for his contributions as a creator, and most of all, for those fabulous DC comics I grew up on in the early 1970s.

Thank you, Carmine.

John Morrow
Publisher

Carmine: No, Donenfeld left first and all of a sudden I became the Editorial Director!

CBA: *Did they just drop it in your lap?*
Carmine: That's it! Jack said, "You have to run it now." That was it! So from then on, I was plotting. I plotted the *Wonder Woman* series bringing together Dennis O'Neil and Mike Sekowsky—they'd sit in the room with me and I'd plot it, Mike would go back and draw it and Denny would dialogue. We did three or four that way—the I-Ching series. Then there was the Deadman thing. I didn't create the character; Arnold Drake had a tah-do with the company and he left and suddenly I'm plotting "Deadman" for about four or five issues with Neal Adams drawing. The guy who did the dialogue was Romance editor Jack Miller.

Then there was *Bat Lash*. I didn't plot the first one but it was so badly written that I rewrote the whole script over the finished drawings of Nick Cardy. That series I plotted until the very end. It was my favorite.

So there I was plotting, I was Editorial Director, running meetings, and running everything. I worked sometimes from eight in the morning until 11 or 12 at night. It was a rough schedule. Then I would go out on the road to work out the distribution problems—plus going to California to sell animated shows to Hanna-Barbera. I continued as Art Director, Editorial Director, and then, *boom!*—I ended up with the

Publisher job, too! Again, I kept taking on job after job after job. Also, in all that time as an executive, I didn't take one day of vacation.

CBA: *Do you remember when a bunch of writers requested health benefits from the company?*
Carmine: I think that was before Kinney came in and the lead guy was that guy who created Deadman, Arnold Drake. I can't verify this because I wasn't there but I understand that Drake went in to Liebowitz and said he wanted to start a union. So Jack apparently said to him, "You get the other companies to join and I'll join." That was the end of it.

CBA: *You came up with a radical idea of hiring artists as editors.*
Carmine: I felt that the company needed artists in editorial positions because all the editors at DC had traditionally been from the pulps; Schwartz, Boltinoff, Weisinger... all came from the pulps and they were not visual people. I felt you needed visual people. That's why I brought in Orlando and Giordano.

CBA: *How did you decide on Orlando? He was untried, yet proved to be your most successful editor.*
Carmine: While I was an artist, he would come up to DC working on a few things and we would just sit and talk. I just listened (because you can learn more by listening than anything else) and Joe was full of ideas.

CBA: *You guys hit it off.*
Carmine: Yeah. I liked Joe right from the beginning. As soon as I was in charge, I called him up and said, "Joseph, do you want the job?" And he said, "Absolutely." And he came down and took it. He was perfect for me; not only was he a raw malleable editor, but I also used him to train talent. He was so good at training young talent.

CBA: *Whose idea was it to do the EC-style Mystery books?*
Carmine: I have to be honest—that was Irwin Donenfeld. He said that he wanted some Mystery books. So we looked through the files and pulled out these old books, *House of Mystery* and *House of Secrets.* I gave them to Joey and he ran with them. He took 'em on. We did that but we were also doing other things because we didn't want to tip our hand to Marvel that we were going to jump into the Mystery line. We had *Showcase* and we were throwing out everything in creation in that book. Meanwhile I had Joe developing these books. Then I put Murray Boltinoff and Dick Giordano on those Mystery books, too, and once they connected with readers, nobody could beat us. Once we came into the field, Marvel tried but they just couldn't catch us.

CBA: *The Mystery books seemed to be doing so well that the Mystery influence permeated the other books as well, even the Super-hero books.*
Carmine: It was all over the place! *All-Star Western* became *Weird Western Tales!*

CBA: *Even* Plop! *had a Mystery influence.*
Carmine: *Plop!* was a favorite of mine and it just didn't make it, but I loved that book. It was developed between Joe Orlando, Sergio Aragonés and myself. We knew what we wanted which was lots of humor but we just couldn't come up with a title. Then one evening we were sitting across the street in a bar, having a drink—Sergio had just drawn a funny story for *House of Mystery* called "The Poster Plague"

written by Steve Skeates—and I think it was Joe who said, "This thing is, like, plopping all over us!" and Sergio said, "That's it! That's the title! *Plop!*" Then we got Basil Wolverton to draw those wild covers! We thought we had a hit on our hands. We really loved that book, and it lasted a while but not long enough. (Now I understand that Levitz has claimed that *Plop!* eventually did sell well but that's kind of hard to believe because I got the final sales figures. Usually you'd receive your final sales figures in six months and it just kind of crept over the line. In those days, you had to have a print run of not less than 300,000 copies and you had to have 50% sales to do decently. *Plop!* never made it.) It broke my heart, but I had to cancel it. I had to give up *Bat Lash,* too, because of poor sales. (I'll tell you something about *Bat Lash,* though: It was a tremendous hit overseas. In Europe, it was the biggest hit around and when I was over there, they asked to keep doing it but I couldn't afford to because it didn't work here. They used to reprint it over and over.)

Above: *Carmine said that this debut issue of DC Special was suggested by DC V.P. Irwin Donenfeld to celebrate Carmine's "final" work as an artist and his ascension to Editorial Director.* ©1998 DC Comics

Carmine Infantino on Archie Goodwin:

"In the passing of Archie Goodwin, the comics world has lost one of the best writers and editors in existence. More to the point— we lost a very good man."

CBA: Bat Lash *had a great sense of humor. A subsequent issue featured Mike Sekowsky doing the breakdowns under Cardy's finish—was that an effort to get away from the humor and get more into the drama?*
Carmine: Mike did *Bat Lash*?!

CBA: *Yeah, he actually did the breakdowns for the origin issue, #6. Joe Orlando seems to remember you being involved with the plotting of Bat Lash's sister as a nun.*
Carmine: But we never got to that. I had plotted a whole thing out. I was going to have his brother be a bounty hunter coming after him. All of that was plotted for later on. Nick was so goddamn good, though. I gave him anything he wanted to do. He was getting ready to quit DC when I took over there. Nick was having problems with Sol Harrison who used to complain that Nick never put enough fishes in his *Aquaman*. He drove the poor guy batty. When I took over, Nick came in and said, "Congratulations, but I'm leaving." I said, "Whoa, where are you going?" And he said they tortured the hell out of him. So I said, "Nicky, give me a chance. I just got here." And he did give me a chance and thankfully he stayed on. The guy is brilliant and so talented. We had a lot of good people coming on board then. I went to that outfit in Connecticut [Charlton] and raided them. I

Below:
A rare teaming of Infantino & Anderson on a Batman story in a mini-comic that—I believe—was a promotional giveaway in the '60s. Other pages follow on the next two pages.
©1998 DC Comics

got Giordano but what I really wanted was Dennis O'Neil, Steve Skeates, and Jim Aparo. I wanted all of those people. I needed change!

CBA: *Did Shelly Mayer tell you about Charlton?*
Carmine: No, that was my thinking. I was watching those books. He was my godfather, I guess, and every once in a while I would call him up and talk to him about some of the people I hired. Shelly told me Dick was not going to make it as Editor. I said that I was going to take the chance and he said, "Go ahead, because you can always drop him later." Shelly was right in his thinking. Everything else worked out fairly well. Then Shelly just wanted to go back to write and draw and not do anything else, but he got me on my feet, thankfully. Then I became President and Publisher.

CBA: *Do you recall a story that Marv Wolfman and Len Wein wrote for* Teen Titans *that was bounced?*
Carmine: I rejected it totally. I remember looking at it. They did that for Giordano, I believe, and after it was done I thought it was terrible. I wouldn't print it. As simple as that. I don't remember any specifics about it now, but I know that I just didn't like it. I used my own judgment.

CBA: *We've uncovered some of the pages.*
Carmine: Nick's art was gorgeous! What's bothered me about Nick is that he's not recognized. It's scary. In my estimation, Nick Cardy and Alex Toth were two of the greatest cartoonists that ever existed. Alex, of course, got some recognition when he went out to the coast to do animation but poor Nick never got recognized and I never could quite understand it. I missed him when he left comics. At one point, I had him just doing covers that were incredible and then he told me that he didn't want to be in comics anymore.

CBA: *Did you push relevance as a trend?*
Carmine: You're talking about *Green Lantern/Green Arrow*, aren't you? That book was dying, so I told Julie to do what he wanted with the damn thing—and I believe it was Denny and Neal's idea to come up with the idea of Green Arrow and the Black Power sort of thing; that's what kicked it off. We did some other things in there but we had to be careful because we had to remember that comics were entertainment. You could put out some intelligent stories but you had to be quite careful.

CBA: *Why was Green Lantern cancelled?*
Carmine: Probably for the same reason other books were cancelled—they didn't sell—in this case, the artist being very late. We had to cobble up the next-to-last issue out of reprints almost overnight. It was a marginal book and the printer's late fees killed the book.

CBA: *Do you remember the book taking heat? Do you recall a letter from the governor of Florida that complained about the Agnew and Nixon satire?*
Carmine: I don't remember any such letter. I would imagine that I would have seen such a letter.

CBA: *It seems that you dealt with just about every single issue except Vietnam.*
Carmine: We did in a way with *The Hawk and the Dove*—only we made it as a Super-hero strip.

CBA: *Did you deal at all with Steve Ditko?*
Carmine: Yeah, Steve came up to see me and I liked him. He's very opinionated, but that's Steve. He did a

couple of books for me but they didn't sell. He could draw, this man!

CBA: *Do you remember the genesis of that idea?*
Carmine: That was mine. It didn't work. I had Steve Ditko come in and I threw the idea at him. I called one the Hawk and the other the Dove. It was a clever idea and Steve wrote it and drew it but it didn't work. In those days, we were not afraid to try anything. That was my promise over there, to just *try*. I didn't care what the hell they were about, just try 'em all. Keep trying. It's the only way you're going to find winners—and we did and I think we had a good time.

CBA: *Was the problem with Dick Giordano that you just didn't get along, or was it what he said—a difference in management style?*
Carmine: Yup, pretty much. It was that and a couple of other things; but I did keep Dick on as an inker. I think he still inks for the company.

CBA: *Right when Dick left, Jack Kirby came in. Did you fly out to California to talk to Jack?*
Carmine: We knew each other very well from the old days. I knew him and Simon very well. I don't remember who called who one day—I honestly don't remember—but I said to him, "Jack, I'm going to be out there on some business and how would you like to have a drink?" He said, "Absolutely." We met in my hotel room. He brought with him some things and he told me how unhappy he was over at Marvel. He then trotted out these three pieces, The New Gods, Mr. Miracle and Forever People. He said, "These I want to do but I won't do them for Marvel," and I said, "Do you want to come to DC? Would you like to?" and he said, "I'd love to." I said, "Okay." And he wrote a contract by hand right there and we signed it. We were in business. It was that simple.

CBA: *He really did some extraordinary work for you.*
Carmine: You bet! He was a great talent.

CBA: *Do you remember Deadman guest-starring in* Forever People? *Did you ask Jack to put him in the book?*
Carmine: I don't think I did. Maybe he tried to juice up the book on his own. I didn't ask him to.

CBA: *You were also seeking other formats. You tried the $1 tabloid books.*
Carmine: I tried everything that I possibly could. Those things, strangely enough, sold well by mail and eventually we sold them out, but when they were out on the newsstands, they never did that well.

CBA: *You tried some black-&-white magazines.*
Carmine: Right. *In the Days of the Mob* and *Spirit World* by Kirby. They didn't work. They just didn't sell.

CBA: *Do you remember a book called* True Divorce Cases *which turned into* Soul Romances?
Carmine: Not good! I wouldn't publish it.

CBA: *Did you want to go up against the Warren books?*
Carmine: The reason we did those books was because we thought that there was more profit margin in those, frankly. With those, the break-even was at about 35 percent —which wasn't bad—but sales came in at 22 percent so that was the end of that. I know that Jack got very unhappy.

CBA: *There were reports that he was so upset with the*

cancellation of the Fourth World that he wanted to quit in the middle of his contact in 1972.
Carmine: That's not true. If he did, he didn't tell me that. First of all, I caught a lot of flak for hiring Jack. He was not liked at DC because of some kind of thing that happened between him and Jack Schiff. There was a bad taste left because apparently he screwed over a number of people, so I put my neck on the line taking Jack on. We tried. But when he left, we left as friends. He felt that he could do better at Marvel again and apparently he didn't do too well the second time. Unfortunately, Jack's writing was not up to par. He could plot well—that's why he did so well with Simon and Lee, because he would plot and they would tie it together beautifully; so I guess his dialogue wasn't strong enough, but I really don't know what the answer was. It just didn't sell. God, I wanted him to sell more than anyone else in the world because I put my neck out, but it didn't work—but neither did Simon on his own.

CBA: *Did you like your job? Wasn't it getting wearing after a while?*
Carmine: It started getting rough after a point because of the hours. Jack decided to leave. He came in and he said that he was going back to Marvel. I wished him well! We were still friends when he left.

CBA: *Why were his books cancelled?*
Carmine: Bad sales. What most people don't realize is that we had to be concerned for distributors. They were part of our company—Independent News. The distributor is advancing money to you all of the time. When you put out a book they advance you the money. They came to us and told us that these books after a certain point started to lose money and we should consider dropping them! That didn't only go for Jack's books but some other titles as well. It's a business!

CBA: *Much as I want to focus on how good the books were and how they deserved to be published, it is still a business.*
Carmine: That's how they viewed it. They weren't concerned with who created what or what this or that man did. They couldn't care less. Once a book didn't do well, *stop!* 'Course, it was costing them money and costing us money. We would usually give a book a chance with four or five issues, and if it didn't make it by the fifth of sixth, than we had to get rid of it. That was the problem. It wasn't only Jack's books but other books as well.

©1998 DC Comics

CBA: *There were three divisions in National Periodicals: Licensing Corporation of America, Independent News, and DC Comics.*

Carmine: We were all a part of one company but they weren't a part of us. Leibowitz was the President of the whole thing. Paul Chamberlin ran Independent News. Jay Emmett ran the Licensing Corporation of America. We each ran our divisions independently. Leibowitz would make the final decisions.

CBA: *So when the company was bought by Kinney National, all the divisions got absorbed by the corporation and you never had anything to do with LCA any more?*

Carmine: We never had anything to do with LCA.

CBA: *But you became President of National Periodicals.*

Carmine: Only the comics. Leibowitz left National Periodicals which consisted of Independent News, DC Comics and LCA. Leibowitz went upstairs to become a board member and I believe that Emmett and Sarnoff took over as head of that division. Then Emmett moved upstairs. All of a sudden, Sarnoff was the only guy sitting there. That's all I remember. Then Wendell left and suddenly I was appointed President of DC Comics.

CBA: *Who was Paul Wendell?*

Carmine: He was National Periodicals' accountant. When Kinney took over they sent over this guy called Mark Inglesias, and he, Wendell and Chamberlain ran the company when Jack Leibowitz went up to corporate. Wendell became President of DC Comics. I reported to him and he was very fair to me.

CBA: *Steve Ross seemed to have a hands-off style of management with the companies that he acquired as long as they pulled a profit. Did you receive much interference from upstairs at Warner?*

Carmine: The "hands-off" policy is pure fantasy. Chartoff Linkletter wanted to license Plastic Man for a movie but Warner was doing Doc Savage and they didn't want any competition. They had the kind of weight that could do it. Then when I sold animation and the movie stuff, I could not make any deal unless Warner got all the distribution rights. So much for everybody working independently.

CBA: *You went out to Hollywood and sold the Super Friends idea?*

Carmine: I dealt the deal with Joe Barbera. That was a great success but Warner had to get the distribution or else there would be no deal. They also got the distribution of the *Superman* movies.

CBA: *Steve Ross had a personal friendship with Gloria Steinem and he supported Ms. Magazine. Did her complaints about the changes to Wonder Woman affect the return to Wonder Woman's costumed persona?*

Carmine: No. I met her when she came down to the offices. She told me that she grew up with and loved the character; but that was it and I never saw her again. Then she went upstairs and I understand they backed her magazine. I heard nothing further.

CBA: *She wrote an introduction to the Wonder Woman collection that complained about how the recent changes deflated the character's importance to girls—y'know, when you put her in that white jumpsuit and turned her into Emma Peel.*

Carmine: I did that. I got news for you: The sales of *Wonder Woman* jumped like crazy. We sold 60-65% with those issues.

CBA: *That's right. It turned into a monthly again. Mike Sekowsky took over, and then, all of the sudden, it turned back into the old costumed character and Bob Kanigher returned as the editor.*

Carmine: What happened was that I plotted the first three issues and then I couldn't do it anymore. I had too much to do. I turned the editorship over to Mike. I should have turned it over to both he and Denny and that was my mistake. I guess Mike didn't want Denny on the thing anymore and Sekowsky was writing it himself. Then it bombed and it bombed badly. After a few more issues I asked Mike what was happening and he said, "I'm trying everything I can but it's just not working." So I took him off the book and he left. That was it.

CBA: *How did Bill Gaines become a consultant?*

Carmine: I can't recall whose idea it was but when they made me the Publisher they made Bill come in to work with me. I didn't mind. Bill was a nice man. We got along. After I left, they just ignored him so he left. One thing he did teach me was to save every scrap of paper, every memo, every document—make copies and save everything, because you never know. And he was right. So anything I'm telling you is fact because I still have the original paperwork and I can back it up.

CBA: *When did you start returning artwork, and do you remember any creative suggestions from Bill?*

Carmine: In 1974, we gave back artwork, increased reprint money, and we raised our rates. Bill really just came in, kidded around and we had lunch. He would look at the books and check the costs from paper to page rates—we went over all the bills. We'd sit and discuss them—the whys, what-fors, and all that.

CBA: *What was Shelly Mayer's role at DC?*

Carmine: I called him once in a while and we just talked. I remember asking him about doing the *Bible* tabloids and he wrote those for Joe Kubert. He also wrote the one about the New Testament but that was never printed. It was in script form—he wrote his scripts with little pictures. He did them all that way.

CBA: *You had to cancel Sugar & Spike because his eyesight got too bad?*

Carmine: That and bad sales. If a book doesn't sell, it doesn't sell. Eventually, *Sugar & Spike* didn't sell.

CBA: *Did Bob Kanigher just up and quit as editor in '68?*
Carmine: Bob wasn't feeling well at the time and he came to me and said, "I've got personal problems and I just can't do the editing now. I just can't." I said to Bob, "What do you want me to do?" And he said he wanted a break for a while. I said, "Okay, you got it." And then I called Kubert in and gave him the books. It was that simple.

CBA: *What made you think of Kubert?*
Carmine: Joe and I grew up together. We were very, very close friends and I also knew what Joe could do. I knew what guys like Kubert and Orlando could do. They had been around scripts long enough to know what to do and how to do it. I was not afraid of putting them on books. At the time the idea of having guys like this on as editors was shocking, but it worked.

CBA: *Did you have a special arrangement with Kubert for* Tor*?*
Carmine: Yes. I went upstairs and got permission. I gave him a letter saying that he owned that character and we were just publishing the book.

CBA: *Were you friends with Alex Toth?*
Carmine: I knew Alex. One time, Joe Kubert brought a story in to me that Alex had written and Joe said to me, "Alex wrote a story I didn't request! What should I do?" I said, "You're the editor. You make the decision." Alex was angered over that. I haven't heard from him since. (By the way, I'd like to take this opportunity to straighten out some unfounded gossip: In the time since I left the company, I've heard the rumor that Gardner Fox had left because I had turned him down for a raise. Nothing could be further from the truth! If Gardner wanted a raise after all his service, I would have given him one without any question. No, he left for a reason that I don't know about to this day.)

CBA: *Whatever happened to Dorothy Woolfolk?*
Carmine: She came in and did some Romance work for us but it didn't work out. The Romance books were dying off slowly and surely. I got Joe Simon in to try and attract the younger crowd but that didn't work. We finally dropped 'em.

CBA: *How did you get Joe Simon into DC?*
Carmine: I knew Joe for a long time, like Jack. We were friends. Joe came in with some new ideas: *Prez*, the Green Team and *Champion Sports*. They all died. It's funny: He was great with Jack and without Jack, his books... Jack was the same without Joe! Maybe because it was a different time. I did put him and Jack together on one issue of *Sandman*— Jack fought with me like hell, he didn't want to work with Joe, but that book sold like a bandit. Oh, how I wanted them to continue together but Jack wouldn't do it. He refused. Joe was willing but Jack wasn't. I could see the team work and I would make any kind of deal they wanted, but Jack wouldn't do it.

CBA: *Did you have a special arrangement with Joe and Jack about the* Black Magic *books?*
Carmine: We bought the rights.

CBA: *In '68, Joe Simon did a book called* Brother Power The Geek.
Carmine: Mort Weisinger was offended by the book and he went to Leibowitz. At that time he had an awful lot of

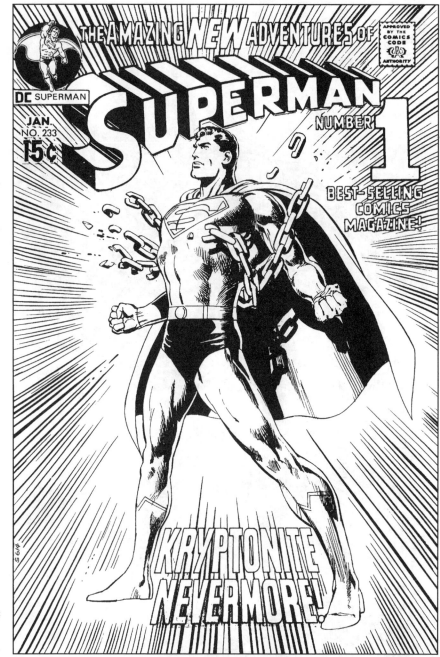

weight and the book was killed! The first issue did so-so, but the second issue was starting to come up in sales. It was starting to do better but unfortunately we had to kill it off.

CBA: *Did Mort want to be in comics?*
Carmine: I don't know. Leibowitz left, Mort said that he'd like to go. I said, "Fine." He went off to write books and had lots of irons in the fire. He was very well off, I think, and he was very inventive.

CBA: *Do you remember the format changes, when the comics went to 25¢ and 48 pages?*
Carmine: The one that really fooled everybody was the *100-Page Super Spectaculars* for 50¢! That one was done because we wanted to try something different. In those days, we were printing 750,000 copies of *Superman* with about 58% sales and that wasn't good enough. They were making money with these books but not enough. So I had to keep trying different things and I wanted to try this one package. I designed this wraparound cover and made Neal do the art. "The World's Greatest Super-Heroes." We followed up with other themes. The strange part was when the numbers first

*Above: *Sigh!* Comics were good back then, huh? Neal Adams' great cover to the Schwartzified* Superman, *#233. ©1998 DC Comics*

Above: *A rejected* Tomahawk *cover by Neal Adams.* ©1998 DC Comics.

that would be a great theme to kick-off a character with. The character's name, "Kamandi," was Jack's idea, but I created the idea of the kid alone in a post-apocalyptic world. That worked out fairly well for a number of issues. That was a good one.

CBA: *Do you remember the books going from 32 to 48 pages? That was a radical move, jumping the price nearly 50 percent.*
Carmine: That was Independent News' idea. They made that decision!

CBA: *What was their thinking—more for the reader's buck?*
Carmine: More for their buck! I didn't find this out until I left the company and it killed me, but they were charging us 12½% for their brokerage fee. Everybody else in the industry was paying ten percent, but we were paying 12½%. That was quite a bite into my profit margin.

CBA: *So it was a sweetheart deal—gouging their own company?*
Carmine: It went into one pocket. Do you remember those *Superman* cartoons from the '40s from the Fleischer Studios? Do you remember the '50s *Superman* TV show? They were bringing in a small fortune and Warner was handling it and my end of that share was becoming minimal.

CBA: *So the distributor made a decision to go 48 pages at 25¢, Marvel follows suit for only one month...*
Carmine: Then Marvel switches around and goes to 20¢, giving the distributor 50% off. When we went to 25¢, we gave the distributor a 40% discount. Marvel goes in and cuts the price 20% and gives the distributor 50% off. *Whoa!* They were throwing our books back in our face! They were pushing Marvel's books so it really became a slaughter.

CBA: *Were there any controls that held you at 25¢?*
Carmine: The price stricture was set up by Wendell, Inglesias, and Chamberlin. Marvel had the 20¢ books and they took the lead in sales. Why they took the lead is the 50% discount so the distributors and wholesalers made more money with Marvel. So the distributors put out Marvel and couldn't have cared less about us. Eventually we had to give 50% off because we were getting slaughtered. We had to drop to 20¢.

CBA: *Did you personally fly out to the Philippines to attract the new artists?*
Carmine: I went with Joe Orlando and Tony DeZuniga, who knew the Philippines pretty well.

CBA: *Why did you want the Filipino artists?*
Carmine: The story was that somebody said that they were going to start a union and they were going to pull all the cartoonists out of DC Comics—not Marvel, just DC. So I thought that I'd better protect myself—I don't know what's going on here. So I went with Joe and Tony and rounded up these artists. Tony and his wife ran it for a while: Nestor Redondo, Alex Niño, Alfredo Alcala, and a bunch of wonderful artists were working for peanuts over there. There was no work for them, actually; so we established with Tony for the artists to get a fair rate and he would get a percentage for taking care of it all. Everyone seemed happy with the idea and so was I. What we found out later was that the game wasn't being played the way we agreed. People didn't keep their word and the artists were being ripped off. So we changed management.

came in on these books, the sales were not good. We were shocked. Then when the finals came in much later, we found out that they did very well. You just never knew with a book until actual final sales came in.

CBA: *Was that an erratic process? Were the figures consistently accurate?*
Carmine: The first numbers would come in after three months. Then at six months you'd get final sales figures, and one year later, you'd get final, final sales. All of this has to be taken into account when you're putting these comics out.

I can tell you how you knew when a book wouldn't do well: If a book came in with preliminaries under 50%, invariably it would drop lower, and if it was over 50%, it would go higher. I always found that to be true.

When the numbers for Jack's books started coming in, the first issues came in at 50% right on the button. Then the next issues would start to go down; 47, 42. I'll never forget those numbers. Then one was 39, and I said, "Uh-oh, this is not good." I put Jack on other books. I created the *Kamandi* book for him after seeing *Planet of the Apes,* and thought

CBA: *Joe Orlando mentioned that it was your idea to have a coffee room where the freelancers could come and shoot the breeze. Where did you get the idea for that?*

Carmine: I remember when I used to go in there as a freelancer: You would go in, give your work, and could only meet the other freelancers downstairs or go somewhere else to have coffee. I thought it would be good to have a place where they would just hang out—set a room aside just for them. It worked beautifully. They came in, exchanged ideas, and looked at each other's work. It was stimulating and it worked like hell. I'd often join them. I also took my jacket off every morning, rolled up my sleeves, loosened my tie and left my door open so anybody could come in. So I kept the connection open all of the time. Anybody could walk in my office if they had a problem. Artists work with their sleeves rolled up all of the time so I made a point of doing that and it seemed to work. It made everyone comfortable.

CBA: *Didn't you miss drawing?*

Carmine: I couldn't as I was laying out all the covers! I still designed every cover we had, and *still* did editorial.

CBA: *Did you work closely with Neal Adams on the cover designs?*

Carmine: Yes. So I found that it was always best to give him a layout and let him embellish it. He would do a helluva job once you gave him a layout.

CBA: *Did you two get along?*

Carmine: No. We argued. He had his ideas and I had mine. He was very contrarian. He wanted to handle Deadman's writing and art. That arrangement killed the book.

CBA: *With the revamp of Superman, did you guys have big editorial meetings planning this stuff out?*

Carmine: Yes. Julie took over the book, putting Denny on it. That was his decision, not mine.

CBA: *Whose idea was it to restart Captain Marvel?*

Carmine: Me. I always loved the character so I ran over to Fawcett and made a deal with them because they liked the idea and had no objection. I think I goofed when I gave Julie the book because I don't think he ever really understood the character. C.C. Beck wanted to be Editor but he never told me. If he had I probably would have given it to him. Julie certainly was busy enough and he didn't need the book. I didn't even know at the time that they didn't get along. Somebody should have said something to me. You can't be all things to all people. Things can go on around you that you don't know is happening.

CBA: *How'd you get Archie Goodwin as an editor?*

Carmine: He just came up. I always liked Archie's work. Then he left me to go back to Warren. He wanted to go and I couldn't stop him, but I told him that my door was always open if he wanted to come back. He's a terrific writer.

CBA: *Do you remember when you first saw Walt Simonson's work?*

Carmine: They brought his work in and when I saw his stuff—whoa!—I said give this guy work right away! That other kid that I was very fond of—Mike Kaluta—oh, I loved his work! He was another one that was going to get work from DC one way or another. And Bernie Wrightson—when he came in and the work was terrific—though I think that Joe Orlando found Bernie. He did *Swamp Thing* and that was wonderful.

CBA: *Whose idea was it to get* The Shadow?

Carmine: That was Kaluta's idea, I think, though it could have been Denny's. Incidentally, Denny was a terrific dialogue man. When I used to plot stuff, I'd get Denny in to dialogue; that was his *forte!*

CBA: *Did you get Frank Robbins into DC?*

Carmine: Yes. Frank was a friend of mine. I talked him into drawing for us as well as writing. He did *Batman* for Julie. That was good stuff. He left DC pretty much after I left for personal reasons—he moved to Mexico and wanted to paint. He had problems with—well, suffice to say that he didn't want to draw anymore and left. We enjoyed having him. He was a terrific writer and artist.

CBA: *Was there a plan to have Jim Steranko do a comic book about drugs for DC?*

Carmine: Not for me. The only thing I remember is Jim talking to me at a convention and complaining that DC was coming out with a character whose name Jim said he owned. It was called *Talon*. I said that I didn't know what he was talking about but I certainly didn't want something that belonged to someone else. I checked with the copyrights and we found that he never copyrighted it; but I still wouldn't use it—it was his. So we changed our name to *Claw*.

CBA: *Do you ever look through the old comics?*

Carmine: No. I have no desire to.

CBA: *Were you looking to emulate Marvel?*

Carmine: No. I didn't want to imitate Marvel. I tried to avoid that.

CBA: *Joe Kubert told me that he bought your art table from you after you accepted the job of Editorial Director. Did you want to stop drawing comics?*

Carmine: I was too busy to draw! When I started, I had my drawing board and my reference files at home and wasn't using them anymore. I was at the office for 12-13 hours a day and then I had to entertain the wholesalers when they came in… I was never home anymore. In fact, at my apartment I had a convertible bed that I never closed.

CBA: *Len Wein says that he talked you into drawing the Human Target story in* Action Comics.

Carmine: Yeah, I remember that one. It was tough for me to do. I had to do it in off-hours and I wouldn't take the money for the thing. I refused to take the money because I felt that it was on company time. DC was paying for reprints since the day I started there. In fact, when I took over as Editorial Director, I wouldn't take any of the reprint money for myself. I'd just kick it back into the pot for the artists. I didn't think it would have been fair for me to have taken it being management.

Among the many other things I did for the company, was stay on top of the *Superman* movie. The first script from Puzo was just not Superman! I went to California and sat in a bungalow at The Beverly Hills Hotel with Mario and the producers. Out of that came *Superman I* and *II*. The producers were so thrilled that they insisted that I get screen credit.

CBA: *How come you always had so many corpses on your covers?*

Carmine: They sold! Some of those Mystery covers

Below and following page: *Licensing work on Batman playing cards showing the Great Designer, Carmine Infantino, at his best.* ©1998 DC Comics.

were our biggest sellers. Y'know who didn't get enough credit? Murray Boltinoff was such a fine editor. Whatever I put him on, he did well. He sold very well. He was one of these guys who is not heralded at all. I really loved him. He and Bob Kanigher... Bob created more characters than anyone in the business, with little credit!

CBA: *You started doing comics that had a blurb on the debut issue that said "First DC Issue." Newsstands would shy away from first issues as they were untried, but you appealed directly to the collector.*
Carmine: They seemed to sell well with that blurb. We were absolutely trying to appeal to the collectors market, but we couldn't forget our mass-market sales.

CBA: *Did you have an deal with Phil Seuling to sell books to him at a discount, starting the direct market?*
Carmine: Sol Harrison used to deal will Phil—I had very little dealings with him. Sol did all the dealing. But Phil started the comics shops, didn't he? The whole reason I allowed the deal was because there would be no returns. Sol came to me and told me they wanted to buy books at a greater discount, sell them around the country, with no returns. I said okay, but as long as they paid for them outright. Slowly but surely their numbers built and kept building until there were all those comics shops.

CBA: *You joined the board of the Comics Code Authority. Were you pushing for liberalization?*
Carmine: I think so. I felt that the old Code was pretty outdated and it needed to be brought up to date. I joined when I became Publisher and went down to the meetings.

CBA: *Marvel jumped in and did three issues of* Amazing Spider-Man *without the seal stamp.*
Carmine: I wouldn't do that. I had to get the proper specialists in to make sure we were saying the right thing about drugs. I didn't want to just throw the thing out there. We had a psychiatrist work on the thing when we did those *Green Lanterns.*

CBA: *Were you looking to liberalize the Code so you could also do more "weird" books?*
Carmine: Well, that word in the title sold books and we tested the Code with it and they didn't balk. We used it often.

CBA: *Were the CCA meetings boring?*
Carmine: Yeah, they were dull. I just sat and listened. There was one meeting when the printer was there and he complained that there were too many books on the stands—it was 1975—and I suggested that we all cut back to 20 books each and we'd have it out to see who could do better. The printer agreed and so did everybody else except Stan. He said, "My books sell, so I'm not pulling back." That was the only meeting I remember having any kind of confrontation.

I don't know if I covered with you the last year that I was with DC. The printer came to me in 1974 saying that there could be a paper shortage for next year and Marvel was going to put out 60-70 books. They could knock us off the stands, so I matched them book for book. I had to cover my rump. Of course, we lost money, and they lost money, but I wouldn't relinquish my space on the stands. That's what got the guys upstairs upset, because I covered myself that way. But I feel that I did the right thing then and I do so now. Once you lose your rack space, you're dead. I stand by my decision.

In 1974, DC was making a lot of money, especially from publishing. That year, we won every award comics had to offer, plus we were neck and neck with Marvel. We did so well that my staff and I were given stock options, and we did it with one-fourth of the staff of today's DC.

CBA: *So then in January of 1976, you were called upstairs and were out in the same day.*
Carmine: I had just returned from an intense promotion during Christmas of the *Superman/Spider-Man* book, all through California. I was ordered upstairs and was informed they no longer were happy with my efforts. I wasn't too happy with their less than thrilling attitude towards comics. I was happy to move on.

And another point: They removed my name from the *Superman* film credit—and they denied me my options! So I left for California. While there, my mom suddenly got ill and I had to return to New York. That's the way the ball bounces!

I'm more than comfortable to let history judge my publishing past. As for my present, I am very fortunate. I only deal with people and things I like and respect. ⓓⓒ

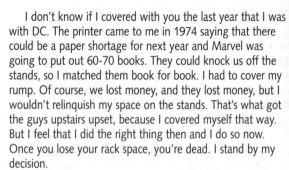

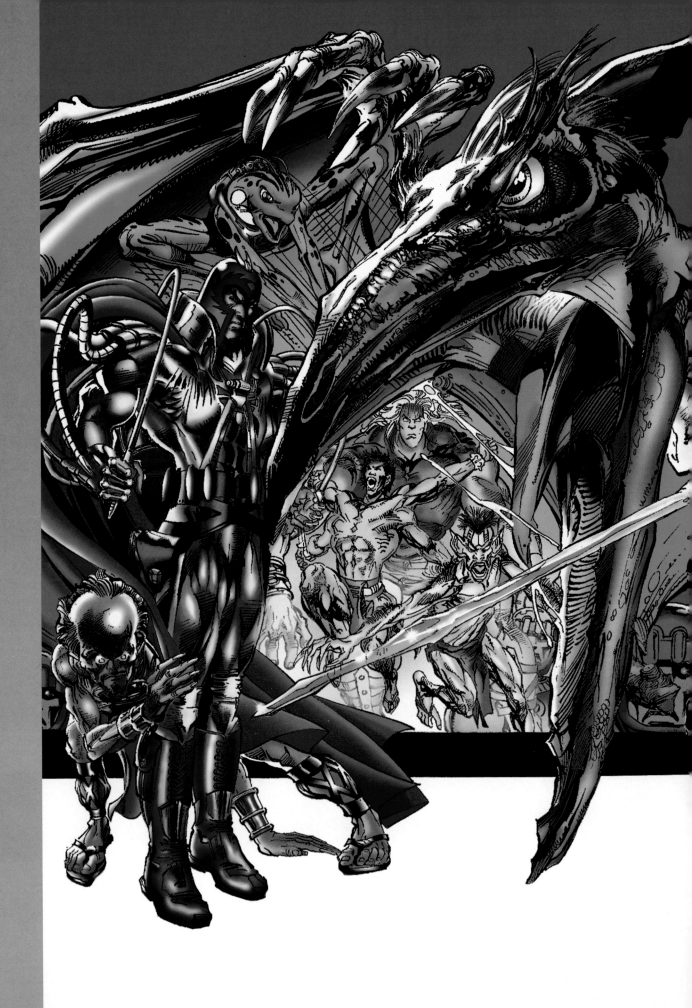

Orlando's Weird Adventures

Interview with that man of mystery, Joe Orlando

Conducted by Jon B. Cooke

This interview was conducted via telephone on February 19, 1998. It was copy-edited by Joe.

Comic Book Artist: *You started at DC as a freelance artist in 1966?*

Joe Orlando: I was drawing "The Inferior Five" and I became friends with Carmine Infantino. He was sharing an office with Jack Miller and I was delivering my work to Jack, who was editor of *Swing with Scooter* and *The Inferior Five.*

CBA: *You had primarily worked for EC beforehand?*

Joe: Yes, I was working for *Mad* magazine as an artist and previously I had been doing Science-fiction and Horror material for EC. I enjoyed doing all types of material, though my favorite was Science-fiction.

CBA: *How come you came over and did work for National? You were doing less work for EC?*

Joe: E. Nelson Bridwell was working as an assistant editor at DC and was submitting material as a freelancer to *Mad.* I had illustrated some of Nelson's material; he liked my art enough that when they were looking for an artist to do "The Inferior Five"—Nelson's creation—he suggested that I do it and I was happy to oblige.

CBA: *Did you aspire to become an editor?*

Joe: I had been freelancing for 16 years and although I was successful, it was a tough way of making a living. I found myself working seven days a week, 16 hours a day. When you're freelancing, you don't want to turn anything down or you might lose a client. So you keep on taking all the jobs offered. Juggling deadlines, stressing out and never taking a vacation, I found that I was very happy to take an editorial job at DC. In the early Jim Warren issues of *Creepy,* I was the story editor and I liked it. So when Carmine asked if I'd work at DC as an editor, I considered it. He asked me before it was known that he was to become the Editorial Director, so I wasn't sure if he was pulling my leg. Fortunately, he had confided in somebody else about his promotion and I heard about it through a fellow artist. When he asked me the second time, I was sure he was serious. Now I knew this was a serious offer and I jumped at it.

CBA: *When the initial offer came through, was it for you to edit a specific number of books? Dick said the agreement was for eight books.*

Joe: I think it was seven or eight books, but half of them were reprints. So our workload wasn't as heavy as it looks. I proved myself as an editor and they gave me more books and an assistant. Then I was putting out 13 or 14 books.

CBA: *Mark Hanerfeld was your first assistant?*

Joe: Yes, I was sorry when he decided to leave, and then

Paul Levitz came along, who became my best assistant.

CBA: *And Allen Asherman was your assistant, too?*

Joe: Yes. Very dedicated.

CBA: *Did Carmine express to you his philosophy about having artists as editors?*

Joe: We certainly discussed that aspect of editorial and in

Above: *A very young Kris Adams (Neal's daughter and manager of Continuity) appears in the great Adams' story "Nightmare" in this issue of* House of Mystery. *©1998 DC Comics*

looking back, many times we were asked to do impossible things by writer/editors who had no sense of the visual—to do things that wouldn't work and have to argue our way out of it. We just thought that as artists, we would do a better job working with talent. We did meet with a lot of resistance when we got up at DC.

CBA: *From who? The writer/editors?*

Joe: Yes, and some of the freelance writers. There was this clique at DC. Every editor, for some reason, had acquired a clone, the freelance writer who got most of the work out of that editor. That writer acquired a lot of authority and could influence the editor as to whether you worked or not, sometimes acting as editor. I think it had become a very exclusive club, that after a time was not meeting the market needs.

CBA: *Were you aware of the writers' movement which demanded health benefits from the company?*

Joe: No, I had no knowledge of it, though later I became aware of the movement. I believe I worked with anyone who had talent and filled my needs.

One of the first books I got to edit was *Stanley and His Monster* and in the beginning, I decided to change it into three short stories instead of one issue-length story, after I read a few issues. I realized that it took 24 pages to get one joke. So I made up my mind that it was going to be three eight-pagers with good premises ending up with a good pay-off to a good joke. I wanted to use Arnold Drake because I understood that Arnold made considerable contributions to the development of that book and I felt I owed him—but I was told that he was in Europe. I waited as my deadline got closer and closer and it led to my famous fight up there with Arnold that kind of made my reputation as a character. Arnold returned to the States—I had never met him—but when I did, he came across as a pushy guy who acted like he owned the place. He was friends with all the staff, and on a first name basis with the publisher. I was really pissed by this time as I had only three weeks to the deadline and I didn't have a script which I had to get to an artist. I kept sending telegrams to Arnold, but I never got answers. When I complained, I was told, "No, no. You have to wait for Arnold." So when he walked into my office, I tried not to insult him, but I did premise the idea of doing three short stories that would speed up the creative process and give me the opportunity to divide the scripts among three artists, so I would have my chance to make my deadline. We argued and he pointed

his finger at me and said, "I say that it's going to be one 24-page story!" I looked at him and said, "You're really saying that?" And he said, "Absolutely!" I said, "You know that I am the editor." And he said, "And I don't care who you are—you don't know who I am." I said, "Okay. Arnold Drake, go f*ck yourself because you're off the book." Arnold was taken aback. "You're telling me I'm fired? You know, I'm going to the Publisher! I've been here for twenty years!" So Arnold stormed into the Publisher's office.

CBA: *To Leibowitz's office?*

Joe: No, Irwin Donenfeld's. (Carmine hired me, Leibowitz interviewed me, and Irwin Donenfeld gave me a cover test—guess which cover sold the most? Carmine told me that I did not impress Donenfeld, but that he had told Donenfeld that he was sticking by me.)

CBA: *What I'm really trying to get at is the concept of "Artist as Editor." You and Dick Giordano in creative ways did some really innovative and good books.*

Joe: To Carmine's credit, he always gave me projects he knew I could handle. He gave me complete freedom and then he pushed me to the limit.

So, Arnold storms down to the Publisher's office and I was called in. The Publisher is sitting there with his advisors who were the print buyers, distribution reps, and the V.P. was there. All eyes were upon me and I was on the spot. I knew that if I did not impress Donenfeld this time, I was through. Arnold was sitting there with his arms crossed and a smug smile across his face with his hat on. He always wore his hat in the office (I think it was because he had a bald spot). Donenfeld looked at me and said, "Joe, did you tell Arnold

to go f*ck himself?" I said that I did and he said, "Well, I don't think that kind of language should be used in an office. It's terrible, deplorable and you should apologize to Arnold." I said, "Well, did Arnold tell you the reasons why I got so angry?" I told them and when my explanation didn't go over too well, he said, "You work that out with Arnold." And that told me right away that I couldn't fire the guy. I said, "With all due respect, I will apologize to Arnold *if* he takes his hat off." I went on to say that because in a million years I would never walk into your office with a hat on my head. I would have it in my hand. Some giggling started and Arnold made a lame joke that he had the hat on because he was Jewish, but then came the silence. Arnold looked at the Publisher and said, "Irwin, do *you* want me to take my hat off?" Irwin said, "Take your hat off." And I said, "I apologize for telling you to go f*ck yourself, Arnold." I knew that I had made a hit with Irwin because that night I had a date with a really gorgeous lady. I was trying to impress her, and we were sitting in this restaurant and the waiter comes over with a bottle of champagne and says, "Mr. Orlando, we are honored to have a famous cartoonist like yourself eat here. The champagne is compliments of the house." Even I was impressed, then I looked across the way from where we were sitting and there was Irwin in a booth. He winked and gave me the high sign. The lady did not see this—she was very impressed.

CBA: *Dick Giordano was Donenfeld's last hire and you were Carmine's first hire. But Dick says that you were in the office a couple of weeks before he was.*
Joe: Well, I was freelance so I was able to come on board immediately. I never quit *Mad.* I was still working for them and the only reason I later stopped working for them was because I had gotten a divorce around that time. My "ex" worked at *Mad.* Bill Gaines, bless his soul, was so good to artists, but he was even more solicitous of his staff. It seems that I annoyed my ex-wife when I delivered my work so I was asked to deliver my work through the mail room. I felt really stupid, and they would whistle me in when her door was closed, and I would sneak into Feldstein's office. After a while I just couldn't take that crap and I quit.

CBA: *Did the freelance work include advertising?*
Joe: Some advertising work: Storyboards, illustration. I worked very hard—the divorce wiped me out financially.

CBA: *You did a lot less drawing when you took the position at DC?*
Joe: Yes. I became involved in my job and Carmine and I became very good friends, and we still are. In the course of our friendship we discussed our philosophy of comics and what we thought about them, how they should be done, and why DC was taking second place to Marvel. It seems that the editors at DC were so institutionalized, coming off all of these wonderful accomplishments—taking credit for the invention of the super-hero and maintaining it, and acting like no one else could do a super-hero as well as they did. DC had sued Fawcett over Captain Marvel and won. They felt invincible. During the industry criticism of EC for wrecking the business, they never bothered to read EC, and reacted to what they read in the papers. They were getting their asses kicked in by Marvel at the newsstands and they were not reading the Marvel books—never analyzing or trying to figure out what the competition was doing. They treated their competitor with total contempt. You would talk to these people and they wouldn't know what was going on in the business except at DC Comics. The editors had this

great little gentleman's club: Every day a two-hour lunch, they wore leather patches on the elbows of their tweed jackets, sucked on empty pipes, and debated the liberal issues of that day. There was this contempt for the artist by this exclusive club of writers and editors; artists were replaceable.

CBA: *You had a reputation as a practical joker.*
Joe: When you come off of 16 years of freelancing, getting paid for having ideas and being able to make them into reality —it was like a vacation for me! I could take a day off to nurse a cold—you don't do that when you're freelancing. It was a dream come true and I thoroughly enjoyed it. I had all of these wonderful artists and writers, willing to work with me, and was having a great time. Practical jokes? Sure, it was part of the fun—my *"Mad"* sense of humor.

CBA: *The books seemed to reflect that you were having a good time—they were good.*
Joe: Angel and the Ape! Carmine and I would work till 9 or 10 at night, after everybody at DC was gone, and we'd go over the pencils, and we would rewrite the dialogue. Look at

the first issue: Bob Oksner's drawings are brilliant, the pacing is wonderful. We were having fun writing the gibberish of the Ape that only made sense when you read Angel's replies. We would think up a good line and laugh our heads off.

CBA: *With* House of Mystery, *was it your idea to do a take on the old EC books?*
Joe: Carmine gave me the book and I remember that I drew the first cover from Carmine's layout and I only had ten new pages to work with—the rest were old stories that I had to reprint. I had ten pages to make it look like a new offering. I read the stories and most of them were 1940s hokey. I had to use the old stuff because of budget. I decided that I would use one page to present a new character that would introduce the book, which is, of course, from my many discussions with Bill Gaines and Al Feldstein. I knew that they had gotten their idea for hosts from the old radio shows. For *House of Mystery,* I used the host to make fun of the story. I'd say, "Wait until you get to the ending of this piece of drek," referring to the reprint. [laughs] You know that if you sit in the movies for an hour and a half and the payoff turns out to be crap, you get angry. You're not angry because you stayed an hour and a half because it was entertaining up until that point; you're angry because the build-up was fine, but the payoff was crap. Rather than get the readers angry after they had read five pages of a story that turns out to be predictable crap, I would make fun of the payoff so it made the reader feel as smart as the host.

CBA: *What do you think made the books sell?*
Joe: The host character's attitude and the covers.

CBA: *Did you seek out Neal Adams for the covers?*
Joe: Yes, I sought Neal. Bill Gaines told me a long time ago that the best-selling covers he had published were ones that

depicted boys in danger. He got the idea from an illustration in Mark Twain's *Tom Sawyer* where Tom was in a graveyard and witness to a murder. That concept, in many different ways, worked over and over again. Neal did the best covers for *House of Mystery.* Many times he would walk in with a sketch that he had thought up himself and I would often get a story written for the sketch. It was a fun way to work—to have that kind of rapport with artists, writers, and creative director.

CBA: *Did you guys collaborate on the covers?*
Joe: It depended. Sometimes I would come in with the idea and other times the artist would. Once we were working together, I couldn't tell you now who did what. Some covers I remember—like the one with the boy under the bed with water around was all-Neal. The guy running who looks like half-man, half-bat was all-Bernie Wrightson. At this point, it was a bunch of guys who understood each other and I was the point man. They knew that I would be receptive and since my sales were good, I could go to Carmine and get almost anything by that was good.

CBA: *For a while there, you got Gothic in your covers, with women fleeing the castle. You went totally Gothic— you even started* Dark Mansion of Forbidden Love, *Gothics in novel-length comic form.*
Joe: That's because at that time, the Gothics in the paperback market were doing so well. I studied the covers on the paperbacks and they always had the woman in the foreground, a sinister guy pursuing them, and a house or castle in the background with always one window lit. So that was a formula I used.

CBA: *So that formula took off?*
Joe: Not as well as they should have because they were supposed to replace Romance comics before they were dropped. I edited *Heart Throbs* and *Young Romance.* After you read a Romance comic, you realized that the number one thing was that the male was always the answer to a girl's happiness. It was the farm girl coming to the city for a nice job and meeting a successful executive or an artist or a musician, and they live happily ever after. I started to play around with these basic concepts. Mike Sekowsky, who was a very good Romance artist, wouldn't work on one of my Romance scripts because the premise was too political. I had a romance going on between a liberal young teacher with a '60s counter-culture attitude and a hard-nosed right wing street cop. I started to create new kinds of characters for the Romance books playing with class and educational differences. I would define the characters, premise the story without coming up with an ending, and hand this to a writer. I started to address ethnic differences in Romance comics and was thinking about trying to do an interracial romance. I was also working on getting eroticism in the Romance comics besides just the big kiss payoff. Touchy-feely scenarios like our now-more-assertive '60s heroine running her foot up a guy's leg, under the table, while her boyfriend is sitting there at the table with them—the scene caused the artist to return the script.

I remember having a somewhat vulgar conversation, I can't remember with whom, but it was about editorial. The gist was that this was the '60s and what the hell can be written about romance? You think these girls believe that bells ring when true love happens? They're f*cking in grammar school, so how can we sell them Romance stories?

The *Binky* books became the "girl's" books. At the time, Archie comics were really selling, and Carmine came to me and said, "Joe, do you want to take them on? We've got to do something! You used to do *Binky.*" And you know the *Binky* style—I drew *Binky* in the old style—which was semi-realistic and not the *Archie*-style of drawing. Having grown up reading about the pulps and that it was a business where one publisher would get a good idea and everyone else jumps on the trend, I studied the *Archie* books and noticed that they weren't any different than the *Binky* books except for being drawn differently. So I said, "We'll do *Binky Archie* books!" I hired Stan Goldberg and we shared the same writers as *Archie* comics. Our characters weren't as strong as *Archie* because I really didn't spend the time thinking about them the way I should have, but as far as I was concerned, this was a quick in-and-out operation to make fast money. I analyzed the colors they used in their masthead, the lettering style and the art style and I duplicated them for *Binky. Binky* jumped on the *Archie* bandwagon and sold like crazy! 80-90 per cent sales on a print run. It got to the point where the publisher of *Archie* called up Leibowitz and started yelling, "You tell Orlando to stop using our red and blue in the *Binky* logo!" [laughs] I laughed when Carmine told me about that call, thinking what a great Supreme Court case it would make: "Archie Comics sues DC Comics over the use of the colors red and blue."

CBA: *Did something bad happen to the* Binky *books when they went to 15¢?*
Joe: I don't think it was the price—we were getting 80 percent sales and then one day they came in at 30. The next month it was 20. This was strange and nobody in the office knew why. At first we all sat around thinking the figures were a mistake but they weren't. I still can't figure why all in one month thousands of readers decided not to buy *Binky* anymore. The bottom just fell out of the *Binky* books, sales just stopped, and they were dropped. The Mystery books kept on selling, so it must have been the subject matter.

CBA: *Did you get Howie Post over to work on* Anthro?
Joe: I loved working with Howie. He went up to see Carmine with his idea, and Carmine said, "I have the right editor for you." I was always the lucky guy because I was the one chosen to do the new projects and work with new people. He came up with this wonderful idea that I loved, *Anthro.* The premise was the fight between a prehistoric father and son. I had been reading an author by the name of Vardis Fisher who wrote a history of mankind in fictionalized form, and I loved those stories and I jumped at the chance to edit *Anthro.* The *Anthro* stories had a great sense of humor and a lot of prehistoric reality. DC should reprint that book. It's timeless.

CBA: *Another book that demands reprinting is* Bat Lash. *Was that created by committee?*
Joe: It ended up that way. The first story was written by Shelly Mayer and Carmine didn't like it. Carmine's idea was a tough Western gunfighter with a gentleman's soul who liked good food, flowers and women. So we both rewrote the premise and then I turned it over to Dennis O'Neil for the final rewrite. After that I used Sergio Aragonés to lay out the plots and Denny would dialogue it over Nick Cardy's pencils.

CBA: *Was it your idea to do it more realistic than how it came out? Your house ads had a grim "Spaghetti Western" look to them.*
Joe: Carmine came up with that ad—before we knew what the book would look like. A lot of gimmicks came from my favorite Italian movie, *Big Deal on Madonna Street,*

where the characters spend hours busting through a wall in a weekend robbery and breaking through into a kitchen where, being Italian, the thieves check the refrigerator and sit down and taste the pasta and beans, like it, and eat instead of rob. In another scene, Marcello Mastrioni steals a camera using a fake broken arm cast hanging from his neck, using his real arm to steal the camera. This gave me the idea for a *Bat Lash* opening splash: Bat Lash's enemies are outside a saloon where Bat is trapped. He has two broken arms wrapped in casts; he cannot defend himself, so they think. But he comes out and blasts them because he had two sawed-off shotguns in his casts strapped to his arms! The Code made me take that out because they ruled that I was showing young people how to commit a robbery.

CBA: *Did you have a lot of trouble with the Code?*
Joe: We would have negotiations over my books all of the time; one of the pleasures I derived from editing was to test the Code's rules. I would come up with story ideas that, to give you one example, would depict this man totally beaten to a pulp, pieces of flesh falling off, and then it would turn out to be a robot. I could then argue with the Code, "It's a machine!"

CBA: *You said in an old interview that you weren't particularly happy with the humor in* Bat Lash. *Still feel that way?*
Joe: It was beautifully drawn by Nick Cardy but he pushed it more to the humor than to the straight. He tipped it a bit too much for my taste. He would focus too much on the humorous side of characters and stray from the main storyline.

Above:
Sergio Aragonés submitted this delightful "script" to editor Joe Orlando for a Romance story in Young Romance. *We include the other 9 pages, reduced from their letter-sized rendering (sorry about that, Sergio, but you are a "marginal" artist!) on the following three pages. Joe tells us this is the typical Aragonés writing format.* ©1998 DC Comics

pg.2

pg.3

pg.4

CBA: *You had Sergio Aragonés work on the book. Did you get him over from* Mad?

Joe: Sergio and I were friends from back in the *Mad* days and if you look in those old *Mad* issues, we were second-stringers in a way, getting one-pagers and only once in a while one of us would get a feature. We both felt that we were getting passed by and not getting the kind of material that we knew we could do. So we were buddies in misery. When I got the job at DC it was Sergio who came visiting me saying, "Well, Joe, how about some work?" So I thought about how I could use Sergio. Maybe he came up with the idea that he could plot Romance stories for me. He did and I would have a writer dialogue them. He went on from there to Mystery stories, *Bat Lash,* and of course, *Plop!*

It was the foresight of a man like Carmine who, number one, hired me—which allowed me to hire Sergio. Do you think that the old DC publishers would have hired Sergio Aragonés to draw? Maybe now because he's a proven winner, but not when I hired him! Would anybody have hired Sergio Aragonés as a writer? They would look at me like I was crazy and say, "What, are you crazy?" Did I get that attitude from Carmine? Absolutely not. Carmine loved Sergio and recognized his sense of humor and obviously recognized my talents, Dick Giordano's abilities, Kirby's abilities.

CBA: *I received the original sketch of Abel. What made you base the character on Mark Hanerfeld?*

Joe: I started out basing it on the biblical Cain and Abel but then I turned to the people that were around me. It's just a writer's trick to take people's personalities and inject them into your characters. Mark stuttered when he got nervous. He was short and heavy so Abel was short and heavy. Abel was a good counterpoint to Cain who was tall and thin.

CBA: *How did you get on* Brother Power the Geek?

Joe: Carmine called me into his office and told me I was Joe Simon's editor. Joe had *Brother Power the Geek*'s first issue written and drawn so I just did the paperwork. I didn't think that it was my kind of book but it was Joe Simon! Can I give him corrections?! Not me! Am I going to stand in the way of the man who originated Romance comics? So *Brother Power the Geek* did not become the Newsboy Legion but it was fun working with Joe.

CBA: *Was it your idea to revive The Phantom Stranger?*

Joe: That I had fun with. Carmine was always looking for things that had a supernatural premise to give me because in his mind I became the guy who could make supernatural things work. For a while, the Mystery books were the best-selling books at DC, better than the super-heroes. With Neal Adams working on *The Phantom Stranger,* I could not go wrong.

CBA: *What was Mike Sekowsky like?*

Joe: Like Jekyll and Hyde; he could be very nice or very mean. I was very friendly with Mike. When he suggested that he would like to be an editor, I said, "That sounds like a good idea." He was intelligent. I went to Carmine and suggested that he think about Sekowsky as the *Wonder Woman* editor. I assumed Mike would give up the penciling when he became Editor. That was not the case. Now as editor he approved his layouts as finished pencils and handed them to Giordano to ink. It was too bad, because Mike was a terrific penciler when he put his mind to it. He was his own worst enemy.

CBA: *At one point, you had 17 books. How the heck did you find time to read anything?*

Joe: I gave every story the attention it deserved because I worked many hours. When you're having fun, hours don't exist. I was getting weekends off and that was enough for me! I was going in the office at around 9:30 and staying until 10 or 11:00. Go out to dinner and go back. Carmine would always be there after I left. Those late nights were when we would take some stories apart. I would concentrate intensely on books like *Bat Lash, Anthro,* and *Swamp Thing.* The Mystery books had a big inventory. I would call in a writer (and I was working with three or four writers at the time and I knew all the cliches). Jack Oleck would come in with 20 ideas and he would go home with 20 stories to write. I found out that the most important piece of work an editor can do is not line-edit but idea-edit. At that point, you have either a good story or a lousy story. We would work through a full day, bring lunch in, and not stop until I examined every premise and every character. I would always put a twist on them so if his character was an 50-year-old man, I'd change it to a woman. If it was a present-day story, I'd make it 18th century. He would sometimes scream at me for creating these problems for him but I was making sure they would be our stories. We'd do this once a month and have an inventory of 20 stories, just from Jack alone. I worked differently with each writer, depending on their needs and temperament.

With Mike Fleischer on "The Spectre" sometimes all I did was come up with the Horror premise; then it was up to Mike to create the crime that set the premise off. We would come up with the idea of a guy being turned into a log and then being put into a sawmill and screams would come from the log as it was being buzz-sawed.

CBA: *You've mentioned that you had a real-life incident that led to those gruesome stories?*

Joe: I was living up on the West Side and my wife was eight months pregnant. We got held up in the daytime. We were pushed up against the wall of a church and they were kids, about 14. My wife started to cry and shake and she opened her pocketbook and I gave them all the money I had in my pocket. Then they walked away so arrogantly, so slowly that I got incensed that I couldn't do anything about it. I ran around looking for a cop and I suddenly realized the loneliness of being a victim. All that anger came out and it clicked with Fleischer's needs and so we created some nifty Horror stories. Jim Aparo's art was the greatest for this series.

CBA: *With the Code changes, you could use the word "Weird," and boy, you used it everywhere!*
Joe: I started using the word and Carmine decided that "Weird" sold anything. *Weird War, Weird Western, Weird Worlds, Weird Mystery.* We were pals and would share ideas.

The day that Carmine came in and told me that they had to put ads in *Plop!* for the magazine to survive was the day that *Plop!* died. It was never understood by the marketing department or the distribution salesman (who would come around saying, "Joe, what kind of name is '*Plop!* '? That's a terrible name! It sounds like crap!" I'd say, "*That's* the idea!").

CBA: *Did "The Poster Plague" start the idea for* Plop!?
Joe: No, I bought Steve Skeates' story for one of my Mystery books. I had the idea to do *Plop!* I was looking for material at the time. I remember Carmine, Sergio, and me sitting in Friar Tuck's, a bar across the street from DC offices, and we were trying to think of a title for a Humor magazine. We were sitting around drinking and Sergio suggested the title. Just think of it, there has to be two other insane people agreeing with him that *Plop!* is a good title for a Humor magazine!

Nobody gives Carmine credit for having a sense of humor but he really does laugh a lot. Carmine always loved the early *Mad* comic book. All of us agreed that there was an opening for a satirical comic book. Carmine negotiated with Bill Gaines (who was our corporate advisor) that I could try to create a satirical comic book. I had Sergio Aragonés illustrate "The Poster Plague" in his style, ran it in *House of Mystery,* and it was a success. Now I had a direction for *Plop!*

CBA: *What's the idea behind Gaines as a consultant?*
Joe: The idea that since he was the publisher of *Mad*—a fabulous moneymaker—he was to spread his magic around and help DC create some best-selling books.

CBA: *One of the biggest criticisms of Carmine's tenure is the tendency to cancel books after only six or so issues.*
Joe: Do you think he made those decisions by himself? He would be sitting around with these people who were supposedly advising him in matters of distribution and business. Carmine was primarily an artist and he had all these business people telling him what to do. I think that he was more at ease with artists like me than with businessmen.

CBA: *Was Jonah Hex the anti-Bat Lash?*
Joe: That was John Albano's concept. He came in with the story and I contributed to the character as it went on. It's an old idea—Jekyll and Hyde, Two-Face, a very tried-and-true concept. John and I had rules about Jonah Hex. You were only supposed to see his face when he was terrorizing somebody. Ordinarily he would look like a handsome normal cowboy but people took it over who did not understand that premise and Hex went around looking like the Phantom of the Opera all the time. Remember the first story "Welcome to Paradise"? That was influenced by *Shane* and you couldn't get across that love story with the ugly side of his face—it's always in shadow in that story. It's a visual representation of Cain and Abel; of what we are. We have our good side and our bad side.

CBA: *Suddenly you had all these Filipino artists working for you.*
Joe: I brought them in. I had a really good artist working for me, Tony DeZuniga. Another reason why I became a good editor is because I would pay attention to people who couldn't speak English too well but who could draw. When they showed me their portfolio, I never told myself that it was going to be too hard to work with this guy because he's not English-speaking—but I heard that over and over again from others. That argument, that it's just too much work and I gotta get home by 5:00 p.m., would not have allowed us to have Jose Garcia-Lopez. I went down and wrote letters, vouching for him, had to find a place for him to live. It takes time away from my own life—but this guy will now do anything for you, will not leave DC because I'm there, and will not go to Marvel no matter how much they will pay him—he had a lot of offers—but that's how you get that loyalty and that's how you get people knocking themselves out for you on books.

I think that Alex Niño was a genius.

CBA: *Where did Arthur Suydam come from?*
Joe: He's a kid from Jersey. I gave him a script out of my inventory that he kept for an entire year. He delivered three pages after one year. They weren't bad but they weren't spectacular. Any other editor would have thrown him out of the office. I just went along with it, saying, "Nice to see you," like I'd seen him just last week. "Are you ready for another script?" (laughs)

CBA: *How seriously did you consider Suydam to take over* Swamp Thing?
Joe: Very seriously. But it's a whole book and, well, he did take a year for three pages though he

pg.5

pg.6

pg.7

pg.8

pg.9

pg. 10

was still in high school. Those were the chances that I took. To me, I was in the great position of being able to say, "Well, so I'll write the three pages off." So I could take those chances.

CBA: *You turned* Adventure Comics *into an anthology book. In #426, you reached Nirvana.*
Joe: I got a lot of criticism for the series "Captain Fear" because I got dates wrong or something. I was interested in the Caribbean and Haiti and I wanted to create an Indian hero, because you know that the Caribe Indians in the Dominican Republic were decimated through slavery. They tried to get them to work in the sugar fields and they couldn't. That's when they started bringing in the Blacks from Africa. The Indians just died off, not only from disease but also from imprisonment. Using that as a premise, I wanted to create an Indian hero and it didn't work out too well. The script didn't work but the art was beautiful.

CBA: *You had some great artists working in that run. Alex Toth, Gil Kane…*
Joe: Did you see that story Gil Kane drew where he made fun of Carmine and me? He put us in the story as evil editors and we thought that it was funny. We had a good time with that and they were some very funny drawings.

CBA: *Did you give up drawing pretty much when you started editing?*
Joe: I would draw once in a while, doing a one-pager in the Mystery books. And I had a heavy hand with the young artists. I would tutor them but did nothing with the older artists because they were already great. I have this strong gift of analyzing work and being able to tell what is working and what is not. That's why I'm teaching at the School of Visual Arts.

Everybody, including myself, needs an editor when you deliver your work because you're just so close to it that you sometimes miss the obvious. You need an editor who is aware of art as well as writing. I think that I'm a strong plotter and I have an ear for strong phrases. I could find things wrong in the scripts and in the art and could make suggestions.

CBA: *Did you enjoy your time at DC?*
Joe: I loved it.

CBA: *What was your greatest joy?*
Joe: To see talent bloom. Absolutely. To see a little scared kid turn into an accomplished artist—to see Bernie Wrightson become a renowned artist—was something I loved. I also liked getting awards for my work. I enjoyed that.

The physical layout of DC was encouraging to a lot of ideas and a lot of interaction with writers and artists was because we had a room they called the Coffee Shop. We have to give Carmine credit for creating that one. In it was a coffee machine and a little sandwich machine. Anytime you wanted to take a break from your office, you went there and inevitably you would find three or four writers and artists sitting around a table arguing about a given character or looking for work or badgering you into making a decision to create something new so they can work—or giving you an idea. I thought that was wonderful. It doesn't exist anymore because space is such a premium, but it was a laboratory for ideas.

CBA: *Is the story true that Carmine was out in an afternoon—BOOM—outta there?*
Joe: That's true. He was in the middle of an editorial meeting with us and I remember him saying that he was going to fire all of us if we didn't get our books out on time—his usual threat—and he was called upstairs in the middle of the meeting. Then he came down and said, "I've been fired." We laughed—a Carmine joke—but it was true. He took his coat, and left. They said that they would send his things after him. And he has never set foot on the premises again.

CBA: *Is that being treated fairly?*
Joe: At the time I said, "My God, they used a goddamned meat axe on him."

CBA: *You seemed to move into the new regime and continued to be an important part of the company.*
Joe: I was lucky all the way. I was there at the right time in the right place. I look back and begin to doubt how much talent it took. [laughs]

CBA: *Did you look on that era as special years?*
Joe: Absolutely. It was a true high. I didn't do drugs so doing those books was like a high for me. DC

Due in stores May 6, DC is publishing **Welcome Back to the House of Mystery,** *a 96-page one-shot comics collection featuring some of the best stories from the Joe Orlando-edited* House of Mystery *and* Plop! *Included are Jack Oleck and Neal Adams' "Nightmare," Steve Skeates and Bernie Wrightson's "The Gourmet," and the notorious "His Name is Kane" by Mike Friedrich and Gil Kane (a story discussed in the above Joe Orlando interview and by Gil in a recent* Comics Journal *interview), plus numerous other classics. There's also a new cover by Bernie Wrightson. Hey, at least someone in Corporate is recognizing the need to reprint this great material!*

Previously unpublished, here are six pages from an unfinished House of Secrets story penciled and partially-inked by the legendary Jeffrey Jones and written by Marty Pasko in 1971. (See page 172 of this Collection for a photo of Alan Weiss modeling for this very story!) Our thanks to the artist for his consent to publish most of the eight-page story, supplied to us courtesy of Albert Moy. Art ©2000 Jeff Jones. Story ©2000 DC Comics.

CBA Collection Extra!

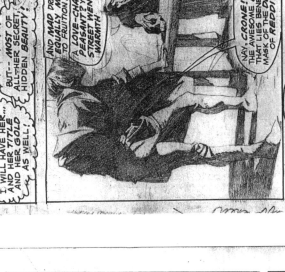

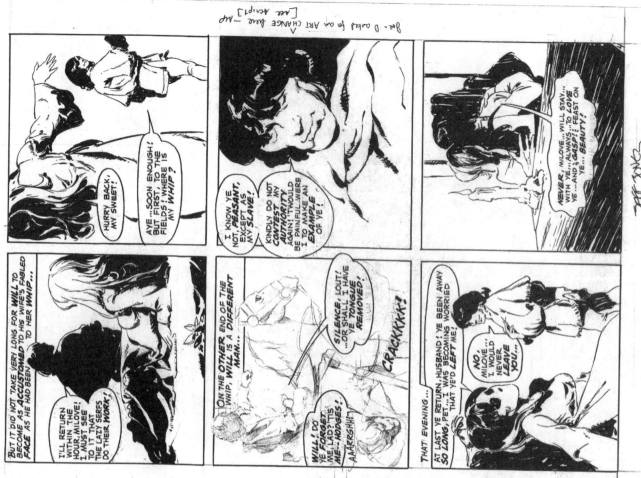

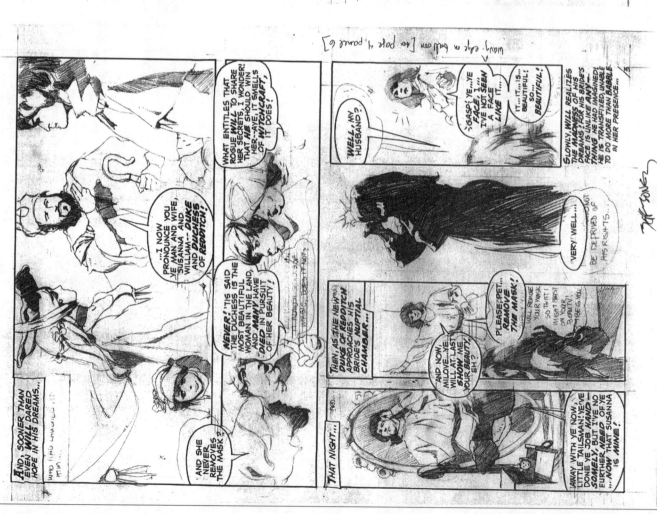

Ruining the West & Loving It!

Possibly the Greatest Comic of Them All: *Bat Lash*

by Tom Stewart

In 1968, a curious house advertisement started running in DC Comics. It featured a gangly figure, in silhouette, stalking toward the reader, with the legend: "Bat Lash. Will he save the West, or ruin it?" *Yeesh,* another Western. Wasn't *Tomahawk* bad enough? This guy did look strange, though; a little less kid and a little more rawhide—and really pissed about something. Maybe this *was* something different.

At the end of the '60s, one could feel that the usual comic book Western, the *Rawhide Kid*s, the *Two-Gun Kid*s, and all the other kids that were scattered around the comic book West, were dying. They might take a few more years to keel over, but as the months passed, they began to look more and more quaint against the background of Vietnam, riots, and Sergio Leone films. That was what Western comics needed—a bit less John Wayne and a little more Leone.

And in rode Bat Lash, skirting the John Ford tradition like Leone films skirted Monument Valley. Born out of an editorial need to compete with Marvel Comics with something different, and the decision to call in a brilliant young cartoonist to see if "he had any ideas," Bat Lash has been referred to as the first of the anti-heroes in comics, groundbreaking in story and art, and one of the best Westerns in comic books.

In 1968, Carmine Infantino, newly-installed Editorial Director of DC Comics, and his editor Joe Orlando were looking for something new. Marvel's inroads into DC's stronghold were at last being noticed (like the horse notices the fly) and it was felt a slate of new books would fill the

"hero gap." Westerns were popular at the moment, with the "Spaghetti Westerns" of Clint Eastwood breathing new life into a genre that had fallen into kiddie fodder. Why not try that same approach in comics?

This was when the young cartoonist was invited to pitch his ideas at a restaurant to Joe and Carmine—and cartoonist Sergio Aragonés had *lots* of ideas as to where to take a Western series.

Sergio explained: "They called me and said 'Sergio, we need a Western, and we need a cowboy called Bat Lash. Think about it.' So I did… The way I work, things pop in my head pretty fast, so as I was sitting with them, I was describing how the character was. So *Bat Lash* was born right there, in the restaurant."

And *Bat Lash* was different.

"That was one of the things they wanted," Sergio said. "They wanted to be 'different,' a different Western, but they didn't know how, so I came up with a guy that had good taste for food and music, and loved flowers and nature—and was a crack shot."

So Sergio wrote the first story, roughly laying out the pages and scripting it as he went. The finished art chores went to artist Nick Cardy. Cardy had been known for his long runs on *Aquaman* and *Teen Titans*, as well as his imaginative covers on those series. He brought considerable skill and feel to the strip, doing some of his best work at DC.

Sergio said, "I did, as in my cartoons, rough layouts, always with a note to the artist, 'please disregard my drawings,' because it's easier for me to draw the stories then to write it. (It's) easier to explain the situations."

The first story appeared in *Showcase* #76. It featured a devil-may-care character, a peaceful, violence-hating man who seemed to attract trouble wherever he went. He was a man who seemed to want to be left alone—with the exception of various females that crossed his path. He was the most shootin'-ist peace lover that ever rode into the comic book West. And he had a sense of humor…

"…But he was no clown," Sergio said. "The idea when I wrote it was that he was man with a sense of humor, but was not a clown. He would do things that will make other people become the butt of humor, but not him.

"There was one issue I didn't write at all (#2); I think I was moving to the West Coast. Nick Cardy wrote it. I was surprised, because he made Bat look like a clown. He drew all the characters so cartoony, falling in bathtubs, and hanging from roofs… It really hurt me a lot, because I didn't want anything like that. The humor should be the result of Bat Lash's action. I think that's the only issue that he's out of character."

"Comics were different then," Sergio said. "If a story was late, and they had a friend over there, they would give the story to them. They would take it wherever they wanted to without even telling the author, because they didn't think it made a difference. There were a couple of things that hurt; suddenly it was, 'Wait, I didn't do that.' They would change

---

Above:
Nick Cardy chose this Bat Lash cover as his favorite work for DC Comics. Note the difference with the printed version. ©1998 DC Comics.

For further insight into the creation of Bat Lash, be sure to read this issue's interviews with Carmine Infantino, Nick Cardy, and Joe Orlando.

Thanks to Sergio Aragonés, Dennis O'Neil, Mark Evanier, and Tori Allen-Williamson for their help.

the whole thing completely. That was… disappointing."

Showcase hit the stands in the Spring of 1968. Two months later, *Bat Lash* #1 came out, this time with a new member of the team, writer Dennis O'Neil.

"I was brought in by Carmine and Joe, with Sergio also involved," Denny said. "I worked from the plots Sergio sent in, adding my own slang to it here and there. I loved working on the character—one of my favorites."

Sergio said that he needed help: "At the time my English was even worse then it is now [much laughter] and Dennis added that wonderful Western slang. The stories and the plots are all mine though. My writing was very loose, and then Dennis would write a Western."

In the comics biz, there is usually a lag time of about three months before preliminary sales reports come in. This means the first issue must have been in the works close to the time the *Showcase* issue was done. But DC went ahead before all reports were in. That was something *new*.

In writing *Bat Lash,* Sergio drew on his love of Western lore: "I am very much enamored with the European westerns. I have always believed there's a difference between the real West and the Western mythology. The myth of the West is much, much better. If you try to make it too real, it becomes just a modern story. I like Sergio Leone, with the mythical towns, like the old TV westerns, the good ones."

And he even drew himself, sort of. "One of the stories I wrote about a really villainous guy (#5); I drew on my little byline a Mexican guy, and obviously a Mexican guy looks like me. I didn't know what name to give him, so I called him Sergio, figuring they'd change it. When Cardy took it, he drew me and called him 'Sergio.' It was never intended to be me, just a guy who was a Mexican."

Also the character of Don Pasqual (#7) is named after Sergio's father. "It's always hard to come up with a good name," Sergio said.

The series also tended to stay away from the usual "Indians as villains" stories used in so many comics and movies. This was on purpose, as long as Sergio plotted the stories. "The reality with American Indians is so different from the lore," Sergio said. "It's the only one that hurt. See, you can play around a lot with the Wells Fargo stuff, and stagecoach robbers and all that, but once you get into something that can damage… It's like telling Polish jokes, some are very funny, but it's racism. I didn't want anything do with the Indians. The reality is too sad. I think the story Cardy did had some [stereotypes] in it, but I avoided them like the plague. If I used them, I would have used them as the good guys."

"Bat Lash was one of the first anti-heroes in comics," Dennis explains, "reluctant to do good unless pressed or paid. I really liked that aspect of his character. I tried to sneak a little philosophy into it; and it was noticed by the fans."

And what future was planned after the meeting of Bat Lash and his long-lost brother? "I wanted Bat Lash to grow," Sergio said. "I was going to take a few liberties with the time period. I was going to jump him a little more towards the beginning of the modern century, parallel to the Mexican revolution. There was a lot of subplots I had in mind… I was going to make it like a saga."

The reason that Bat Lash had to turn in his saddle after only eight issues? "Sales, I imagine," Dennis said. "That's the thing that we most went by."

"It was a difficult time for comics that weren't super-heroes," Sergio said. "Marvel was increasing the Super-hero thing; it was a whole change of attitude. It was the period when the super-hero took over completely."

Was working on *Bat Lash* a special time? "That's one

book I'd drop everything to write," Dennis said. "*Really.* I had a great time doing it."

Is the book fondly remembered by many fans you meet? "No," Sergio said. "I see about as many of *Bat Lash* as I see of *Plop!* If they bring *Bat Lash* up, I know they're a true fan. 'Hey, they know about it!' I'm very happy about that."

So while Bat Lash rode into the sunset, he's gone but not forgotten. The dash for any *Bat Lash* originals that make it to the market is proof of that. One dealer who recently offered a *Bat Lash* half-page (basically one large panel) told me he could have sold it 70 times over.

If any comics series deserves a trade paperback collection, it's *Bat Lash*—even a black-&-white one. And how about a revival for old time's sake? Nick, Dennis and Sergio are still around! Maybe…?

(P.S. Nick Cardy will be a Guest of Honor at this year's San Diego Comic Con—guess who'll be in the autograph line with his set of *Bat Lash*es?!) ^{dc}

[Yeah, and behind me! — *Ye Crusading Ed.*]

Above:
Bat Lash's bounty hunter brother, a Carmine Infantino creation. From Bat Lash *#7. ©1998 DC Comics.*

A Tale from the Swamp

The Origin of Wein & Wrightson's Swamp Thing

While we unfortunately couldn't fit the interviews of the many artists and writers we spoke to who worked at DC in those great years, we have excised some choice comments from Len Wein, Bernie Wrightson (and a few from featured artist/editor Joe Orlando) on the planting of some sinister seeds and the growth of one great horrific idea: The roots of DC's seminal monster hero (before he was defined as a walking tuber!), Swamp Thing. First up, let's see what woeful tale the credited writer, Len Wein, has to tell:

CBA: *What's the genesis of the Swamp Thing story in House of Secrets #92? Was he based on the Heap?*
Len: At that point, I wasn't even aware that the Heap existed. I was rooming with Gerry Conway at the time, who coincidentally was working on the first Man-Thing story, but neither of us knew what the other was doing. It was one of those bizarre things. The idea came to me on the subway on the way into the office. I was going up to see Joe and I had no ideas but—I don't know what triggered it; something came to me and that story grew out of it.

CBA: *Bernie received a full script from you?*
Len: Absolutely. Bernie and I were at Marv's housewarming party and Bernie had just broken up with someone that he was seeing and he was moping. It was a cold Winter's night and he and I went out to my car to talk about life and relationships—we were such old hands at that point, being 20 or 21—and I told him that I had just written a story that had the same feeling as what he was talking about and asked him if he wanted to read it. He read it and said, "I want to draw it." Which was just what I was hoping he'd say.

CBA: *It wasn't Louise [Jones/Simonson] he'd broken up with, was it? She's on the cover.*
Len: No. Weezie, the dearest thing to ever walk the earth and one of the great unrequited loves of my life, was happily married to Jeff at that point, but almost everybody in that story is based on a real person who modeled for the art. Because of scheduling and to get everything done quicker, they photo-shot everything and Bernie worked from photos, the way that Al Williamson always worked for his entire career. The Alex Olsen character is Bernie, the mustachioed villain killed by the Swamp Thing is Mike Kaluta, the heroine was Weezie, Jeff was an incidental character, Alan Weiss was an incidental character. The whole gang lived in that building and we knew that we had to get the story out by Tuesday and so they took photos and worked from that.

CBA: *Did the reaction to the story come from readers or did it start in the office?*
Len: It started in the office, then the mail started coming in. Carmine wanted it to become an ongoing series immediately. It turned out—and this is one of the most prideful moments of my career—that the best-selling book that DC

published that month was *House of Secrets #92*, outselling everything. Carmine said, "This is a hit! Let's do a book." But the story was so personal to Bernie and me that we didn't want to mess with it and it took me a year to realize that I didn't have to do just a sequel to the original story, but I could start all over again from square one with a different character in a modern-day setting. When I came up with that, I went to Carmine and said, "Do you still want to do this?" He said yes and I gave him my new premise.

CBA: *What was the reaction to the coincidence of Man-Thing?*
Len: A lot of people thought that we had copied each other but it's just great ideas coming out at the same time.

CBA: *Did you work Marvel-style with Bernie on the on-going series?*
Len: I did. Bernie, Joe and I would sit down in the office, plot out the stories, break it down very crudely page by page. Bernie would go home and pencil it and then I would dialogue the pencils. Gaspar Saladino, God love him, would letter the first batch of pages and then Bernie would ink.

Next is Bernie Wrightson's recollection:

CBA: *There was another party at Marv Wolfman's house where you and Len talked in a parked car.*
Bernie: I recall Len offered me the "Swamp Thing" short story to draw that night. The deadline was really tight and I remember doing most of the work on a weekend. I had help from Kaluta, Jeff, Weiss, and Louise. I remember that to save time we photographed the whole thing. The bad guy is Kaluta who could make himself look really oily. I parted his hair in the middle and he had this great mustache. Of course, I was the hero because the girl was Louise Jones, Jeff's wife, who I had a crush on and I got to put my arm around her.

CBA: *Did everybody have a crush on Weezie?*
Bernie: Yeah, I think everybody did. She was a hell of a girl who was really sweet and outgoing. She was just a doll; the kind of girl that everybody wished was their girl. She still is a very sweet woman who I just love to death.

CBA: *Was* House of Secrets #92 *a rare example of using live models in your work?*
Bernie: I use photo reference from time to time and I blame Jeff for that. Jeff had some really good cameras, his own enlarger and dark room, and he got me interested in photography. It was just a passing interest but Jeff used a lot of photo reference. I really like the way that the story turned out and I was passionate about it. I had just broken up with a girl at the time and this story really touched that in me, so I just poured my heart and soul into it.

We did the story and I pretty much forgot about it. The

issue came out and apparently it was their best-selling book that month, beating out *Superman* and *Batman*. They got a lot of fan mail on it. Anyway, I went out of town for a week, came back and people are telling me, "It's great news! We hear that you're doing a *Swamp Thing* book!" I'm saying, "What *Swamp Thing* book?" It took an effort for me to remember what Swamp Thing was! So I went into the office and they said, "Yeah, we want to do a book." My immediate reaction was: "What are you, crazy? You want to do a period book?" Joe said, "No, we're going to change it around, update it and retell it in modern terms." I was a little skeptical at first and I really needed Len to come and talk me into it. I needed him to say, "This isn't what you think. This is what we're going to do: a comic book that has a monster for a hero and nobody will have ever seen anything like it. We're going to do our best to make a commercial success without sacrificing any integrity." Once I heard that, it was, "Okay, I'll sign on." The way we approached it, it was a new thing and a pretty innovative idea.

CBA: *Conceptually the book seemed to become a monster movie version every issue.*
Bernie: It seemed to become that after a while. We needed a conflict and he needed a different foe in every issue. It became so that we would sit around and try to come up with the new monster every issue which the Swamp Thing would fight and win the day. I just got bored.

CBA: *Was the Comics Code a problem for you guys?*
Bernie: They sent back the original script for *Swamp Thing* because Alec Holland died and was resurrected. They said, "This means that he is the walking dead and we do not permit zombies." So it had to be rewritten so that Alec Holland did not die. We later got up to #5 or 6 when we received a panicked call from somebody at the Code who said, "You can't do this! This figure is undraped!" They were saying that Swamp Thing was naked! Joe said, "You want us to put purple pants on him?" And they said, "Yes!" Joe went to bat for us and in the face of total boneheaded ignorance went through, panel by panel, from #1 showing that he had always been undraped—he was a monster! It has no genitalia and if it did, you couldn't see it because it was always in shadow. You can't even see the crack of its ass if it even had an ass!

Our final guest, Joe Orlando discusses the birth of the series:

CBA: *What's the genesis of* Swamp Thing?
Joe: I'm going to tell you the story even though there's a difference of opinion between Len Wein and myself, though I think that Bernie Wrightson agrees with me. I was given the job to create books in genres because there would be a slot and I'd be told to take a book on. I wouldn't bring in a concept to get an okay. I would be told to do a Western book or Horror book. So when I was given an assignment to do a new Horror book, I would think about what I wanted to do that was different than the rest of the books that I was doing. I've told this story before but I would read the *Atlantic Monthly* as I rode the bus as it went along Broadway. I was reading this article on the way to the office and it was about famine in the world and how to relieve it. The author said that food was cheap but the transportation to get the foods to areas of the world that needed it was expensive. The article also said that if only we knew how to accelerate growing time for food—plant life—and that was the story idea! Whoever could figure that out could rule the world. We were in a Cold War and if the U.S. suddenly

found the formula—it was the idea for the story. You can come up with a million characters but if the premise doesn't work, you don't have a story. When I was a kid, I read The Heap in *Airboy Comics* and I always remembered him. It's a cliche—a man explodes and turns into something horrible. In fact, the first story was done in *House of Secrets* and I fed to Len the idea from an old EC story that I loved (which I didn't draw) where they took the brains out of this guy and put it into an ape and the last panel is that it's Christmas time and he looks into the window of his home and sees his wife and children celebrating Christmas and there's a picture of Daddy. The family turns and screams and he has to run and leave. I thought that that's such a powerful idea and it's in the first Swamp Thing story.

CBA: *How did you recognize the series potential of that short story?*
Joe: I didn't. That was Carmine.

And so ends our terrifying tale. Be sure to be here for the upcoming "DC's New Blood" issue with recollections by more of the creeped-out creatives immortalized in *HOS #92!* ⓓⓒ

Above:
Comics went crazy from the swamp gas in '71! This issue of The Phantom Stranger, *featuring this dynamite Neal Adams cover, appeared virtually simultaneously with* House of Secrets *#92 (Swamp Thing's first story) and* Savage Tales *#1 (with Marvel's Man-Thing). Hey, isn't that Abby Arcane puttin' the touch on that guy in the foreground?! No wonder that Bog Beast is teed off!*
©1998 DC Comics

Along Came Giordano

"Thank You & Good Afternoon!" Talkin' with Dick

Conducted by Jon B. Cooke

This interview was conducted in Dick Giordano's Connecticut home and in a nearby restaurant on December 27, 1997. It was copy-edited by Dick.

Comic Book Artist: *When did you start reading comics?*

Dick Giordano: I was ill as a child, so my mother and father made sure I had reading material to keep me occupied. My father came home with the first copy of *Famous Funnies* and that got me hooked. I was mesmerized by the art form and started drawing when I was six or so.

CBA: *Did you go to art school?*

Dick: New York City had a progressive school system and I went to art school at the High School of Industrial Art—but they talked me out of taking the "comic books" course, saying that it wasn't a viable field. I majored in illustration and advertising art, and I put together a portfolio (which I have to this day) that's just loaded with drawings of handbags, couches and shirts. Fresh out of school in 1951, I coincidentally walked into an art studio that had just been rented by a comic book writer who recommended that I talk to Jerry Iger (whose shop was still operating at that time). I went over and got a job within minutes, stayed there for nine months, and went freelance thereafter. At Iger's, I did grunt work: Erasing pages and, by the time I left, I was only inking backgrounds. I wasn't very good at it, either. I learned on the job.

CBA: *How did you get a job at Charlton?*

Dick: My father was a cab driver in New York City, and a friend of his had a brother-in-law, Al Fago, who was an editor at Charlton Comics. I went up there at his invitation on New Year's Day 1952 when Fago was visiting his brother-in-law

Special thanks to Pat Bastienne and Paul Levitz for their assistance in getting this interview.

and showed him my samples. I left Jerry Iger shortly thereafter and went freelance, working for Fago. In those days, though Charlton was in Connecticut, Fago was working out of his home in Great Neck, Long Island. We used to drive back and forth and everything was done out of a car. I got a script every week to pencil and ink, and received no interference. I was left alone to my own devices and I learned my craft.

There was a great variety of subject matter to work on: Space Adventures, Westerns, Hot Rods, Romances, but mostly Crime. I did those for a couple of years and then in 1955 Charlton decided they wanted to save money by having their artists on staff. They invited a bunch of people up there, myself include, and offered us a position to work on their premises on a piecework basis. This was offered when work was *really* hard to come by and essentially the choice was for me to either take this and make less money, traveling back and forth every day, or find something else to do. If Charlton was out of the picture, there was no one else who could be in the picture for me because I wasn't ready yet for the other companies. Did I want to do comic books or something else entirely? My choice was to stay in comic books and I commuted to Derby for two years before I decided to move up.

When I moved up in 1957, that was basically to take a staff job as Pat Masulli's assistant (Pat was Managing Editor of Charlton at the time) and I did for a year or so. It was not work that thrilled me. (One of the problems I've always had with taking staff jobs is that I invariably start working with someone whose style of dealing with people is so different from mine that I become uncomfortable.) So I went back to freelancing and stopped working exclusively for Charlton, moving off premises and working at home. I did some work for Timely, for Stan Lee, which was mostly Mystery books while they were being distributed by American News, doing eight-page Mystery stories with Steve Ditko, who was also working at Charlton on staff during this period. Most of the stuff we sold to Stan never saw print, but they paid for them.

At that point I started freelancing, doing a lot of work for Dell as well as Charlton. I did pretty well working as a ghost for Dell as well as working on my own for them.

CBA: *Did you seek a job in editorial?*

Dick: At some point of time, I realized that just sitting at a drawing board, knocking myself out for the rates that existed wasn't going to get me anywhere so I decided I wanted to take an editorial position at Charlton. I just kept throwing myself in front of the owner until he finally noticed that I was lying on the floor in front of him and offered me the job.

CBA: *So you edited 17 books a month?*

Dick: My job was not only to edit the books—first of all, one person can't edit 17 books in a month, even if you spent full-time at it. Most of the books were just traffic-managed. I assigned the scripts, took the scripts, gave it to an artist, took the art and sent it down to the engraver. I never read it, never looked at it. I had no idea. The only books I edited at all were the Action Hero line with *Captain Atom, Blue Beetle,* the Question, etc. A major part of my job was scheduling material through the plant, so not only did I schedule the creative and editorial work to come in on time but also schedule the production aspects. The work had to be engraved, color-separated, and printed. The job had to move from department to department. I spent half of my time in the plant, and half my time in the editorial offices. The upside is that I learned everything that I could possibly learn about the reproduction process so that when I went to DC I knew exactly what I was talking about. I knew how color separations happened, how plates were made, how material reacted on press and what you could and couldn't do.

CBA: *At Charlton, you had quite a creative stable of personnel. There was Steve Skeates, Jim Aparo, Steve Ditko, Dennis O'Neil, Pat Boyette, Joe Gill, and even Grass Green. How did you attract such diverse talent?*
Dick: A lot of those people just came out of a file. Pat Masulli didn't have time to pursue establishing a crew. Some of them came through recommendations. I think Steve Skeates came out of the recommendation of Roy Thomas, as did Dennis O'Neil. I don't know how Pat Boyette came in. I never met Pat but we talked on the phone. He mailed his art in from Texas and he was wonderful to talk to. He was a radio announcer with this great speaking voice that was fun to listen to. He was also a creative guy. There was a very delicate balancing act for me because the people that we had on staff were given commitments that I had to honor. I had to keep them as busy as they wanted to be. Because the staff by that time had shrunk considerably, I had to look for people to fill out the rest of the schedule. In order to get the money to pay for the freelance work, I farmed out a whole mess of stuff—after the guys on staff got theirs—to a studio in South America which I discovered the name and address of in Pat's files. These guys were great illustrators in South America (the Union Studio in Argentina) and all I had to do was send them plain English scripts—they would do the translations into their language—and they would send back finished work but at a *tremendously* lower rate. So I worked out a deal with my boss so that the money I saved there went to Steve Ditko and all the other freelancers I dealt with in New York so they were getting decent, not great, but decent rates compared to what everybody else was getting.

CBA: *What made the Charlton heroes different?*
Dick: With the exception of Captain Atom, not one of the Action Hero line had a power. They weren't super-powered characters but were people who had something: Blue Beetle had the bug, Judo Master knew martial arts, Sarge Steel had a steel fist and a gun, Fightin' Five were just highly-trained military personnel, even the Question just had the ability to cover his face up with a mask that couldn't be ripped off. The concept of super-heroes, then and now, wasn't terribly exciting to me. If you will, I've been faking orgasms for years when it comes to super-heroes because the idea doesn't really appeal to me, but that's what the market wants. I hadn't the choice so I had to learn something about the genre to feel comfortable with it. One of the reasons why Batman is my

favorite super-hero is because he's not *really* a super-hero. For me, it was always hard to get by radioactive spiders or someone who came from another planet.

CBA: *Were you taking on Marvel with your heroes?*
Dick: When I went to DC, they wanted me to respond to Marvel. I didn't have a choice because DC was trying to get back the business that Marvel had taken away from them. At Charlton, I don't think that anybody really cared. I don't think that they put any effort into the Action Hero line and that's why it sold so badly. They didn't do any real promotion or go out and beat the brush to try and get people to recognize that Charlton was doing something that was in line with what the Big Two were doing. We were always badly distributed and there was no store where you could be sure of getting all 34 titles. When I got started at Charlton, no comics readers knew about Charlton comics—unless they were already buying them—because they wouldn't know that they were going to be there or not in the stores.

I was predisposed to accept DC's offer to go talk to them, when it came, because I was unhappy about the Charlton Action Hero line but I can't remember if they had already been cancelled, just about to be, or whether the sales were just so bad that I felt I was whipping a dead horse. Whichever way it was, it was right on the cusp.

CBA: *Who made the first overture from DC?*
Dick: It was Steve Ditko, believe it or not, who made the pitch from DC. Steve and I remained friends throughout those times and I used to go down to a New York office that Charlton rented out and give work to the people who did work for us. (We still had staff artists and a staff writer in Derby—Joe Gill remained as staff writer until he retired.) One time, I went to the city and Steve came over. He had been doing the Question, *Captain Atom,* and *Blue Beetle* for me at Charlton, and he had just left Marvel to do work over at DC. He was there discussing *Beware the Creeper* and *The Hawk and the Dove.* (*The Hawk and the Dove* and *Secret Six* were both developed before I got there.) The first Creeper story was by Sergius O'Shaugnessey who was definitely my writer because he came with me—it was Dennis O'Neil's pen name (he was working at Marvel and they didn't want him working anywhere else).

Anyway, Steve Ditko came up and told me that the people at DC were interested in talking to me about taking an editorial position. He was really the catalyst for that move. I then went to talk to Carmine Infantino. (Carmine had earlier left the company and had gone to California to try and get into animation. Irwin Donenfeld chased him down out there and brought him back to become Art Director.) But I was hired by Donenfeld, not by Carmine. Carmine wasn't in

Above:
Spillane á la Giordano! Ouch! It's Sarge Steel! Whatcha say a story with Sarge versus "His Name is Savage!"? Macho rules! ©1998 DC Comics.

Above: *A rare mix of Mike Sekowsky pencils over Nick Cardy's inks. The first few* Witching Hour *covers are some of the best of the genre.* ©1998 DC Comics.

staff and who could make the transition into this brave new world they were envisioning and who couldn't. They felt that Kashdan was being run by his writers and had very little to offer. Whether this was true or not, I never knew because I never met the man while he was working at DC. Carmine and Irwin had made a decision about how they were going to create a platform from which to launch the new DC so that it would be in the same game that Marvel was. I think it was difficult because DC had so much baggage.

At that point, Marvel was being distributed by DC and was restricted to eight books a month. So we got called in with the idea being to get back our leadership in the industry. Carmine was thought to be one of the few old-line artists who could make the transition. He was always an experimenter and always did interesting stuff—he was a Jack Kirby in a lot of ways, but unsung as most people didn't recognize how good Carmine was at what he did. Our mandate was to create new super-heroes and a line of books that would challenge Marvel's new-found supremacy. We may not have yet!

CBA: *The concept of artist as editor came from Carmine?*
Dick: Carmine was comfortable with artists and so that's why the switch was made from the very dry editors they had there to the artists who became editors. It started with Joe Orlando and myself. Joe Kubert came on shortly thereafter, then Mike Sekowsky and Jack Kirby. The list grew. Somewhere in there, Irwin Donenfeld and Jack Liebowitz were gone. The two sold the company to Kinney National and two people came in who had no idea what the comic book publishing business was all about. Carmine was the ranking executive and all of a sudden he was in charge—although he had no business acumen whatsoever! (He never did develop any and, as a matter of fact, that was probably the biggest reason why I eventually left as editor.) As Art Director and creative person, he was and is one of my heroes, but as a businessman he affected what I was doing and it was totally separated from what I found reasonable to do. It seemed to me at times that he would try to pick my brains a little bit because I had that experience from Charlton but we just rubbed each other the wrong way after a while. Our management style was so different. My style was basically to focus on the things that I wanted to accomplish creatively and then find the people to accomplish those things for me.

CBA: *Did you hear that George Kashdan was one of the editors fired in the purge that was prompted by the writers' demand for benefits?*
Dick: I took over George Kashdan's desk and his books. I only read about [the writer's movement] much later. The guys who were involved never said anything to me about it. There were a few of them that were still there, like Arnold Drake who was reportedly one of the ringleaders. He wasn't doing anything for me specifically and he never mentioned anything to me about a writers' strike.

CBA: *Carmine has mentioned that you were a part of a "package deal" in getting the better talent away from Charlton and into DC.*
Dick: There was no official "package deal," no matter what Carmine says. During the early course of our discussions nothing was mentioned except my coming to work. Later on, into the fourth or fifth meeting, I said that I'd like to bring some of my people with me and Irwin said, "Oh, we would rather expect that." It was very common then that when an editor moves he takes some of his creators with him. It wasn't that "Either these people are coming with me or I'm not taking the job," or they said, "Either these people

charge of the operation but just the Art Director at that point. It seems that they found me through Sheldon Mayer. Shelley was on staff at DC from the time that he retired until the time he died—he was getting paid every week. They were looking for new editors because they had been comfortably sitting on their oars and Marvel sailed right past DC as the industry leader. So DC was looking for ways to get back into the business. They asked Shelley to check around and see if he could find anyone and evidently he bird-dogged me for one of their editors. That also included Joe Orlando who got there about two weeks before I did.

CBA: *So Ditko called you about the DC job?*
Dick: Ditko called and said, "If you're interested, the people at DC would like to talk to you about a position." I called and went up and saw Carmine after hours in the office (I didn't realize until later but they were trying for me not to be seen by the people I was going to replace). Then we met again at Irwin Donenfeld's place in Westport. I replaced George Kashdan essentially. Carmine and Irwin had come to certain conclusions about certain people that they had on

are coming with you or you don't get the job." It was nothing like that. I had already been given the job and accepted the terms. They told me what books they were giving me.

CBA: *Did you get in contact with the Charlton freelancers and say, "Come on over"?*
Dick: I called them when I had a project in and was sure that I had work for them. *Aquaman* was being done very nicely by Nick Cardy and I didn't think that he needed to be replaced. What I think needed to be replaced was the look of the book because it was thought of as being a silly, childish, TV rip-off (though it was the other way around as TV had gotten the character from us); Aquatot, Aquababy, funny walruses, and everything else wandering around. I wanted something a little bit more serious in order to chase Marvel. In many cases the changes I made were changes for their own sake. I think Cardy was a fine artist but if I didn't change the art it would not look as if anything had changed. I did keep Nick on *Teen Titans* for a long time after that—I was in love with his stuff. Still am.

CBA: *Your arrival at DC was ballyhooed.*
Dick: Joe Orlando penciled that drawing of me saying, "Hi, I'm Dick!" and I inked it. I wrote the copy and touted my own arrival!

CBA: *How many titles did you edit?*
Dick: They gave me eight titles when I arrived: *Young Love, Secret Hearts, Secret Six, Beware the Creeper, The Hawk and the Dove, Blackhawk, Bomba,* and *Aquaman.* I was told that *Bomba* and *Blackhawk* were dead books when I was given them. I was there just to mop up and be given a couple of issues apiece. I got Jack Sparling to draw *Bomba* and I think he drew some of the best work of his life.

Blackhawk, I went to the source: Reed Crandall. I never met the man but I called him on the phone and asked him if he'd like to finish off two issues of *Blackhawk.* Either we'll go out in style or maybe revive it if we can get something interesting happening. He said, "Yeah, I'd love to do that." So I sent him a script and never heard from him again. I guess the script wasn't to his liking and he was semi-retired anyway. So when we got close to the deadline, I called Crandall (who lived in Kansas) and asked his mother to please have him mail the script to Pat Boyette who lived in Texas, the closest artist I could find—this was all before Federal Express. I called Pat and told him that he could do whatever he wanted with the two issues because we were dead before we started. He did a nice job.

The Romance covers were the books I was allowed to design and they were the love of my life! That series (*Young Love* #68, "The Life and Loves of Lisa St. Clair") was adapted from a newspaper strip that I developed. Lisa is my daughter's name. The strip pitch never got presented to anybody but I had the first story written and some of it storyboarded. When I got *Young Love* to edit, I went to Jack Miller (whom I happened to like though I was told to ignore him) and gave him my notes and we went with it. And I got my favorite Romance artist to draw it, Jay Scott Pike.

CBA: *You were with* The Hawk and the Dove *and* Beware the Creeper *right at their inception.*
Dick: Actually, I came in as editor right in the middle of The Hawk and the Dove story in *Showcase.* Steve Ditko already had the rough plot worked out. Steve Skeates worked from that plot and came up with a script. The *Showcase* was okay because Steve followed basically what Ditko wanted him to do. But from that point on it was terrible

for them both.

The basic idea for The Hawk and the Dove was Steve Ditko's and that concept was a triangle; father as the moderate and the extremes represented by the two kids, and all the other things were put together to make that triangle work. The powers were discussed secondly. The "hawk and the dove" was, at that time, a term that was being used very often, was very popular and referred to where people stood regarding the Vietnam War; there were hawks and there were doves. These two boys represented such extreme opposites we thought that in order for it to work we had to offset both of their extremes, so we used their father, the judge, to be the third part of that triangle. That was the original idea that we started off with. Their names, Hank for Hawk, Don for Dove, were chosen to make everything clear. It was simple and clear; almost a parable. I'm not sure where Skeates fit in there but I think he leaned towards Hank.

Ditko would pretty much eliminate whatever was in Steve Skeates' scripts that he didn't feel belonged there. At that point, I think that Ditko's agenda was more the furthering of his philosophical views than writing and drawing entertaining stories. *Mr. A,* which immediately followed, illustrates that point to some degree. I have no problem with his beliefs— whether I believe in them or not is irrelevant—I just don't think that comic books *per se* are the proper vehicle for a forum. I don't think we should promote the existence or non-existence of God.

Steve stayed a little longer on *Beware the Creeper* because it had fewer places where one could further a political agenda. My big involvement with this book—the first that I fully edited— was if you read the opening caption you'll see the word 'FLICKER.' The reason that word is there is because they told me I couldn't use it, because if the "L" and the "I" get blurry and run together it becomes... you figure it out! I told them, "I'm using it and you guys are going to have to live with it! I don't edit books with rules!" So they came in

and screamed, "FLICKER! FLICKER!" I said, "I don't care. I'll make enough space between the letters but that word is staying." I had to establish where I was coming from immediately. We were going to forget rules.

CBA: *At the time of your arrival, the DC books really started to open up graphically.*

Dick: Somewhere along the line, you'll find two-page spreads on the second and third pages. Joe Kubert started it, Joe Orlando followed, and I used the device occasionally. We did it because the production department said it couldn't be done. Remember that I worked in production at Charlton so I went into the DC production department and said, "Yeah, it

Above: Alex Toth keeping it simple, clean and beautiful. Hot Wheels is another great overlooked book. Check out #5 with Alex's "The Case of the Curious Classic." *Sigh!* ©1998 DC Comics.

can be done and I'll show you how." That's when we started with the two-page spreads. Production was in control of the artwork. The editors at DC were held captive by the production department because the editors that were there before us—Schwartz, Miller, Boltinoff, Weisinger, Kanigher—didn't know anything about artwork. Production would hand out the inking assignments. Joe Orlando came in with the

two-page spread of a Romance story I inked and they told him, "You can't do that because it won't match up." I said, "Why won't it match up?" They said they couldn't guarantee it and I said, "Bullshit. Just send it through. It'll match up." The only thing you can't do, to this day, is have lettering in the center because the words might go into the spine.

CBA: *As at Charlton, the DC characters you edited weren't super-powered.*

Dick: That's one of the reasons why when we got to The Hawk and the Dove, there was this "Voice." We were talking about, "How are we going to give the characters their powers?"—what's the difference?! They're all stupid ideas anyway! Just have a voice saying, "You have the power and you have to do good!" In my mind it made as much sense as anything else. We could sit down and make it very complicated and people wouldn't be able to suspend disbelief any easier than by listening to a disembodied voice telling the characters what their roles were going to be. Even there I kept the powers moderate. I kept the Creeper's powers moderate also with no super-strength or ability to fly.

CBA: *How was Ditko to work with?*

Dick: Ditko was very unhappy with his situation on *Amazing Spider-Man*. Back then he was easy to work with. As he became more enamored with the Ayn Rand political/social formula, he became a little more difficult to work with. When you're in a hard "Good Guy vs. Bad Guys" world as you are in the comic book industry, you can't let your personal philosophies take precedence over what makes a good comic book story. He became a little bit more difficult to work with. I have no lasting problem with Steve and whenever we do see each other these days (which is very rarely), we're still amiable; it's just that I didn't agree with his feelings and he didn't agree with mine.

I remember an incident (and this really wasn't indicative of anything other than where he was as opposed to where I was): Denny had written a script of *Beware the Creeper* and he wrote something about this character who was described as an "ex-criminal." Steve jotted down a very bold note on the script that "there was no such thing as an 'ex-criminal.' Once you've committed a crime, you're a criminal for life." First of all, that wasn't in the copy. There was no need for him to take that attitude, to take that harsh a view over what Denny had written. Basically what it got down to at that point was that Denny and Steve couldn't work together any more. It had nothing to do with me and I could no longer be the referee. Steve quit the book shortly thereafter.

CBA: *Another talented writer was Steve Skeates—his* Aquaman *was a great book.*

Dick: Steve Skeates worked for me for a long time. *Aquaman* was the closest thing to the way that I liked to work. Jim Aparo and Steve Skeates would come into New York every six months and we would plot out six months worth of work. I would tell them what I was going to be looking for. I told Steve, who had a tendency to overwrite copy, "Write the hell out of it and don't try to hold yourself back. I'll edit it." I'd then send the stuff to Jim Aparo who would pencil, ink and letter, and then turn it in.

CBA: *Why did the covers on* Aquaman *rarely depict the action that went on inside the book?*

Dick: The covers to *Aquaman* were one of the sticky points between Carmine and myself. I had no objections to Nick doing the covers but I had a feeling about covers that they shouldn't lie, a feeling that Carmine didn't have. In order to get by my objection, he set up a system where Nick would come in after I left because I was living in Connecticut—I had to leave at about 4:30 or 5:00. Both Nick and Carmine lived in the city and he would have Nick come in and they would lay out a cover going over the artwork for the book and I'd come in in the morning and find a finished cover. They were great covers—creatively, they were great but they just lied!

CBA: *The* Aquamans *also had their share of corpses on the covers.*
Dick: Carmine just loved dead bodies on covers. He decided that heroes had to be suffering all of the time. Carmine actually did the breakdowns on most of the covers and Neal was the only one allowed to ignore Carmine's drawings to some degree. Carmine used to do layouts on 8^1/$_2$" x 11" bond paper and fill 'em out to all four corners, and the art paper that we worked on just about would allow to use it as the print area. I used to trace his layouts when I was drawing the covers. I don't know how many other people did. He used to do very rough roughs for Nick—Nick wasn't going to listen to anyone about drawing—but Carmine designed just about every cover of every DC comic book. It was very rare when he would let someone else design a cover. I did get a chance to do a couple of the Romance books because he didn't like to do those.

CBA: *Skeates mentioned that you guys got away with stuff in* Aquaman *because no one in management read the book.*
Dick: We were having fun and doing what we wanted to do because Carmine never read the books. As a matter of fact, when he used to do a cover he would just skim through the interior artwork and look for something that would appeal to him. If that couldn't be turned into a cover that worked he would then extrapolate and add something that wasn't in the story at all in order to come up with a cover idea.

I always got positive reaction to the stuff that I did at DC. I never felt unloved or that I was heading in the wrong direction—I always got good, positive response from the fans in the mail and at conventions.

CBA: *You took over* Secret Six *with the second issue.*
Dick: Murray started *Secret Six*, I think. It was an interesting concept but because it had already been set up by the time I had got there I just didn't get as enthusiastic about that book as the others and as a result, in the issues that I did edit, I inadvertently eliminated two people from being Mockingbird by giving them thought balloons that proved that they couldn't be Mockingbird. I enjoyed the artwork that was being done—Jack Sparling and I became fast friends as a result of the work he did for me but I just wasn't into *Secret Six* even though I was into non-costumed heroes. I just didn't have a natural feel for it. The idea that these people were performing heroic acts because they *had* to—each had their own gimmick—and the fact that one of the six was actually Mockingbird without us knowing who, it was really a cool idea, but I just didn't get into it.

CBA: *Why did Pat Boyette leave DC?*
Dick: I don't think that Pat left DC. I just don't think there were any more assignments for him. I couldn't find anything for him to speak of, only a few little things here and there. If he left in a huff, it wasn't with me.

CBA: *You seemed to enjoy the Mystery books.*
Dick: I worked with Joe on coming up with the Abel thing. Joe started up *House of Mystery* first and had Cain, so it

seemed obvious that *House of Secrets* should have Abel, the brother. As aggressive as Cain was, we made Abel that much weaker, a coward, being intimidated by the house, noises and darkness, etc. Physically, we based Abel on Mark Hanerfeld, a DC staffer, and Cain was based on Len Wein.

The Mystery books were my farm system. Mostly I used them to try out new people. When I left DC as an editor, both *House of Secrets* and *The Witching Hour* had a ton of inventory. It was stuff from people that I tried out to see if this guy or that could be useful to us. Sometimes I would put a story on the shelf that wasn't very good. Sometimes it was an experiment that failed. Almost all of that stuff was experimental to one degree or another.

CBA: *You and Joe Orlando got along?*
Dick: Initially Joe Orlando and I bonded because we were the two new kids on the block and at that point we were the only artists that were editors. So we were basically standing back-to-back, protecting each other. It was made clear that we were the new important kids on the block. The other editors either treated us with respect or at arm's length. It was kind of a strange situation. DC was always a very businesslike

WHAT HAPPENED BEFORE...
MELANIE WINTERS RAN AWAY FROM HOME TO ESCAPE ENTANGLEMENT IN HER MOTHER'S WEB OF FEAR, HATE, AND GRASPING AMBITIONS —!
ON HER WAY TO NEW YORK, TO FIND HER ESTRANGED SISTER, MONICA, SHE MET YOUNG JUAN RICCO, WHO LATER, THROUGH A MISHAP, IS JAILED, FALSELY NAMED AS HER "ABDUCTOR"!
BROUGHT HOME TO HER MOTHER AND STEPFATHER, AFTER AN ACCIDENT, SHE AWAKES FROM HER COMA TO WITNESS THE ARRIVAL OF AN UNEXPECTED VISITOR, IN THIS EPISODE OF...
20 MILES TO HEART BREAK
ALEX TOTH & VINCE COLLETTA
YOU! HOW DARE YOU SET FOOT IN THIS HOUSE, AGAIN?
MOTHER!- NO!!
GET OUT OF HERE! GET OUT! BEFORE I HAVE YOU THROWN OUT!
OH - PLEASE!
YOU - YOU, WHO'VE TURNED ALL THAT YOU TOUCHED INTO TRASH .. YOU! YOU'RE NO GOOD!
STOP IT, MOTHER! STOP!
FILTH BREEDS MORE FILTH!
HELLO-MOTHER...
G-113

Above: *A beautiful example of Alex Toth's Romance work, inked by (yow!) Vince Colletta.* ©1998 DC Comics

place. Arnold Drake always came in with his hat, a tie and a jacket. Joe and I were there essentially to loosen things up. Not that I didn't wear a tie and a jacket—I did until I retired in 1993 (and I haven't worn a tie since).

He had the same amount of books as me to edit: Eight. Because he started *House of Mystery*, it was natural for Joe to help me start a companion book. *House of Secrets* was an alternative to *House of Mystery*, rather than an echo.

I wasn't or will not be the kind of editor who makes all of the creative decisions. I want to hire the people who make the right creative decisions and get a variety of ideas instead of just mine. When an idea doesn't come to one of the creative people I put in that position, I invariably have to sit down and help work out a new idea. Good, bad or indifferent, none of my books looked like each other. Even *House of Secrets* and *The Witching Hour* weren't that close. *Secret Hearts* and *Young Love* were different points of view.

CBA: *What was behind the* House of Secrets *revival?*
Dick: Joe Orlando and I were involved in developing *House of Secrets.* We both came up with the character Abel. Goldie was my son's invisible friend. We were able to do whatever we wanted to do. It was flying upside-down and having fun. The haunted House of Secrets came from a lunch Joe, Carmine and I had together. The idea was that the house itself is alive and thinks that Abel is just stupid and silly. So it would slam windows on his fingers and he knows the house is after him all of the time. That was the whole idea behind the book. The stories were just incidental, but the fun I had was with the bridges. I enjoyed the bridges very much in *The Witching Hour.* I enjoyed having Alex Toth do most of those bridges for me—he did a great job. Most of them were written by Marv Wolfman, Len Wein and Gerry Conway. They used to hang around the office all of the time. Even those issues look like they had themes; they weren't written as a book. I used to order a bunch of stuff and then I would go through the inventory and compile this month's *The Witching Hour.* I would find three stories that had some kind of thematic connection and add up the page count. Then I'd say, "I need a one-page intro, a two-page bridge between these stories, a one-page bridge between these, and a half-page close-off," and give the three stories to one of the writers.

CBA: *Neal did some great covers for you on the Mystery books—did you seek him out?*
Dick: When it came to covers, if Neal was around I'd just give him the work. I'd give him the book that we were putting together and he'd come up with a cover that would make the book work. Neal would come up with a quick sketch in a minute. One of the advantages of Neal was that for most, if not all of the time that I was at DC, Neal was in the office across the hall from me. He was on the premises even though he wasn't required to be there. He had a small room with an Artograph. He'd do one of his small sketches, bring it in for my okay, put it in the Artograph, blow it up and draw it.

CBA: *Did you hit it off with Neal Adams?*
Dick: Neal Adams and I were the "young Turks" there. We bonded immediately and we decided to make things happen. Neal got to DC before me so he was already hounding the production department. He used to go in there and give them a hard time every day to get better color work and good cover separations. It got to the point that Jack Adler liked so much what Neal was doing that he wouldn't make a move without discussing it first with Neal. Jack was in charge of color and Neal was doing every thing he could to keep him challenged.

CBA: *Alex Toth did some outstanding work for you.*
Dick: Toth and I were real friends. We were buddies on the *Hot Wheels* book. We couldn't have been closer. At that time I was inking some of his Romance stuff and was his editor on *Hot Wheels.* On the fifth issue of *Hot Wheels*, we completely threw out the script that we had bought and I let him write something that he really wanted to write, "The Case of the Curious Classic." He was in love with that car in the story, the 1937 Cord, and so was I; I was a real car buff. He went to a car show and took pictures of a Cord on a lawn, and even sent me a bunch of photos. (Remember, years later, the Human Target in *Action Comics*? He drove a Cord and to draw it we used for reference the photos Alex had sent me.) So we both got our jollies out on that story.

Alex has always said that he was always searching for the simple statement. He was trying as an artist to make the drawing as simple as possible so that it will be clear. So I have a letter from him thanking me for editing his stuff. I took out things that he put in that he didn't want to be there. I was able to anticipate his need to make a simple statement and I helped simplify the work. I was really proud that he had noticed what I had done, especially because he was always one of my heroes.

Alex did the character designs for the *Hot Wheels* cartoon for Hanna-Barbera and I know he was having problems. He had been doing *The Witching Hour* bridges for me for a while but that was a modest amount of work. So I just called and asked him to do the comic. So he did some character sketches and said he'd like to take a shot at it. I gave him Joe Gill's scripts only because Joe was such a vague writer that you could make changes without even Joe realizing that you made them. I know that Alex was going to make changes because he has his own way of looking at things which doesn't necessarily jibe with the writer's ideas. So we got some pretty decent stuff in *Hot Wheels*. On the fifth issue he called and said, "This is my last issue so do you mind if I tell my own story?" I said, "Joe's been paid for it, so go ahead. If I can get somebody over here to listen to me, I'll pay you too." The amount of money we pay for an extra script isn't a big deal—and it turned out to be the best story of the bunch: Eight panels on every page and he didn't skimp on anything.

CBA: *Alex seemed to have a successful gig in animation. Why did he work for you?*
Dick: For the most part, I don't think that Alex ever needed the work. I think that he enjoyed doing comics. He was tentative about this brave new world we were concocting which was completely different than the one that he had grown up in. He was used to a business where the artist basically took orders from an editor, got a full script and did whatever was in that script. You didn't dare make a change. He didn't really believe that we were becoming more flexible. He now had in mind the same kind of stories, approaches and details that he had earlier but he didn't want to believe that we were coming closer to the way that he thought. Every once in a while he would feel good about it but then would say that, no, it's not what he wanted at all. It was all in his head, whatever it was.

Alex is the closest thing we have to a genius in this business.

CBA: *You also inked a lot of material when you were editing. How did you accomplish all of that work?*
Dick: I felt that the freelance work—my inking—and the editing were both part of the same job. I was able to turn administrator off and creator on when I needed to, and when I would go into the office, turn 'em the other way. I'd get up at 4:00 A.M. and draw until it was time to take the train to New York. By the time I got back home, I was gone; just wiped out. I would do one page of inks in the morning.

How I did freelance art while maintaining an editorial job at DC is that I'm pretty fast at what I do and I'm disciplined so that whatever time that there was available, I'd find a way to make use of that time. I learned my discipline and my speed while working at Charlton.

CBA: *What was Mike Sekowsky like?*
Dick: Mike Sekowsky was very often called "The Wild Russian" by a bunch of people. That comes close to an art description. He was a big bear of a man—wild hair. Though I never saw it I was told he had a fitful temper, really angry. Evidently everybody else did! We were having a ball on that *Wonder Woman* book! I really enjoyed that work! Everyone says that, "Well, Adams has to be the best stuff you inked." I enjoyed the work I did on Sekowsky more. I enjoyed it more and thought it was more creative in a lot of ways. Adams'

stuff was for me, mostly tracing—he solved most of the problems so I was just there to put ink on his pencil lines. But Sekowsky was different. Even though I knew it was a rip-off of the *Avengers* TV show and I knew so at the time, it was fun! That was also part of this relevance thing that involved DC at the time—for some reason Carmine was so enamored of it—he got rid of powers, got rid of costumes (which I did with *Teen Titans*—that wasn't my idea, but Carmine's). Same thing with *Wonder Woman*. It was decided that she wasn't to have a costume any more. We changed it so she always wore white sweaters and slacks. They took away her powers so we had to contrive stories like crazy. I don't know what we did to make her a non-Amazon!

CBA: *After you resigned as editor, one of your* Wonder Woman *jobs had a bad guy who looked suspiciously like a certain publisher.*
Dick: I went to our files in the office and dug up whatever photos we had on Carmine and used him as a heavy. I don't know if he ever even read it but he never said a word about me using him as a villain.

Above: *Alex Toth submitted three cover proposals for* Witching Hour *#1, all rejected. One saw print on the back cover of* The Amazing World of DC Comics *#1. Another is shown above. Where's the third one? Seek and ye must find!*
©1998 DC Comics

CBA: *What happened to Jack Miller?*
Dick: He was accused of stealing stuff from the library and was fired, which I thought was pretty silly. The artwork routinely was stolen by everybody, including me! I got some *Aquaman* pages because I wanted them—they were going to shred them up! Len, Marv and Mark Hanerfeld built tremendous art collections by going into DC after school, working for free in production, and they'd pick up some artwork before they left. Artwork wasn't returned to artists in those days—it was destroyed.

CBA: *You had an impact at DC but you didn't stay long.*
Dick: I was only at DC for two years the first time around though it may seem a lot longer to people. My books died with me when I left. Part of it was a difference in management style between Carmine and myself which led to my dissatisfaction and I had to leave. Carmine wanted someone who did things his way and I wanted someone to do things my way. He was the boss. I didn't disagree necessarily with what he was trying to do but I just disagreed with his methods. He believed in punishment as incentive for people to do good work and I didn't. That's really basically what it comes down to. Punishment meant saying, "You want to work

here? You want to get paid? You got to do it the way we want you to do it." I would try to present the same idea but by saying, "This is a great way to do this. Everybody will love it. You'll have fun, we'll all have fun." It was a different approach to getting the same ends. It's not that I wanted an end result different from Carmine's. We're talking about creative people who aren't hamburger flippers or the average guy on the street. Some people in the creative community are pretty strange—probably I'm pretty strange but I just don't notice it—but they don't notice that they're strange either. So you have to deal with them in a totally different way to get them to function, produce and feel as if they're making a contribution to something, because therefore they will do the job better. Carmine believed in laying out rules and regulations, and holding out your paycheck as a reason to do things his way. The fact that you can do it that way doesn't mean that you should. The end result is not as good as it could have been if he had played a little softball. That was my opinion. I don't know if we'll ever find out who was right. When it became a seller's market, the creators weren't any better at it than the publishers were in terms of being arrogant and hardheaded. I'm not sure that Carmine wasn't right. I'm just saying that I had to leave because I didn't feel comfortable.

At that time, *Superman* and *Batman* were DC Comics and everything else was sort of cannon fodder; stuff to bring up the rear. Joe Orlando had a pair of Romance comics, I had a pair of Romance comics, and both sets sold pretty much the same. None of them were exceptional or making a good deal of money for the company. *Superman* and *Batman* were where the money was.

CBA: *How did you know if your books were selling?*
Dick: In those days we didn't have sales figures given to us as we did in later years. Every editor had a cork board with their books' cover proofs pinned up. Sometime during the night, Carmine or somebody would turn over the cover and write a figure down for that particular title. It wasn't numbers but a percentage, but we weren't given the print run numbers so we never knew how many we sold. I didn't pay too much attention to the numbers because I had no way of comparing them to anything that made sense to me. They dropped *Strange Adventures* with Deadman when it was selling 125,000 copies and that wasn't enough to keep it going.

I wouldn't take the Publisher's Statement numbers to church. I'm not sure where they came from but I'll tell you one thing I know for sure—because I can't get in trouble. At Charlton, they just made them up.

CBA: *Do you think your books received the support they deserved?*
Dick: I think that they supported the books to the degree that they could. I think that I had as much information as anybody else. I think that Carmine was trying often to get me to change my mind about what I was doing creatively by showing me other things that I could be doing. My take on Romance books was basically do them as modern day fairy tales—the beautiful princess meets the prince and they live happily ever after, with some trouble in between A & B. Joe Orlando's approach was relevance. He had women who worked in some sort of a social agency in the ghetto and with basically the same kind of end result where the man and woman get beyond their problems and get together. His were grim and gritty and mine were fairy tales. Well, Carmine evidently felt that Joe's approach was superior to mine. In retrospect, looking at sales figures years later, I realize that the sales figures were basically the same in both

books. But what happened was that Carmine gave me inappropriate figures—or figures that I could only interpret that I was going in the wrong direction so that I would go to Joe's way of doing things. I think that Carmine was trying to be kind and gentle in a way, because that wasn't his normal style to try to influence things by trying to manipulate numbers—generally he would say to either do it his way or get out—and he didn't do that. He tried to change my mind in other ways. I was told that the sales numbers on *Aquaman* were very low and I'm scrambling around, making changes and trying to get sales figures back up when actually they weren't bad according to what Paul Levitz told me when he found the sales figures years later. He as a fan of *Aquaman* enjoyed the magazine and told me that it was selling quite well, as well as some of the other books.

CBA: *Was Carmine in the right job?*

Dick: Carmine really had no business being where he was. It's really hard to blame somebody for finding himself in the position of one day being Editorial Director, the next day Publisher, and the next day President. I mean, nothing changed in-between. Nothing prepared him to be President and Publisher. It's just that the people who took over the company said, "Who's in charge here?" and they found out it was Carmine who was the only person left. Leibowitz left. Donenfeld went and the Art Director remained. "Make him Publisher and President!" He's not going to say that he's not qualified for that. He wasn't prepared for it and he really didn't know where to find the information. He got somebody out of Kinney National's group of executives that showed up—you should have seen these guys, all out of Hathaway shirt ads. One of them literally had an eye-patch! The other one in charge was a marine that was just out of the service and never stood any less straight than a wall.

CBA: *Did Carmine see you as a threat to his position?*

Dick: I've been told that Carmine did perceive that I was interested in becoming Publisher of DC but I had no interest at all. If he had just asked me, I would have saved him all of his concerns. I didn't want his job or anything near it. I was satisfied with what I was doing.

Since I've been in this business, my concern was always, very honestly, the understanding that I'm lazy and the only way that I can work as much as I can is by not thinking it's work. So that means that I only do things that I *like* to do. That's very selfish but I don't like to do certain things. When I got to the point where I didn't feel that the creative end of my job was as fun as the administrative end at DC, that was the beginning of my withdrawing to get out of the company.

CBA: *Did you quit DC?*

Dick: Emotion has played a large role in any business decision I made. I quit DC. The last piece of business that Carmine was doing to irritate me in trying to make me quit—I could tell that all along—was he came in and told me to fire Gray Morrow because of a story Gray drew. I said, "No," went back to my office, sat down for a few minutes and thought about it. I went back into Carmine's office and said, "I quit." The fact of the matter is that when I left, Gray Morrow was still there! So I knew that it was just a set-up, nothing more. It wasn't real. At that point, it felt like I wasn't doing what I wanted to do here and I was running into too many pressures that didn't appeal to me. It was a little childish and self-serving but, hey, I didn't want that.

When I came back into my office, I said to Neal, "Let's go to lunch. I just quit." Continuity Associates was born that

same afternoon. We had already been doing some commercial work together on the side (I don't know where I found the time to do it—don't ask!) and I said, "Well, I want to get out of here, and a studio sounds like fun, but I don't want to do it right away. I don't want to replace one pressure with another pressure." Two days later I attended an editorial meeting and I was contributing just like usual. I had another month to go before my "retirement." Carmine came up to me later and said, "Gee, Richie, I can't get over that. You're still in there working." I said, "I'm getting paid until November 4, and I'm going to work until November 4. After that, I'm gone and you don't have to worry about me." He was kind of surprised. I wasn't helping Carmine or myself. I was just doing the job.

So pretty much I stayed home in my studio downstairs one year to lick my wounds—I felt the need to catch my breath. Julie Schwartz was my editor for that one year and he was wonderful. Called up every day and said, "Got enough work? Need a check?" Whatever. Julie was right on top of it. He still is. We were roommates, sharing an office at 909 Third Avenue. I did all the Batman work—Bob Brown,

Above: For a dead guy, Boston Brand sure can move! Another innovative Neal Adams cover, from Strange Adventures #214. ©1998 DC Comics

Irv Novick, and Neal's stuff—*Justice League, Green Lantern.* So I calmed down over the year and Neal finally called and said, "Let's go." That's how we started Continuity.

CBA: *Right after you left DC, Jack Kirby came in.*

Dick: Jack knew from square one that somebody else was going to draw the Superman heads because of requirements to make the licensing have a consistent Superman image. Jack didn't object to it. After the fact, everybody is objecting to us having changed it but that was part of the deal. He was being paid more money for a page rate than anybody else at the time. Carmine was trying to beat Marvel by getting Jack Kirby, their co-creator. He thought we could get there faster by having Kirby on our side. Sales on the Fourth World books weren't bad by today's standards but they were bad then, based on what we were paying Jack. Carmine didn't want to admit defeat. It cost him a lot in pride and honor to have gone out and gotten Kirby and then have to say, "I'm sorry, we can't go ahead with them." I think that Carmine was looking for a magic bullet, but Kirby wasn't it.

It wasn't so much sales were plummeting as Marvel was widening the gap. Our sales held even but they were on the rise. There's nothing wrong with that unless you're the industry leader and the upstart now has a 2-to-1 market share.

CBA: *What was your editorial style?*

Dick: I knew what I wanted to do and picked the people who knew how to do that. So I didn't have to get too involved in the creative process. You can't. An editor cannot control the creative process without affecting the work in a negative way. You can't get into the faces of the people while they're doing the creative work. You can advise them before they start; you can give them helpful "tips" along the way, but you can't control the creative process without hurting it.

What I did instead was maybe impose one way per person. I tried to create an environment for each creator so that they could do their best work. If that's hands-off, than I was a hands-off editor. I always said that one of the major jobs of an editor is to create an environment for the creators. Not surprisingly, one of the most important aspects of the creative process is the pat on the head as a show of love. Without it, creators have a tendency to feel unloved. Of course that's obvious, but imagine sitting there by yourself, perhaps it's 1:00 in the morning and you're working and there's no one around you. You start imagining things about what "they" are doing to me. The reason that happens is because "they" didn't set things up properly so he wouldn't think about that. My job was to relieve the freelancer as much as I could from any thoughts except the work so that if it was a pat on the head that he needed, I gave him the pat on the head. If it was having a check as soon as he finished, then he had the check. It required on my part that I learn something about each of these people as individuals and not treat them as a collective bunch. That is where Carmine and I differed. Carmine believed that everyone ought to be taught to toe a line, a line that he drew. Everyone had to do it his way. Whether the line is arbitrary or not is irrelevant. The fact is that everyone is not going to toe the same line. There are some things that work for artist "A" that won't work for artist "B" in terms of getting them to do the work well.

So for example, I remember one of the places where Carmine and I went head-to-head was concerns about clarity in storytelling. I agreed with him that there was a problem at DC at that time. Some early Neal Adams work was a real prime example—you really didn't know where to look next on some of those pages. It was confusing. Carmine's solution was to mandate how paneled pages were to be laid out. It was an absolute law; it had to be done this way. And he made photocopies of all of these rules, put them on my desk and said to send them to the freelancers. Months later he came into my office to talk to me about something and he sees the pile of photocopies still where he put them. So when he sat down I said, "I think that there are many more ways than one to solve a problem." There was nothing wrong with the storytelling in my books because I straightened everybody up, one way or the other, but I did it without always resorting to his new rule. There are things to be said about keeping everything contained within a panel in terms of clarity but sometimes clarity can be awfully boring. It depends on who's doing it.

CBA: *Why did you work in comics?*

Dick: I *wanted* to be in comics. So did Neal Adams. So did Joe Kubert. So did Gil Kane. It's not that we didn't want to do anything else—all of us experimented here and there—it's just that comics offered more of what we wanted to do. ⓓⓒ

The Story that Haunted Julie Schwartz

The Tale behind "The House that Haunted Batman"

Editor's Note: *It is to my chagrin that there are a number of interviews and features which should have made it into this magazine, but didn't. Russ Heath, Murphy Anderson, Howard Chaykin, Ric Estrada, Alex Niño, Bob Haney, Frank Robbins, Ralph Reese, John Severin, and Ramona Fradon are but a few who got short-shrifted because—well, you have to understand that this issue started as a 52-pager and is now nearly twice that size. I regret not discussing the contributions of Murray Boltinoff who did a number of fine books during this era and I'm ashamed to say the interview tape with Jim Aparo was accidentally destroyed. Also badly damaged was my taped interview with the great editor himself, Julius Schwartz, but I confess it wasn't an adequate interview. Julie didn't have much to say that he hadn't already and, gracious as he was, he couldn't conjure up too many tales of the office. He told me he had no interest in company politics and prided himself on just doing his job (and an excellent one at that). But just as I was to retreat—crestfallen—after grilling him for nearly an hour, Julie pulled out a nugget: A story untold, given for our pleasure from the Great Editor himself. Thanks, Julie.*

Comic Book Artist: *Did you see Neal Adams as a new style for DC?*

Julius Schwartz: I don't worry about style. I just look at how the artwork looks—if I like it, I like it. I don't know if Neal told you this story, but I will: Neal liked to work with new talent and Len Wein and Marv Wolfman hadn't become pros yet but they were very anxious to get started but evidently they were too afraid to ask for a job. So they did a Batman job on their own. I vaguely recall that the team worked with Marv doing the plotting and layout and Len doing the dialogue. In other words, Marv was the stronger plot man and Len was the stronger dialogue man. They wrote a story called "The House that Haunted Batman" all on their own and they were almost afraid to tell me about it! They brought it into Neal because they wanted his opinion. Neal read the story and liked it so much that he took it upon himself to draw it by himself, not knowing whether I'd even be interested! That was certainly a positive factor for Neal: Taking a job and doing a 15-page story, not knowing whether he was wasting his time or not.

As history can be a matter of perception, the other participants in our tale see things differently, each in their own way. Being the pitbull my Publisher says I am, I tenaciously tracked down all the other players to get their side of this sordid tale. First, it was Len Wein:

CBA: *Do you remember the story behind "The House that Haunted Batman"?*

Len: That was basically how Marv and I got introduced to Julie. We came up with an idea for a Batman story. We mentioned it to Neal who we used to hang out with—he wasn't that much older than the rest of us so we were all a part of the gang. Neal said that it was a great story and he wanted to draw it. So we did the story on our own. Marv and I wrote the script, Neal drew it and when it was finished, we presented it to Julie. "Here's your next issue! It's done." Julie had a conniption. "How dare you do this? I didn't assign it!" We said, "Read it. If you don't like it, we'll eat it." He read it and said, "All right. It's the next issue." So we went from there. Julie was full of bluster. You don't become the best editor there is without recognizing something that has value.

Above: Looks like an unused Batman cover with pencils by Neal Adams, but we haven't the foggiest what issue it was intended for! Any ideas, Batmaniacs?
©1998 DC Comics

Julie said, "Whether it went through channels or not, it's a great story and I'm running it."

Then, Marv Wolfman:

CBA: *What's the story behind "The House that Haunted Batman"?*

Marv Wolfman: That was a fun one. Len and I were both Batman fans and we both wanted to see him back the way he used to be, dark and mysterious. This was during the "New Look" Batman. We came up with the idea of a real dark mystery and Batman would be much closer to the way that he used to act in the 1940s. We plotted it spec and tried to sell it to Julie. He first said, "Well, let's have this giant ping-pong ball machine in there which Batman and Robin would be put into." We did that but Julie finally said, "No, this is too dark for the type of material we're doing." So the story was killed. We showed it to Dick Giordano because we thought that it was a great story and couldn't believe we didn't sell it. Dick loved it and he showed it to Neal Adams. Neal loved it so much that on his own he spent about a year drawing this story without letting Julie know about it. In the meantime, he was starting to change the look of Batman on *The Brave and the Bold,* giving him the longer ears and making him the more mysterious character—it was just on his own because it was not in the writing. In the meantime, he was secretly drawing this story. When he finished, he brought it into Julie and said, "Here's something that I've been working on on my own." Halfway through reading it, Julie says, "Wait a minute! I know this story! It's by Marv and Len!" At this point, he bought it because they'd since made Batman dark again. So by the time that it came out, it was not a revolutionary story but when we plotted it it was.

Neal did the story absolutely on spec because he knew that it would sell. At this point in his career, because he was so good and so much in demand, he knew that whatever he did would sell. But this was done as an absolute top secret. It very well could have backfired. Julie could have said, "Screw you all." But Julie isn't that type of guy. He was mad as hell but when it comes right down to it, it was a good story and he went with it. If it was a bad story, he probably would have killed it.

Finally, the artist himself, Neal Adams, gave me his reply. After I subsequently shared some excerpts from the above participants, he revised his comments to read:

CBA: *Do you remem-* ber a story called "The House that Haunted Batman"?

Neal: Well, now that I've read all your notes from Len, Marv, Julie and my own first, off-the-cuff response, I've put my "memory thinking cap" on and reconstructed the whole thing.

First, yes, the boys did show it to Julie and he editorialized over it and suggested the ping-pong ball thing… which wasn't executed very well and seemed more like the TV show and *not* like the rest of the story. The reason I was shown the script was that Julie had (finally) rejected it.

I felt it was quite a good story and a "real Batman story," so without telling Len and Marv, I pitched the story to Julie. He told me, "*They* should be in here, arguing the story." I said, "You rejected their story." Julie said, "If you like the story so much, why don't you go ahead and do it?"

I asked, "Then will you buy it?" Julie said, "I'm not promising anything. Take a chance."

You might think I was taking a gamble here, but I wasn't. Julie was saying, "Put your money where your mouth is." He would never have rejected it if I drew it after that. He's simply not that kind of guy. Still, it was a surprise when I handed it in. By the way, to set the record straight:

1) I had penciled only the first half when I showed it to Julie (not yet the ping-pong sequence).

2) I had already done some Batman stories with Denny by the time Len and Marv approached me (or so says my memory).

3) That sequence I showed Julie took about three months to jam it out between my other work. I would have to say the first new/true Batman writing was done by Denny (if you except *The Brave and the Bold* reworking that I did). I feel that Len and Marv were first to recognize and be inspired to work in the new Batman direction Denny and I initiated. I think that we have to say that Denny created the new wave in writing for Batman. ⓓⓒ

Cracking the Code

The Liberalization of the Comics Code Authority

by Amy Kiste Nyberg

Drug abuse was a fact of American life by 1970—a fact that could not be acknowledged in comic books of that period because their content was strictly governed by a set of standards, adopted by publishers in the mid-'50s, known as the Comics Code. Three issues of *Amazing Spider-Man* changed all that.

Les Daniels tells in his history of Marvel that Stan Lee, Marvel's Editor-in-Chief, received a letter from the Department of Health, Education, and Welfare asking the company to do a story about the dangers of drugs. In *Amazing Spider-Man #96-98*, Spidey learns that his college roommate is a drug addict. Because the Code forbade any mention of narcotics or their use, the story didn't get Code approval, but Marvel decided to go ahead and publish the story anyway. Lee recalls that the story got favorable press nationwide, "and because of that, the Code was changed."

The publishers apparently considered Marvel's request to be allowed to publish their special issues at a June 1970 meeting of the Comics Magazine Association of America (CMMA), the trade organization responsible for overseeing the Code. That led to a discussion of whether the time had come to change the Code, led by the representative of Marvel's biggest competitor, DC's Carmine Infantino.

Their conclusion: "It was decided each publisher, after discussions with his editorial staff, should prepare any suggested revisions he saw fit, and these should be submitted to the Board for its consideration at a subsequent meeting."

However, the board rejected Marvel's request with this statement: "In the meantime, the Code Administration's ruling that no stories shall deal with narcotics addiction shall remain in effect."

While Marvel's defiance of the Code Authority was the impetus for the Code revision, the time was ripe for modifying the 1954 Code. The Silver Age of comics resurrected and revamped the '40s super-heroes for the baby boom youngsters who were now teenagers. This new breed of super-heroes, as many have noted, represented a departure from the traditional formula; the god-like beings were replaced with super-heroes who had all-too-human flaws.

These super-heroes were creatures of the '60s, a decade very different from that occupied by the Golden Age super-heroes. To keep pace with the times and to maintain interest in the Super-hero genre, publishers added "social relevance" to their comics. The leader in this respect was a DC super-hero team consisting of Green Lantern and Green Arrow. Comic book historians Will Jacobs and Gerard Jones note that the characters served as "a mouthpiece for [writer

Amy Kriste-Nyberg is an assistant professor in the Department of Communications at Seton Hall University. This article is based on excerpts from her book, Seal of Approval: The History of the Comics Code *(1998, University Press of Mississippi).*

Above: *The paramount. Rejected* Green Lantern/ Green Arrow #76 *cover art by Neal Adams.* ©1998 DC Comics

Dennis O'Neil's] own 1960s radical orientation."

Infantino, then Editorial Director at DC, admitted to *The New York Times Magazine* in May 1971 that the push for relevance was a last-ditch effort at keeping the super-hero alive. "*Green Lantern* was dying," he said. "The whole Super-hero line was dying... We started interviewing groups of kids around the country. The one thing they kept repeating: They want to know the truth. Suddenly the light bulb goes on:

Above: *Go figure why they requested Neal Adams do a redraw on this cover of Green Lantern/Green Arrow #77.*
©1998 DC Comics

ground comix. These were actually the first comic books to escape the constraints of the Comics Code. The product of the counterculture that flourished in America in the late '60s and early '70s, undergrounds originally were available only by mail order or directly from the artist. Eventually a network of retail outlets, including alternative record stores and book-stores, along with head shops, was created for distribution. A whole new alternative comics culture was established, with its peak years coming between 1968 and 1974.

It was not the intention of the underground comix to compete with mainstream publishers for their audience. Rather, the underground artists, who grew up with comics, found comix to be the perfect medium to express their defiance of social norms. What better way to demonstrate their disdain of conservative taste than to pervert what the public perceived as children's entertainment?

They represented no real challenge to the comic book industry. Their limited circulation posed no economic threat and also meant that there would be no public confusion about their product and those labeled "comix"—but undergrounds had established that there was a new adult market for comics, a generation that had grown up with comic books and were open to the possibilities of the form.

Work on Code revisions began shortly after the June 1970 meeting of the CMAA, and the association's board of directors reviewed specific provisions in a special meeting called December 7, 1970 for that purpose. The President of the CMAA, John Goldwater, noted that he had always taken the position that if times and circumstances warranted it, changes in the Code should be considered and made.

He added: "However, such changes should be carefully considered, so that the self-regulation program, which has served the industry effectively for more than 16 years, should not become ineffective."

Revisions were discussed and approved for most of the text of the Code at that December meeting, and the publishers agreed that the new Code would go into effect February 1, 1971. Many restrictions on the presentation of crime and horror were liberalized. Ghouls, vampires, and werewolves, prohibited under the original Code, would now be allowed as long as they were "handled in the classic tradition such as Frankenstein, Dracula and other high caliber literary works… read in schools throughout the world."

Revisions dealing with sex also reflected relaxing of the strict morality imposed by the '50s version of the Code. Although illicit sex acts were not to be portrayed, they could now be hinted at. While rape still could not be shown or suggested, seduction could be intimated (although not shown).

The Code provisions for advertising remained unchanged. Unlike other magazines, which relied heavily on advertising revenue, the revenue derived by comics publishers for advertising was negligible. Nearly 95% of revenues came from newsstand sales.

A lengthy preamble was added to the 1971 Code reaffirming the publishers' commitment to act responsibly in publishing comics. It praised comics as an "effective tool" for education and instruction and also noted the comics' emerging role as a contributor to "social commentary and criticism of contemporary life," recognizing the move in the industry to incorporate contemporary issues into storylines. Code changes were explained as necessary to making a positive contribution to "contemporary life."

While wording of some sections of the Code was modified, format of the Code remained unchanged, with emphasis remaining on the depiction of crime and authority figures.

Wow, we've been missing the boat here."

O'Neil sought to introduce fantasy rooted in the issues of the day. Stories tackled problems such as overpopulation, racism, sexism, and judicial due process. However, the Comics Code made crafting such socially-relevant stories very difficult. Under the 1954 Code, comic book characters lived in a perfect world where good and evil were supposed to be clearly defined and where figures of authority were never corrupt. This vision was not consistent with the social unrest that reverberated through the '60s, when the Vietnam War, the Civil Rights movement, the Feminist movement, and other protests questioned the very structure of society. The 1954 Code didn't acknowledge that the world had changed.

To bring an element of realism to comics, the publishers needed a code that adhered to more contemporary standards. Despite its short run, lasting only 14 issues, *Green Lantern/ Green Arrow* helped open the way for a challenge to the outdated rules of the Code.

It's important to recognize one other influence on the industry in its drive to revamp the Comics Code—the under-

Comic book standards defined the reader as a child, and there was no acknowledgement on the part of the CMAA-member publishers that the medium should move beyond content suitable for an audience of all ages.

These changes were approved by the publishers at their meeting in December, but the publishers could not agree over the wording of Part C, which gave the Code administrator broad powers to interpret the Code for "all elements or techniques not specifically mentioned" in the Code. That debate was carried over into the board's meeting January 28, 1971. National had proposed amending that section of the Code by adding a second paragraph that would read:

"It is not the intent of the Code to prohibit the treatment of such realistic problems as drugs, generation gap, poverty, racial relations, abortions and political unrest handled in an instructive positive fashion. This provision shall not be unreasonably invoked."

The debate centered around the interpretation of the Code over stories involving drugs and abortion. Although the amendment was supported by Charles Goodman, representing Marvel Comics, and Carmine Infantino, representing National, three other publishers opposed its adoption, including Goldwater (representing Archie Comics), Leon Harvey of Harvey Comics, and John Santangelo, representing Charlton Comics. The proposal failed, and Section C of the Comics Code remained unchanged.

At a meeting February 1, 1971, the association formally approved and implemented the new Code. Goodman, speaking on behalf of Marvel, promised that after the publication of the three *Amazing Spider-Man* issues (cover-dated May–July 1971) the company would not publish any comic without the seal of approval. The minutes specifically state that the meeting was called "to receive assurances that the members would comply with the Code in the future."

New provisions on the issue of narcotics were not part of the 1971 Code when it was released in February, despite the protests of Marvel's Lee, who had already chosen to release the *Spider-Man* story without the Code seal of approval.

"We can't keep our heads in the sand," Lee told a *New York Times* reporter. "I said that if this story would help one kid anywhere in the world not to try drugs or to lay off drugs one day earlier, then it's worth it rather than waiting for the Code Authority to give permission."

And while DC supported revisions of the Code to permit stories on drugs, Infantino was critical of Lee's decision to proceed without Code approval. "You know that I will not in any shape or form put out a comic magazine without the proper authorities scrutinizing it so that it does not do any harm," he said, "not only to the industry but also to the children who read it. Until such a time, I will not bring out a drug book."

He told the *New York Times* that he would seek not only Code approval but also the approval of knowledgeable authorities on drug abuse before bringing out the magazine.

When the new guidelines on narcotics were issued in April 1971, they were not a formal part of the association's code, according to a story in the *New York Times,* but the Code administrator, Leonard Darvin, maintained that they carried the same force. The CMAA was testing the waters to see what impact the new standards would have. "I think we have to go through the experience of using the guidelines to see how they work," said CMAA President John Goldwater. "When we've had the experience, we'll either add or subtract and then incorporate them into the Code." Infantino praised the addition: "I feel it's a great step forward for the industry.

I think this can prove that the medium that was considered junk for one generation will be the jewel for the next. It can explore the social ills for the younger generation and help them decide how to direct their lives." It's not clear when the guidelines were incorporated into the Code proper, but they were later published as part of the Code standards.

The liberalization had less impact on industry output in the '70s than one might expect. Part of the reason for this was that the push for "relevance" in comics died not long after being introduced. It's been suggested that relevance failed to catch on because audiences wanted more allegorical and escapist entertainment from their Super-hero comics.

The content of some comics did change under the 1971 Code, however. For example, the relaxing of the restrictions on vampire and werewolf stories led to publication of a number of these types of stories, prompting some publishers to propose this amendment at an October 27, 1971 meeting: "No comics magazine shall use the word vampire or werewolf in its title, or bear illustrations of such characters on its

continued on page 63

Above: *Another unused cover by Neal Adams for GL/GA. This one from issue #78.* ©1998 DC Comics

Featured on the next four pages are 16 of Neal Adams' gorgeously tight thumbnails for a forgotten Batman story seen originally, we think, in finished form as a Peter Pan comic. We tried to get the continuity right but think we're missing a few pages. Can you help us with a color xerox? There's a free issue in it for ya! ©1998 DC Comics

Takin' Ten with a Regular Joe

Interview with the great cartoonist/editor/teacher Joe Kubert

Comic Book Artist: *In the mid-'60s, sales for Marvel were picking up and DC was dropping a bit. Did you personally feel the pressure to at least check out Marvel's books and see what the appeal these books had?*

Joe Kubert: No. When I became Editor up at DC, my criteria for what I wanted to do was strictly based on what looked good to me and how I felt. It was intuitive.

CBA: *When you became Editor of the War books in '68, there seemed to be a sudden infusion of relevance. Oddly enough for a WWII book, you made it contemporary—"Stop the War, I Want to Get Off."*

Joe: I felt very strongly about that, that's all. I had been asked to edit books by Carmine Infantino. He had taken on the job of Editorial Director and asked me—we had known each other for a long, long time—and he was one of the few people that I had socialized with while we were growing up. So we knew each other pretty well. When he asked me to come in, one of my criteria was that I was free to do what I wanted. If I was going to be restricted, I wasn't even going to start. There were other directions that I could have gone into that I was thinking of. At the time, I was just coming off the syndicated strip *Tales of the Green Beret* and there were other places that I was considering. Carmine said, "Joe, you can do anything you want."

As a sidebar, when I said, "Okay, I'll do it," Carmine kind of pulled me over to the side and said, jokingly, "Y'know, Joe, now that you will be working here in an editorial position, maybe it's a good idea to start wearing a jacket." I've always dressed kind of slovenly, I guess, so I said to Carmine, very quickly, "If I have to dress in order to do this job, you can take this job and shove it." Carmine said, "No, no. I was just kidding." But that was my relationship with him so he understood that I could do pretty much what I wanted to do— that was the basis for my taking the job. What I did was those things that felt good to me.

When I did the "Make War No More," I felt that what I was trying to do in some ways was similar to what Harvey Kurtzman

IF I COULD TAKE MORE'N "TEN" -- I'D BE IN SAN DIEGO, TOO!

REGARDS TO THE '80 SAN DIEGO CON --Joe KUBERT

had done. The Kurtzman War books had a feeling of realism and what a guy in the Army has to go through—closer than anything I had read before. To some degree, Sgt. Rock was always written that way by Kanigher, but I felt that it needed perhaps a little more of a definitive push in that direction.

CBA: *Were you a reluctant editor or did you lobby for the job?*

Joe: Neither. I became an editor because Bob Kanigher (who had been the editor for a long time) became ill and was no longer able to continue in that position. Because of the fact that I had worked so long with him on the books—I knew the books so well—Carmine had asked me to take over the editorial chores.

CBA: *When you went to the syndicate job, did you really leave DC?*

Joe: Oh yeah. Absolutely. I had to stop at DC completely. Doing a syndicated strip is a completely time-consuming job in terms of deadlines. The pressures are absolutely extraordinary. That strip has to be in the newspapers every day. If you miss a day, it's two days that you have to make up so you have to double up in order to be where you were before. Taking vacations? Forget about it unless you can get somebody to cover for you. I was doing the lettering, penciling, inking and coloring—everything—so it was a full time job. In comic books, the deadlines are stringent but nowhere near as severe as with newspaper syndication. You can sneak an extra day or two in bringing your work in late and still get away with it for comic books. But if your strip isn't there in the paper when its supposed to be, you're in a hell of a lot of trouble.

CBA: *Did the pressures get to you after a while? I noticed that Jack Abel did some inking in the later strips.*

Joe: Yes. I just couldn't maintain the amount of work that I had and I asked Jack to do some inking when I went on vacation.

CBA: *When you left the syndicate, did you immediately go back to DC and request work?*

Joe: It was about that time when I left the syndicated strip that Carmine asked if I'd be interested.

CBA: *A small irony of your career is that Neal Adams suggested you for the syndicate job and your absence at DC opened up an opportunity for his comics work.*

Joe: I don't remember how that worked out but it was funny because at the time that Neal had recommended me, we didn't even know each other. It's nice to have guys like that in your corner.

CBA: *Was getting to know Neal invigorating?*

Joe: Oh, yeah. Neal is a terrific guy and somebody that I consider a very dear friend. We had a hell of a lot of fun together, along with some very interesting and invigorating discussions.

CBA: *When Carmine became Editorial Director, was there an optimistic atmosphere?*
Joe: Very much so. First of all, he hired editors who were artists—Joe Orlando, Dick Giordano. Most of us coming in were art-oriented and it was a hell of a lot of fun. Carmine gave us a lot of freedom. Most of us previously were complaining as artists about the fact that the writers and the editors were so ill-informed as far as the art aspects were concerned. All of us artists were chomping at the bit to get into editing and Carmine gave us the opportunity.

CBA: *Were you aware of the writer's "rebellion" in the late '60s? Bill Finger, Otto Binder…*
Joe: Bill Finger I had known for years. Otto I hadn't worked with. Arnold Drake I knew well. But most of these guys I did not socialize with—these were the guys that I'd meet, talk to whenever we met up in the office. No, I didn't hear much about any rebellion.

CBA: *Would you say that there was a correlation between the purging of writers and editors at DC with the hiring of artists as editors?*
Joe: Purging? I don't think so. I think that perhaps the editors were a bit more selective as far as the writers were concerned from the standpoint of the art itself. But I wouldn't call it a purge.

CBA: *Suddenly Gardner Fox, Bill Finger, Otto Binder weren't getting work anymore.*
Joe: Julie Schwartz was still there and he was very much a writer-oriented editor. I don't remember that being the case at all.

CBA: *You were living in Dover at the time?*
Joe: Yes. The arrangement I had with Carmine was that I would come in maybe two or three times a week. I could come in after the rush hour traffic and leave before the traffic. So I was willing to take the job. It was great. I did my work, I had my place, and that was it. I didn't really involve myself with office politics because it just didn't interest me. I would hear all kinds of things going on but I was pretty much oblivious to it all; out of the loop.

CBA: *Did you deal with the freelancers through the mail?*
Joe: Most of the guys I dealt with, except for Russ [Heath] who worked out of Chicago or John Severin out of Denver, were guys who came into the office—one of the reasons I had to be in the office.

CBA: *It came as a real surprise to me when you mentioned in the Comics Journal interview that you had little interest in the War material.*
Joe: That's perhaps too strong. It isn't that I didn't have any interest in the material. Rather, some surmised that I had a particular interest in War. It's not that I had a disinterest in it. I wasn't particularly interested in it. It was just another assignment, just another job or story that I was illustrating. No more and no less. I have an interest in the work that's under my hand at that particular time. Any job or strip that I got, whether it's a War or Super-hero or Horror story—whatever it was—I tried to invest myself 100% into, emotionally and mentally. That's where I got my greatest pleasure. The biggest kick you get out of doing this work is when you real-

ly put yourself into it 100%. That's the best part about being able to draw. That's my attitude with every job that I get. So it's not a matter of being interested in one genre over another. It's just that every job that I do, I give it my all. I'm going to do reference, I'm going to get as much background and as much feeling about the story content that I can so I can put that into the work.

CBA: *When you became editor of* Sgt. Rock, *you also became writer?*
Joe: For a short period of time, although I would have preferred to have written consistently. I don't consider myself a good writer, but I get the greatest pleasure from being able to control as much as I can on a project. When I started with *Sgt. Rock* writing the stories it was very pleasurable because I was able to have more control over the work I was doing.

CBA: *Immediately the emphasis started on the visual. You started immediately with the double-page spread on pages two and three. Was that an intentional trademark that you wanted to set up for all of your books?*

Above: St. George takes on the Hammer from Hell. Joe Kubert's story and art from Star-Spangled War Stories #147. ©1998 DC Comics

the BRAVE and the BOLD

Above: *Rejected Neal Adams cover art from* The Brave and the Bold #84. ©1998 DC Comics

Joe: I don't know about the trademark. I'm certainly not the first artist to have used that device—but I've always felt that in doing the kind of work that we do, cartoonists should take advantage of the fact that if you do a dramatic or impactful illustration, the larger you make it, the more effective it becomes. If you do a dramatic shot and squeeze it into a little panel, it ain't gonna be that dramatic.

CBA: *Neal Adams was mucking around with Jack Adler in the production department, pushing better standards.*
Joe: Neal was always a gadfly. He was a guy who was always trying to push the envelope.

CBA: *Did you get inspiration from his efforts? You started to use Zip-A-Tone…*
Joe: I had done that before. I had tried pencil work combined with grease pencil/inking. When he was still editing, Kanigher and I had tried different things like doing the whole story in black-&-white (as long as there was a reason for it), to give it a different look and more interest. Bob and I felt that what you want to do with each subsequent issue is to

create something different visually that the reader will not expect, something different with a twist—so they would come back and want to see more. He would do it in the story, and I would do it in the illustrations.

CBA: *Other artists used the same format—the page 2-3 spread. Did you dictate that in most of your books?*
Joe: Yes. That was described in the script. When I was editing, I felt that it was important for the script to be a complete one rather than giving the kinds of freedoms and responsibilities that a Marvel script does. When the artist got the script, the double-page spread was written in. So was all the dialogue, text and captions.

CBA: *Your letter pages were very friendly and intelligent but you could also criticize yourself. Did you feel that readers deserved respect and to be given honesty instead of hype?*
Joe: Absolutely. I felt that it was important for the reader to know that as an editor I was trying to put the best product together, and if it doesn't come across that way to the reader then I want to know why. I was responsible for the letter page for some time when I was editing and I then gave the entire page over to Bob Kanigher.

CBA: *You published a lot of letters from servicemen who were in the Vietnam War. Were you starting to get the feeling that the war was questionable?*
Joe: More than that. What really struck me and Bob from the servicemen's letters was the fact that what we were doing in a comic book was being perceived by a lot of these guys in the Army as real stuff. They believed that there was a Sgt. Rock and that really knocked me out. We put together stories that had credibility. A G.I. could identify with the characters.

CBA: *Did you appreciate Dick Giordano's influence at DC after he came over?*
Joe: What I like most about Dick is that he's a professional. His attitude was the same in teaching here at the school. He's a no-nonsense kind of guy, very analytical and very much disposed to knowing exactly what was going on in the business and communicating that to anyone who wanted to do work for him or was thinking of getting into the business. His books reflected that. He was a complete and total professional.

CBA: *Do artists make good editors?*
Joe: I don't think that an artist or writer *per se* makes the best editor. It has to be a combination of both since the medium is such a visual one. Bob Kanigher has a tremendous graphic sense despite the fact that he can't draw specific details (though he's a terrific abstract and non-representational painter). He writes in pictures which is great for the artist. It's important for any editor, especially in our medium, to have both a graphic sense and the ability to write.

CBA: *Was Carmine's experiment successful?*
Joe: I thought it was. I think that the time during which those guys were there—Dick, Joe Orlando, and the others—was overseen by Carmine and the books took on a brighter look and a more interesting look than they had before.

CBA: *Did you do cover conferences with Carmine?*
Joe: Always. Carmine always had input on the covers. Carmine was the guy who was Publisher and Editor-in-Chief. My responsibility was for about ten different books—and

those covers were my responsibility but I was also doing covers for any number of other books. Carmine would call and ask, "Joe, do you have time to do this cover?" I was doing five to ten covers a week. If the cover had anything to do with a story, he would describe the story. If he had an idea for a cover that had nothing to do with the story, we'd discuss that and I'd go home and do it.

CBA: *Were you overworked?*
Joe: [laughs] No, I was never overworked. I've always been fortunate that if I felt it was too much, I'd cut back somewhere. To some extent, it was an unhappy experience, especially when it came to *Tarzan*. That book probably leaves the biggest lump in my stomach. When I started out, I did all the writing and drawing and that was very pleasurable—it was like revisiting my childhood. I loved what Hal Foster did on *Tarzan* before he went on to *Prince Valiant* and it was one of the first things that got me interested in being a cartoonist in the first place. I was editing a number of books but then I found that the time and responsibility of editing all of those books made it difficult for me to complete my work on time. It was then that Carmine had taken a trip to the Phillipines and had gotten a line on a bunch of artists including Nestor Redondo, a fantastic artist. They suggested that because I couldn't do them myself anymore, that I get some of the best of these new artists to illustrate *Tarzan*. We felt that the storytelling qualities were perhaps lacking with a lot of the Filipino artists so I would breakdown the stories as much as I could. I did them on letter-size paper and then sent them off for them to do. The unhappy part of it is that despite the fact that Nestor and a lot of the guys who were working with him were outstanding, terrific artists, it still wasn't what I had pictured—it still wasn't what I wanted to do and it was terribly frustrating.

CBA: *So it was your loss of control?*
Joe: Yeah. I think that's true.

CBA: *There was a time when you first became editor of the War books that you did a lot of corrections.*
Joe: I wasn't doing it because I had the power and I wasn't doing it because I wanted to insult anybody. The changes that I made were done because I felt that the work had to be consistent—the characters had to be recognizable.

I'm probably most proud of the relationship that I had with Sam Glanzman simply because he gave me the best work he had ever done.

CBA: *How did you become aware of Sam?*
Joe: I think Sam had been working for one of the other editors at DC at the time. He showed me the stuff he was doing. I felt that he did outstandingly the sea stories in which he was personally involved—they're so personal, so terribly personal! You can tell by reading them that these are stories that he actually experienced. I insisted that Sam write these stories because when he did them they were so real, credible and touching. I felt that nobody could write that material better than Sam. He always felt, "Get somebody else to write—I can't write this stuff!" He would always belittle himself for some weird reason. His work was so effective, so appealing. When he would bring in rough layouts, they were absolutely magnificent. He'd say, "No, this is just the roughs," and he'd go home, work over it and polish it. He'd bring back the finished art and it would seem to be missing something—the kind of immediacy that his sketches had. Next time he came in and he says, "I'll go back." I said "No!

Above: *Neal Adams pencil sketch from the Neal Adams Portfolio, Set "C" envelope cover. Tarzan ©1998 ERB, Inc.*

You're not going to take them back! I'm publishing these roughs!" They were the best stuff that he did.

Sam's just a terrific artist. I don't know if you're aware, but his brother is one of the top illustrators for *National Geographic*, Louis Glanzman. One time Sam brought me down to his brother's house in South Jersey, and it was a thrill because he had a whole studio filled with the paintings. I think that Sam's work can sit right alongside of his brother's with no diminishing effects.

CBA: *Did you assign him a specific number of stories to deliver?*
Joe: No. He knew how many pages of work he wanted to do. He limited it to five pages a story and he had *carte blanche*. He could do anything he wanted. I did the same thing with Mike Kaluta! Mike was fascinated with Carson of Venus. He was so in love with it—I saw the sketches he did—and he said, "All I want to do, Joe, is the story page by page just the way Burroughs wrote it." I said, "Do it!" And, of course, he did! Because it was such a labor of love, he did a beautiful job on it.

CBA: *Do you have any affinity for Enemy Ace?*
Joe: Not particularly. I thought that it was an interesting concept which was initially Bob Kanigher's idea. I thought interesting to tell the story from the "enemy's" point of view, especially WWI where war was fought in an entirely different manner than subsequent wars. I think that the character was a good one but I didn't find it particularly appealing.

CBA: *How was the Unknown Soldier created?*
Joe: Probably as a result of Bob Haney and I just banging the idea around—probably more his than mine.

CBA: *How about* Firehair?

Joe: That was my idea. I just felt that I would have really liked to have done Firehair as a series. It's nothing original—a white boy being raised by Indians. But I just felt that it would be a good vehicle to tell some interesting stories, taking place during the settlement of the West—a Western told from the vantage point of the Indians.

CBA: *Was one of the reasons you were interested was that you wanted to do reference on Native Americans?*

Joe: Yup. I have done that. It would've been a project over which I'd have had a lot more control than if I was just illustrating someone else's Western script; an opportunity to do the research and get into the characters a lot more deeply—a lot more interesting for me.

CBA: *How would you rate yourself as an editor?*

Joe: Gee, I dunno. [laughs]

CBA: *You were able to elicit some great work. Russ Heath did that magnificent "Easy's First Tiger" story.*

Joe: Wasn't that fantastic? And he wrote that! I feel that the job of an editor is not so much to control but to direct. I know that when I was Editor and someone really had his teeth into a project that he'd like to do, artist or writer, I'd try to have him do it. It means that it's not just another job. He really wants to do something that he has some sort of feeling about and that's going to come out in the work. I'm for that.

CBA: *So you wanted to get more continuity in the Sgt. Rocks—for a time there were story arcs.*

Joe: Bob had been doing the stories for such a long time that it's easy for any writer to fall into formula and I think that—to some extent—Bob was doing that. I thought that perhaps a change of pace and more depth in story might work.

CBA: *What happened with Russ Heath? Did he just tire of doing the series and want to move on?*

Joe: Russ Heath is someone that I've known for a long time and been my friend for I don't know how many years—but I came very close to killing him. At the time, Russ had a deserved reputation of being awful with deadlines. It's very difficult to publish a monthly book when you're getting a story every six weeks. Russ would miss these deadlines and it was just absolutely impossible to maintain any kind of schedule for the books. It came to a point where I said, "Russ, we're friends. We'll socialize. But you're never gonna work for me again." That's the way it was.

CBA: *Did you prod DC to get the Tarzan license?*

Joe: From what Carmine told me, DC was able to acquire the rights to publish but the Burroughs people had told Carmine that they wanted me to do *Tarzan.* I was very flattered and had wanted to do the strip since I was a kid—

especially as done by Foster. That was when DC took the book and on that basis I became Editor. It was not something I sought.

CBA: *But you obviously relished the book once you got the job. Did you want to do your interpretation or go right back to the source?*

Joe: My whole intent was to do a book that would generate the same kind of reaction from the readers that I got when I first read *Tarzan.* So I did go back to the source and reread all 26 *Tarzan* novels and also went through all the old material that I loved when I was a kid when I read *Tarzan.* I went through it all over again to find out just what it was that I could incorporate into my stuff to make it work. That was my approach.

CBA: *Did you enjoy editing a whole family of books?*

Joe: I didn't even think about it. They grew like crazy. [laughs] I'd be doing a book and Carmine would say, "Well, we got a couple of more books that we'd like you to do." I said, "Fine. I'll take them on. Whatever I can do, as much as I can do." I never really thought about it too much.

CBA: *What was the story behind* Weird War Tales?

Joe: Just another comic book with a twist. The concept of the book's interior was mine—have some sort of weird incident occur and then spin off into the stories. There was about six pages of original material which was the opening and the closing and all of the other material was reprints. We selected stories with an eerie motif. We used a lot of reprints.

CBA: *Did Carmine's management style help or hinder the company?*

Joe: I think it helped the company. Carmine was probably the most conscientious guy in his job that I have ever come across. Carmine was married to that business. It was his mistress, his wife, his family. He thought about the job 24 hours a day. I couldn't have done it. I wouldn't have done it. It was his whole life. Lemme tell you how much: There was a time when he was so involved in the managing, directing and publishing, that he found little time for drawing. He had his studio setup in his apartment in New York and he told me that he had done so little drawing that he was going to sell all of his stuff; three or four filing cabinets filled with his reference material (photographs of every subject that you can think of), art table, chair, taboret, lamps—everything! I said, "Carmine, if you're going to sell it, let me know what anyone else will pay you and I'll buy them from you… I don't want that stuff going just to anybody." And that's what happened. I met whatever offer he received and I took everything. I still have all that stuff. It's still the bulk of my reference file. And I'm drawing at his table.

My relationship with Carmine has always been excellent. I consider him a friend and an extremely talented person. Maybe that's where he made the mistake; devoting himself so completely and so incredibly to the business. He slept, ate, and drank that business and I don't think that the business itself rewarded him as equal to the efforts that he put into it. ⒹⒸ

Can Lightning Strike Twice?
C.C. Beck & the return of the Big Red Cheese

by Paul Charles Hamerlinck

Editor's Preface: DC Comics' revival of the World's Mightiest Mortal during Christmastime 1972 contained all the elements for a phenomenal commercial and artistic success. As the relevance trend in comics waned, a wave of nostalgia for more fantastical and innocent material surged; and riding high on that wave was Captain Marvel and his enduring charm, as people yearned for the simple pleasure of reading good, wholesome comics. Despite the character's complete absence from the reading public for nearly two decades, a cynical and jaundiced world begged for his resurrection; and in the public's demand of quality comics, DC saw quantities of money to be made.

When *Advertising Age* asked DC Publisher Carmine Infantino in February 1973 what the motive was for reviving the character, he said frankly that Captain Marvel might help create a "resurgence of the comics industry" by generating "big enthusiasm in the trade and at the consumer level."

DC brought out big creative guns for the revival, recruiting the consistently-excellent editor Julius Schwartz to helm, who in turn took on board two of the best writers in the field, Dennis O'Neil and Elliot S. Maggin, to scribe—but the trump card was the return of *the* Captain Marvel artist and brilliant storyteller C.C. Beck to draw the adventures of the Big Red Cheese.

House ads and the fan press ballyhooed the debut of *Shazam!* as the comics event of the decade and on every level, from the company's financial projections to the young reader's anticipation, earmarked the book for outstanding success.

The first-issue sales did not disappoint, as the *Advertising Age* article (titled "Capt. Marvel returns (!) to lead comics revival") trumpeted: "Carmine Infantino, National's publisher... said the first issue's 600,000 press run is 'practically a sellout in just over a week, and wholesalers are calling for more.' The initial press run, he added, is 'larger than any other in contemporary (comics) publishing history."

Naturally, big plans for the good Captain were immediately put on the front burner. "Based on *Shazam's* success," *AA* explained, "they now plan to revive the rest of the Marvel Family—Captain Marvel Jr. and Mary Marvel—in the third issue, before spinning them off on their own, again." There was also talk of a TV show, and new marketing approaches were implemented with the $1 tabloid books. "Retailers want profits from comics," one official said, "and this will offer big profits."

Needless to say, many retailers are still awaiting those big profits as their large inventories of *Shazam!* #1 turn yellow with age in the bargain bins—and readers are still hoping for an appropriate revival. Despite all the elements for glory and unprecedented sales and promotion, *Shazam!* failed

P.C. Hamerlinck is editor of the fanzine devoted to the Big Red Cheese, FCA – Fawcett Collectors of America

artistically. Every single creative involved has expressed disappointment in the printed product. What went wrong? Hopelessly biased editor of FCA (the Fawcett Collectors of America fanzine) P.C. Hamerlinck attempts an answer through these quotes from artist C.C. Beck:

"Twenty years after Captain Marvel disappeared, I got a call from Superman's publishers. The same people who ran Captain Marvel out of business were reviving him and wanted me to submit samples of my artwork in competition with some other artists whom they were considering.

"This was somewhat silly, it seemed to me. I had not had to submit samples of my work since I had first appeared as a callow youth at Fawcett's door 40 years earlier—but I sent Carmine Infantino a drawing of Captain Marvel as Rip Van Winkle with a long white beard, a rusted musket, and a look of wonder on his face.

"Carmine loved it. Julie Schwartz loved it. So did E. Nelson Bridwell and Sol Harrison. DC sent me two very poor scripts.

"I drew them up; they loved them. They sent me more scripts. Each one was worse than the one before. I drew them up, trying not to wince too much. After I had drawn about a half-dozen issues, I received two scripts that were so completely worthless that I refused to illustrate them. They were 'The Invasion of the Salad People' and 'The Incredible Capeman.' I returned them.

"Then I went to New York as guest of honor at Phil Seuling's annual 4th of July comic convention. I was introduced to fans by Bruce Hamilton and received a standing ovation. But I was not cordially greeted at DC. It seems I had forced them to call in Kurt Schaffenberger and Bob Oksner to draw up the stories I had returned. I had upset their huge sausage grinder which turned out comic books as mindlessly as a robot.

"DC made me a generous offer, however. They said that I could write my own stories and, if they were accepted, I would be allowed to illustrate them. I wrote one and sent it

Rip Van Marvel. Sample drawing submission by C.C. Beck which clinched the DC assignment.

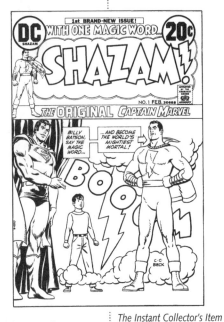

The Instant Collector's Item that never was. Carmine Infantino told Advertising Age *that this issue's press run was "larger than any other in contemporary (comics) publishing history."*

Above: *Time-lapse cartooning. This handout was given out to fans by C.C. Beck during his convention appearances in the late '70s. ©1998 DC Comics*

to them.

"About six months later it was returned to me completely rewritten in DC style: Filled with flying figures, heroic poses, and meaningless mob scenes. All the villains and other interesting characters had been removed. I sent it back saying I wanted nothing to do with it.

"I have never been asked to do any work for DC since."

— C.C. Beck

(excerpt from his soon-to-be-published biography by P.C. Hamerlinck)

News of DC Comics reviving Captain Marvel in the early '70s was met with great enthusiasm, especially when it included the announcement that the Big Red Cheese would be drawn by his original artist, C.C. Beck—but in many ways, the arrangement seemed doomed from the start—the chances of DC, Beck and *Shazam!* possibly achieving any success together was slim to none.

The major factors working against the comic book's success included: 1) the fact that DC, the very company that originally drove Marvel to his grave in 1953, was reviving the character; 2) Publisher Carmine Infantino was banking that nostalgic fans would carry *Shazam!* to the top of the comic book best-seller list; 3) Headstrong editor Julius Schwartz, whose greatest success was in modernizing super-heroes, was working under pressure to live up to the hype and publicity DC gave for the revival; and 4) Putting equally head-strong writer Dennis O'Neil, a writer known for his "relevant," semi-realistic contemporary stories, and rookie writer Elliot S. Maggin on the series. Beck, Marvel's first and arguably greatest artist, was returning to comics not out of need but out of love for the character and his desire to see the hero he helped pioneer be handled properly by his new publishers; and the character's naive, innocent, good-natured ways of the '40s suddenly being tossed into the very different, alien world of the '70s.

The combination of these elements seemed to be too much. After several issues of *Shazam!* and a collector's edition, things had already begun to crumble. Beck argued back and forth with Schwartz about the poor quality of the scripts he was receiving and that he wanted more control of the character. O'Neil and Maggin didn't want Beck altering their scripts.

Shortly thereafter, Beck went to the aforementioned con, and it was there that he returned two scripts to Sol Harrison, DC Vice-President and Production Manager. Beck told him that the stories were inappropriate and he refused to draw them. The stories were both written by Maggin.

Beck returned to his home in Florida, expecting to be contacted soon. A lengthy time passed. He learned that the two stories were given to two other artists to illustrate, Bob Oksner and Kurt Schaffenberger.

Some dust had settled and both parties were ready to give it another try. DC invited Beck to submit a script of his own. Beck did just that and immediately sent them a story he wrote. Many months passed. Finally it was returned to him,

completely re-written by E. Nelson Bridwell. Beck sent it back and said he wanted nothing to do with it. He never heard from DC ever again.

Earlier, Beck had tried to re-write the "Cape-Man" story, but said it was impossible. He complained that all the scripts he had received from DC, especially the later ones, were completely out of character. He was also unhappy with the handling of Cap's alter-ego Billy Batson, claiming that neither O'Neil or Maggin knew that the original appeal of Captain Marvel came from the emphasis on Billy, with Cap used sparingly. Beck said in an interview I did with him in 1979 (published in *FCA – Fawcett Collectors of America* #54) that the DC stories were "too juvenile" and the writers made Billy infantile and stupid.

Maggin and O'Neil disagreed, as did editor Schwartz, stating in *Inside Comix* #6 that his writers "are one thousand times better than C.C. Beck" and "I value my opinion one hundred times more than C.C. Beck's in regard to stories."

Beck's concern for the character's handling in DC's revival was clear. He felt the new stories were uninteresting, involved a lot of pointless action, bad jokes, and that Cap and Billy were made out to be imbeciles. Here was Beck, a man intimately connected with the success of the character originally, who knew what constituted the makings of a great Captain Marvel story: Minimal use of violence, less use of Marvel and more use of Billy. His advice fell upon deaf ears.

Beck voiced his displeasure that DC's policy was to "change and degrade everything and run it into the ground." He often referred to the DC stories as "a hodge-podge of junk."

Neither Maggin or O'Neil felt Beck's comments were justified. O'Neil claimed ha and Maggin did "extensive research" by each reading at least 100 old Fawcett stories. Schwartz also felt Beck's comments were out of line. Schwartz told Joe Brancatelli for *Inside Comix*: "What gives Beck the right to say he knows more about Captain Marvel than anyone else? I object to C.C. Beck taking credit for anything and everything about Captain Marvel."

In the text piece "C.C. Beck — The Shazam Man" in the *Shazam! Limited Collector's Edition* (#C-21, 1973), the writer states that Beck was willing to return to Captain Marvel… providing DC stuck to the original concept and didn't try to make the hero into a modern-day, relevant super-being. "We went right along with his thinking." Sadly, it was never the case.

Beck's attempt at salvaging the poor scripts with edits and re-writes caused an uproar with Schwartz and the DC writers. O'Neil felt Beck took too much liberty with his material and that Beck was "encroaching his area." Maggin felt the same, saying, "I'm the writer of the book, not C.C. Beck."

Schwartz made it candidly known that Beck had no right to change stories completely. "When we first talked," Schwartz said, "I agreed to let him make minor changes he thought important to the stories and the character, but I never gave him permission to change things like he began to do. You couldn't recognize the scripts. I'm the Editor, and it's my job to re-write scripts, not his. He was telling us how to run things. He forgot we hired him, not the other way around."

Beck denied these accusations, claiming that Schwartz gave him permission to go ahead and make changes he thought were important. "If they gave me permission to change things the way I'd have liked them, God knows, I would have done it," Beck said. "The stories were terribly in need of style and continuity. Julie knew I was only getting back into comics out of love for the character. It wasn't the money—it's about the same as it was in 1940—but I felt I wanted to be in on the revival. Everyone guaranteed me the character wouldn't be changed significantly."

The bottom line why Beck was removed was because both he and Julius Schwartz wanted complete control over *Shazam!* and the direction of Captain Marvel.

Beck felt bringing back old Fawcett writers like Rod Reed and William Woolfolk (Captain Marvel's most prolific writer, Otto Binder, had absolutely no interest in being involved with *Shazam!* or DC) and having the book produced in a shop setting similar to his and Pete Costanza's studio back in the Golden Age would have produced a better product.

"The scripts were rotten," Beck said. "I don't see why they didn't let me go out and get in touch with Rod Reed and Bill Woolfolk. I'm sure I could have worked up a much superior product with a shop. But National has this policy of the editor is always right, and consequently, the stories turned out as they did."

Schwartz said no to a shop set-up, pointing out he had spent more years in the business than Beck and that such a set-up wouldn't work in today's environment. As the editor he was under pressure to make the book a seller and wanted full responsibility for the direction and sales of *Shazam!*

"Julie knew I wanted to set up a shop to handle the whole thing," Beck explained. "If I had been able to set up the shop, the stories would have had much more continuity and they would have been better. Everyone takes credit for Captain Marvel, but no one wanted to handle the responsibility for keeping the character good. I was more than willing to handle it, but Carmine Infantino felt that the editor should handle everything."

So ended yet another dark episode in the history of Captain Marvel and DC—the first being the ridiculous lawsuits from the '40s and '50s. I have often wondered what the results of Captain Marvel's revival at DC would have been had Beck been given more control over the book featuring the character he knew like a best friend. We will never know.

I also wonder now if Infantino and Schwartz—while logical that they would defend their own work and stand by the work of their writers—when looking back at that time, if perhaps they would of handled things any differently?

Beck, a man of enormous talent and integrity, must be admired for his strong convictions and not compromising his ideals and standards to DC. He truly cared about the character.

Beck told J.G. Pierce in 1975's *Fantasy Unlimited* #26: "I don't feel bad about being out of work but I do feel sorry for poor old Captain Marvel, who is now being once more put to death by the same people who put him out of business back in 1953." C.C. Beck died November 22, 1989. He was elected to the Will Eisner Hall of Fame in 1993.

Beck said, "The writers made Billy infantile and stupid." From Shazam! *#5. ©1998 DC Comics*

Cracking the Code

continued

cover." The motion was tabled at that meeting and defeated at the board's February 28, 1972 meeting. On June 19, 1973, the association clarified the use of the words Horror and Terror, specifying that while those words could be used in the body of a story, they could not be used in the title of the story. The prohibition of those words on the cover of comic books continued as well.

Horror comics had been banned under the 1954 Code, a move aimed in large part at the genre's most successful publisher, William Gaines. The eccentric head of EC Comics had been a thorn in the side of the other publishers for his outspoken defense of Horror comics and his popularity as a spokesman for the comics industry with mass media covering the comic book controversy in the '50s. His testimony at the Senate investigation of the comic book industry in 1954, where he debated with Sen. Estes Kefauver over whether a comic book cover featuring a man holding the severed head of a woman was appropriate for children, was front-page news all across the country. But Gaines was no longer a factor. His difficulty in getting distribution for his comics, even after he dropped his Horror line, and continuing disputes with the CMAA led him to quit the business entirely and to focus exclusively on publishing *Mad*, which was outside of the authority of the Code. In addition, the success of Warren's titles spurred the publishers to reconsider the Horror ban.

Roy Thomas, then at Marvel, recalls that in 1970 the publishers were looking for new markets. "Super-heroes couldn't do it all," he said. And while Marvel could have published Mystery titles like those of DC under the old Code, Thomas noted: "We wanted to go further and felt the Code was holding us back.

"The fact that the moment the Code was changed, Stan told me to create a vampire super-villain, shows that we were indeed chomping at the bit. I'd had my *I, Werewolf* idea long before, too, and it soon became *Werewolf By Night*." Comics also became somewhat more graphic in their depiction of violence and sex, and occasionally the Code Authority issued memos interpreting the regulations. One such memo was issued April 13, 1974, and clarified the definitions of "excessive bloodshed and gore" as well as warning publishers about their treatment of sex. Darvin wrote:

"Running or dripping blood, or pools of blood, are not permitted. A very small stain around a wound may be acceptable, but must be kept to a minimum. There must be no impression of gore in any areas of objection by governmental and private agencies concerned with children." The memo also cautioned publishers that the topic of rape was forbidden, that the Code prohibited any illustration or dialogue that indicates a sexual act is actually taking place, and that homosexuality or any suggestion by illustration, dialogue or text was strictly forbidden.

Another memo, dealing with the topics of drug addiction, nudity and alcohol, was issued in 1978. The memo, written by Darvin, noted that stories showing or describing any kind of drugs, including marijuana, had to definitely state or show it being a harmful substance. Publishers were also violating Code standards of nudity by submitting art work that showed nude buttocks or "so insufficiently covered as to amount to nudity." Darvin warned publishers that such representations were not allowed under state statutes that legally defined nudity. He also warned against showing the drinking of alcohol and instructed publishers to avoid gratuitous display of signs or scenes showing liquor, beer, or wine.

Despite its softened stance, the 1971 Code represents a lost opportunity for the industry. The publishers were generally content with the *status quo* and unwilling to risk their economic health on experimentation that would challenge the public's perception of comic books. The Code's reaffirmation of comic books as a medium intended for children effectively shut the door on the possibility of attracting a broader audience for comic books and restricted the artistic development of the medium.

Next issue: Marvel's Second Wave '70-'77!

The Battle Over "Jericho"

The Controversy Surrounding *Teen Titans #20*

Opposite: *The evocative, beautiful splash panel by Nick Cardy to the unpublished version of* Teen Titans #20.

Editor's Note: *Comic Book Artist had intended to showcase the set of pages we've thus far uncovered of the rejected* Teen Titans #20 *story (as described below), but we've decided to first put out a public appeal for the pages still missing. With luck, we will be featuring the entire issue as originally drawn by Nick Cardy and written by Len Wein and Marv Wolfman in the upcoming "DC's New Blood" issue. So if any art collectors have the unpublished pages (or photocopies) still missing from our set, we ask them to mail us photocopies. To keep up our end of the bargain, the owners will each receive a free year's subscription to CBA and our undying gratitude. We are in dire need of the following pages of Cardy's art:* 2-6, 8, 12 and 13. *Any and all photocopies of original art pages from the published version of TT #20 would also be appreciated and rewarded handsomely.*

While the entire nation was undergoing a transformation of conscience, debating the vast issues of race, poverty, war, consumer consumption, gender equality, pollution, and the Vietnam War, DC Comics was undergoing its own tumultuous changes, foremost the effects of a loss of readership to Marvel Comics. To survive the competition of TV, comics had to speak to kids in their own language and DC couldn't seem to find a sincere voice. In an effort to win back the fleeing readers, DC sought to establish a niche with readers as *the* relevant comic company—but sometimes the very issues they exploited would come back to bite the company.

Filling the void left by the writers' purge, the new generation of creators contributing to DC was part of the same activist, protesting generation that questioned the push-button issues of the day. Sometimes these (usually) liberal beliefs were contrary to DC Management's and an inevitable generation gap developed. No incident better expresses the tense division of ideology between the new wave and the old guard than the events surrounding *Teen Titans #20*—but the issue may not be, if you'll pardon the expression in an article centered on race relations, so black-&-white.

Marv Wolfman and Len Wein were looking to do stories with impact that went beyond "funny books" and they decided to deal with a perennial American crisis—the shame of bigotry and racism—in the pages of *Teen Titans.* "Len and I, being young liberals," Wolfman explained, "didn't understand why there were no Black super-heroes—though neither of us were Black—but we lived in the real world and there were certainly Blacks all around New York. So we proposed a story featuring a Black super-hero. Dick Giordano, the editor, loved it. At that time, the company was still being run by the original owners and Dick gave this story to Irwin Donenfeld, Vice President of the company, who also loved it."

Donenfeld has no recollection of the incident and Giordano recalls little about the pitch, though he did give the go-ahead on the script. Wolfman and Wein delivered a story that Giordano remembers "was a little preachy, if memory serves." Wolfman described the tale: "The story was about the Mob taking advantage of Black anger by using and

manipulating a teen gang. Somebody goes against the gang and tries to stop them. He preaches the Martin Luther King line that people can't resort to guns and violence. At the end it turned out the masked super-hero is the brother of one of the gang kids."

Neal Adams remembers the story had a heavy-handed agenda. "It was full of racist remarks, reverse racism, with a tremendous amount of lashing out by young, White liberals—'I'll fix those three hundred years of racism, you White honkies!' type stuff. It was simply too much!" Wolfman sees the tale differently. "At the time it was a very controversial story, though when I read it now I can only think, 'Gee, our writing wasn't very good.'"

But, according to Wolfman, Donenfeld saw potential and said, "'Make this a two-parter and make it even more hard-hitting. Go all the way.' He understood that the market and the world was changing." And production went ahead: Nick Cardy penciled 23 pages and began to spot ink the story entitled "The Titans Fit the Battle of Jericho." Carmine Infantino describes the work as "Gorgeous!" and Wein concurs, saying, "It was one of the best art jobs that Nick Cardy had ever done." Wolfman says Cardy "really worked hard on it because he thought that it was an important story." Cardy said, "After all these years I really don't remember [events surrounding the incidents]." But a problem arose not because of the art, but the choice of controversial subject matter.

"The problem was that after we did the script," Wolfman said, "after it was accepted, after it was penciled, inked, lettered and colored, Donenfeld left and there was a new publisher." "I remember looking at it and I rejected it totally," Infantino explains. "Giordano had okayed the job, I believe, but after it was done, I thought it was so terrible that I wouldn't print it. It was simple as that. I don't remember any specifics about it now, but I know that I just didn't like it so I had to use my best judgement."

Giordano also forgets some aspects: "I really don't remember what irritated Carmine, but Neal was right across the hall from me and, with the offices not that big, Carmine would come to the doorway—without coming in—and say something like, 'Richie, I looked at that book, I don't like it and we're not going to publish it. Get a new story.' And he walked away."

Wein recalls, "At the last minute Carmine got gun-shy and was afraid that we wouldn't be able to sell the book in the South and that all these terrible things would happen. So he just pulled the issue and said, 'Nope, we're not going to do it.' This was less than a week before the book was supposed to ship to the printer." And, Giordano said, "The cover was already done and printed so it had to have 'Jericho' in the title and something to do with the action on the cover."

Something had to be done. Fast. "Neal across the hall hears all of this and comes in," Giordano says. "We both had this wonderful relationship at DC in being able to communicate without talking—sometimes you almost had to do that. So after Carmine had thrown the art back in my lap, Neal came in and looked at them. He said, 'What are you going to

Above: *The hero revealed: Joshua makes a speech from the rejected* Teen Titans #20. ©1998 DC Comics.

do?' I said, 'I don't know. I'm going home and I'll think about it. Tomorrow, I'll decide.' I came in next morning and there were seven pages. He had stayed up all night, penciling them."

"I was sought out by individuals as the 'defender of the faith,'" Neal explains, "and I was handed the script by an irate Len and Marv with the request to read it and see if there was anything wrong with it because Management was being crazy and they stopped the job. I read it and felt that it was going way overboard in that it offended White people just as People of Color had been offended for hundreds of years—this was not cool; I could defend it, but not in the face of total rejection. This was a comic book medium and this was the *Teen Titans!*… [the story] was simply too much! First I offered to edit it down to try and save it, but my edit was rejected."

Wein remembers, "They wouldn't accept a new version of the script and they ended up doing an entirely new thing that came out in place of what we had done." Adams "volunteered to rewrite the entire job," Wolfman recalls. "He did and it was still killed. At that point we all understood that it wasn't being killed because of bad writing, but because

it had a Black super-hero in it." Adams says he went to Management to plead for the salvage job: "I said, 'Look, why don't I do this? I will rewrite the story (use as many pages as I can) and let's agree that the guys went overboard, but this is not a reason not to ever give them work again."

"Basically what Editorial was saying," Adams says, "was not to give them any more work because they could not be trusted. I said, 'This was simple enthusiasm, so let's not throw the baby out with the bathwater. I will rewrite this story and I will pencil it. The situation has gone too far so let's just back off. I'll patch up the story.'"

The issue was now getting the job out, so Giordano says he asked Adams, "Can you finish it in time? Carmine is breathing down my neck." Whether Adams stayed up all night writing to salvage Cardy's art or drawing the beginning of an entirely new story is debatable, but one aspect is not in contention: The future of writing team Wein and Wolfman was in serious jeopardy at DC. "I spoke to Len and Marv but they were riled up," Neal said. "I said, 'I'm going to redo the story and we're going to take those references out.' They went, 'What do you mean!? Come on, Neal, don't you think it's unfair?' I said, 'Guys! Yes, you're right, but they don't want to give you any more work in the future because of this. This is very serious business! I need you guys to back off for now.' They said, 'Oh, that's not fair! This is just bull-shit!' I was trying to make peace and it didn't seem to be working. I wanted those guys to work at DC in the future and I couldn't let it go on, so I had to make an arbitrary decision and follow through with the offer I made to DC. So I indeed finished it and gave it to Cardy to ink. Carmine finally accepted it and it wasn't long before Len and Marv began writing again for DC." But some of Cardy's original pages did make it into the final version. "They used about five pages including the cover," Wolfman said, "but they threw a blue tone over the Black characters on the cover so you wouldn't know necessarily that they were Black—though if you look carefully, you can see that they are."

There was lasting damage to the writers' reputations at DC. "From this point, Len and I were both blacklisted at DC for about two years," Wolfman says, adding, "Later on, I used the name Jericho as a Titan in the *New Teen Titans*. While it had nothing to do with the original Jericho story, I was determined to use the name." But occasional jobs made it into their hands from sympathetic editors. "I was able to write the origin of Wonder Girl [and some Mystery tales], for instance," Wolfman said, "because Dick and Joe Orlando would give us short stories under the table."

Neal saw a more positive repercussion: "I think this incident later sparked the decision editorially to accept the Black Green Lantern, and maybe we should have dedicated that story to Len, Marv and Joshua."

A fair assessment of the controversy—even if there was a "right" or "wrong" in this incident—can't be made until the entire story (either Cardy's pages and/or Marv's script) is found and published. Did Marv and Len go "overboard" with virulent racist dialogue, or was management "gun-shy" about dealing with the racial issues (and what would have been DC's first Black super-hero) in comic books? It is our sincere wish that the owners of the "lost" pages will come forward and share their treasures with the rest of us. *CBA* hopes to publish the complete story when they see the light of day.

When Jack Kirby came to DC in the early '70s, his obligations included producing a line of black-&-white magazines intended to appeal to adult audiences. While his In the Days of the Mob and Spirit World made it to the newsstands (albeit for one issue each), an aborted project called True Divorce Cases was initially developed and later refined into an all-black romance title, Soul Love. While the project was abandoned, copies of Jack's stories survive and we're proud to feature pages (sans the splash—which can be found in The Jack Kirby Collector #23) from the tale, "Dedicated Nurse." Inks by Vincent Colletta. Courtesy of and art ©2000 the Jack Kirby Estate. Soul Love ©2000 DC Comics.

The King & the Director

1971 interview with Jack Kirby & Carmine Infantino

Conducted by Mark Sigal, David Rubin, Paul Hock, and Marc Bigley

This interview took place on January 31, 1971 in the offices of National Periodical Publications. It appeared in the fanzine Comic & Crypt #5, 1971. Comic Book Artist has attempted to track down the editors of C&C for permission to reprint but to no avail. C&C credited the help of Emanuel Maris, John Shyke, and Marc Bilgrey in getting the interview, and prefaced with the comment, "The interview is more a casual discussion, which is exactly what took place; just the four of us sitting in Carmine's office talking with him and Jack Kirby."

Comic&Crypt: *How did you both get started in comics?*

Carmine Infantino: I got into comics the same way Jack did; we were kids of the Depression. Now you gentlemen don't know the Depression, or what it was about. It was a period when you starved; your family starved. There wasn't enough food to go around. This was an outlet for us, a field open to us, and like those who went into prizefighting, we went into comics.

Jack Kirby: I feel the minority people had a lot of drive and went to entertainment or anywhere energy was involved.

C&C: *Who did you start off with first?*

Carmine: We both started off with Harry Chesler many years ago. He was a packager—used to package comics, and he used to cheat you like crazy. You were lucky to get paid at the end of the week. It was more fortunate then, as there was time to begin. Now you either have it or you don't—but then there were always little outfits where you could begin, learn, and grow.

Jack: Back then I worked for *Famous Funnies* and I did cowboy stories for one of my earlier jobs. I also was with—!

Carmine: Yeah! He started that way, and you got nothing for it, but you didn't care. It was a chance to work, a chance to draw, and that's all we cared about.

C&C: *Were you in a group of independent artists who sold their stories to the publishers?*

Carmine: No, I worked for Harry for a while; then I went to Quality, erasing pages and doing backgrounds. Those were the days of Lou Fine, and Reed Crandall on *Blackhawk*, and the genius Jack Cole started on *Plastic Man*. I used to erase pages all Summer just to get a break to start, and that was the beginning.

C&C: *You seem to be best known for [Adam] Strange and* The Flash. *Which did you enjoy more?*

Carmine: To tell the truth, I did not like doing westerns, or, strangely enough, *The Flash*. As for Strange, I enjoyed him at first, but I really liked the Elongated Man. I'm sure this goes for you too, Jack; the ones you're best known for aren't the ones you like best.

Jack: The ones I began weren't the well-known ones. I began Manhunter and Mr. Scarlet, which just faded out. Every strip I did was a challenge, as I'm sure it was to Carmine; but I feel what Carmine is trying to say is that he especially liked one thing but we couldn't always do that. We did what they gave us to do.

Carmine: I could never do a sci-fi story the way he could.

C&C: *But your speed concepts and futuristic cities were amazing.*

Carmine: Did you see the ones he did?

C&C: *But you're two different types of artists. You can't—*

Carmine: This isn't what I'm trying to say. This is not what I enjoyed the most. I enjoyed the Elongated Man because of the satire in there. Well, let me say something. Back in the early days there was quite a lot wrong with my drawing and every once in a while I would go up to this fellow in the city. We'd talk and he'd help me—but the most important thing he helped me do was think, and I feel he was one of the best around. When I went up there, he used to stop his work and look at my stuff and give me suggestions. That person was Jack.

Jack: Well, I'm not going to take credit for that. Carmine was and is a fine artist, but back then Joe Simon and I used to have an apartment up there. All the guys got together and I think we helped each other actually. That was the main purpose back then as none of us had a school; we became each others' school. There were things that Carmine knew that I didn't. It was an exchange and that's basically how artists learned back them. We took standards from each other.

C&C: *Just what was your relationship with Joe Simon? How did it start?*

Jack: It started the same way all things did in the industry. Some guys gravitated to each other and Joe Simon and I met, liked each other, and decided to work together.

C&C: *In a lot of your books, you started the sort of panel within a narrative. How did you get the idea for that?*

Carmine: The reason that was done was because we wanted to get as much motion as possible going, so that when you put that little box in with the silhouette of the batter pulling his bat back, in the next panel you had the follow-through which kept the flow of motion.

C&C: *But how did you get the idea [for "Strange Sports Stories"]? Was it a brainstorm of yours or what?*

Carmine: Well, Julie Schwartz, the Editor at the time, told me to go home and make the book look different.

C&C: *Did you enjoy doing that particular series?*

Carmine: Yes, I did. Maybe it was the sports angle to it. I could design stadiums and futuristic basketball arenas, and the storyline made you think. Every book was a challenge.

Jack: I think you hit on the right gimmick. I feel that sports books are the toughest books to do. To do it in the first place is a challenge. To do it effectively was an achievement of some kind. I never had the opportunity to do it but I still feel that it would be a challenge.

Carmine: I must have penciled a page a day on that stuff. That's how rough it was because you had to make sure the action followed through. If you didn't, the thing didn't work. It looked terrible. The bat was back and on the next panel, the ball connected. Then the ball moved out. The thing I enjoyed most was when somebody said I want it different.

C&C: *We've noticed that some comics are featuring covers by you. Do you ever feel like getting back to the drawing board?*
Carmine: Jack, do you want to answer that for me?
Jack: Well, I feel essentially Carmine will always have the urge as anyone involved in a creative activity does. I think it's a matter of circumstances and if Carmine had the opportunity and the time…!

C&C: *What led you into becoming Editorial Director?*
Carmine: An accident. I was drawing here. I think I was drawing the Batman and Deadman. It was during that story that the second guy at Marvel was slaughtering National. I think his name was Kirby or something, and the gentleman who happened to be in charge at the time asked me if I would care to stop in and help re-organize. We discussed it and I finally did. I thought it would be interesting.

C&C: *Well, you tried the "New Trend" books. They failed but I read them all and I thought they had possibilities, especially* Bat Lash.
Carmine: In *Bat Lash* what bothered me the most was that I wrote it. I plotted every one of them and Sergio [Aragonés] took it from there and wrote them down. Then Denny [O'Neil] would dialogue them later.

C&C: *When a friend of mine met Mr. Weisinger, he was told by him not to go into comics; that it was a dying field. He told him rather to go into painting and to get out of comics.*
Jack: You should have told him not to knock anything he hasn't tried.

C&C: *Was that the type of attitude that was around then?*
Carmine: No, I think it was a personal attitude.

C&C: *Has the atmosphere changed? Are new ideas welcome?*
Jack: Yes. It's a different company today. If a company feels that there is an essential need somewhere they get the right executive to fill that need. In other words, to expedite that need. You use that need to revitalize the company. Comics are in a transition, as far as I see it. I think this is the most interesting time for comics.

C&C: *How long have you had the idea for the* New Gods?
Jack: Well, I guess for several years it's probably been in the back of my mind, but I've never sat down and worked it out though I've always known it's been there.

C&C: *Do [the] Forever People come from the same place as the New Gods?*
Jack: Yes, but they don't call the things you see the same things that I do. In other words, I would say great or swell, and you guys would say cool. It's not New Genesis to them, but Supertown. That's how they see it. There is, though, a lot more to it than that and I think you guys are going to find it pretty interesting.

C&C: *According to sales, the Super-hero book is on the rocks.*
Jack: I pay attention to the sales occasionally only because I plot the books, and sometimes the sales are my only link with the fans. I feel that the Super-hero surf is going somewhere. What I'm trying to do is follow its exact trail; that's my job. I want to entertain you guys and find something new for you—if not just for you, for myself—the challenge of my job is to keep me from getting bored. I feel that if I would want to buy my own book, I have met that challenge.

C&C: *The themes in* New Gods *and* Forever People *are expansions of the old themes from Marvel. It seems that you had more ideas, but they wouldn't let you continue with them.*
Jack: That's more or less true. It's not that I was cramped, but there were limitations which stopped me from going on. Over here I have the chance to go beyond them; I feel that whatever story there is to this "gods" business, the "new" gods or the "old" gods, I feel that there is a story to them. I

Above: *The one that started it all—at least for Ye Ed. Jimmy Olsen #133, Jack Kirby's first '70s DC comic book.*
©1998 DC Comics

STRANGE STORIES OF THE DNA PROJECT

THE ALIEN THING!!!

THE FIRST GENETIC STRUCTURING TO RUN WILD IN THE LABORATORY ALMOST PROVED TO BE THE LAST!!!

WHEN IT QUICKLY EVOLVED TO ADOLESCENCE, THE DNA PROJECT FOUND TROUBLE ON ITS HANDS!! THE BATTLE WITH IT LASTED FOR A DAY!!

HERE GOES A GAS GRENADE!

IT WAS FIRST "DNALIEN" THE PROJECT HAD PRODUCED!! IT GREW FAST!--AND HOSTILE!! NOTHING SEEMED TO STOP IT!!

PAF!

TRANQUILIZING GAS SEEMED TO SLOW DOWN ITS MOVEMENT--BUT NOT THE MATURING PROCESS!!

HERE IT COMES! LOOK OUT!

SOMEHOW, ITS METABOLISM WAS WILDLY ACCELERATING!!--EMITTING GREAT BURSTS OF BRIGHT, SEARING, DAMAGING ENERGY!!

Above and opposite: A Tale from the DNA Project, Jimmy Olsen #143. Uninked pencils by the King, Jack Kirby. Don't forget to check out the ad in this issue for The Jack Kirby Collector, the premier magazine devoted to the comic book legend (and our sister publication to boot!). ©1998 DC Comics

feel that there was an actual replacement of the "old" gods by new ones which are relevant to what we see and hear. In other words, Thor may have been great in medieval times, but I feel somehow that we have transcended. Once it had a certain glamour, but now we need a new kind of glamour. Not that it isn't fantastic, but we don't see it in the same light anymore. I think we see things differently, the same things with an altered interpretation. You know what Thor looked like, what Mercury looked like, what Zeus looked like, and all the rest of them. It's like everything that's done and seen. What I'm trying to do is show the things that haven't been done or seen. We have our "new" god today—technology. A new way of looking at things that I have got to represent. How do I represent that new technology? I've got Metron. How do I represent the kind of feelings we have today? Maybe some of us are analyzing ourselves, trying to find out why we're a violent society and how we could be non-violent, so we all become Orion. Why do these feelings live like that inside of us? Not only do we associate ourselves with them, but these are conflicts. But why do we have conflicts like that inside of us? So we try to analyze it, just like Orion does. That's what the gods are. They are just

representations of ourselves. At that time, you take a crummy Viking, remove the glamour, and what the heck was he? Some poor guy in bear skins who never took a bath. He had a beard with lice in it and he says: "Look at me, I'm a really cruddy object"—and I felt the same way. The G.I.'s feel the same way sometimes when they're sitting in some hole but suddenly he says: "What the heck am I doing? What am I a symbol of?" And then he begins to idealize the version of all the bravery that goes into the fight. Maybe he begins to see himself as Thor and his captain as Odin. Then he sees what he's fighting for. He sees why he's in that hole, why he's in the dirt, why he's dressed in that stupid uniform. It's not only functional—it's symbolic of what he is; he comes into a whole new world and he feels pretty good about it. That's what it's all about—to make everything we see and know around and in us, and give it some meaning; and the gods are nothing more than that. They are making us see some value in us and we have—we have that value. So in order to express that value, we make "new" gods. We can't be Thor. We can't be Odin anymore. We're not a bunch of guys running around in bear skins; we're guys that wear spacesuits and surgeon's masks. A surgeon is godlike because he handles life and death. If you want to idealize him that's the way to do it. A nuclear physicist is Metron. A mathematician is Metron. A guy who works a projection booth in a theatre is Metron. We're trying to know everything and we've got the equipment to do it. That's where Metron's chair comes in. It's one of our gadgets. That damn chair can do anything!

C&C: *There is so much meaning in the strip. I read it and I enjoyed it but I couldn't lace all these things into it, but it's there.*
Jack: It's there because I'm trying to interpret us. Nothing more than that. I'm trying to interpret what we're in. What kind of times we live in—and we should have these versions. I can see this guy in a space suit. There is no reason why he shouldn't be able to go to Mars. Maybe in '75. Because we can do it. The materials are there. They'll be common—and to put it all in one word that's Metron—and New Genesis. You name it. That's New York or Chicago; just an idealized version of that. It's the city.

C&C: *Did you ever mention this to Marvel?*
Jack: No. I was involved in what I was doing there and I feel that this would never have fit into what they were doing. This is a whole new interpretation and it cannot be told with shields and swords; it must be done with what we know and deal with what we worry about.

C&C: *So was Thor; when it came out as a mythology in the olden times it was relevant and real to people then, because people were using the same things: swords, shields, etc.*
Jack: Yes, Thor was very real to this guy in the Middle Ages, and not only that; if you think about it, Thor was a religion as well. Thor is not a comic book story—Norse mythology was a religion, just as Greek mythology was. I was being superficial when I did Thor and if I showed it to a guy who was really involved with it he would tell me it wasn't good enough.

C&C: *Why?*
Jack: Suppose I was to make an interpretation of things you really believed in. It would be weak because those things are on such a grandiose scale, I can't draw them.

C&C: *Who would you classify as your favorite artist?*

Jack: Well, I like them all, especially if they have their own distinct style. Neal Adams is one, Steve Ditko is another.

C&C: *Any of your favorite comics work being done now?*
Jack: I like anything that is trying to do something different. Anything that tries to put new life into the strip, or upgrade the medium is doing a good job.

C&C: *Who thought of the black-&-white books?*
Jack: I don't know how these things start. They start with everybody. It might have been in your mind too!
Carmine: No. It was in yours. It is a completely new approach to the visual medium. It will be composed of photographs, drawings, and writing. It's very different.

C&C: *Isn't it something like Gil Kane's* Blackmark *book?*
Carmine: Nothing like that at all! This will be larger-sized books with black-&-white material.

C&C: *How big are you going on this? About 150,000?*
Carmine: No. Much more.

C&C: *That is what happened to* Savage Tales. *They only printed 150,000 and they were hard to get. Neal Adams told me that Marvel dished out quite a bit of money because they were trying for a quality effect. They spent $6,000 instead of the usual $3,000. I don't know if it's true or not.*
Carmine: I'm going to tell you to look at Jack's books and make up your own mind.

C&C: *With the black-&-white books, are you trying for an adult market?*
Jack: I am trying for a universal market. It's going to be rational for the adults and exciting for the kids. In other words, if an adult picks it up and he analyzes it as an adult should, he might find it interesting whereas the kids will have the costumes, the action, the strange atmosphere which I think every strip needs. Fantasy is interesting because it is a projection, an idealized version of everything we see and hear. I think that is what makes it interesting. For instance, if you see a tank I've drawn, or a car, it could never work, but it's an interesting looking object. If you want to analyze my machines, they may be nothing more than a fantastic typewriter or a pencil sharpener.
Carmine: This is the beginning for comics. Only comics not as you know them. This is a whole new world; that's why I'm here. That's why Jack is here. On June 15, the first book we were talking about comes out. July 15, the second will be coming out. We're doing our own thing. Jack wouldn't be here if we were doing what everyone else is doing.

C&C: *Some comics, like* Superboy, *don't have the same flexibility, or even attempt it—as long as they sell.*
Jack: They are not made for a universal market. They are not aiming for my market.
Carmine: First of all, the *Superboy* and *Lois Lane* books—*Lois Lane* is made for the "girl" market. *Superboy* is the same thing. It's at another level, though. You don't mess around with a book like *Superboy,* which is selling over 500,000. That's not saying what we will do tomorrow. I don't know. Jack will develop his own line of books. It will have Jack's stamp. We have some other stamps. You'll buy these or you won't—but to turn out [only] one stamp in a company, I can't feel is very good.

C&C: *Did you like Gray Morrow on* El Diablo?

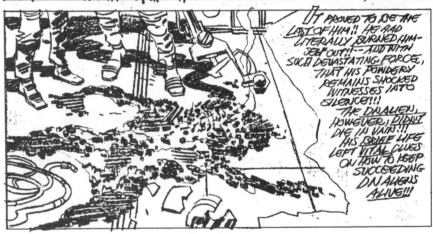

Carmine: No, I did not like his artwork. I told him I didn't. That does not mean that Gray is not a talented man. I thought that Gray should be on other things that he could do well.

C&C: *What did you think of his work on* Witching Hour?
Carmine: Beautiful. That's Gray's field.

C&C: *Are you considering making the new books monthly?*
Carmine: I don't know. If Jack's books turn monthly, can Jack do all of the work by himself? I'm not going to ruin him. I'm not going to spread this guy so far that it'll destroy him—and I won't let anybody else do his characters. Nobody touches his characters! He knows what he's doing with them.
Jack: *Silver Surfer* was taken out of my hands. I originated it because I had a reason for the Silver Surfer. Nobody else had a reason for him; I knew the Silver Surfer. Nobody else did.
Carmine: Jimmy Steranko was offered the *Fantastic Four* and he turned it down. He said he wouldn't presume to follow Kirby.

continued on page 85

Archie's Comics

Archie Goodwin talks about DC in his last interview

Conducted by Jon B. Cooke

What follows is the final interview that Archie Goodwin gave before he passed away on March 1, 1998. It was conducted via telephone on February 20, 1998, while Archie was preparing to leave on what became his last day in the DC offices. While I was not able to get a transcription to Archie before his passing, Dennis O'Neil was kind enough to do an initial edit, and the final transcript was approved by Anne T. Murphy, Archie's wife. Very special thanks to Anne, Dennis, and Paul Levitz.

Comic Book Artist: *I'm doing an issue devoted to DC Comics between 1967 and 1974.*
Archie Goodwin: Right.

CBA: *I'm starting with Dick's arrival in '68 and ending with your departure in '74.*
Archie: Right.

CBA: *I've chosen your departure kind of arbitrarily but in the hopes of basically discussing why a lot of creative talent was leaving DC at a period of time. Anyway, where were you working before starting at DC?*
Archie: Let's see: I think I was probably freelancing at Marvel.

CBA: *Is that when you were doing* Iron Man?
Archie: And the *Hulk,* and some other stuff. Yeah.

CBA: *You did some great Hulk stories, I thought.*
Archie: Yup. Or was that later on?

CBA: *No. That was '72 or '73. What made you go over? You seemed to jump around from company to company a lot.*
Archie: Yeah, I would always try to get out before they caught me.

CBA: *[laughs] What do you mean? Caught doing what?*
Archie: Just a joke. I think I maybe suffered from a short attention span a little bit, so I could do something for a year or two but then I began feeling the itch to move on. I always find new offers tempting. It's great if you're doing something that you really, really like but it's also great to somehow have something shiny and new

Convention sketch of Manhunter by Walt Simonson. ©1998 DC Comics

waved in front of your face, too. While I had been doing freelance writing for Marvel, I got the offer from Carmine Infantino of DC to take over three of their War books that Joe Kubert had been editing. Since he was taking on *Tarzan* and a couple of other projects he didn't want to continue working full-time on those. I had been away from editing—and away from War comics—since I did *Blazing Combat* at Warren, so it was a tempting new opportunity.

CBA: *Did you follow Kubert's War books at all? Did you have to play catch-up?*
Archie: Not too much. Back in those days there were not so many comics being published that you couldn't go back and re-read and pick up on stuff pretty well. You could also kind of keep up with the stuff. Kubert's books were always interesting, visually exciting books so I had a fair idea of what was going on in those.

CBA: *When you went into the job, were you looking back at Blazing Combat or were you seeing this as an entirely different thing? Were you going to follow Kubert's lead or did you want to try something new?*
Archie: No. I wanted to do a bit of a mixture of both. The format of the books involved continuing lead features which I'd never tried with War material and they also included some short stories thrown in as well—and I could kind of do *Blazing Combat*-style short stories and yet also get to try the longer-form material of the continuing characters.

CBA: *If memory serves, you did "The Losers" with Johnny Severin doing the art.*
Archie: Right. Robert Kanigher was writing it.

CBA: *Did you say, "We're going to establish continuity"? It never had continued stories before.*
Archie: That was one of the things I tried to get going into all of the books with the on-going characters. If you're going to have continuing characters, I felt that there should be some continuing continuity. [pause] What else would you have but continuing continuity?

CBA: *[laughs] The Dept. of Redundancy Dept.*
Archie: Yes.

CBA: *You also worked on* Star-Spangled War Stories. *You wrote that?*
Archie: I think I wrote the first few. Later on, Frank Robbins took over the writing on that stuff, but in the beginning, I wrote the "Unknown Soldier" feature when I took over *Star-Spangled War,* and I wrote the "Haunted Tank" feature in…

CBA: *G.I. Combat.*
Archie: …*G.I. Combat,* of course.

CBA: *Were you a fan of Russ Heath's "Haunted Tank"?*
Archie: I was a fan more of the artwork than some of the stories. I thought that the very best DC War book was *Our*

Army at War with Sgt. Rock which Kubert had edited. I don't think that anything I did in the other War books ever reached the level of some of the Kanigher/Kubert/Russ Heath Sgt. Rock stories—but I did some interesting things.

CBA: *Gee whiz, but some of the back-up material was outstanding, Did you approach Alex [Toth] to do "Burma Sky"?*
Archie: Yeah.

CBA: *How do you approach a short story like that? Did you have Alex in mind?*
Archie: Oh, yes. You know, Alex Toth, Flying Tigers, gotta do it! In that case, it's like me being a fanboy. To me, having Alex Toth do any kind of airplane story, it's a joy for me. If I see a chance to do something like that, I will. He did a really fabulous job on it. And I thought it was a good story, too.

CBA: *Did you initially call him and say, "I have a story idea. Do you want to hear it?" or did you send him a full script?*
Archie: That's a good question and I don't know the answer. Often my method of working with artists, particularly on short stories—but even on longer stories—is to kind of find out if there's something in particular that you would like to draw, some subject that you'd like to do, some kind of scene that you'd like to see, and then try to work that into the material. I give them something that they really get enthusiastic about. And I don't know if I talked to Alex about doing something or if he suggested doing the Flying Tigers or if I just did the script and said, "Would you be interested in doing this?"

CBA: *Were you happy with the results?*
Archie: Incredibly happy.

CBA: *What other artists did you seek out to work with that come to mind?*
Archie: I worked with George Evans, Tom Sutton (who I thought did several really nice War jobs for DC—including some he wrote himself), a Scottish artist named Ken Barr…

CBA: *He originally worked with Kubert, right? For a period of time, then he disappeared. That's what first made me buy your War books as a kid—seeing the Simonson story "UFM" and Ken Barr's work. Did he live in Scotland?*
Archie: No, he was over here.

CBA: *Do you remember him coming into the office or was it by mail?*
Archie: It was usually… back then, people actually delivered jobs to the office. Sometimes they'd have to mail them in but a lot of the times they did deliver the work to the office.

CBA: *Ken was predominately a Science-fiction artist?*
Archie: No, he was just a good general illustrator. His background in British publishing was some Science-fiction but he had done a lot of the British War comics.

CBA: *After working for you, he pretty much disappeared from the comics scene in America?*
Archie: Well, he worked for several other publishers. He did work for Marvel—a lot of covers for Marvel's black-&-white line later on, he didn't just work for me.

CBA: *Did you discover Gerry Boudreau and Walt Simonson?*
Archie: I think Walt made a trip to New York to show his work and he showed it to several different editors. I think Joe Orlando was the first editor to actually give Walt a job and I may have been the second or third person. Gerry was someone that Walt knew from Rhode Island. They had worked together on a project. So I tried Gerry on writing some of the material as well.

CBA: *Do any other short stories come to mind? Was that Wally Wood story yours?*
Archie: I tried to get Woody but I don't think I ever got…!

CBA: *There was an aviation story, "Spitfire."*
Archie: That may have been Joe's from a slightly earlier era.

CBA: *Did you enjoy working on the War books? Was it all you wanted it to be at the time?*
Archie: Yeah. I enjoyed working on them. I think I felt like I was never able to top the level of what we managed to do on some of the *Blazing Combat* material, but it was interesting to do.

CBA: *You dealt with issues—there was a Joe Orlando-illustrated story in* Blazing Combat *that comes to mind that took place in rice paddies about Vietnam, it was contemporaneous… 1965, I think you came out with the book and Vietnam was starting to pick up. Did you want to deal with real issues, either covertly or whatever in the War books?*
Archie: Yeah. As much as I could. The trouble with doing Vietnam War stories back then was there wasn't a wealth of research available like now where you can find anything you want about Vietnam. A lot of what you had to do on Vietnam was to dig out of the newspapers and some news magazines a little bit of research and then kind of extrapolate—if this is happening, what's really going on? What is it really like? My personal feelings were that we shouldn't have been there but at the same time my feeling was also that what I'm most interested in is telling the story of the people who get caught up into the war, whether it's a war we should be in or not.

CBA: *I think that there was a moment in one of the letter pages where you confessed that you purposely left off the blurb "Make War No More." Was there any reason behind leaving it off? Why did you take it off?*
Archie: I felt that if I'm doing a comic book, selling it, and it's a War comic, I felt uncomfortable with that as a message at the end. That was a personal thing.

CBA: *Did you receive any heat for it in the office?*
Archie: No.

CBA: *Did you go back to it or did you just stop using the bullet altogether?*
Archie: I just stopped using it. I felt like if the point of my story was "Make War No More," they'll get that. I didn't need that. It was something they added to the books under Joe Kubert and it was probably a worthwhile thing to do. It slugged home a certain message but it was just something

Convention sketch of Manhunter by Walt Simonson. ©1998 DC Comics

Above: *Evocative page by Russ Heath for* Our Army at War *#212. Archie calls Sgt. Rock by Heath the best DC War comics.* ©1998 DC Comics

that I felt uncomfortable with so I dropped it.

CBA: *Did you ever sit down with Joe Kubert and go over the books? Did he give you any pointers? He was obviously doing a lot of the books and you came in to take them off his hands—did you talk to him about them?*

Archie: Not a great deal. We were kind of a mutual admiration society and he didn't try to direct me and stuff but he would continue doing covers for me. If I asked advice, whether technical or how to deal with a writer or artist or something like that, he was always great with helping me out.

CBA: *He came in a couple of days a week. Did you come in every day?*

Archie: No. For a while, we alternated; on the days Kubert didn't come in, I would be in using his desk with the same assistant.

CBA: *Allen Asherman was your assistant?*

Archie: Mostly I worked with Jeff Rovin.

CBA: *You also worked on* Detective Comics. *How'd you end up with that?*

Archie: After doing the War books for about half a year, Carmine Infantino, the Editorial Director, said that Julie Schwartz was going to do *Strange Sports Stories* again and wanted to give up one of his books, and it was *Detective.* Of all the DC characters, Batman was probably the one that I liked best, so I jumped at the chance to do something with Batman.

CBA: *You really made an impression right off. Did you request Jim Aparo for…?*

Archie: That was the plan. The problem was that as a writer and editor, I was not as efficient as Aparo and I couldn't keep up with Jim's time slot for when he could do the book. So I began using other people through no fault of Aparo's but through my inability to keep matching his schedule. So I had stuff by Dick Giordano, Howard Chaykin, Alex Toth, Sal Amendola…

CBA: *Did you have to talk Alex into doing a Super-hero story?*

Archie: No. He had always wanted to do a Batman story and, in fact, he would occasionally still like to do a Batman story.

CBA: *Would you seek him out for one?*

Archie: We work at it, we work at it. He's a little less casual about what he does in the way of a story now.

CBA: *What was you favorite experience working on* Detective? *Was it the Manhunter or the Batman stories?*

Archie: It would have to be the Manhunter material.

CBA: *What's the genesis of that?*

Archie: You had three Batman books at the time. You had *Batman, Detective Comics* and *The Brave and the Bold.* Each one of them had a different editor. The ongoing *Batman* book was Julie Schwartz's, *Detective* was mine, and *The Brave and the Bold* Murray Boltinoff edited. *The Brave and the Bold* was a team-up book and obviously the *Batman* book was the major Batman book. [In] *Detective* you sort of tried to do Batman stories that fell in kind of a "detective" vein but you'd usually have a back-up feature as well. My taking over the book, I decided that I couldn't make a lot of changes in Batman and what was being done with him because this was not the major book to make Batman changes in. So I thought having a back-up feature that would take on kind of its own continuity and create some excitement on its own and not be totally out of whack in a book called *Detective* would be a good way to go.

CBA: *How did you come up with the idea for Manhunter?*

Archie: At the time, Jack Kirby's Fourth World material was coming out and in the packaging of them they reprinted a lot of Kirby's earlier stuff, and they reprinted some of the earlier Manhunter stories that he had done. I just thought it's a cool name: "Manhunter, he stalks the world's most dangerous game!" It just seemed like a neat idea that fit into this "detective" format and yet was quite a bit different from the way Batman approached things. Although Batman is a manhunter of sorts.

CBA: *Thinking about it, it really was a mystery that was unravelling. Walt has said that it wasn't necessarily Paul Kirk to begin with but became Paul Kirk?*

Archie: First we were going to do just an all-new character but then we began thinking, "We've got this kind of neat character. If we call him Tom Schmutz, it doesn't make him a better character, it doesn't gives us a past history to draw upon or anything." It just began seeming logical to just kind of extrapolate out of the Kirby character.

CBA: *You say "we." Did it start off as a collaborative effort? Was Walt in on the beginning with the first story as co-plotter?*

Archie: We go back and forth on that a little bit. My memory is that yeah, we pretty much… when I work with any artist, I try to collaborate with them—draw them into the process. My memory is that Walt would always be contributing stuff to the plot. He's a great storyteller. His memory is that I did a full, typewritten plot and maybe even some thumbnails and things like that. And it was not until maybe the second or third episode that we stopped writing plots and just began discussing the stuff. So that, for me, is lost a bit in the shrouds of time.

CBA: *You didn't last that long at DC. Was that just wanderlust or…? Why did you leave DC after only about 18 months?*

Archie: One, I got an offer from Warren to come back and edit a couple of his titles which I found interesting and wanted to try. At the same time, I also felt that DC was falling behind in terms of giving back original artwork to the creators. Marvel began doing it, Warren began doing it, most other companies started doing it and we could not get DC to return people's original artwork—they insisted on keeping it. So it began making it harder to work with a lot of the better artists and again, being a thing I felt uncomfortable about—if I was getting an offer from someplace else where they would give back the original artwork which I felt should go back to the artist then I certainly felt more comfortable about going in that situation.

CBA: *In your memory, Marvel was returning original artwork in 1974?*
Archie: Yeah, they started doing it.

CBA: *I thought DC was the one who did it first.*
Archie: I don't think so. That's not my memory.

CBA: *And Warren was returning artwork?*
Archie: Warren started doing it, yes.

CBA: *Who was first? Was it by request from creatives?*
Archie: Around that time in the mid-'70s, they formed this organization, the Academy of Comic Book Arts, and a lot of issues came up in meetings we'd have, and return of artwork became a very important issue.

CBA: *You did attract some very fine talent right when you started off with Warren. I'm doing a Warren issue down the line and I hope to be able to talk to you about that then.*
Archie: Certainly, I'd be happy to.

CBA: *In a nutshell, how would you characterize your time at DC? Was it a good time?*
Archie: Yes, it was. I think that Manhunter is one of just several projects that I've worked on that I consider a highlight in my career. It is something that I may never be able to top in a lot of ways. To have done that and for DC to have given me the opportunity to do that was great.

CBA: *What made Manhunter so special beyond the team-up of two people who worked so well together—was it the finite storyline?*

Archie: It didn't start out to be a finite storyline but I knew long enough in advance that I would be leaving so that Walt and I could plan to bring the series to an end. We checked with Carmine, the Editorial Director, and Julie Schwartz, who was going to take the book back, to see if they would go along with our doing that and they were fine with it.

CBA: *There must be some gratification that the character has never been revived.*
Archie: Well, the character has.

CBA: *It has?!*
Archie: Several times. It still remains the version that people tend to remember.

CBA: *Did you have a hand in the revivals?*
Archie: I did in one of the last ones that fared no better than anyone else's.

CBA: *Where was it revived?*
Archie: It was revived as a title called *Manhunter* as part

Above: *Rejected cover for GL/GA #87. What was the problem to make Neal Adams redraw the entire cover with nominal reposturing? ©1998 DC Comics*

of the *Zero Hour* spin-off.

CBA: *I probably just assumed it was that Steve Englehart thing [Justice League of America #140-141].*
Archie: No, but Steve did some Manhunter stuff, too. I think John Ostrander and Kim Yale did a Manhunter as well—but the main reason I decided to try it one more time was just to make sure to do one that had nothing whatever to do with the version that Walt and I had done.

CBA: *To backtrack just a little bit, was your idea to do the opposite of the War books—you really didn't do continuity, you did arguably—well, not Elseworld stories—but you now currently edit* Legends of the Dark Knight *which is very self-contained.*
Archie: I did more self-contained stories. I tried to give them a slight, spooky, supernatural edge even though they usually have an explanation at the end.

CBA: *Did you try to get Neal Adams to illustrate any of your stories?*
Archie: Probably.

CBA: *Do you remember one of the stories that credited "Story Idea" by Neal Adams?*
Archie: There was one story called, I think, "Night of the Stalker" that Steve Englehart did the dialogue on and Sal Amendola and his brother had plotted. Neal may have given them some advice on that.

CBA: *So you don't remember what his specific contribution to that was? The cover wasn't done first? It was by Neal.*
Archie: No, the cover was done after the story.

CBA: *So you gave quite a bit of warning to DC that you were leaving? Months?*
Archie: I said that I'd like to leave after we finish the Manhunter material.

CBA: *So obviously it wasn't "Nope, forget it. Pack up your stuff and go."*
Archie: No, no, they were very cooperative and we parted on good terms.

CBA: *Did you see changes—beyond the non-return of artwork—that were taking place at DC at the time that made Warren more fun to work at, more interesting to work at? There seemed to be an exodus of talent at DC. A lot of the good artists went over to Warren: Bernie Wrightson…*
Archie: Warren had gone through a period where he almost went out of business but fought his way back and became a stronger company, a better-paying company, and he started giving back artwork and all, too. So yeah, they were able to lure artists.

CBA: *You were with Jim Warren at the inception, right? You were there at the beginning of Creepy, Eerie…?*
Archie: Yeah. I didn't become Editor until about the fourth issue; but I was writing most of the stories at the beginning.

CBA: *How long did you stay with Warren on your second tenure there?*
Archie: Not very long. [pause] My status was a little less independent than I thought it was going to be when I took the job and I didn't feel comfortable working with the other editor, Bill Dubay.

Above: Some self-portraits by Archie Goodwin. Do you have any "Little Archies"? Please consider sending a photocopy to CBA because we're doing a special section devoted to anecdotes about Archie, featuring his unmistakable cartoons.

CBA: *You returned to DC after Epic? Pretty much during the '80s, you were at Marvel?*
Archie: Yeah.

CBA: *When did you return to DC?*
Archie: That would have been 1989.

CBA: *I'm sorry if I'm too forward asking this but how is your recovery? Do you feel that you're going to be editing more books in the future?*
Archie: I'll probably be editing the same amount of material in the future.

CBA: *Are you enjoying your responsibilities?*
Archie: Oh, very much so. DC is right now the place to be. It's a great company to work for. The people that run it still have connection and feeling with what we do. Paul Levitz comes from an editorial background. Jenette Kahn comes from a publishing background. They like doing commercial work that does well but also appreciate and like doing projects that are just good projects—and I think that more and more that will count for more and more in comics.

CBA: *I have to say as an aside that I really do very much enjoy your book. I can't say that I buy every issue but it seems to be an art-driven book and that's what I've always bought comics for. You did a Michael T. Gilbert book a couple of years ago, and I go back and buy the Gil Kanes, the Russ Heaths, and I find that of contemporary comics—of which I buy very few contemporary Super-hero comics—yours is consistently the one I do buy.*
Archie: It's a pleasure because of the variety on *Legends of the Dark Knight.* You can afford to go wrong on an episode or two. But you can also play around and try some interesting choices that you probably wouldn't be able to do on a book where you're involved with setting the continuity and running the characters' lives.

CBA: *That again gets back to your old run on* Detective. *In a lot of ways, that was really the cool thing. I remember some of my peers not being happy with Alex Toth's story—but [laughs], wait a minute! We got an Alex Batman which we would never normally get! A "Super Friends" Batman, maybe. It was cool that you almost had the Elseworlds idea, way back when.*
Archie: More of the *Legends* kind of thing, I think.

CBA: *Yeah, right. So it wasn't stuck—there's something eternal about the character that was neat.*
Archie: But also that's partly that you're trying to find a market niche for your own book so you don't want to—if you're doing one thing in a Batman book, you want to have slightly alternative programming in the other book.

CBA: *Well, thank you very much, Archie. I appreciate this.*
Archie: I enjoyed it.

CBA: *Thanks very much. Have a good weekend.*
Archie: You're welcome. Bye-bye.

CBA: *Take care. Bye.* Ⓓ

He's in Heaven

Jim Warren remembers Archie Goodwin

Archie Goodwin was 27 years old when he arrived at Warren Publishing Company.

When we first met, face-to-face, my impression was that Archie was a combination of Wally Cox and Woody Allen. He seemed shy. I wondered if he had the right stuff to work with a wild bunch of writers and artists, not to mention the temperaments and eccentricities of our office staff. I had hoped that beneath that cloak of presumed shyness there was some know-how and ability. Eventually I discovered that beneath that cloak of shyness was… nothing.

Nothing but talent.

Nothing but incredible skills.

Nothing but a supreme command of comics.

Delicious layers of it.

It's been said a thousand times that Archie was multi-talented—that he could play every position. It's true; he could—but he could also function well as a blanket of calm and reason over the madness and disorder of creating and publishing.

When things got tough, when things got chaotic, when no one knew quite what to do, or in what direction to go, Archie would walk into the office—and as soon as I saw him, I knew everything would be all right.

Archie and I are from different parts of the universe. But I soon discovered that we had, aside from comics, something very much in common in our personal lives.

Fred Astaire.

Not his dancing (as much as we both loved it).

It was his singing.

Archie loved the songs Fred Astaire had sung in his movies and Broadway shows. I did too. We both collected old recordings of Astaire's singing. Until I met Archie, I never knew of anyone who was an avid fan of Astaire's singing voice. It was as if we were the only two people on earth who shared this feeling. I once jokingly said to Archie that if a three-day convention were held for all the fans of Fred Astaire's singing, Archie and I would be in an empty auditorium, staring at each other for 72 hours. He looked at me, shook his head, and replied, "Not so, I know two others; one is in Nebraska and another in Guam." And I believe he did.

The Archie Goodwin I knew as my editor, writer, art director, artist and production manager was a curious combination of capability and calmness. He was a natural. He made it look easy. To me, he was the Joe DiMaggio of comics—a champion with dignity.

He stayed with us for a few very good years before going over to Marvel. On the day he left, I wished him well, gave him a hug, and as he walked out the door, I felt like calling out, "Shane, Shane—come back, Shane!" Anyone who remembers that movie will understand.

Toward the end of his life, Archie went through an awful, awful time. If the ancient Greeks were right that the gods envy and punish the gifted, then Archie Goodwin is prime evidence.

He was uncommonly gifted. And he gave those gifts to those who worked with him, to those around him, and to millions of readers and fans throughout the world.

Our industry mourns a champion.

— Jim Warren, Warren Publishing
March 1998

Jim Warren was publisher of Creepy, Eerie, *and* Blazing Combat, *the first magazines that brought attention to Archie's great writing and editing talents. This remembrance was shared with Archie's family and friends at the Goodwin Memorial on April 7, 1998.*

Superman and Batman thumbnails for DC's tabloid comics by Neal Adams. ©1998 DC Comics

Special Thanks
John & Pam Morrow
Beth Cooke • Roy Thomas
Ben, Josh & Danny Cooke
Ina Cooke & Nick Mook
Andrew D. Cooke & Patty Willett
Arlen Schumer & Sherri Wolfgang
Bob Yemerian • Sam Gafford
Ed Hatton • Tim McEnerney
Roger Brunelle • DC Comics
Cory Adams • Kris Adams
Neal Adams • Bill Alger
Jim Amash • Jerry Bails
Bill Black • John R. Borkowski
Bob Brodsky • Ian Cairn
John D. Coates • Les Daniels
Steve Ditko • Evan Dorkin
Kevin Eastman • Dave Elliott
Mark Evanier • Mike Gartland
Archie Goodwin • Gary Groth
D. Hambone • Mark Hanerfeld
Charles Hatfield • Bob Heer
Randy Hoppe • Tom Horvitz
Richard Howell • Carmine Infantino
Tony Isabella • Patty Jeres
Mike Kaluta • Gil Kane
Chuck Kim • The Jack Kirby Estate
Peter Koch • Richard Kyle
Batton Lash • Paul Levitz
The Mad Peck • Don Mangus
Frank Miller • Albert Moy
Anne T. Murphy • Dennis O'Neil
Joe Orlando • Rick Norwood
Bud Plant • James Robinson
Allan Rosenberg • George Roussos
Jeff Rovin • Fiona Russell
Marie Severin • Joe Simon
Phil Straub • Mike Thibodeaux
Anthony Tollin • Alex Toth
James Van Hise • Jim Warren
Al Williamson • Words & Pictures
Bernie Wrightson • Tom Ziuko

**Dedicated to
Archie Goodwin**
1937-1998
*For making editing
an artform*

Who was Mike Sekowsky?

Talking to friends of the Neglected Artist/Editor

by Tom Stewart

On assignment for *CBA*, I spent a month or so calling the friends of Mike Sekowsky (and a few people who might fit that description only reluctantly), and digging through old comics in order to get some idea of the neglected Artist/Editor of DC Comics, and the art that *everyone* has an opinion about.

His friends recall that Mike didn't talk about himself much; not at all if he could avoid it. A large man, tall and quiet, very shy in his relations with other people, Mike was hard to get to know. "He was hard to compliment," said Mark Evanier, comics writer. "For the first six months he knew you, you couldn't get him to look you in the eye. He didn't take compliments well," mostly mumbling thanks and looking for a way out of the whole awkward situation.

Mike started in comics in the early '40s, probably at Timely. His first assignment for the young Stan Lee was drawing a strip called *Ziggy Pig and Silly Seal*, one of many forgettable funny animal comics coming out at the time. He soon graduated to other strips at Timely, such as Gus the Gnome, Black Widow, *Young Allies* and *Captain America*. He worked there on and off through the decade.

Sekowsky probably worked at just about every company putting out comics during the '40s and '50s, drawing every kind of strip, under his own name, and helping out other artists, like his long-time friend, artist Joe Giella.

"I was a kid 17-18, inking a six-pager, and I lost it somewhere on the subway," Giella remembers. "I thought Stan was gonna fire me! This guy, big guy, comes up to me and says, 'I'll pencil it for you, [if you] give me the script.' He penciled it, I inked it, and Stan was happy. He saved my ass on that one!

"That was Mike Sekowsky. He wouldn't take any money for it—not at all. He said, 'Just do it for someone else sometime.' We became real close after that."

And a lot of other artists owed Mike a thanks for similar saves. Evanier explains, "There's a lot of stories where right in the middle of say, a Gil Kane story or something, it will suddenly become Sekowsky for a few pages... Mike had a great respect for artists. If you were in trouble, he'd pick up a pencil and start helping out right there. He never worried or cared about money."

Mike worked for Atlas throughout the '50s on everything that came along, from Westerns to Teen Comedy, to Romance, to Funny Animals. "You name it, he did it," Giella said. "Mike could do it all. He was fast, and *good*; it was all good stuff."

Just how fast was he? "Let's say you gave Mike and Jack Kirby the same script page, and two hours to draw it," said Evanier. "If you came back in an hour, Jack would have half the page drawn, but Mike wouldn't have started. There might be some guide lines, a few sketchy lines, but that'd be it. Mike would spend the first hour-and-a-half planning the page, and the last half-hour drawing it. And it would be terrific stuff."

He had to be careful, though, not to turn in the job too early. At times, an editor might look at the pages, shake his head and say, "You're rushing, Mike. Slow down and take your time." So next time, he would finish the pages, then hold onto them for a few days before turning them in—and, of course, the editor would say, "Much better; see what you can do when you take your time?"

How was inking Sekowsky? "Mike's pencils were dark," Giella said. "He had a very deliberate, strong style—good control over the pencil; everything was there. The problem was the drawing wasn't as accurate as one would want. His proportions would be a little off but a good inker could fix that, no problem—but boy, was he a layout man! That's where he really excelled. He could lay out a story, and utilize a panel to its fullest. He wouldn't fake backgrounds; not at all. Mike was a terrific designer."

All of which would help him out on the series he's most well known for, *Justice League of America*.

Mike had been working for DC since the early '50s, penciling on their War, Romance, Space, and Mystery titles—everything except the Super-hero titles. In 1959, after successful revivals of *The Flash* and *Green Lantern*, Julie decided to bring back the Justice Society in a new form, the *Justice League of America*. Gardner Fox would write, and Sekowsky would pencil.

Why was Mike chosen for the title? Well, he was probably one of the few artists to navigate between almost all the DC editors at the time. The editors were always happy to have Mike on a title, "because they knew it'd come in on time, or earlier," Evanier said.

"Mike was a speed merchant," Giella said. "He was *fast*. In the time I did one page, Mike could do four. Not inking, just penciling. You need to make a deadline, you call Mike, and he was right there."

"Mike enjoyed *JLA* at first," Evanier said. "It was a challenge that he liked, figuring out where everything would go—but after a while, he got bored with it, and he felt the writing wasn't as good. Then, when DC changed the page size, Mike felt he just couldn't draw it with the same quality."

Mike went on to draw some 66 issues of *JLA;* 66 issues of hundreds of super-heroes, wearing hundreds of different costumes. He quit several times before they found someone to replace him.

Artist Dick Dillin took over after Mike left the title, staying on the book for a run even longer then Sekowsky's.

Evanier again: "When I told Mike that Dick had passed away, he said, 'Yeah, that book would kill anybody.'"

Mike Sekowsky became an editor in 1968, taking over the titles that had been edited by Jack Miller. Mike had wanted to make the move into editorial for a while, and the

Thanks to the many patient people who helped with this article: Jerry Bails, Mark Evanier, Joe Giella, Dennis O'Neil, Joe Orlando, and Dr. Michael J. Vassallo.

promotion of Carmine Infantino to Editorial Director cleared the way. Overnight, artists were promoted to editors, and Mike was assigned *Metal Men* and *Wonder Woman*.

Wonder Woman at the time was one of DC lowest selling titles, and it limped along on memories of former glory. Enter Mike Sekowsky who had been playing around with an idea for a series for about a karate chopping female and her Asian guide. He injected this into *Wonder Woman*, stripping her of her traditional costume and powers, and having her train in the martial arts. Sales increased (how much we don't know; records are spotty at best) and so did controversy about the change. Older fans were unhappy at the wholesale changes, but new fans were attracted to the new, hipper style. During the run, Sekowsky replaced Dennis O'Neil as writer, writing most issues (some of the best of the run) before leaving the book.

Mike had also taken over Supergirl in *Adventure Comics*, trying to bring some life into that series—but he couldn't quite make lightning strike twice. After working on Supergirl for several issues, Mike left the title, and left DC. (Without Sekowsky, *WW* reverted back to her old powers and costume, to be more in line with a planned TV series.)

Why did Sekowsky leave? One DC editor at the time said Sekowsky was a great guy, especially when you got to know him. But, when he was mad... So, Mike had a temper? "He sure did," Evanier said. "Mike had an ego. He was a big, loud guy when it came to his work. He thought he was good (and he was), and he didn't think he was appreciated as much as he should have been."

After a long-running love-hate battle with Management, with Mike feeling that his work and input were not appreciated, he left. Around this time, the artist also developed health problems with diabetes—and alcohol.

Did Mike have a drinking problem? "Yeah, that's true," Evanier said. "He'd pretty much licked it by the time he moved to the West Coast. It was no secret.

"Mike was big, pale, very pasty guy. He wasn't doing all that well with his health... He had his good days and bad. I mean, 30-35 years in the business, you're bound to have times when things just don't go right. "

Mike went to work for Marvel, penciling the Inhumans and *Super-Villain Team-Up*, but his work was not up to Sekowsky standards; sickness and alcohol took their toll. Bill Everett was called in to redraw parts of an Inhumans story. Mike left comics to move to the West Coast and into animation design for studios like Hanna-Barbera.

Mike produced new comics stories after ending his run at DC and Marvel in the 1970s—most of them Hanna-Barbera comics for the foreign market—then later, one-shots for DC (including a little-heralded return to the *JLA),* and a few stories for independent publishers like Eclipse & New Media.

"Mike could be very bitter about his time in comics," Evanier said. "He didn't want to talk about it much."

But he still had his sense of humor. "At Hanna-Barbera, there were a lot of new guys coming in around my age who remembered Mike's work from the *JLA* or *Wonder Woman*. They kept coming up to him to meet the Great Mike Sekowsky and they all said the same thing: 'I didn't like your art when I was a kid but now I love it.' It got to be a running joke around the studio. Mike procured a number dispenser, like they use in a bakery, and he put it up over his cubicle with a sign that said 'Take a number to tell me how much you used to hate my work but you love it now.'"

"One thing we never really saw," Evanier explained,

"was his really twisted sense of humor. There's some of that in "Jason's Quest," a little of it in *Wonder Woman*, but we never saw a whole story... it's really too bad."

In 1981, Mike's friends tricked him into going to the San Diego Convention to watch Alex Toth receive the Inkpot Award, the annual award given to honor achievements in the field of comics. Mike was reluctant to go, reluctant to see the his old co-workers again. He sat through the tribute to Toth, then heard his name announced.

"There was this big ovation for Mike as soon as his name was announced," Evanier said. "He broke into this great big smile. The award meant a lot to him, but I think the ovation meant even more.

"As he passed by Julie Schwartz's table, Mike whispered something to his former editor. I collared Julie afterwards and said, 'All right, what'd Sekowsky say to you?' Julie smiled: 'My page rates just went up.'"

Mike Sekowsky died in 1989. ©

Above: *All new! All mod! The breathtaking arrival of Mike Sekowsky's unforgettable Diana Prince with inks by Dick Giordano.* ©1998 DC Comics

Mike Sekowsky's Mod

The Oddness of the Artist/Editor's work

by Garrie Burr

"It was a time of anarchy, yes, but also a time of sowing ...seeds of hope and the future. Those seeds are continuously sprouting in the most unexpected places, and there are a lot of them still under the soil.... Keep an eye on those verges at the side of the concrete road... those margins at the side of that colossal text, that thrust of rationality and falsification..."

— Peter Whitehead, liner notes to the soundtrack album "Tonite Let's All Make Love in London" (1968)

As controversial as the historical events of the '60s remain, so too does the debate over the quality of Mike Sekowsky's work. Certainly his art never catered to the more-popular tastes of comic book fandom, even with his earlier high-profile work on the *Justice League*. Compliments, when they come, sometimes border on back-handedness.

"The debate on whether Sekowsky was the right person for the job did not even end with his death, but continues to this day. He had a highly personal sense of anatomy," Paul Gambaccini wrote in his introduction to the first *Justice League Archives* volume. "Mike's real triumph was in giving *Justice League of America* an identifiable look, which helped give the book its unique nature. Issues after he left are generally less distinctive and less memorable, and there may be a cause-and-effect relationship."

Mark Waid's biographic material on the creators of the *Justice League* said: "Though never one of comics' more polished artists, Sekowsky more than compensated for his never-graceful style with impeccable and dynamic storytelling."

Gerard Jones and Will Jacobs wrote in *The Comic Book Heroes*: "Often maligned for his strange interpretation of human anatomy and his blocky lines, Sekowsky had an intelligent sense of storytelling that was fluid and dynamic, and that would soon serve him and DC very well."

Put these together and you see a dichotomy in feelings about Sekowsky's work—graceless yet fluid, unpolished yet dynamic—a mystifying "something" there that becomes quite appropriate when used for his "mod" material of the late '60s.

"Mod" itself is a fashion quite difficult to put a finger on, mainly because the essence of mod was change. Dave Marsh wrote in *Before I Get Old:* "Pure mod was based not just on being one step ahead but on staying there..." This was also as good a definition as any of the late '60s. Greil Marcus noted this change in December, 1969 for *Rolling Stone* (reprinted in *Ranters and Crowd-Pleasers*): "In London, in the '60s, when styles on Carnaby Street changed by the day, when each new group was thrilling, when America looked to London with envy, joy, and, really, wonder, what one saw was a mad pursuit of every next day, and what one saw looked like the most complete freedom the world had ever known."

Sekowsky's "written-drawn-and-edited-by" tenure on revamps of *Wonder Woman, Metal Men,* and Supergirl—as well as his original *Showcase* concepts "Jason's Quest" and "Manhunter 2070"—survive as not only products of that time but, unlike all-too-many other comic books published then, as timeless truer pictures of what was really going on. His work merely appeared to be escapist adventure stories, but the pace at which his adventures moved kept rhythm with the staccato beat of the late '60s—a time that just couldn't stand still.

Sekowsky's "something," then, becomes clearer: His fluidity represents the change of the time, his "lack of polish" is the constant newness, and the dynamism of his storytelling is the wonder and the mad pursuit of the unknown future. He truly was a modern, a mod.

Of course, Sekowsky's best works of the late '60s could represent the fullest ideal of any fashion era, "freedom of expression," but his freedom is—more-appropriately for the late Sixties—"freedom of expressiveness."

It's the free expressiveness of his drawings that cause the finger to waver over the 'something' that makes his art work. Though it's quite simple to look at a comics page and say "That's Sekowsky," it's more difficult to pick out examples on that page of what makes such a pronouncement so obvious. His years in the trade offered him constant practice in a variety of work in a variety of genres. The tricks of that trade, and how well he learned to use them for his own purposes, become quite apparent here.

He's not an action artist *per se*—his figures aren't constantly coiled in the midst of movement—yet there's, again, "something" about it: The delicate blockiness, the figures always expressive with hands, smiles, the way a knee is bent, etc. Reading Sekowsky's pieces is like watching a method actor exhibiting such intangibles as inner strength or a sense of humor.

Also subtle—and surprising—are the arrangements of his story panels. Cinematic sequences, three consecutive panels denoting a single action, are rare. Sekowsky's camera seems to be hand-held, constantly rotating around a group or person or place. The most frequent shot of all in his repertoire is the montage, but that by its very nature means "nothing is the same." The only consistency in his layouts and page design is that they're consistently inconsistent.

Some of the inconsistencies may be explained by the fact that Sekowsky was a "from-the-gut," intuitive storyteller, but his choices in style for panel to panel were often the best choices for what he wanted to say.

Despite the inconsistencies, his stories are far from confusing. There's never a feeling of "where do I go from here?" Sekowsky knew how to properly identify each essential character for the reader, as well as the place and plot, before moving on with the sequence—however it appeared. You get the feeling he didn't really know beforehand, and that feeling spills over into the excitement felt reading his stories.

Until his work appeared under his own editorial regime, his art remained under the control of others' scripts and too-tight inkers. Once he was loose, on his own, you not only didn't know what was going to happen to his characters on the next page, but you had no idea what that page would even look like. There's a feeling of discovery here, and the joy of discovery he imparts is enough to push the reader forward. It isn't the placement of characters within a panel that does so. It's the art and story together.

Toward the end of his work on others' scripts, Sekowsky appeared to be experimenting with layouts, going off on pages of slanted panels. Perhaps he was influenced somewhat by the popularity of the young Neal Adams. Whatever the case, once he started working on his own he settled back into a more-conservative style, using not much more than the usual blocked panels. Possibly this had something to do with his previous lack of experience with writing the words. Once he'd become accustomed to writing *and* drawing, he began to occasionally go after something new.

The opening sequence of the "Return of the Amazons" story in *Wonder Woman* #183 is an eye-opening piece of work, for example. Diana flees into the London fog during a montage of events from the previous issue. Exhausted, she stops in time for a properly-clad Amazon warrior to call her name. More ambitious is the opening scene in the first of the "Detour" two-parter (*WW* #190). Sekowsky placed one montage within the frame of another—bringing the past and present together—and while imparting a sense of disorientation similar to Diana Prince's, it remains straightforward and simple to follow.

Who knows where Sekowsky could've gone from there? We'd never know, as this was about the time that some kind of trouble was evident with his editorial regime. Soon after, *Wonder Woman*'s stories would be (according to the production numbers) stories assigned and begun much earlier. Whatever the problems, if his life and the times could be seen in the work—the essence of life is forward movement as is the essence of Sekowsky's stories on the page—then it makes sense that he'd keep plowing toward whatever it was he saw just ahead.

What he saw is important here, because I doubt that Sekowsky was part of the youth movement, that he listened to modern music, or dressed in the latest fashion. He undoubtedly soaked up what he observed, though—even if only with the knowledge that it was part of his job.

Although he was one for fashion, he wasn't one for being fashionable. His work stands out because he drew things that probably never were, but his people talk like people always talked. While the younger artists and writers tried so hard to be 'hip' and 'with-it,' their results often felt forced. Having Batman mention, for example, Big Brother and the Holding Company, feels similar to seeing a picture of your uncle wearing a tie-dyed T-shirt and raggedy bell-bottoms. The Teen Titans were at least more of an appropriate age for such references, but their colloquialisms nonetheless felt phony. There's very little topical 'grooviness' in the speech of Sekowsky's characters. It all feels true and there was a greater need for truth back then than the world realized.

Greil Marcus, again, from the same 'End of the Sixties' essay, writing about The Rolling Stones' "You Can't Always Get What You Want": "Dreams of having everything, right now, are gone; ("Let It Bleed") ends with a song about compromise with what you want, with a celebration of learning to take what you can get, maybe even what you deserve, because time has passed, and the rules have changed."

Above: *Yet another tear-filled, yet well-designed cover by Mike Sekowsky & Dick Giordano. These really are good books and quite worth the search (and a tough find they are!).* ©1998 DC Comics

Sekowsky agreed that the rules had changed. "I personally feel that too many of DC's stories are still being written and plotted for the year 1940 instead of 1970 . . ." he wrote in the letters column of *Wonder Woman*. By this he didn't mean they needed to tackle issues "torn from today's headlines"—instead he'd focus on the humanity inherent in heroes. In a way this fits his 'education' at the Alex Toth 'school' of comic book art—one of the lessons there being, according to *Alex Toth* (Kitchen Sink, 1995), "strip it all down to essentials and draw the hell out of what is left!"

Sekowsky followed many of Toth's 'rules' in depicting the stories, but there was something similar going on with the plots and words therein, as well. Strip the super-heroes and their stories down to the essentials. Give the reader just enough characterization to make what's going to happen more believable—these weren't character-driven stories, they were more Hitchcock-like.

With Sekowsky's stories the magic was in the real world and all you had to do was look at things from a different angle; you didn't need super-powers, just yourself.

Wonder Woman gave up the old magic, but didn't give up living, and found what pain there was to be human, but

Above: *She's got the look! A beautiful example of the great team of Sekowsky & Giordano. Dick says inking Mike was a career highlight. From Wonder Woman #178. ©1998 DC Comics*

what joy, too. "As an Amazon princess—as Wonder Woman—I had perfect control of my emotions! As plain Diana Prince, I'm human… too *darn* human!" (*WW* #182) Here she was referring to being swept away by a good-looking guy, but the implication runs deeper than that. Was she removed from something else, like humanity itself, when she had her powers? When she goes to ask for help of the great heroes of myth she finds them to be far from willing, and perhaps more like what she and the other JLAers had been than she'd care to admit. "You're not heroes—you're children!" she scolds. "You play games while a world burns! You are a disgrace to the word Hero!" Later she reveals the gist of her anger… "It is because of (heroes) and the example they and others like them set to make it a better world that we do what we do now!" (*WW* #184)

"Others like them" could include Sekowsky's re-fashioned Metal Men—who became human in appearance, but in the process lost their identities, their personalities. No wonder their father went mad and tried to kill them. Unfortunately, though they were more 'human' than before, it was difficult to tell one from the other. Or perhaps that was the point. There were some good bits too: The idea that they hide "in plain sight" from humanity and, most especially, that the other humans—Mister Conan, their mysterious benefactor, for one—were more cold and machine-like than the metal band ever were. Like Wonder Woman's boutique, though, their more pop individual identities were soon lost in the action; unlike the boutique, the missing identities were mourned. The special magic that had been the original Metal Men could not be duplicated, but if Sekowsky had been given more time, perhaps it would've been replaced.

Supergirl, too, lost some of her magic. She'd also lost a father-figure, literally, in the retirement of Weisinger. Her universe was no longer so well-defined. She'd become an orphan angel again, this time in strange places she never could've seen in the same old familiarity of her cousin's backyard. Her attitude under Sekowsky was: "I have these powers—and while sometimes I wish I didn't—and could live a normal life—I have to use them to help humanity as long as it needs me!" (*Adventure Comics* #402)

And speaking of humanity: One thing Sekowsky undoubtedly learned from his Teen Humor-genre work was to make the characters topical, but believable. You have to concentrate on the more-universal traits that remain constant, no matter the fashion of the time. If it's difficult to find consistency in his layouts and storytelling style, it's apparent that there's nonetheless a consistent theme to his work that lies somewhere around: "No matter what we look like we've got the same basic needs underneath." Yes, he stripped away the super-powers, but only to show more clearly how close to us

in the basics are the Dianas and Karas and Tinas. And if they're really so similar to us, then how much simpler would it be to follow their heroic examples in deeds?

Where so much of the late Sixties was involved in pointing out the differences, where the question that mattered was "Whose side are you on?" Sekowsky was pointing out the similarities, and sometimes with the most subtle of voices. For example, *Adventure Comics* #399 features Supergirl helping out a football player who's forced to throw some games if he wants his girlfriend to remain unharmed. What's never mentioned in the story is the fact that the player and his girlfriend are Black. This isn't a token statement paying lip service to discrimination. It doesn't matter what race he is, he's got the same feelings as anybody else. It doesn't matter here what you wear, or what you look like. What matters is "what you do."

What Sekowsky did can best be seen in his two most 'human' series: "Jason's Quest" and "Manhunter 2070." Each series, especially "Jason's Quest," contains his typical non-stop action with one event piling on top of the other. As the '60s seemed to be one darn thing after another, Marcus' "mad pursuit of every next day," so, too, did Sekowsky's storylines for every one of his series keep moving on into what seemed unknown even to him.

In the *Metal Men* you'd have witches calling up the final darkness in one issue, followed by a phantom of the movie studio, and then a quick trip to a suspiciously undemocratic eastern European country—which was assisted, of course, by a suspiciously familiar mad scientist. Wonder Woman faced a different mad scientist, but she was soon up against the God of War, and then onto the trail of a teenage runaway and her master's leash, a talking frog and a manic-depressive witch. Not to be outdone, Supergirl was assisted by the same witch when she faced a warlock, and then she was off to blackmailing gamblers, Phantom Zone leprechauns, and a mouse, with the only stop along the way for a change of attire.

"Jason's Quest" was all about finding the magic you never knew was there: Your real identity. In his case, his previously-unknown reality was in the form of a lost twin sister—and so were Sekowsky's other series, at their heart, quests for identity. Even "Manhunter 2070" who, though ostensibly travelling down the mean streets of space for both the bounty and for the welfare of others, more specifically sought to provide a protection from pirates. He'd needed protection himself when he was young so, in that sense, Starker the Manhunter keeps finding his "self" that *might've* been.

It's also appropriate that these pirates, the criminals of a thousand worlds, emulate the past, making the present (our future) a nightmare. In other words: His criminals weren't up-to-date in their fashion; they followed the same tired cliches as much as Sekowsky avoided them.

No, he wasn't an innovator.

He followed new trends, rather than set them—but while he stood in line with the rest he did his own unique little dance to the life; steps no one else could follow. Unlike comics of today, which reflect more the world within itself, referring more to their own various universes and 'histories' than the one in which a whole new audience might dwell, Sekowsky's comics took the real world on. As he wrote in *Wonder Woman* #189: "…it's to today's readers that we must cater to, not to a bunch of old fuddy duddies who only look back… "

That's why his stuff is still real. It didn't matter that he wasn't a member of the youth movement, that he didn't speak, like, groovy. What mattered was that he didn't look back. He looked out, and stayed mod. ⒹⒸ

The King & the Director

continued from page 73

C&C: *Let's say ten years from now the same thing happens at National that happened at Marvel, where your books are selling very well and all of a sudden Jack Kirby says he wants to retire.*
Carmine: Then I wouldn't presume to do those books, because nobody could do them as well.

C&C: *You'd drop them?*
Carmine: Yes. Wouldn't it be better for us to drop them then for the books to die themselves?

C&C: *How could somebody like Marvel drop the* Fantastic Four?
Carmine: It's going to die anyway.

C&C: *I know.*
Carmine: Would you rather die at your zenith or at your low end? First of all, he's not going to retire in ten years anyway; I wouldn't let him.
Jack: Second of all, I think that even if I did retire, the comics would continue with the same feeling.
Carmine: He is planning to develop people for these books in case the need comes. He wants people developed to follow his thinking.

C&C: *Who got the idea for the Neal Adams* Green Lantern *book? The sales are dropping. I know they went up and*
now they're dropping a little bit. I don't know how true it is.
Carmine: Who said that?

C&C: *Neal Adams. I heard that you are keeping it for prestige. I'd like to know how it got started.*
Carmine: The *Green Lantern* was ready to be turned out when we were told to drop it, even though I wanted a few more issues. I said to Julie: "There's something you wanted to try. I want this book as different as you could possibly make it." We sat down with Denny and came out with it. The book was slowly rising. It went real high at one point. Then it sagged off again. If this book can give to us the public relations, if it can take this business and give us the solid citizen reputation, it should have not been considered junk, as it used to be. It will be worth everything we are putting into it. ⑩

Above: *Carmine Infantino (left) and Jack Kirby at a '70s comics con. Look for Vanguard Productions' book,* The Amazing World of Carmine Infantino, *an autobiography/art book by the artist designed by ye ed and due in June 2000! Tell Vanguard I sent ya!*

The Greatest!

Neal Adams on his masterpiece, *Superman vs. Muhammad Ali*

Conducted by Arlen Schumer
Transcribed by Jon B. Knutson

Below: *We found this partially unused full-body image of Ali and Kal-El in Neal's thumbnails, though the upper-body portion was adapted for the book's final two-page spread. Art ©2000 Neal Adams. Superman ©2000 DC Comics.*

[Editor's Note: *I may be in the minority fandom opinion on this, but I've long felt that Neal Adams' Superman vs. Muhammad Ali was his best work for DC Comics. Ever. It appeared on the stands in late 1977—just as I was losing interest in comics, and Neal's storytelling and technique simply blew me away. So I asked Neal and my pal (interviewer/designer/historian extraordinaire) Arlen Schumer, if they could do a brief interview about the story behind the story. In phenomenally short turnaround time, Neal gave us the definitive interview on the project, Arlen sent us original art and the tapes, and transcriber*

Jon B. Knutson finished the transcript in record time. CBA presented an edited version of the transcript—about half the size of this interview—in CBA Special Edition #1. What follows is the entire transcript, illustrated with plenty of new artwork. This interview was conducted in Neal's Continuity Studio on Nov. 12, 1999.—JBC]

Arlen Schumer: *Let's start with the cover: Originally, this project at DC Comics was going to be drawn by Joe Kubert, and for whatever reason, the Muhammad Ali people weren't happy with the likenesses, and somehow the idea came up, "Maybe we can get Neal to work on it."*

Neal Adams: Clearly, DC was having a problem with likenesses, and Ali's people weren't happy, so they had me take a try. They were happy with my likenesses, and basically, that was the turning point, and the reason I got the project.

When I saw Joe's original cover (he hadn't done detail to the background) with the two figures, I thought, "Gee, you know, no matter what I do, I don't think I'm going to come up with a better layout than Joe." So I essentially took his layout, and just put my own drawing into it, and if somebody recognizes the pose of, say, Superman as not being a typical Neal Adams pose, it's a Joe Kubert pose, adapted to my style.

Arlen: *I remember looking at this at the time, thinking, "This cover doesn't quite look like Neal."*

Neal: I wanted to keep Joe's name attached to it, and by using his layout, I paid homage to it. Because this is a classic Kubert layout: The one foot up, and the shoulder. The big question that entered my mind was, I knew it would have a wraparound cover, so how do I then make it an event? And I thought, "Why don't I put famous people on the cover watching the match?"

Arlen: *Kubert's layout had a generic audience.*

Neal: I don't think he was focused on the audience at that point; he was looking to get a layout done, and just show the main figures. So, I started to put in some famous people. Naturally, the President would be there if the Earth is in jeopardy, as would various other people—and for some reason, it caught on at DC Comics. They thought, "Well, why don't we put famous people there?" The logic says make it an event. So, I started to do that. I didn't have any idea what I had let myself in for. [*laughter*] I simply had no idea.

Arlen: *What do you mean? You knew you had to do likenesses....*

Neal: If you count them, I think there's something like 170 different likenesses there. For a cover, that's a lot of drawings. You don't really do that—but I guess I was caught up in it, in that, for instance, I had just met Kurt Vonnegut and I thought, "Gee, Vonnegut would be at this fight." Certainly Ali's trainers would be there, and of course, if Superman were there, Lex Luthor would be there, [*laughter*] and Batman would be there... well, by the time I got that stuff going, we got carried away—it just turned into this ball of string that I just couldn't unravel. And it got to the point where I was saying, "If there's a circle there, I ought to put a person there... where do I stop?" [*laughter*] Where does it end? Well, it just never ended, we just kept on going and going and going.

Arlen: *As a former employee of yours, I remember one of your lessons in drawing was, when one has to do a crowd, design it in such a way that you suggest a crowd....*

Neal: That was one of those times that I should've stuck with one of my own rules! [*laughter*] Once the idea was presented up at DC, the question was: Should we get permission from these people to put them on the cover, or should we not? My feeling was, "I don't see

Devoid of type, here's Neal's fully-inked front cover for his masterpiece Superman vs. Muhammad Ali. Note the presence of Mick Jagger in the lower left-hand corner. The singer was later replaced by Don King in the final version. Special thanks to Continuity employee and friend Tom Ziuko for making us a copy of this treasure. Courtesy of Neal Adams. ©2000 DC Comics.

why we'd have to get permission. If it was an editorial decision, that essentially these people would be at this thing, if you put drawings of people on a comic book cover, it's just a comic book. You're not really saying anything or implying anything, so I don't think there's any reason for it." Well, for whatever reason, it was decided, "Well, why don't we ask anyway?" Maybe it was the publicity….

Arlen: *And thus, the biggest can of worms was opened.*

Neal: The logical thought was that everybody would say, "Yes, who cares?" And certainly, a majority of people said yes. There were people who decided not to say yes… why, I have no idea. Assuming that they would say yes, I went ahead and put them in. So, then we started to get responses (and most people were very cooperative, and very generous, and I'm sure that even the people who rejected the idea were very generous and very cooperative), some just decided on that day, "I don't feel like giving my permission." You know, it's sort of a flip of a coin. They just said no, or yes, whatever.

So, there were people I just left out—but there were other people I'd already put in there. For example, John Wayne decided he didn't want to be in it, but I'd already drawn him. So I decided, "I don't want to take him out, but on the other hand, I don't want everybody to know it's John Wayne." So we put a mustache on him. So, if you look very carefully on the front cover, you'll see a guy with a mustache sitting right next to Johnny Carson, and sure enough, that's John Wayne with a mustache. You'll see next to Ron Howard, is a guy with a mustache—that's Fonzie [*Henry Winkler*] with different hair and a mustache.

Arlen: *So, basically, anybody with a mustache is somebody that didn't give approval? [laughs]*

Neal: Well, I can't guarantee that! It becomes a game to look around and find people who might not have given permission. We tried, but it got to be like a silly joke after a while. I thought, "Oh, God, what are we doing?" So, there were a whole bunch of people I

really had to put aside, if I had to take them out, but in some cases, did the mustache thing. So there are, again, over 170 people on this cover… big, big project! The two figures in the middle? The easiest part of the cover! [*laughter*]

Remember, I had to have photographs to work from, and I then had to draw these people so small, yet the likenesses had to be there so people wouldn't come to me later and say, "Gee, that doesn't look like so-and-so." It's a professional thing to not miss the likeness. Also, all the people who were not stars on the cover, but people I liked, I didn't want to disappoint them, and put them in such a way that you couldn't recognize who they are. So the game with this comic book, of course, if anybody can find it, is to play that little game of "Find out who all those people are."

Arlen: *Whose idea was it to do this comic in the first place?*

Neal: I think it generated like lava, from some swamp beneath the earth, and it suddenly appeared. [*laughs*] My memory says that Julie Schwartz had something to do with it, and of course, without knowledge, I'd love to give Julie credit for the whole idea, but I guess you'd have to ask him. Certainly, when I heard it, I thought it was a great idea. I mean, just the concept… yet, at the same time, the logical question is, "How do you have a human being fight an alien—Superman—and how do you justify such a battle?" We had to come up with an answer.

Arlen: *Let's back up for a minute. Once you did your thing, and were approved, in a sense, as the artist, were there any other creative people involved?*

Neal: Denny O'Neil was certainly involved, and both Denny and I had to be approved, not by DC Comics or by Muhammad Ali, but by Elijah Muhammad [*head of the Nation of Islam, the American Black Muslim organization*]. Elijah Muhammad had to decide whether or not we were okay to do this book. Remember, Cassius Clay had accepted Islam as his religion, changed his name to Muhammad Ali,

Below: Preliminary version of the legendary cover featuring Neal's likenesses of at least 17 celebrities who ultimately declined to be used. Note the ringside use of Telly Savalas (smoking, no less!) who was easily transformed into Luthor. Another treasure found by Tom Ziuko and courtesy of Neal Adams. Art ©2000 Neal Adams. Superman ©2000 DC Comics.

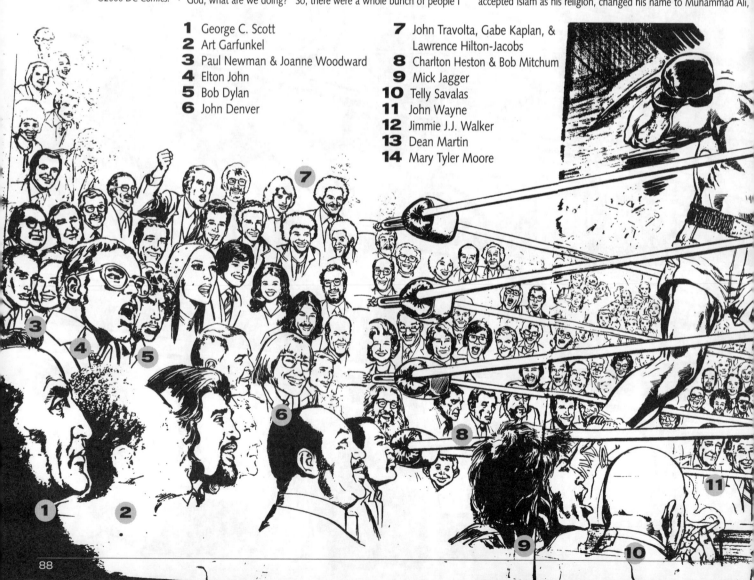

1 George C. Scott
2 Art Garfunkel
3 Paul Newman & Joanne Woodward
4 Elton John
5 Bob Dylan
6 John Denver
7 John Travolta, Gabe Kaplan, & Lawrence Hilton-Jacobs
8 Charlton Heston & Bob Mitchum
9 Mick Jagger
10 Telly Savalas
11 John Wayne
12 Jimmie J.J. Walker
13 Dean Martin
14 Mary Tyler Moore

and essentially put himself under the guidance of Elijah Muhammad. So, here we were in this curious situation, that once the artwork was approved by the Ali people, the question was, were we approved by Elijah Muhammad? And there was really only one way we could be approved of by him, and that was for us to get on a plane, go to Chicago, be driven by limousine to the home of Elijah Muhammad, set out in the windy plains of Chicago, through a gate, and up to his rather elegant house.

Arlen: *This is just you and Denny?*

Neal: Just me and Denny, led into a parlor, very Turkish in design, surrounded by columns and couches around the edges—and Elijah Muhammad came out, said hello, got into a phone call, was called away, and left—and we were excused!

Arlen: *That was it?*

Neal: That was it.

Arlen: *He just had to physically...?*

Neal: See us, I guess, I don't know! [*laughter*] I think, in spite of the fact that my personal history comes from many different back-

grounds, I think the map of Ireland was on both Denny's and my face, and perhaps that's what swayed him. I don't know, whatever it was, we seemed like friendly guys. I think it was just a... ritual. I think that he felt responsible to Ali, and was looking after him, and why not meet the people who were going to do this, and see if they're okay? It seemed a little odd to us. [*laughs*]

Arlen: *The book came out in 1978. Your last comic for DC before this was "Moon of the Wolf," which was published in early '74, which you had to have drawn, let's say, in late '73, after "The Joker's Five-Way Revenge." From that point on, you pretty much thought that was it for you and DC, in terms of concrete artwork.*

Neal: Right. Remember at that time, I was dealing with Jerry Siegel and Joe Shuster [*fighting for Superman's creators to receive recognition and a pension from DC Comics*]. That became a rather intense time for me. At any rate, I had a contract for *Superman vs. Muhammad Ali*, I also had an agreement with DC Comics that I get a very, very small percentage of overseas sales. I don't believe that any other comic book artist has ever gotten that.

Arlen: *This was really the first mainstream DC comic you did that was not work-for-hire?*

Neal: Not as work-for-hire, but under contract. It wasn't a great contract, but it did have stipulations in the contract that were valid for people to have, and I let everybody know what was in there.

Arlen: *At the time, this was DC's highest-priced original comic book, I believe. The format was established from those dollar editions, so this was really the first "prestige format."*

Neal: It was meant from the beginning to be a success. In the end, whether it was a success, I don't know.

Arlen: *How come you don't know?*

Neal: No, I don't know the sales in the United States. I know that all around the world it sold very well.

Arlen: *So you were approved as the artist, Denny was approved as writer, Julie Schwartz is the editor.*

Neal: Now, I participated in the outline, and it turned out, in the middle of the project Denny could no longer work on it, so essentially, Julie Schwartz dumped it into my lap to finish.

Arlen: *We've got some script pages so we know it was written as a traditional script.*

Neal: Up to a certain point. Remember, this is a 72-page story. You don't write it all at once, you do it in parts. Midway into it, Denny was unable to finish, so Julie asked, "Do you want to finish it? You know the story better than anybody else." I said, "Fine." He said, "Have the remainder of the script in here Monday." [*laughs*]

Above: *Joe Kubert's cover art for his version of the book, a design Neal retained in homage to the great artist/editor/mentor. ©2000 DC Comics.*

Ringside Seat

John Workman remembers *Superman vs. Muhammad Ali*

As I recall, by the time I had started working on staff at DC in 1975, there had already been an ad printed in certain comics promoting the upcoming *Superman vs. Muhammad Ali* tabloid-size book. It featured artwork by Joe Kubert. At some point, a logo was needed for Ali and Sol Harrison gave me a pencil rough with instructions to do the finish at home and to bring it in to the office the next morning. The finished logo would then be shown to Ali's people for their approval. I'm not sure, these 24 years later, who had done up the rough, though I believe it was either Sol himself or Joe Orlando. There is an outside chance that it could have been Carmine Infantino's handiwork, since I remember doing a few things (including the "square-jawed" Batman face with the 1960s-style lettering that adorned *Detective Comics* for a few issues) that were based on Carmine's concepts.

When I got to the Staten Island apartment that I shared with Bob Smith, I looked at the logo rough and was appalled to find that there was the very real possibility that Muhammad Ali's name had been misspelled. Knowing that my brother Bill would have the necessary information, I phoned him out in Washington State and found that someone at DC had, indeed, messed up Ali's name. My brother corrected the spelling and I did up the logo. The next morning, Sol Harrison put it in for stats and took the copies to show Ali's people. Because there seemed to be no further need for my original, I took it back home with me… at least until a few weeks later when Jack Adler was looking around for it and I told him that it was in my possession. He was happy to find that it hadn't disappeared or been misfiled and told me to bring it back. I did.

As things progressed on the book, a couple of interesting stories circulated through the office. The first one concerned Joe Kubert. Evidently, the group that represented Ali's interests was not happy with the "scratchiness" of Joe's art. I had seen evidence of such attitudes when I was still out in Washington. Bob Smith and I had once attended a symposium on comics at Western Washington University and found that, along with the moderator and cartoonist Russ Meyers, we were alone in our liking of Joe Kubert's art. Everyone else attending the symposium was unanimous in their intense dislike for the Kubert *Tarzan* artwork.

The result of this rejection of Joe Kubert's work was that Jenette Kahn (who had since assumed the duties of DC Publisher) and Sol Harrison presented to Ali's representatives samples of the work of every artist that they could possibly get to do the work on the book. After looking over the samples, Ali's guys agreed that *Superman vs. Muhammad Ali* should be drawn by Kurt Schaffenberger. The DC people were not happy with this and successfully lobbied to have Neal Adams as the book's artist. In retrospect, it's understandable that Kurt Schaffenberger (or Curt Swan or Murphy Anderson or a ton of other comic book stalwarts) should be seen as being representative of what the general public thought of when comic books came to mind. But there was already a drastic change taking place at DC as the "fan" element came to prominence. Kurt Schaffenberger was not a "fan favorite," but Neal Adams was. The strange thing was that Neal's work encompassed the dynamic energy so beloved by the fans while his stuff also appealed to the much-larger group of comics buyers that would make or break *Superman vs. Muhammad Ali*. Neal was, in the end, the perfect choice.

The second bit of information that swept through the corridors at DC concerned Neal's intent to create a *Sergeant Pepper* cover with tons of famous people pictured in the audience. There was word that the Beatles had given their enthusiastic support and that they would be reunited on Neal's cover. Carol Fein lined up the DC staffers in the hallway near Sol Harrison's office and we had individual Polaroid photographs taken so that Neal could use them as reference when he drew each of us into the crowd scene. I remember going to a party at Jenette's and looking at the work-in-progress cover that Neal was doing. Once, he brought it into the production department and I made a Xerox copy of what he had done to that point… including drawings of several celebrities who decided against being on the final version of the cover. When I went to seek Neal's advice about going over to *Heavy Metal* (Neal had suggested to *National Lampoon* Art Director Peter Kleinman that I would be a good Art Director for *HM*), he was sitting in the Continuity Associates office working on fight scenes between the Man of Steel and Muhammad Ali. Seeing Neal draw is a fantastic experience.

I was working at *Heavy Metal* when the book finally came out. I have to admit that I was bothered a bit by not being at the press conference wherein the DC staffers got to meet a somewhat reticent Muhammad Ali. I dropped in at DC and was given a copy of the book. Somebody told me that the print-run was 400,000 and they expected it to do very well.

We were kidding Neal a lot in the production department as the original deadline came and went. The joke went around that Neal would finish *Superman vs. Muhammad Ali* right after he completed the work on *Superman vs. Joe Louis*. After seeing the finished book, we were all happy with it and we figured that the long wait was worthwhile.

Arlen: *He wanted you to write it up full-script?*

Neal: Of course. Any work that I've ever done for DC Comics, I have to write full-script. I wrote the "Deadman," and a couple of issues of *The Spectre* that way. [*laughter*] Believe me, Julie Schwartz gives no dispensation to anybody. He's a very, very tough editor.

Arlen: *Up until this point, nothing is drawn, right? It's all script?*

Neal: Right, and because this is the way it was established, I basically had to say at DC Comics—contrary to what anybody may say, this is the deal that was made—I said, very clearly, and it was agreed, "I cannot be on a deadline on this book, because I'm no longer taking up space at DC Comics, I'm really not pushing myself forward as a comic book artist, I have to make a living, I have a studio, I have to fit it in between whatever else I do." It turned out my partner, Dick Giordano, was the inker on the book, and so he would ink the pages as I would do them, but it was very, very clear from the beginning that they could not be on a deadline. Everybody agreed that it would be fine.

Arlen: *Again, do you remember what year this was?*

Neal: Probably 1976, something like that. That was the way we proceeded, and I must admit, I proceeded slowly. But on the other hand, if you just look at that cover, you'll get some idea of the kind of work that went into doing this book. So, I did it when I could. It got to a point, a half a year, eight, nine, ten months later, people were asking, "When is this thing ever going to get done?" I did work on it whenever I could, but it's one of those books that if you look at it, you go, "Boy, this guy really busted his ass on this book." And I did!

Arlen: *Did DC make a mistake promoting it too far in advance?*

Neal: I'm sure they didn't say it should be out, but they certainly said that we were doing it. I don't know what their promotion was. My agreement with DC Comics was that I couldn't commit to a deadline, and it was agreed it would be done when it was done. That was the agreement—the full measure of the agreement—and it took a year to get the thing done! If there was a deadline, certainly the book would've been pulled long before the year went by. Everybody agreed there was no problem, and it was a big project to do.

Arlen: *The ironic thing is that Ali was champion when the project was announced, and in a bitter irony, by the time the book came out, he was….*

Neal: In between his second championship and the third. Then, almost on

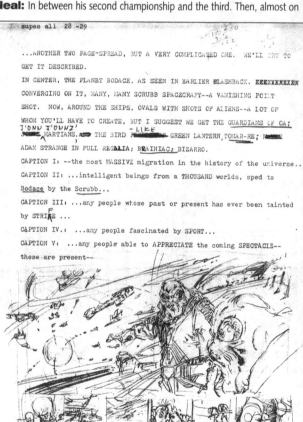

Above: *A page of Neal's revised script, complete with thumbnail. Note the use of Adam Strange and Alanna in the bottom right panel. Courtesy of the artist. Art ©2000 Neal Adams. Adam Strange & Alanna ©2000 DC Comics.*

the occasion of the book's release, he won the championship back a third time. So, I actually liked that the coincidence worked out very nicely. I had no problem with it. It was clear the book was very popular all over the world. It appeared in more languages than you can possibly imagine, and it was very, very popular. Superman, of course, is a popular character around the world; Muhammad Ali—even though he got rapped in the United States—you must remember that Ali is the champion of the world. He was certainly the champion of people whose color isn't exactly white; and for people like myself, he's our champion, too, because he stood up for what he believed in, and was willing to go to jail for it.

Arlen: *And he forfeited his crown.*

Neal: These are not small things. People do make light of them, but I don't. I really feel very strongly about it.

Arlen: *Actually, they don't make light of him now.*

Neal: They did, they don't so much now. I'm doing the cover for *ESPN* magazine featuring the 100 greatest athletes in the last century, and you can pretty much guess about right where Muhammad Ali is located. In fact, I was asked by *ESPN* to do it very much like the cover for *Superman vs. Muhammad Ali*, because the editor remembered that book. So, there are some people out there who've seen it, and have a certain amount of respect for it, which is pretty gratifying after all these years! One wonders why DC Comics hasn't reprinted that book, or in some way, promoted it.

Arlen: *At the time, other than a couple of* World's Finest *stories, and maybe one or two back-ups, you never really got to draw Superman per se.*

Neal: That's true. That's interesting, isn't it?

Arlen: *So, what was your emotional connection with this? Were you a fan of Muhammad Ali? I mean, you respected him, but going into this, knowing it was going to be this massive project, what was your feeling about it?*

Neal: Well, first of all, I'd established a certain amount of connection with Superman, because of the covers I'd done (and I will admit to anybody there are a lot of covers for Superman that I did that were not really good covers or good layouts, but there were some that I did like). One of the things I felt I did with Superman, over time, was make him younger and more athletic, somebody whom you could admire a little bit more as a trim, attractive human being. I'd done enough Superman work that I could present a Superman I was happy with, somebody more athletic, younger, more vital. My Superman could be at least comparatively equal to Muhammad Ali, so I had these two guys who physically looked fairly equal. Beyond that, I really liked Ali. I was totally offended by the way the press and a lot of people treated the man. You know, it's not the brazen side of

Ali that's important, it's that—in the middle of his life—he changed. Not necessarily because of religious conviction, but because he *stood* for something, and he brought attention to the problem: How many black guys are named after their slave owners, how many times do they take on superficial names? He led the way. More than that, he stood up for himself in a political way, and again, willing to go all the way to stand up for what he believed in. You know, an awful lot of people didn't. But here was somebody who was worthwhile. How do you turn it into a comic book story? Well, I guess you have to believe it, and that's what I did: I believed it, and I bought the whole story.

Arlen: *Muhammad Ali is a real, true super-hero—that's a thing that defines him.*

Neal: And compared to Superman—well, Superman's an alien, isn't

he? [*laughter*] So, if you want to be close to one of them, you've sort of got to be close to Muhammad Ali! I felt very much that way—not alienated from Superman, he's an icon—but Superman is, after all, not of this Earth, you know? We love him as a super-hero, but I think that, in some way, their individual statures made them equal, in some weird kind of way.

So, we started off with a bang, and I thought, "Well, you know, I have a story here, how do I begin this story and make people go, 'Woof!'?" So, I did this first double-page spread, which had to be significant. It had to show some part of America... you know, I think in comic books, if you really have the opportunity to say something, you really ought to say something! This is a neighborhood in the Bronx, or Brooklyn, or....

Arlen: *It's got that Bronx feel: Jerome Avenue. Were you working from photo reference, or did you make this up?*

Neal: No, in fact, I'm so familiar with the territory that though I was going to go out and take pictures, I thought, "You know, there's not an ideal place. But I know!" As much as I say to people,

"Research, research, research!"; in this case, I thought, "Maybe I could put it together, and if I couldn't, I'll go out and walk around and see what I see." I mean, the black lady in a blonde wig, I *know* that lady! She lived down the street, and why she wore that blonde wig, I have no idea—but I *know* her! The guy looking at her suspiciously while she's rummaging through the food, with the cigar sticking out of his mouth? That's somebody! There's little things in there, things that I don't really talk about, but—you see those initials in the concrete?

Arlen: *"JC and VM?"*

Neal: That's Jesus Christ and the Virgin Mary! [*laughter*] Nobody knows that, and it's a joke in bad taste, but bad taste is part of it! It's like, "What is that?" and some jerk in the neighborhood goes, "Yeah, I wrote that... you know what that is?" It's one of those... you know those funky little whales that they put in these little bathtubs, these plastic tubs, and they float around and squirt a little water out, and kids go, "Oh, I want that, I've got to have that!" and the mother doesn't pay any attention? The guy's walking by the girl, and she's got a little patch on her pocket that says, "Randy," there's all these little things... for me, I was saying, "Yes, in the first page, you're going to see Superman and Muhammad Ali, and you're going to see this down shot, but we're going to take you right into a neighborhood, wherever you look in this picture, you're going to see something, and you're going to think about it. You look in the upper left-hand corner, you're going to see pigeons flying out over a building, and somebody's got an old pigeon coop. You'll see the kind of buildings that are there, you'll see the lamps, the kind of fire hydrants, everything you see will be real, in a comic book format, and then we can go on from there."

Arlen: *In many ways, this is the epitome of what you are about, as an artist in the field, this is what you brought to comics.*

Neal: Then didn't it deserve my best—or the best that I could do? Garbage bags and garbage sitting on the side next to a car, leaning up against the car, the poor son-of-a-gun that's going to come out and try to drive that car away, and all the garbage falls down....

Arlen: *Garbage that looks like garbage, people who look like people, realistic settings that look real. These inks, this is all Giordano with Terry Austin backgrounds? Give us a clue....*

Homage to the Greatest!

In late 1999, the art director of *ESPN* magazine (a periodical well-regarded in the field for its cutting-edge design) contacted Neal Adams and requested his artistry for a planned special edition of the sports magazine, featuring a celebration of the top 100 athletes of the past century. Confessing a life-long affection for Neal's *Superman vs. Muhammad Ali* cover, the art director asked for a homage of that breakthrough work. Taking on the assignment, Neal and his staff at Continuity worked under a crushing

deadline, producing a full-color wraparound cover (featuring *ESPN*'s choices for the two greatest athletes of the last century, Ali and Michael Jordan, and the likenesses of over 100 sports legends in the audience), and a double-page interior spread spotlighting the career of the greatest boxer of all time. Thanks to the help of Neal, Tom Ziuko (official *CBA* cover colorist), and the staff at Continuity, *CBA* is proud to feature the line art for that cover [bottom], a repro' of the finished cover [left], and the interior spread drawn by Neal [above].

But before you go looking for this back issue in your neighborhood library or dentist's office, be forewarned that this *ESPN* just might be one of the rarest Adams collectibles around. This "Thrillennium of the Millennium" number was sent only to subscribers for the holidays—*hmmm,* there's a marketing idea!—making it a very special edition indeed. Of note to comics aficionados, the magazine also features spreads by Jack "*Mad*" Davis (featuring Babe Ruth), Kyle "*Why I Hate Saturn*" Baker (depicting Michael Jordan), and Todd "*Spawn*" McFarlane (rendering Wayne Gretzky), making the issue a veritable comic book/sports fiesta! [All illustrations ©2000 *ESPN* magazine, courtesy of Neal Adams.]

Above: Courtesy of Todd Klein, this page and opposite feature the partial unlettered inked pages seven and nine respectively. ©2000 DC Comics.

Neal: Here was the magic: Not to take anything away from Dick, but when Terry Austin inked his backgrounds, the thought that immediately came to mind is, "I can put anything in these backgrounds, and Terry will ink it." Terry was around the [*Continuity*] studio, and he suffered the brunt of my eagle eye, so he was very, very careful, but he was always—always—conscientious, and he was always hard at work. Terry never, never gave anything short shrift. I knew that if I did all this stuff, that Terry would ink it, and Dick would be glad to leave it to Terry to ink, he could focus on the things that he had to focus on. So, I put these things in, confidently, where-as perhaps—in another time—I knew if Dick was inking it, and he had another background artist, I would never get these kinds of

backgrounds, so I could take the chance to do these things, and Terry would lay them all in. And he really, really did it—I mean, he just did a fantastic job.

Arlen: *Neal, I've got to tell you, even these figures... this doesn't really look like Dick's inking. This is all his inking? Did you go in and ink some of this?*

Neal: I'll tell you, part of the joke between Dick and myself on this book was, in spite of the fact that I love Dick as an inker, there were times with this book that I felt he was inking it too fast. [*laughs*]

Arlen: *Now it can be revealed! Neal, this always bothered me, because I knew this was not Dick's inking!*

Neal: There were certain things that I inked myself because I felt personal about them, there are other things where Dick would come in the morning, and I'd be sitting there, going over his page, and tightening up his pages, and he'd stand there and go, "What are you doing?" and I'd say, "Well, uh... I'm just tightening up this stuff a little bit, Dick!" Dick would then say, "Well, that's fine," and he'd walk away. It was this understanding, that if I felt that strongly about it, then he didn't mind my going ahead and doing it. So, you'll see an awful lot of Neal Adams in the inks. Up until the end, I said to Dick, "Gee, I'd like to ink the rest of the book," Dick inked it all the way through. On the other hand, I was the kind of pain in the ass that would go over all the pages and make sure they were tight enough.

Arlen: *Your whole alien design is reminiscent of some earlier work. You never finished the "Kree-Skrull War," [laughter] but this was sort of your intergalactic sequel to that with so many designs that resemble characters from that* Avengers *run.*

Neal: Between you, me, and the fence post, I would love to have finished the "Kree-Skrull War," because I think that was a project that would've been, should've been done. You can't go very far in this comic book and not find Neal having fun—it's all over the place, all you have to do is turn the page!

Arlen: *Were you happy with the reproduction [on* Superman vs. Muhammad Ali*]? Was this the best DC could do at the time?*

Neal: Sure, this was toilet-paper comic books. I mean, nowadays, we'd look at this with a jaundiced eye, because we get good quality reproduction. We worked within the medium, all comic books looked like this. Within the medium, if you do your job right, even in spite of all that, it's going to look good.

Arlen: *In the late '60s/early '70s, reproduction in newsprint comics actually seemed better. In the mid-'70s, it went downhill.*

Neal: No. Understand the difference between what you're talking about, and that is that in the '70s, when we were still printing with letterpress presses, which means metal plates were pressing the image into the paper. Nowadays, we essentially put the ink on the late, and it's separated by oil and water, and we "lick" the surface of the paper with the ink, so the dot or whatever it is appears only at the size it appears. Here, we're pressing the ink into the paper, so every time you have an edge on a color, and this is a good example of it, if you have a tone, right at the edge of the tone, the letterpress pushes into the paper. The same thing with lettering. If you remember the time, this quality-wise was well above that quality, because we were using more colors than other people, at least I was. We were using white as a color, which is hardly ever done in the comics.

Want to know what it's like for Neal to have fun? This page [pg. 15—see fourth thumbnail, CBA Collection pg. 91]! [laughter] You'd think there's something mundane in a scene with policemen lining up, holding people back—but for me, the challenge is take a mundane situation and make it interesting. That's what I used to do when I did my Ben Casey comic strips—I learned this process of how you take something that's not that interesting and make it interesting by the way you do it. So, any time we've calmed down and the characters are talking to one another, I would find ways of making that panel interesting... the cops lined up in front of the people, the way it's colored, the way you can feel the sunshine of day on the situation, you can see the cops become a symbol of what happens when cops hold people back.

©2000 DC Comics.

Arlen: *Gaspar Saladino never lettered a comic of yours, if I remember correctly. There's something about his lettering throughout the book that—this is just personal—I find a little off-putting. It's a little bigger, it's bolder....*

Neal: I don't have that problem. Whatever it is that Gaspar does, to me, he makes the lettering lyrical, and I have reasons that I like certain letterers. You could say that my favorite letterer is John Costanza, because he was trained by Kubert, and I've always really loved that Kubert lettering. As the classic comic book letterer, I consider Costanza to be the best. I had Gaspar letter for me on *Jerry Lewis* and *Bob Hope* comic books, and the thing I liked about his lettering was it was very lyrical, and very easy to read, and it didn't steal weight away from the art. What it does, for me, is it takes lettering outside the story that's being told, and it allows the story to be told by itself, and it's not—it doesn't pretend to be integrated with the art, and I like that. I have such an affinity for Gaspar's stuff, and like it so much, that I felt here I had a ponderous, long book, I'm going to pick somebody that's going to keep the lettering light. Another thing, too: Letterers I like tend to be artists on their own, so they tend to have more respect.

Arlen: *Being that this was an oversized comic, do you remember how big the original art was?*

Neal: It wasn't 150% of the page size, I think it was something like 15% larger. It really wasn't gigantic. Remember this: I always draw quite tightly. You can tell from my layouts that I have no trouble with drawing small. The second was, once again, I had Terry Austin doing backgrounds, and he is very meticulous. I had no problem with, "Well, the page is big, it's going to be reproduced big, are the backgrounds going to hold up?" With Terry, they held up. I had no problem with that. I don't know that I'd do that with another background guy. You look at some of these backgrounds with the Zip-A-Tones, and all the fine linework....

Arlen: *Is that all Terry Austin?*

Neal: It's all Terry, absolutely.

Arlen: *Because this is your space design, I remember when I was working for you, this is your EC/Wally Wood...?*

Neal: I think you'd have to say it's Wally Wood's space design. [laughter]

Arlen: *That's what I meant. As we proceed....*

Neal: Here's another thing, too.

Arlen: *Page 18.*

Neal: Yeah, this is a great example of Denny's writing, where he picks up from Muhammad Ali's own way of speaking, and created this page of writing, and of course, it's a simple-enough looking page, but I would be in very difficult shape if I didn't understand this stuff, so I had to do a fair amount of studying... the idea of stepping backwards and throwing a punch, if you really have to get across that idea, or not. Remember that lots of comic books are done—this is not intended as a criticism because artists have reality to deal with—are done off-handedly. If you're going to show a guy boxing, well, perhaps it's not necessary to learn the art of boxing to do it. That's not how I work. So, when you look at my drawing, and you're seeing boxing going on, you're actually going to see boxing, that's what's happening on the page. I don't feel comfortable having somebody coming up to me later on and say, "That page you did on boxing had nothing to do with boxing." I don't like that, I don't like those conversations, so I'm very conscientious about those things.

Above: Thumbnails to pages 18-19. Courtesy of the artist. Art ©2000 Neal Adams. Superman ©2000 DC Comics.

Below: This thumbnail image was not used in the final book. Courtesy of the artist. Art ©1999 Neal Adams.

Arlen: *But Neal, it's the same thing you cited as a concern in Terry's work!*

Neal: Well, yeah.

Arlen: *I mean, why should this be any different?*

Neal: Again, it's a source of joy. I've got this little kid in me that giggles when I do stuff and it comes out right, and I step back and look at it and say, "Right. I like that." This little chuckle comes out.

Arlen: *Let's see, we're up to here, with the thumbnail, it's a beautiful little....*

Neal: Isn't it interesting how it's possible—if you really pay attention—to get some very interesting design work into something as simple as having rockets launch? There's a personal, quiet pride I take in this rocket launch shot.

Arlen: *But this is like you had photo reference. Did you?*

Neal: Interestingly enough, no.

Arlen: *No? [laughter]*

Neal: It's one of those times where you go, "Boy, photo reference. No, if I can knock it out without it..." Okay, if you fail, then you pull

out the reference, but you look at the layout, and you go, "I know exactly what to do with this layout, I got it." It's sort of like drawing on clouds. You see an elephant in a cloud, and you can actually sit down and make a sketch of it, and you've got an elephant, and maybe you didn't know how to draw an elephant quite right, but somehow, the cloud helped you. In a way, when you sketch things out, the sketch itself—by its freeness—will give you hints as to what to do.

Arlen: *But Neal, what I was going to say, your accumulated years of studying photographs enables you to draw without photographs, and almost subconsciously you're pulling it up, where it ends up looking like a photograph, from the years of experience of....*

Neal: And there's the quiet secret, isn't it?

Arlen: *Right.*

Neal: If you do work from photographs... well, heck, same page, upper left-hand corner, total photograph, tracing from a photograph.

Arlen: *"You are what you eat" when it comes to drawing, you surround yourself with photographs and looking at life, you're going to end up drawing photographically.*

Neal: Well, it's a tool you can learn from. There are a lot of art students—and a lot of artists—who decry the use of photographs. I think they're very foolish when they do that, because artists aren't born in a vacuum, they don't grow up without having input. The question is, how valid is your input? Are you going to make false markers, to say, "I'll do this, but I won't do this"? If your goal is to do a good job, then why should the things that are supplied to you be limited by other people's opinions? So, using photographs becomes almost foolish not to use, when there's a reason for it. Here, on page 20, we have a photograph... I didn't even draw it. I just pasted it in. It's the UN Building. Yes, I took some white paint and I took a side of the UN Building out that I couldn't see clearly, because I wanted to make it clear it was the UN Building—but did I need more for that panel? It was just fine, it worked great. The robots? I love robots. Remember, this was a time when people weren't doing very good robots. [*laughs*] So, I got to play with robots on pages 21 and 22. But what was interesting about the robots was not so much the robots themselves, but the relative size of the robots compared to he men—they were a really great size to work with. I didn't get to play with them very long, but this idea of running between the legs and making the robot bend over, and punching the robot in the ass, I thought was pretty cute. Smashing the robots. Once again, I guess Dick got involved in the inking, Dick and Terry together. Not too much Terry here, but I guess Dick felt obligated to do a lot of the inking on these robots. Here's an example of what has now become standard for the business. Now, you'll have people who do robots fantastically. In those days—geez, I hate to say things like "those days"—but in those days.... [laughter]

Arlen: *Are you talking about these chrome-like effects? They're very well done.*

Neal: Nobody did them.

Arlen: *But also, drawing—once again—drawing machinery realistically, as opposed to designing, like Kirby's. This looks like you could see the joints and the way things bend, and fold. Nowadays, people draw robots like this, like they could be real, but that's really a thing you innovated.*

Neal: Well, here's another little thing: You see this, on this double-page spread where Superman smashes these robots? You see the lettering over here? This—for today—would be nothing, the way the shadows of one letter fall on another. To get DC Comics to agree to do drop-outs for these letters was like pulling teeth. [laughter] There was no room in the DC universe for that sort of thing. Times have changed.

Arlen: *This is the big 24-25, the Hun'ya establishing shot.*

Neal: Yeah, here's this thing... we don't have a thumbnail of that one. The thumbnail was done separately on another piece of paper. This was a problem, because it's not your typical layout... you've got two guys that are normal-sized, then you've got a bad guy that's normal size, and you want to present the bad guy—the big bad guy—and you want to show a relative size that, essentially, the character's going to end up in the ring with the other guy, so he can't be so big as to be impossible to conceive, but he has to be sufficiently big enough that a normal human being would look at him and go, "I'll never be able to fight this guy!" If that's the case, essentially, you have three normal-sized people, and then one slightly bigger, and then you have a vertical page... how do you handle that, and get across the impact of it? This was my solution. Other people would have other solutions, but I can tell you, it seems like a simple problem—not a simple problem at all, everything being the same size. It's always nice to have something big and gigantic, and some things that are small to display.

Arlen: *Actually, you'd think maybe the cliché way to approach it, if you want to make this character Hun'ya big, is you'd shoot it from a low angle, make him big looking up at him, but in that case, you'd have to shoot him from the back, because you want to get their response.*

Neal: Right.

Arlen: *But the fact that you made him seem big by looking down on him is what makes it off-beat and memorable.*

Neal: But that's—in a way—all these little problems we're talking about is artists' solutions, that you go along saying, "Gee, I've got the time to do this, and I'm doing this nice commercial work, now I can turn to this." Probably the reason that page was not on this page of layouts was that I didn't have the solution at that point. When I finally did have the solution, I couldn't find that piece of paper, so I found another piece of paper, and I did the solution on that; but I gave myself that grace. One of the things that I do, often, is if I'm not happy with the solution, I'll go on—not very far—but two or three pages on, and give myself a chance to percolate the idea and see what's going to fit this best. For any problem, there's possibly a thousand solutions, of which maybe 100 are good. Then, to go down and pick the right one that fits into this story correctly, and does all the things that you wanted to do—and sometimes they're the simplest ones, you know, you've got Godzilla above the city, it's really not hard to figure out what the hell to do—but something like this, it is a problem, and I would guess that's the reason that thumbnail's not here.

Arlen: *Your spaceship designs—which are unique to yours—what have been your influences? They're somewhat reminiscent of things, but yet they're unique, and I've always wanted to know, when you*

go to do spaceships, what are you drawing from? They don't really look like the Wally Wood ships, they don't look like the Kirby ships... I'm just curious.

Neal: Remember: Here we're talking about a deficiency in Terry Austin, which you're going to hardly ever find me do: One of the things that Terry does is he kind of makes things look like Tinkertoys, because he outlines everything. So if you look at my sketch of that ship, it has a sleeker look than what Terry ended up inking. Now, what I found as I was doing these things was that Terry was doing this kind of "klunking" these things up, and I had to find a way to overcome that, I had to find a way to sleek things up so that—even though Terry may have inked it the way he inked it—I could sleek it out. Very, very hard.

Arlen: *You see, this looks like Austin's inks, these look like yours.*

Neal: They're not.

Arlen: *That is Austin inking?*

Neal: That is probably Dick. The logic is Dick did that. But these outlines are all Terry. So, here we have this problem. Now, how often have I had the problem of doing spaceships? Well, remember, I'm a science fan, and so I know what the possibilities are, I know what solar sails are, and I know what all the booster rockets looked like, and how all this stuff works. So, the opportunities that present themselves up in comic books up to this point are not very great, but in this book, I had opportunities to sit and design. I could initially start this concept of making my own designs. I thought, when I started, I stumbled a little bit, but I got an opportunity very soon on to do a lot of different design work, not necessarily using these immediate pages, but to come to it. We can talk about it then. Here's Hun'ya punching the wall—of course, it's one of my favorite panels, and a lot of other people's favorite panel. A lot of people will talk about that... there's a lot of times that you'll see—even now—artists will handle a big guy this way, the way this is done. He somehow seems compact, his effect is not so much like a car is exploding, but somehow you really get a sense of power. That is the origin of that particular thing. Also, the way

Below: *Neal's robots in action. Thumbnails to pages 22-23. Courtesy of the artist. Art ©2000 Neal Adams. Superman ©2000 DC Comics.*

Below: *Neal's version of The Hulk, Hun'ya, throws a tantrum. ©2000 DC Comics*

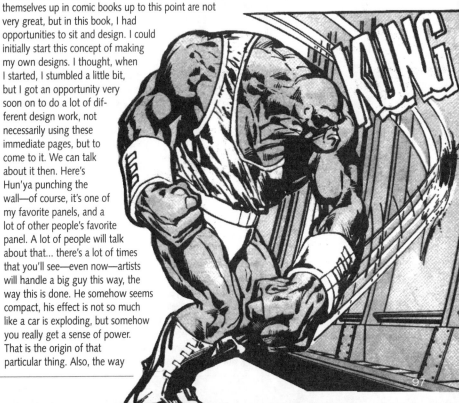

Hun'ya is put together, very, very compact and very powerful. Another photograph of Muhammad Ali....

Arlen: *I always thought that you never really got to draw the Hulk, but I always got the feeling that this is your...*

Neal: Yes!

Arlen: *...kind of Hulk.*

Neal: Well, that was obviously of some inspiration. One of the things that I get the biggest kick out of was all these different designs of these spaceships. It wasn't so much that I was designing spaceships, that the spaceships had to seem as if they came from different cultures. So, as you look at them, certain spaceships look "klunky," certain spaceships look sleek, certain spaceships have a solar sail feel to them, some of them are flying saucers... So here, even though they're small, if you start to look at them individually, you start to spot things. There's one over here that looks like a snail. Here's one that looks like it's from *2001: A Space Odyssey.* Here's one that looks like a rocket sled by Gil Kane. A lot of different things, very simple ships, energy in front of them. There were a lot of ideas, and as they get smaller and smaller, you kind of go, "Well, they're just shapes." No, each one of them, as you go smaller and smaller, was something—and, because I had Terry Austin inking, he wouldn't let me down. He nailed them all. This, in the upper right-hand corner, is an extension arm of this spaceship that—if you follow the perspective and see it goes off, in effect—there's another captain sitting with a crew, there's a whole crew sitting at that ship, and it's like an arm of the ship that can detach and fly away. So, this is not just, "Here's an interior of a spaceship," here is some kind of structure that you can look at and go, "Gee, what the hell is that guy doing?" You start to examine it. It's sort of like... I guess maybe a part of me is infected with this Wally Wood thing, Wally Wood used to do things for *Mad* magazine that, wherever you looked at on the drawing, you'd see something else, and do these little things in the corner, that if you read the thing five times, you'd find something each time.

Arlen: *That's what made Mad.*

Neal: Right, and in a way, that's what I do... periodically, I'll do something where if your eye drifts someplace, you see something else.

Arlen: *You put the work in, I mean, the blood and the sweat...*

Neal: Oh... not the blood and sweat; never blood and sweat—fun! It's always fun. Here, we've got two aliens talking to one another, and their brains are floating inside some kind of gelatinous crap in their head. [*laughter*]

Arlen: *I think that's great.*

Neal: It's funny. Ah, the stadium... throwaway panel. People lined up for miles to go up to that stadium, and it's floating in the air. It's a throwaway. Alien TV commentators floating around in these pods... this is the kind of stuff that—only now—we're starting to get to, artists are doing this sort of stuff. I don't know if we went into this one: You get more aliens viewing what's going on and Jimmy Olsen is the narrator. On page 31 in the foreground is Howard Cosell, while Jimmy—in the background—is doing an imitation of Howard Cosell. [*laughter*]

Arlen: *Yeah, you even wrote down "Howard Cosell" in the thumbnails.*

Neal: But the reason it's there is: If you read the copy, it's very clear that Jimmy is doing Howard Cosell, and here's Howard Cosell in the foreground, giving him that kind of eye. In the upper right-hand corner, the panel, another throwaway panel, looking at aliens. Well, it is a throwaway panel. Accept that, accept that. Here is grumpy dad, [*laughter*] here's his son, here's a little kid, here's mom, and the right-hand side, there's somebody in the family kind of moving away because dad is farting and making bubbles behind him [*laughter*] and this character is moving away, because he doesn't want to smell the farts, while the other teenagers in the background are fighting, and the neighbors are looking at the TV set.

That was the thing about this, too: I met—since we've had a studio in Hollywood—people who do special effects, and I was in a couple of guys' studio, the Chiodo Brothers, very good special effects people. I noticed on the wall, around the bookcase, they had *Superman vs. Muhammad Ali.* I said, "Gee, that's real nice, you've got *Superman vs. Muhammad Ali.*" One of the Chiodo brothers, I forget which one, said, "Don't you know, Neal? That book is in *all* the special effects guys' studios!" I said, "Why?" They said, "Well, any time we need to do aliens, all we do is flip open the book, and you've got pages and pages and pages of aliens!"

Arlen: *It's like a sourcebook.*

Neal: Pick a panel! I thought that was pretty funny. And sure enough, there are aliens everywhere. What is there to say about this, Angela Dundee and... I tried to stay close to the characters, I forget the name of this... oh, here it is, Angelo Dundee, Herbert Muhammad, Bundini Brown... this is one of the panels where I hit portraits, I used photographs, I drew from the photographs, and Dick didn't ink it very well. [*laughs*] So, I was like, "Dick, these are the guys we have to suck up to!" [*laughter*] "Come on!" But he just knocked them out. [*snaps fingers*] "Noooo!"

Arlen: *I like your little baby thumbnails, things are interesting. What is this?*

Neal: These are just pages of script that I've had, with all of these thumbnails, and I tried to just align them with this page. What had happened was, the way this story was going—and this is a conference that Julie and I had—that things were being added, and we didn't have enough for the back end of the story, and since Denny wasn't involved at that point, I was having to make decisions as to what to leave out, and what to put in, because we had events we had to put in, and in order to fit those events in, we had to leave some other stuff out. Part of my writing technique is to do little sketches like this, to structure the story. These are not really layouts, they're quick roughs, to get a story structure to pace the story, to find out where I am in the story, and how many pages I have left, and what to do, and I started to number the story based on that, so basically, what you have here—in effect—a re-pacing of the story, and decisions on what to leave in and what to take out. My goal was to leave as much of what Denny had done that was specific to the exact story, and to only take those things out that didn't allow us to get to the end. So it worked out pretty nicely. I kept a lot of really good stuff. Here is another example, on page 34 and 35. This is something that I owe to Bob Kanigher, and I freely say it. Bob did a story about this idea of standing, even when you're out cold.

Arlen: *A Sgt. Rock story?*

Neal: Sgt. Rock.

Arlen: *Yeah, getting a boxing story.*

Neal: A boxing story,

Above: *Down for the count. Evocative full-page splash.* ©2000 DC Comics.

where the idea is that you have what he called a "fighting heart." The idea is that if you have a fighting heart, then even if you're out on your feet, you don't go down. I thought, "Gee, that's a great idea." I know when I read it, when Kanigher did it, I thought, "Of the things I like about Kanigher's stuff, this idea of a fighting heart... that's a very... I can understand that, that you go beyond yourself, and then your body takes over, and because you refuse to go down, whatever happens to your body, you just stand there and be punished!" A very good idea.

Arlen: *And it fits Superman.*

Neal: It's Superman's persona. He may not be the greatest athlete on his planet, but he is certainly... part of what makes Superman what he is, is that, in spite of the fact that he's Superman, his own personality makes it impossible for him to give up. So to have this fighting heart, and to have him get punished like this, I thought was a very good dramatic thing—so I punished him. I had Ali: And there's some shots in here that I'm very, very happy with—middle of page 35, when Superman lunges forward, and Ali socks him, and his head goes back like that—you just feel the shot. It doesn't matter what happens to him after that, you know that he's taking it, and he's just taking it and taking it.

Arlen: *Once again, Neal, it was realistic hitting, unlike comic-book hitting. You were true to boxing, and hitting and impact.*

Neal: But overall, the idea that he wouldn't go down, and that Ali's choice was to walk away from it, and only after Ali was declared the winner would Superman's body allow him

Left: *Neal cites the influence of Robert Kanigher and Joe Kubert's "fighting heart" Sgt. Rock story, "What's The Color of Your Blood?" from* Our Army at War #160, Nov. 1965. ©2000 DC Comics.

to fall down, I think just really... it's one of my favorite story ideas and contributions to the story.

Arlen: *Also, looking at the art...*

Neal: I say my contribution to the story, but of course, it was Kanigher's contribution to the story! And Bob, if you're out there listening to this interview, I want you to know, this is all yours, baby! [*laughter*]

Arlen: *But Neal, also, I want to draw attention, artwise, to the cape... your understanding of the way the material folds, and even the impact, some of these images, because of the design—top of page 35—Superman's cape drapes over the body, the way it folds, it adds to the motion and the impact of what's going on.*

Neal: It's interesting in the story, a small contribution... I decided that it was a great idea for Superman to fight in his costume, and you could say, "Well, I'd rather see Superman in boxing trunks, fighting," but there's time enough for that... we have Ali fighting like a boxer, and I thought, "Well, here's a good opportunity to make a statement." So, essentially the statement that was made was made by Jimmy Olsen, and that was the reason that Superman is fighting in his costume was that, except for only minor changes in skin color, aliens found that humans looked exactly alike, and I thought, "Gee, I like that one." [*laughs*] That was good. So, that was my excuse for keeping his costume on, I thought it was a pretty good excuse and a pretty good statement.

Arlen: *Then we have the fantastic full-page overhead shot of Superman on the stretcher being taken out. Again, just everything about it... the Zip-A-Tone floor... makes everything jump.*

Neal: I've got to tell you, that was Terry Austin again. That was not my decision. It was Terry's decision, a really good decision. I can tell you that people who had been used to Superman for many, many years at DC Comics really, really, loved this page, because they'd never seen Superman just smashed up like that before. We got some really nice drama out of it, the excitement... this is the kind of filmic drama like I'm talking about, where Jimmy's making his way through the people, and there's a big *meleé*, Lois Lane is running, and here's Hun'ya, watching it happen, and something is clearly

going through his head.

Arlen: *A beautiful, silent panel.*

Neal: Is it because he's watching Lois Lane go by? Is he thinking he's going to kill this guy? What is he thinking in this panel? And it's not until the end of this story that we discover the kind of things going through his mind.

Arlen: *Neal, at what point do you take over the story? Was it a concrete, "He only wrote up to page 37," or...?*

Neal: I think it was a process. Remember, these are things I believe Denny would've done had he continued. If you're writing a story, and you get up to page 40, and you have a given number of pages left, you have to edit yourself, take it back, or the editor does it, and then you start to edit it. That process wasn't available to Denny, so that was the process that I took over by taking things out and adding other things back in. In a way, it was an amalgam. One thing drifted over into the other, and the story got finished. There are pages in here, for example, that Denny wrote that I kept that are later on in the story, because they're so powerful, and they fit the story. Other pages I took out because we didn't need that event. It's more the event wasn't needed, and it slowed the pacing of the story down, and we needed to get other events in. Certain things—the big close-ups of Muhammad Ali, where Muhammad Ali is yelling—Denny looked that stuff up and wrote that out in sequence, that's really great. This was a page that I felt I'd made a particular contribution to in a writing sense, this idea of... because I'd done that Kanigher thing, I thought it would be really interesting to have this ship take off and do this little conversation... "Yet these soldiers stand in silence, until the ship disappears from sight, and in their hearts, there is a special place for this alien warrior. And when fighting men sit around and cook fires on distant outposts, they'll tell about the man who would not fall down." I liked that piece of writing, it's very nice, I think.

Arlen: *Well, it shows how things become legends. This was a spectacular panel, on page 41... Ali, the roar of the crowd....*

Neal: Well, here was a very, very difficult page, if you think about it. We had a number of panels to do, and we had to bring the bad

Below: Neal's thumbnails to pages 44-45. Courtesy of the artist. Art ©2000 Neal Adams.

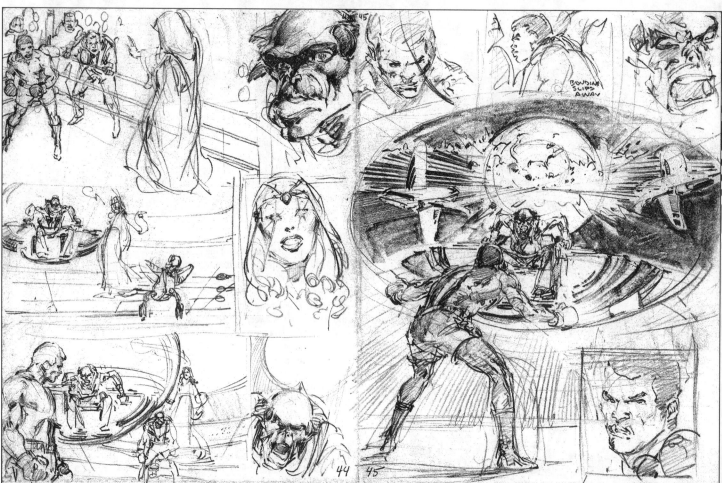

guy into the fight. Then, on the very same page, we had to bring the good guy into the fight, and we had to give them an equal balance, and we wanted to focus attention on them, yet we had all this other stuff going on; we had the weighing in, the mentor in the ring. One of the things you do as a comic book artist is you make decisions based on what goes on in a page, what you will emphasize. Very often, you'll get a situation where something is important, and something else is important, and how do you balance those things out? How do you find the room on the page to do that? Sometimes, it's very, very hard, and you really have to... in this case, I didn't feel there was much opportunity to change, to give something short shrift, so I found a way—through composition, through lighting—to really focus on these two events, while not losing anything otherwise. But this book is rife with that, I mean, I'm not saying to people, "Go out and buy this book, that it's a great comic book." For me, it's the best comic book I ever did.

Arlen: *Well, Jon Cooke agrees with you, he thinks this is the best thing in the world. Do you feel that, this is your best single...?*
Neal: I would have to say that. I've been asked lots of times, but I must admit, even I enjoy reading this book over and over again.
Arlen: *There's nothing like it, so it's unique just on that level.*
Neal: It's also a strange idea. People say, "*Superman vs. Muhammad Ali?!?* What the hell is that?!?" But it really works out to be a pretty good story.
Arlen: *But in a way, it's classic, because didn't every now and then, Superman met a real person, in the '60s there was a John F. Kennedy story, in the '50s, he met Steve Allen... I mean, Neal, there was a comic book tradition to Superman meeting celebrities.*
Neal: If there were more stories like this, I'd be reading Superman more often.
Arlen: *Not like this, what I'm saying is, this was a modern... I think that's also what made it great, is it made perfect sense, "Oh, yeah, Superman and Muhammad Ali, sure." We're at the big full-page of... I forgot the name of this character, she's an ethereal....*
Neal: She's a symbol, she acts as a symbol.
Arlen: *And again, nice Zip-A-Tone.*
Neal: This was one of Denny O'Neil's ideas, even though I shortened up some other stuff, this is a very, very strong idea, and I made sure I kept this very fully. Also, I had fun with the aliens in America. But this seems to come out of nowhere. The story's gotten very gritty, and in some ways, very plodding and moving along, and suddenly, this thing comes out of nowhere. I think it's a really interesting story surprise. Very strong element...

Here we have—and this is sort of very critical to the story—we have, now, we think Superman's gone, or something's happened to him, and now we have Ali by himself. So, now we have the two characters split up, and now they're doing their own thing. Of course, the villain shows his evil side, and we get to do this great double-page spread of Ali blowing his mouth off, and it's one of those things like, "What am I going to do with this?" I came up with a design technique where, basically, I used three photographs in the background in high con—which totally set the production department off the deep end [*laughter*] at DC Comics... "What are we going to do with this?!?" Because, of course, these photographs appeared in black, so we had black on black, and so they went nuts.
Arlen: *But Neal, how different was this from your second "Deadman" cover with the eagle in the background... you know what I mean? I'm just saying, that was just a color hold....*
Neal: That's right, that was a color hold. But that was for a cover. I could work with Jack Adler. This was for the production department—not so good. But by that point, I had gotten sort of special dispensation. [*laughter*] You know, they knew they were going to expect the unusual, and that I would give it to them, and they were going to have to deal with it, so nobody came walking up to me saying, "This is impossible." They just looked at it and said, "What are we going to do with this?" I basically told them what to do with it. What's interesting about this is, essentially, it almost has nothing to do with the art. The art is there the way it would be in a magazine, as in a magazine illustration, it's the words that matter, and the words are what it's all about. They don't show Ali in the greatest light in the world, because Ali's use of the language left something to be desired. Yet, for building critical mass, this really was great!

[*laughs*] I thought, "Well, all I can do is decorate the stuff," and that's what I did. I used photographs as much as I could.
Arlen: *This is some of the best... [laughter]*
Neal: I don't think this one on the right was inked all that well, but I got to tell you, when Ali used to do that thing where he'd screw up his face, and he'd start breathing through his nose and panting, and woofing, and I thought...
Arlen: *But you pulled it off!*
Neal: I thought I could not do it.
Arlen: *I think this adds to it, part of the beauty of the book is that you never knew what was coming next, so all of a sudden, this spread just blew people away when they saw it.*
Neal: And then we discover that...
Arlen: *There's thumbnails here... page 48, 49....*
Neal: Then we discover that suddenly, Bundini Brown is acting like a hero, we don't know what the heck is going on, and he's doing a "James Bond," and he's doing it very, very well. We didn't hold on that very long, we did it, and we're going, "What the hell is that?" Storytelling-wise, it was a really nice twist. Later, we're going to reveal that's Superman, but for one page, we get all this really nice James Bond-type action, and then you go back to the fight.
Arlen: *Which again makes this whole book feel like a movie, I mean, that's part of the twists, the turns... it wasn't just a straight, linear narrative. You weaved in and out.*
Neal: I would've loved to have seen this as a movie. There was a little part of me that was saying, "Boy, you know... Ali's the right age, you get the right actor, would this make a great film?" We lived in an America at that time where it just wasn't about to happen.
Arlen: *And yet, later that year, after this came out, the first*

Above: *Line art portrait of the one-time World Heavyweight Champion from Neal's recent* ESPN *assignment. Courtesy of the artist. ©2000 ESPN magazine.*

Below: *A kiss for luck. Panel detail. ©2000 DC Comics.*

Superman *movie with Christopher Reeve came out.*

Neal: Yeah.

Arlen: *So it's not like they weren't making* Superman *movies.*

Neal: It's not like this couldn't have been the second film.

Arlen: *Right, right.*

Neal: That would've been way too much to hope for, but it's the kind of thing where you go, "I don't know, I'd have a good time watching that movie."

Arlen: *Part of what's wrong with Hollywood is they don't realize they've got a movie on paper, in a sense, planned out for them, and all they've got to do is film it, so to speak.*

Neal: Twenty years later.

Arlen: *Anyway, this, the kick—again, this was covered in the* Neal Adams Sketch Book... *I think stuff that was covered probably will not be in this article—but you know, you went into a nice whole discussion about this drawing.*

Neal: From this point of view, once again, this is, in effect—two pages back, we had Bundini Brown—now we're back to Bundini Brown, and once again, the design work... I was getting off. At this point in the story, we're on page 51, I may have felt I was practicing, but when I got to page 51, I felt really comfortable with the design work. I was feeling very good—even though I wasn't necessarily given the opportunity to do design work—I was much more confident the way this escalator works up into the ship, and the energy field, and the ships on the outside, and this interior of this room here... I felt very, very comfortable doing that. I think, in some ways, I cut my teeth on some of the space design stuff in this book, and I felt very comfortable when I got to this point. So, from here on, the spaceships and the other stuff get more confident. Even though it was of a given style—a style I wouldn't do now—I still was doing it confidently, the strokes were bolder, they were cleaner, the shapes were even kind of bolder... this kind of stuff in here with these... taking a design, and moving the camera around and finding it, like on page 52, panel 3, here was a vast design that we just isolated a given area and took the picture, and you can imagine taking the camera and moving it to the right, and moving it to the left, and seeing all the other design elements of the ship... they're still there, because in my mind they're there, and in your imagination, you can see them. I was

much more comfortable, very, very comfortable with this stuff. These spaceships—I had decided what these aliens' spaceships looked like in general, so I was clean on that.

Arlen: *Neal, how influenced were you—because this came out a year after Star Wars—how influenced were you at the time by the impact of that movie coming out?*

Neal: I think you'd have to say I was influenced only in that you had this kind of transition between The Day the Earth Stood Still, Wally Wood-type of spaceships that were these pointed bullets that fly off into space....

Arlen: *And then you had* 2001.

Neal: Well, 2001 was very mechanical in nature. Even though it was interestingly designed, they had a lot of interesting design elements, it was very industrial looking.

Arlen: *Lucas brought back the fun with spaceships.*

Neal: Yeah, in effect, if you look at the contrast between 2001 and then George Lucas' stuff—and I have to say that George Lucas' stuff essentially was very basic, it was all triangles and circles—what it, in effect, said to you was, "There's a wide, vast difference between what you can set up in space." Even though you knew from literature and everything else that once you got into space, you're basically free to design anything you wanted, you didn't believe it. You bought the Wally Wood spaceship, that had to look like a bullet or a rocket. Now, we saw other people doing it, and we saw, "Wow, there's a lot of freedom, you can basically do whatever you want." So, their technology is based on solar sails, it's basically a ship that has various functions, and one way or another, there's a sail. Maybe different designers designed the ships, they come from different companies or whatever—the lesson, of course, that we learned was, "Hey, there are other ways to do this... yeah, you can shape them like bullets, but they're not really bullets, they're designs." So, if you have a culture that's into sleekness, you can make them sleek. If you have a culture that's into klunkiness, you can make them klunky... you can make them balls, you can make them flat walls that fly forward... it didn't really matter. So, here was, essentially, the call to freedom was out there. Was I the first to do it? No, no—but I certainly had a lot of fun!

Arlen: *Page 54, 55?*

Neal: Here I'm well into the semi-reality of Superman. Once again, I had only done Superman covers. Now, I'm really beginning to enjoy the Superman character. Once I got through that fight, and I had that cape move, and I did all the stuff that you mentioned with the cape, I'm realizing, "Hey, I can really use that cape. It's not Batman's cape, it's a very different cape, it's a piece of cloth on this guy's back that can fit his form, I can really play with that. I like that." It's very, very enjoyable. So, now we're at...

Arlen: *I've always loved Superman kissing his fist. That's a great...*

Neal: Of course, you don't have to see the next scene.

Arlen: *Yeah. But, Neal, interesting again, like a movie, the cutting: This is how a great director would do it: Kissing his fist, and then you cut to....*

Neal: At least a good director.

Arlen: *Yeah.*

Neal: I got a lot of fun out of this. Now, each time we cut back, in a way, the story is developing each of the characters. We're seeing Superman develop, he's doing his job. We're seeing Ali face the situation, that he's doing his job.

Arlen: *Step up to the plate.*

Neal: He's stepping up to the plate. He's deciding that this is going to end, that he's going to win. No matter what the bad guys do, he's going to win this fight. Even in the first panel, one of the things that I tried to do was to show...

Arlen: *We're on page 56.*

Neal: ...at the top of the panel that, here was a small man punching a big man, and the effect of his punches is not to knock the guy away, but he can wear him down, so those two punches, if you look at it, essentially the first punch to the gut really doesn't make the other guy do anything, but you still feel from that little turn of his foot that he's felt the impact. In the second drawing, he's tried to throw a blow, his jaw has been slammed together, he's felt it in his brain, but there's not that kind of comic-book action to it yet. You're starting to get it, the little guy is fighting back, and he's got a chance,

AS LUTHOR ONCE SAID, "THIS IS GOING TO BE LIKE TAKING CANDY FROM A BABY!"

so now the bad guy is also getting it... just while you're getting it, the bad guy gets it! That realization comes into his face, and he decides to be a real bastard, and he decides he's going to attack the Earth—and so, I had this fleet of spaceships going by the red spot on Jupiter...

Arlen: *Page 57..*

Neal: ...which I got such a bang out of drawing—and look at this U-turn they make! [*laughter*] This is reminiscent of some experiments that Jack Kirby did with perspective that I really liked, where you'd do angles that seemed so odd, where at the bottom of the page, you're looking at something front-on, and at the top of the page, you're looking right under its underbelly.

Arlen: *You know, Neal, when I look at this, I also think of the Sentinels going into the sun, full-page. It's almost like the flip side of that. But again, accurate use of Zip-A-Tone at the right moment for that graphic impact.*

Neal: Is Neal having a good time? I was having a good time.

Arlen: *Then we have this last scene, in the chin.*

Neal: Then we get to...

Arlen: *Page 58. Again, Neal, you talk about this in the sketchbook, you know, about how you wanted to re-position Superman.*

Neal: In effect, to re-introduce him—and that was the idea of this... here, I had an opportunity, in this nice, big, comic book, to focus on Ali, to really show you Ali, in this fantasy background that made you buy him. Now, here, I had the opportunity to take Superman's powers away, and then give them back, and to have him glory in the power. So, it wasn't so much that I just had him fly out of the ship—that was enough fun, if that's all I got to do, that would've been enough—but to then have him take on this gigantic space fleet, and to have some trouble taking it on, and to bounce off a force field, and to realize that here was Superman taking on a battle that maybe he wouldn't win, but he was going to fight it as Superman.

Then, we come to my favorite spread in the whole book. Oh, man... would anybody not want to be given the opportunity to draw these three panels? I can't even imagine. Any artist, just to be given the opportunity, it's just so... I had such a great time, because here was—if you were Superman—oh, *man*, wouldn't this be something? And then you got bashed? Then we get back to the fight... is Superman dead, what's going on?

Arlen: *Neal, at this point, you're hitting us over the head. It's like, again, you paced the story where we're getting these giant full-page spreads, full-page panels. I remember reading this, and again, what could keep coming next?*

Neal: And I wasn't going to let up, either.

Arlen: *The classic knock-out, knocking out of the ring. And again, it's all in the thumbnail.*

Neal: Right. The thing about the knock-out was, I thought, "Well, I've shown you two panels already where you see him hit the guy... how's he going to do a knock-out that you're going to believe?" Because the guy is this mountain! So, what he does is run across the ring, and he uses his fist like David and Goliath, his fist becomes the stone, and he hurls it at this guy with such ferocity—I mean, you see his whole body bends back, this is a seven-foot long punch, and smashes this giant in the face, strong enough to knock him out of the ring, you believe it! You look at him go back, and you look at him run forward, and you look at that hand

down there, and you know he's got to pull it from the ground, and he smashes this guy, and—for one of the few times in comic books—you believe that this has happened, it's like "Yep, he did it... he knocked him out of the ring."

Arlen: *A classical spread.*

Neal: The crowd explodes.

Arlen: *You know, Neal, maybe another artist would've used this format to do a bunch of double-page spreads, you paced your double-page spreads out only for the effect.*

Neal: Where it was deserved, I did it. Where we could get the impact. I mean, this panel alone here, in my opinion, was worth a double-page spread.

Arlen: *Page 64, top panel.*

Neal: I just had so many opportunities. But if you examine that panel, you can have a lot of fun just going from character to character to character, and seeing these guys. It's not this panel, but there's another panel that we passed earlier on with one of the aliens so taken by what's going on, he grabs another alien and throws him up in the air in joy! [*laughter*]

Arlen: *We'll have to find where that is.*

Neal: Anyway, so now we're back to Superman, he's doing a great job, beating the aliens, but now he's got a problem: He says he's disabled nearly half the fleet, but how can he stop all of them, because he's done... he's used it all up. So, he decides he's going to trick them into thinking they've beat him. In their zeal to destroy the nearly-invulnerable Superman, they—in effect—line up to blow him away, all at once, and he takes the opportunity to just make a living rocket out of his own body, and fly through their ships... oh, was that fun! Man... if I had fun

Above: Step aside, George Lucas! Neal's intergalactic traffic: A full page splash from Superman vs. Muhammad Ali. ©2000 DC Comics.

Below: Neal's favorite spread in Superman vs. Muhammad Ali. ©2000 DC Comics.

Terry Austin vs. Muhammad Ali
The Inker meets The Greatest!

As I remember, it was a sunny afternoon in January 1978 when I punched the down button on the wall of Continuity Associates and waited for the elevator to arrive. Neal Adams, ambling past, spied the copy of *Superman vs. Muhammad Ali* under my arm and asked, "Where ya goin'?" "I'm going to the big press conference and get Ali to sign my book," I replied as the elevator door opened. As the doors slid closed between us, Neal said, "Uh huh," in a tone indicating he figured I had about as good a chance of returning with the autograph of the Man of Steel himself.

I walked a few blocks over to the Warner Communications building and hooked up with my good buddy Al Milgrom, then an editor at DC Comics. I related Neal's skepticism as we traveled to an unfamiliar part of the building, eventually entering an immense room with a ceiling somewhere in the stratosphere. At one end was a stage with a podium cluttered with microphones from all the New York radio and TV stations. A photo of the champ wearing a Superman cape was affixed to the lectern; hanging behind was a huge blow-up of Neal's cover of *Superman vs. Muhammad Ali*.

The atmosphere in the room was electrically charged, packed with a great rolling sea of humanity. I could easily identify the reporters, cameramen, Warner executives, and less expensively-dressed DC employees—but who were the hundreds of others jammed into this vast enclosure? Looking around at all the happy, laughing faces, charged with anticipation and excitement, I realized we were all there united in purpose: To bask in the glow of one of the most celebrated and charismatic personalities in the history of our planet. That, and we were all there to see a show.

For those of you readers too young to remember, Ali became a celebrity based not solely on his boxing skills—which were considerable—but by virtue of the force of his personality. Cocky, confident, outspoken, and controversial, Ali was the consummate showman, as much a force of nature outside the ring as within. A hush fell over the crowd as we braced ourselves for the whirlwind about to descend into our midst.

Ali strode to the podium accompanied by cheers and deafening applause. As I remember, the first question was something innocuous like, "Champ, how do you feel?" The assembled multitude collectively breathed inward as if to soak up the essence of the man like a sponge. "Fine," Ali replied, without any vocal inflection, staring unblinkingly at some distant point over our heads. The crowd tittered nervously. The next question may have been, "Are you ready for your next fight?" to which the champ answered, "Yes." At this point the energy level in the room plummeted to zero and the faces of the onlookers fell with it. Every question that afternoon was answered with a flat unemotional yes or no by Ali, with none of his characteristic braggadocio. We might as well have been watching a poorly-programmed Ali robot. With an air of infinite sadness descending, the questions soon dwindled to a trickle, and the heavyweight world champion left the stage to a smattering of weak applause. To no one's surprise, no footage from the press conference would air that night on any of the New York news broadcasts.

Dejectedly, I looked to Milgrom to get us out of there, since I had no earthly idea where I was. Allen led me over to a side corridor and stopped. We talked quietly about the fiasco we had just witnessed and about how not one of the questions had had anything to do with the comic book that was ostensibly being promoted.

Just about then we looked up to see a phalanx of burly guys coming down the corridor toward us and in the center was Ali. To my horror, Allen stepped right into his path and said, "Champ, I'd like you to meet one of the artists who worked on your book!" That's when everything went into slow motion for me. Muhammad Ali stopped, turned his icy stare straight into my eyes for a moment, nanoseconds that seemed like an eternity; and I saw his hand coming up from his side, moving in my general direction. "I'm dead," I remember thinking, "Who's gonna phone my mom and tell her that the champion of the world punched her son so hard that his brain flew out of the top of his skull and is now being searched for above the acoustic ceiling tile in the Warner building?" Unbelievably, that lightening fast hand stooped, extended in a gesture of friendship. As I shook the champ's hand, for the first time that afternoon, there was a genuine twinkle in his eye as he looked into mine, and he smiled as if to reassure me that the real Ali had been there the whole time, he was only playing possum for the crowd. Then, everything sped back up again as he swept the book from my hand, signed it, and he was down the corridor and gone. I looked over to Allen, seeking confirmation that it actually happened, and there was good ol' Milgrom grinning like a loon.

"So, did you get Ali's autograph?" Neal asked when I arrived back at Continuity. "Sure," I replied jauntily, tossing the book onto his drawing table. "Maybe you wouldn't mind signing it too, if it isn't too much trouble." Neal may have flown to distant galaxies on an adventure with the champ, but I was privileged to share a moment with Muhammad Ali in the corridor of a glass and steel tower in the heart of Manhattan.

with that first drawing of Superman, imagine how much fun I had on this one!

Arlen: *It's like, "Can you top this?"*

Neal: Oh, really!

Arlen: *You kept topping it.*

Neal: And had fun all the way, all the way. Here, I've got Terry Austin inking spaceships for me, putting in all the crap that I want to have in there, what a great time! Hun'ya, suddenly, that expression that we saw on Hun'ya's face on page 68, pays off... he turns on the bad guy, smashes him, and the next panel, we see all his minions, all the bad guy's minions, stand there and they all agree with our chief bad guy, it's like, "You've disgraced us, you son of a bitch." To me, if I saw that in a movie, I'd buy it... I'd buy it. You can say whatever kind of hokey things you want to say, but this is something that...

Arlen: *But you know, the classic element of turning the so-called "bad guy," bringing him around...*

Neal: Well, turning what seems to be the brute into the intelligent, feeling character that he always was, but he's been used, you have the true story of a warrior. So, here we see Superman floating in space, rescued by what was Hun'ya, obviously wearing royal robes, and is doing fine. And then, the story calms down. I did this intentionally, even though it was hokey. I slowed the story down, and I stopped the story, and I said, "Okay, let's just wind this story down, baby." There's nothing I do about the layouts that I do to excite you, simply just to tell the story between these characters, and move the story to its end. And I really wanted this idea to happen that Ali guesses that Superman is... in a way, I felt—and I think we all felt—that we wanted a true equality between these characters right at the end; and I think that by guessing Superman's identity, we sort of create that.

Arlen: *Brains and brawn, not just brawn.*

Neal: Exactly.

Arlen: *Because you know, Neal, there's a running subtext to this whole thing, the white man against the black man.*

Neal: And that's the thing that I felt was the strongest challenge of all, was that, in an honorable situation, you put these characters together, they can fight each other and still be brothers, and that's the important story to be told. You see it in sports all the time, that's part of the thing that's so great about sports, is that the competition is meaningless except as competition—it has nothing to do with fighting, it has nothing to do with prejudice—it has to do with the joy of sports. In effect, that was a really good reason to put them together. Why did I do this story? Why was I so intrigued, and why was I in love with this story, no matter what anybody would say? I've had people criticize this story, saying, "Why did you want to do this *Superman vs. Muhammad Ali*, it's sort of ridiculous." Not for one second is this story ridiculous, it's a terrific story. It was a pleasure doing it. As far as I'm concerned, Superman and Muhammad Ali are the greatest. Two Jewish boys from Cleveland, Ohio, and the black heavyweight champion of the world, that's what it's all about.

Arlen: *So Neal, why hasn't DC treated this well, or reprinted it?*

Neal: I'd be curious about the answer to that question myself. I'd be curious, because I think it's a good job, it deserves to be.

Arlen: *First of all, DC owns it... is the original art still around?*

Neal: I'm sure they could reprint it, it has nothing to do with the original art. Dick has some of it, I have some of it... that was part of that time, was to get artwork returned, and one of the things that we were very, very strong on was to make official the return of that original art, so everybody was aware of it, so that made a very strong case. I mean, there are certain turning points in the industry that are significant, relative to this book, that underline a lot of what went on. The original art has nothing to do with it. I question whether or not... I'm not so sure that DC Comics didn't make a sincere effort to get it reprinted, and maybe permission was not achieved.

If somebody in *ESPN* magazine can remember this book enough to have me do the centennial cover, certainly there are people out there remembering and it means something to them.

Arlen: *That's my point: it's a shame that it always seems to be people outside of the company that get it, and the people in the company don't get it, but on the other hand...*

Neal: Yeah, but pretty much the success of *Green Lantern/Green Arrow*, you know, Aquaman, I don't know what happened to him, he's got one hand. [*laughter*] I don't know how many Flashes there are, it doesn't seem as though the licensing ability of these characters is being held intact, and the things that we love about them continues on. Maybe it's all become mashed potatoes after a while.

Arlen: *The success of this tells me that, if your work were treated with the care, and reproduced well, there's a market for it if this thing was done as a hardcover.*

Neal: I don't think anybody questions whether or not there's a market for it, I think that sometimes they question whether or not they want to do it, I don't know. It's very hard to read other people's minds, I don't get it.

Arlen: *After this book came out, do you remember what the reaction was? You said you don't know how it sold.*

Neal: I had the impression from DC Comics that the sales were disappointing—but I have to tell you, between you, me and the fence post, if you read the article that just recently appeared about how distribution was done [*CBA #6*], then...

Arlen: *It's another victim of affidavit return fraud?*

Neal: I would say this is another victim of that, I would say that... the way I get my copies is there are certain stores—I did this in California—there was a store in California that puts them out every once and awhile, and I said, "Look, I'd like to get some of these copies, do you know anybody that has them?" And the guy said, "Well, I happen to have a box in the back of the store, and I usually sell them for a little more than the cover price, but if you want to buy them, you can go ahead and buy them." So, I bought 20 copies. Now, how come that guy has 20 copies in the back of his store somewhere, mint condition? And I gave them to friends. All I know is that around the world, it did great... if sales were disappointing in the United States, after all, haven't they always said that about my books? "Deadman," *Green Lantern/Green Arrow, X-Men,* "Sales were not as good as we expected them to be." I wonder how that's possible, and I wonder how come I keep going to conventions and signing mint condition copies of these comics? Somebody has to put that together.

Marvel's "Amazing-Man"

Celebrating Gil Kane, our great cover artist, and the Heroic Ideal

Besides the obvious presence of Roy Thomas, Barry Windsor-Smith, Mike Ploog, and others, the two most prominent artists showcased in this issue who *permeate* the contents are two of the great old masters of comicdom: Bill Everett and Gil Kane. Our beautiful cover (drawn for us by Gil) represents a dual homage of sorts: One to Bill Everett and his creation, Amazing-Man; but primarily to celebrate the glorious collaborations between Gil and Roy Thomas, most of which were inspired in some way by Bill's *A-Man*, which include some of the most well-remembered strips of the '70s—*Warlock, Captain Marvel,* and the origin issue of "Iron Fist." In our interview, we asked Gil what was it about *Amazing-Man* that attracted the artist.

"First of all," Gil said, "it was early on in the history of comics. [A-Man first appeared in *Amazing-Man Comics #5,* Sept. 1939.] Part of the Amazing-Man's character is that he was raised by monks in Tibet, and that appealed to me right away. One of the monks' tests (to measure his maturity) was to tie his hands and throw him in with a snake, which he killed with his *teeth!* But the part that I liked was that he stood there, bound to a stake, and they threw knives at him. One knife struck him high on the chest and another struck him in the throat. He sagged but didn't die. So they bandaged him but it healed right away! I just loved that whole idea, loved the resilience, loved the anger—the character was always in a rage, and taking on the Amazing-Man persona, he became insane and a homicidal maniac! I just *loved* it!

"Bill Everett only did about four or five issues that I cared about—either he left it or I did— and some other guys took it over, but it was never the same. Those first four or five issues were the inspiration for everything I did in terms of storytelling. I always wanted characters to suffer but not to die, understand? So I always had my characters wounded grievously but they would never surrender. They would sink to their knees but somehow *weather* it.

"There was that sustained sequence that Steve Ditko did with Spider-Man trapped under the machine, which I've mentioned in a million interviews: I always thought that that was absolutely my whole sense of what a hero should be. A hero should not be merely tough and have anger; what he should have is resilience and nobility; some quality of rising above the situation, something above what anybody else would be able to do in terms of self-sacrifice and to achieve some- thing. That is what I always thought a character should be like and those panels of Spider-Man just absolutely said the whole thing. To me, it was just a perfect demonstration."

"When Spider-man finally lifts that giant machine over his head," we observed, "it's a very Gil Kane-like figure."

"I see when that final effort comes," Gil said, "it is a wrenching effort where muscle fibers tear and the effort is so severe, it's *inhuman!* But you have to understand the penalty he is paying in stamina and strength and wear and tear. *That's* what I always want to leave the reader with and that's why I believe in prose and captions in comics because what I just told you, in just so many words, couldn't be drawn well enough. A caption has to be added to say what I just said, the cost in physical terms— the severity, the pain, the inhuman effort. *That* I feel would give a proper context to the picture."

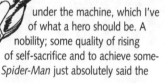

"All your work seems to reflect what you just said," we offered. "The ideal, the profound sacrifice."

"Yes, it does," Gil continued. "Gary Groth, my best friend, has always felt that I could do some sort of serious comic. When *Maus* came out, he said, 'Jesus, you were born over there, you were in World War II, why don't you do something like that?' But I don't have any interest and I don't think I have the capacity for it. What I have a capacity for is that I've been marinated in romance all my life. I grew up reading and absorbing all of the great classic romances of my age. I grew up with *King Kong, Gunga Din, The Lone Ranger, Jack Armstrong, Superman, Batman, all* of that stuff! I used to see the serials, so I was inundated with romance! On top of that, every movie was romantic or melodramatic. Even if they were excellent movies with perfect personalities, all of them were *romantic.* I grew up that way and was conditioned. I don't read any of that stuff anymore—I haven't in *years.* I read non-fiction, books on sociology, literature, history, and anything you can think about. But my first impulse when I wanted to work would be to do, for instance, *The Ring of Nibelung, King Arthur,* because I'm at my best in that sort of material. It's in my blood—epics and myths.

"I wish I were more commercial and guys would carry me around on their shoulders, but they don't! And the truth of the matter is, I'm not terribly interested in possibly getting somebody to like me more. The things that I like to do, I like to do. Somehow or other, I pour that into whatever I do every opportunity I get (if they give me the opportunity)."

Gil Kane is *our* hero, and as we extend our heartfelt thanks and gratitude to him for his superb contribution of the amazing cover and for a lifetime of extraordinary achievement, we just wish he'd stop working so hard and *let* us hoist him on our shoulders (and with his height, we'd never get out the door!). Inside you'll find a bounty of work by Gil, from thumbnails to finished work. Huzzahs for the Great Kane! (Also, thanks to the wonderful colorist Tom Ziuko for his great coloring jobs on both the *CBA* and *A/E* Kane covers!)

We also hope you enjoy the touching Bill Everett Tribute in our pages, showcasing an interview with his daughter Wendy, and a photo album (with greeting cards drawn for his family), plus a reminiscence by Bill's friend Mike Friedrich. Now, let's get cosmic! ⚡

Above: *Inspired by Roy Thomas' take on the Broadway musical* Jesus Christ Superstar, *and Gil Kane's devotion to Bill Everett's* Amazing-Man *comic book character, Adam Warlock was truly a "New Age" Marvel super-hero. The team melded Jack Kirby & Stan Lee's "Him" and "High Evolutionary" concepts and took them a leap forward. Jim Starlin would later take it even a step beyond, exploring Catholic theology and the concept of self.* ©1998 Marvel Entertainment.

Making Mine Marvel, 1970-77
Becoming a Friend of Old Marvel Bullpenners

If you were around for the first issue of *Comic Book Artist*, you know that I'm a huge fan of the DC books between 1967-74. Not all of 'em, mind you, but starting with Jack Kirby's Fourth World books and on down, I was hooked. And what I liked best was the overlapping continuity that Jack brought to the titles, some of it seeping over into Julie Schwartz's great Superman books. What I didn't realize was that Jack was attempting a "Marvelization" over at the Distinguished Competitor and that he had left a legacy over at that garish, slightly tawdry line called Marvel. Well, a trip to a flea market and a chance encounter with both *Avengers Special #4* and *Captain America Special #1* changed all that. But (sigh) I'll dispense with the boring reminiscence and get to what *CBA* does best; go to the source, after a brief word.

What distinguished Marvel's Second Wave from the previous Kirby-dominated Marvel Age was not only Jack's absence but the lingering power and dominance of his and Stan Lee's concepts. It was what was accomplished by taking Lee & Kirby's ideas as a *starting* point which made for some slammin' comics. Cases in point: The collaborations of Roy Thomas and Gil Kane—specifically *Warlock*, *Captain Marvel* and "Iron Fist." Roy shared with me his take on the teaming of Thomas & Kane:

"One of my all-time favorite collaborators has to be Gil Kane, who's also become a good friend over the years," Roy told me recently. "We had known each other slightly since the 1965 New York Comicon, and we would exchange a few words here and there, but we never really talked. Then in 1969 we wound up doing *Captain Marvel* together, and we really hit it off. He loved the story I had plotted only a couple of days before he walked in and said he'd like to see what he could do with Mar-Vell; and I, for my part, loved the dynamic, spare way he drew the story. We even redesigned the costume together. I still have the splash panel, inked by Dan Adkins, hanging in my foyer. After that first story, we co-plotted the other four *CM* issues we did together, some of which were originally Gil's idea. The last issue, in which a man in an apartment-house maze turns out to have been an inmate of a Nazi concentration camp, had real power, and it was basically Gil's idea.

"After *Captain Marvel* we worked together whenever we had a chance. Gil's always saying he was 'never anybody's first choice' for an art assignment, but he's wrong there. He was very definitely my first choice when I thought of the basic idea of *Warlock*, which we then developed together. He was the first artist I thought of working with when I wanted to do "Iron Fist"; in that case all I had was a name and a general martial arts theme, so when Gil suggested we plunder the Amazing-Man origin for Iron Fist's background, I really got into it. We did a Ka-Zar origin that was a thing of beauty, and his two early issues of *Conan* were not only beautifully drawn but were very good sellers.

"In some ways the height of our collaborations was *The Ring of the Nibelung* at DC. Once again, Gil was my (and original editor Mike Gold's) first choice. That series of four books was so good that it went right over DC's head, and I think they were shocked when we started getting all these great notices from opera reviewers. I wasn't. *The Ring* was a work of real integrity, and no one could have done it any better than Gil.

"From time to time Gil bemoans the fact that he's overly identified with Green Lantern. I can understand his feelings, I guess. But Gil should be proud of the fact that, after four decades of artists who have drawn the Hal Jordan Green Lantern, there is absolutely no one whom people think of in connection with that hero before they think of Gil Kane. Only the Neal Adams *Green Lantern/Green Arrow* period even rivals it, and that's primarily because of the super-relevant subject matter, not even Neal's artwork.

"Bill Everett and the Sub-Mariner. Jack Kirby and the Fantastic Four. Steve Ditko and Spider-Man. Gil Kane and Green Lantern. That's not bad company to be in, you know?"

There's good company also to be found in the following pages. Roy and I have obviously hit it off famously in the last six months or so, and I would not have such a concise issue devoted to his era as Editor-in-Chief at Marvel (and beyond) without his very-much appreciated help. This one's for you, Roy.

This one's also for those Bullpenners and freelancers who did not make it into the issue but shared their time and efforts: John Romita Sr., Marie Severin, Don McGregor, and Dave Cockrum. The issue proved *so* big, that we've decided to follow-up with "Marvel Phase 2" for our next issue, where their interviews will finally appear (with a few more surprises).

Let's start our tour with a stop in Stan "The Man" Lee's office…

Above: Night Nurse #1. Cover art by the late Winslow Mortimer. Worth $25 a pop? Nah. But the epitome of "fun, fun, fun" at Marvel? You betcha! Linda Carter rocks! ©1998 BWS.

MARIE SEVERIN 101

THIS IS IT! YOUR **MARVEL VALUE STAMP** FOR THIS ISSUE! CLIP 'EM AND COLLECT 'EM!

Stan the Man & Roy the Boy

A Conversation Between Stan Lee and Roy Thomas

An *Alter Ego* **Extra!**

What follows is less an interview and more a conversation between the two most prominent creative forces working at Marvel Comics in the early 1970s: the legendary "Smilin'" Stan Lee and "Rascally" Roy Thomas. The discussion was conducted via telephone in two sessions during May 1998.

Stan Lee: What on earth could you possibly ask me that hasn't been asked before?

Roy Thomas: *The magazine's theme for its second issue is Marvel from 1970-77, but still we'll need a little background from the '40s through the '60s.*

Stan: You just ask and I will answer.

Roy: *You started working at Timely as a teenager under Joe Simon and Jack Kirby. Were both of them counted as editors, or was it just Joe?*

Stan: My memory is not the best, but I thought that Joe was the editor and sort of Jack's boss. I got that feeling. Generally, Jack would be sitting at the drawing board drawing and chewing his cigar, muttering to himself. Joe would be walking around, chewing his cigar and mumbling, and also handling whatever business there was to handle under Martin Goodman.

Roy: *So you didn't see Joe draw a lot?*

Stan: No, but I know that he did draw. I didn't see him draw a lot at all.

Roy: *When Simon & Kirby left Timely in 1941 to go to work for DC with the deal that had them doing "Boy Commandos," "Sandman," etc., was there some bad blood between them and publisher Martin Goodman? Or did he just accept the fact there was more money to be made over at DC?*

Stan: I would imagine there had to have been some bad blood, or why would they have left? I have a feeling that there was some problem. Either Martin found out that they were doing work on the side, or they started to argue about who owned Captain America—both of these things may be wrong, but it was something like that. There was some unpleasantness.

Roy: *John Buscema once told the editor of* Comic Book Artist *that, sometime in the late '40s, Martin Goodman once opened a closet door and discovered "an enormous pile of discarded (but paid-for) art that was never published."*

"Now look, you guys, this is the graceful effect I want you to achieve as Thor rescues the nurse from Loki's magic tornado...."

John says that Goodman promptly put all the staff artists on free-lance status. Do you recall that?

Stan: It would never have happened just because he opened a closet door. But I think that I may have been in a little trouble when that happened. We had bought a lot of strips that I didn't think were really all that good, but I paid the artists and writers for them anyway, and I kinda hid them in the closet! *[laughter]* And Martin found them and I think he wasn't too happy. If I wasn't satisfied with the work, I wasn't supposed to have paid, but I was never sure it was really the artist's or the writer's fault. But when the job was finished I didn't think that it was anything that I wanted to use. I felt that we could use it in inventory—put it out in other books. Martin, probably rightly so, was a little annoyed because it was his money I was spending.

Roy: *The revival of Captain America, the Human Torch, and Sub-Mariner in the '50s was done, everyone assumes, because of the success of the Superman TV show. Bill Everett told me in an interview how some TV producers approached Martin Goodman and Timely in 1954 about a Sub-Mariner TV show to star Richard Egan. Bill said comedian Herb Shriner was part of the deal, and that Arthur Godfrey put up the money. Bill mentioned a producer named Frank Saverstein or Saperstein. Did you know anything about that?*

Stan: No. It's a funny thing: Martin never discussed business deals with me, and that would have fallen under the heading of a business deal. This is the first that I've heard about it.

Roy: *You were just the peon that kept things running? [laughs]*

Stan: I was just the guy in the other room, trying to do the comics.

Roy: *A couple of years after that, the American News debacle happened—that's when Timely/Atlas collapsed. Bill told me that someone forewarned him. Did you have any warning that this total collapse was coming?*

Stan: Absolutely not. The only thing I did know was that Martin had given up his own distribution company and had gone with the American News Company. I remember saying to him, "Gee, why did you do that? I thought that we had a good distribution company." His answer was like, "Oh, Stan, you wouldn't understand. It has to do with finance." I didn't really give a damn, and I went back to doing the comics.

And then, very shortly thereafter—maybe two weeks later—the American News Company went out of business! We were left without a distributor and we couldn't go back to distributing our own books because the fact that Martin quit doing it and went with American News had got the wholesalers very angry—I don't know *why* it got them angry, but this is what I heard—and it would have been impossible for Martin to just say, "Okay, we'll go back to where we were and distribute our books."

It ended up where we were turning out 40, 50, 60 books a month, maybe more, and the only company we could get to distribute our books was our closest rival, National (DC) Comics. Suddenly we went from 60, 70, 80 books a month—whatever it was—to either eight or 12 books a month, which was all Independent News Distributors would accept from us. We had to try and build ourselves up from that until we eventually went to Curtis Circulation.

Roy: *Didn't Independent have a contract that basically said that in order to start one new title, you had to drop something else?*

Stan: I don't remember that for a fact, but that could very well have been the case. I know that it was very tough for us; we were down to almost nothing.

Roy: *That's the period when Jack Kirby came back to Marvel. Jack mentioned in an interview [in* The Comics Journal *#136] that he came to work offering his services when people were literally moving out the furniture. Do you recall that?*

Stan: I never remember being there when people were moving out the furniture. [*chuckles*] If they ever moved the furniture, they did it during the weekend when everybody was home. Jack tended toward hyperbole, just like the time he was quoted as saying that he came in and I was crying and I said, "Please save the company!" I'm not a crier and I would never have said that. I was very happy that Jack was there and I loved working with him, but I never cried to him. [*laughs*]

Roy: *During that period when you put out very few books, did you feel that your days in comics were limited and that maybe the whole thing was going to die?*

Stan: Believe it or not, I think I felt that way until we started Marvel Comics. I *never* thought that this thing would last! [*laughs*] When did I start? '40? I think it was the third issue of *Captain America.*

Roy: *That would have been in very late '40 or early '41, in terms of when the issues left the office. Less than a year later you became the temporary editor; that lasted for decades. Now, skipping ahead to 1961: The story has often been told of this infamous, legendary golf game with Martin Goodman and [DC President] Jack Liebowitz in which Liebowitz bragged about the sales of* Justice League of America, *and Goodman came back and told you to start a super-hero book. Was that story really true?*

Stan: That's absolutely true. He came in to see me one day and said, "I've just been playing golf with Jack Liebowitz"—they were pretty friendly—and he said, "Jack was telling me the *Justice League* is selling very well, and why don't we do a book about a group of super-heroes?" That's how we happened to do *Fantastic Four.*

Roy: *Was there any thought at that time to just bringing back Cap, Torch, and Sub-Mariner?*

Stan: No, I really wanted to do something new. You probably heard this story: I wanted to quit at that time. I was really so bored and really too old to be doing these stupid comic books; I wanted to quit. I was also frustrated because I wanted to do comic books that were—even though this seems like a contradiction in terms—I wanted to do a more realistic fantasy. Martin wouldn't let me and had wanted the stories done the way they had always been done, with very young children in mind. That was it.

My wife Joan said to me, "You know, Stan, if they asked you to do a new book about a new group of super-heroes, why don't you do 'em the way that you feel you'd like to do a book? If you want to quit anyway, the worst that could happen is that he'll fire you, and so what? You want to quit." I figured, hey, maybe she's

right. That's why I didn't want to do the Torch and the Sub-Mariner; I wanted to create a new group and do them the way I had always wanted to do a comic book. That's what happened.

Roy: *I assume that Joan said this after you were given the assignment to do the super-hero group and not while you were doing the monster books.*

Stan: It was after I told her that Martin wanted to do a super-hero group but I thought that I would say to him, "Forget it. I want to quit."

Roy: *So you were actually thinking of quitting instead of doing the* Fantastic Four? *I hadn't heard that before! That would have changed comic book history.*

Stan: Maybe. If Martin hadn't come in to me and said, "Liebowitz said the *Justice League* is selling well, so why don't we do a comic book about super-heroes?"—if he hadn't said that to me, I might've—in the next day or two, I might've just quit.

Roy: *Timing is everything.*

Stan: Luck, too.

Roy: *By* Fantastic Four #1, *you had developed what later came to be called "the Marvel style." But you were doing this all along for some monster stories, some time before this. How far back does that go?*

Stan: You mean just doing synopses for the artists? Was I doing them before Marvel?

Roy: *I know that you did it for* Fantastic Four. [Stan's synopsis for *F.F.* #1 is printed in Alter Ego, *Vol. 2, #2, backing this issue of* CBA.] *So I figured with Jack as the artist—and maybe Ditko, too—in these minor stories that you mostly wrote, along with Larry Lieber, you must have been doing it since the monster days.*

Stan: You know something, Roy? Now that you say it, that's probably true; but I had never thought of that. I thought that I started it with the *Fantastic Four,* but you're probably right.

Roy: *You probably didn't write full scripts for Jack for "Fin Fang Foom."*

Stan: I did full scripts in the beginning, but then I found out how good he was just creating his own little sequence of pictures—and I did it in the beginning with Ditko, too—but when I found out how good they were, I realized that, "Gee, I don't have to do it—I get a better story by just letting them run free."

Roy: *The amazing thing is, not only could you get Jack and Steve to do it, but that other artists who had always worked from scripts—Dick Ayers, Don Heck, and others—could also learn to do it and be quite successful with a little training from you.*

Stan: I will admit that a lot of them were very nervous about it, and very unhappy about being asked to do it. But then they loved it after a while.

Above: *"The Man" in recline. Photo of Stan Lee in his Marvel office taken presumably by New Wave French film director Alain Resnais when the two collaborated on an abortive film project, "The Monster Maker," in the early '70s. The pair went on to develop another (ultimately unfilmed) movie script, "The Inmates," in 1977. This photograph appeared in James Monaco's book on Resnais' career,* Alain Resnais, *published by Oxford University Press, New York, 1978. A chapter examines the "nonfilms" of Resnais and Lee. (The photo in the book is uncredited.) Kudos to Roy Thomas for supplying a copy of the book.*

Roy: *I think that John Buscema, too, thought it was a little strange at first, but got to really like it. Then, when someone would give him a full script, he didn't like that.*

Stan: Absolutely right. John Buscema is amazing. He was never thought of—it's not the popular idea that he was the most creative guy, storywise. And yet, he was as creative as anybody else—probably as creative as Jack. Well, *you* worked with John.

Roy: *Sure, quite a bit:* Conan, Avengers.

Stan: He only needed a few words. He didn't even want a big synopsis; he wanted the skimpiest outline, because he wanted to do it his way. And his way was always great!

Roy: *I remember plotting the first story of this villain called the Man-Ape in* The Avengers *with him for five or ten minutes over the phone. I wanted to give him more, and he said, "Nah, that's enough." [laughs]*

Stan: That's exactly what he did with me. And I was never disappointed.

Roy: *How did you feel about being distributed by Independent? Especially after Marvel became successful, were you antsy to get out from under?*

Stan: It would be like if you were working for Ford, and General Motors was selling your cars! I could never prove it, but we were sure—it's just human nature and psychology—that National Comics wasn't working as hard to sell our books as they were to sell theirs. Even more, it was the fact that we were only able to do so few books in the beginning, which meant we had to let a lot of artists and writers go. That was always the worst thing that could happen.

Roy: *I do remember when we began particularly to have suspicions during the* Not Brand Echh *days, when every issue of that book seemed to sell, until the one where we had a takeoff on Superman on the cover. Suddenly the sales went down! [laughs] In the early days, it's now well known that Larry Lieber, your brother, wrote the dialogue for a number of stories, after they were plotted by you and drawn by Jack or whoever, on some series like "Thor" and "Iron Man."*

Stan: Well, it's in the credits and I always put his name in. If not, I'd say, "Plot by Stan Lee." Larry definitely did the first "Thor," and he *may* have written the copy for "Iron Man." What I did was give him the plot and he wrote it.

Roy: *Was it that you were just too busy, or did you just think that it wasn't that important that you do the dialogue?*

Stan: Both. And you know that both "Thor" and "Iron Man" were only 10-, 11-page stories and not a feature book. I was very

busy and I liked the way that Larry wrote, and so I thought I'd give him a shot at it.

Roy: *The mere fact that people assumed for years afterward that you did the dialogue shows that he imitated your style pretty well. The thing with Larry is that he was just a little slow.*

Stan: He was like Romita; he was never the fastest one.

Roy: *We used to say that if we'd change* Rawhide Kid *from monthly to bimonthly, Larry would just take twice as long to draw it. [laughter] I'll never forget the day I walked into one Marvel office not long after Ditko quit, and here's John Romita drawing* Amazing Spider-Man *and Larry drawing the* Spider-Man Annual *and Marie Severin drawing "Dr. Strange," and I joked, "This is the Steve Ditko Room; it takes three of you to do what Steve Ditko used to do."*

[Production Manager] Sol Brodsky told me that, right from the start, you thought Spider-Man was an important character, even if he was just in the last issue of Amazing Fantasy. *But Larry Ivie, someone else who worked there at the time, feels that you considered him a throwaway character. Did you feel that Spider-Man was big from the start?*

Stan: I'm trying to remember, but I think I must have felt that he was a good character or I wouldn't have fought so much to do him. I wanted to do Spider-Man as a book, but Martin wouldn't let me. Therefore I sneaked him into the last issue of *Amazing Fantasy.*

Roy: *Because Goodman said that spiders wouldn't sell?*

Stan: He said three things that I will never forget: He said people hate spiders, so you can't call a hero "Spider-Man"; then when I told him I wanted the hero to be a teenager, as he was in the beginning, Martin said that a teenager can't be a hero, but only be a sidekick; and *then* when I said I wanted him not to be too popular with girls, and not great-looking or a strong, macho-looking guy, but just a thin, pimply high school student, and Martin said, "Don't you understand what a hero is?" At the same time, I also said that I wanted him to have a lot of problems, like that he doesn't have enough money and he'd get an allergy attack while he was fighting. Martin just wouldn't let me do the book. Normally, I'd have forgotten about it, but when we were doing the last issue of *Amazing Fantasy*, I put it in there. So I must have felt that he was important somehow, or I wouldn't have bothered.

Roy: *You started right off joking about super-heroes being "long underwear characters," so it had a different tone at the very beginning. It was obvious that there was a lot of thought going into it. I noticed that the day I bought it, in 1962.*

Stan: I don't know if there was *that* much thought, or if I was just uninhibited when I wrote it.

Roy: *There could be that, too: the opposite!*

Stan: There wasn't much thought in anything, because there wasn't *time* to give anything that much thought; we were working too fast!

Roy: *Sometime, not too long before that, you had some alien "spider-men" in a story you did with Jack.*

Stan: Maybe. I know Jack once said that he had done a Spider-Man comic years ago and said that I had copied it. I never saw it and, to this day, I don't know what was going on.

Roy: *C.C. Beck and Joe Simon worked on the Silver Spider, but there are few similarities, it seems to me, between the two. Besides, there had been The Spider before, anyway, in the pulps.*

Stan: That's probably what influenced me with the name. I used to read *The Spider* pulp magazine—which of course was nothing like Spider-Man—and I always thought that it was a dramatic name.

Roy: *The funny thing is that the pulp Spider was more like The Shadow; he didn't have any kind of web. But when they did the movie serials, he had a costume that had webbing on it.*

Stan: I didn't see the serials. When they started to do the *Spider* paperbacks a few years ago, whoever the publisher was sent me a letter asking if I'd give some sort of testimonial for the book. You know I'd always write a few lines for a book, and I wrote that it's great to see *The Spider* back again. I thought it was nice and tried to do what I could to help those books sell. One day not so long ago, I got a letter from Jay Kennedy, the Editor-in-Chief at King Features, and it said that in the Spider-Man newspaper strip I must not use the term "The Spider" in the title, in one of the coming-next-week blurbs. I wrote something like, "The Spider at Bay." They protested and thought I was trying to pull a fast one. Since then I don't use the term "The Spider" anymore.

Roy: *Various people like Gene Colan, Frank Giacoia, and Mike Esposito started wandering over to Marvel in the mid-'60s, and they used pseudonyms. Was this so DC wouldn't know that they were working for Marvel?*

Stan: Maybe not in every case, but as far as Gene and Frank, I don't think there was any other reason for them to use different names.

Roy: *Everyone's heard tales of you physically playing out stories, jumping on tables, and acting out "Thor" stories.*

Stan: I used to enjoy doing that. I always had a lot of energy in those days and it was hard for me to sit still. I think I never really grew up and I loved acting silly. I got a kick out of it. Writing comics—you know how it feels, but maybe you don't feel that way—writing at the typewriter, hour after hour, got kind of boring. I would do whatever I could do to jazz things up. I liked to feel that there was excitement in the air at the office. If I could sing out loud or play my ocarina—I was the worst player in the world, but at least it made a lot of noise.

Roy: *Maybe I'm more inhibited because I'm short, and as a high school teacher for several years, I had to get the students, some of whom were taller than I was, to take me seriously.*

Stan: [*laughs*] Being a teacher probably toned you down!

Roy: *When you started those letter columns with that friendly tone, were you inspired by the EC letters pages?*

Stan: No. You know what inspired me? When I was a kid, there used to be these hardcover book series like *The Hardy Boys, Tom Swift, Tom Sturdy,* but nobody ever heard of the one I read: *Jerry Todd and Poppy Ott.* I think Poppy was a friend of Jerry Todd's who was spun off into his own series. They were not periodicals or magazine but real books.

At the end of each book, there were letters pages where the writer, Leo Edwards, would write a little message to the readers and print some of their letters with answers. He had a very informal style, and the books themselves were wonderful because they were adventure stories. But unlike *The Hardy Boys* and the others, there was a tremendous amount of humor—the way I tried to do with *Spider-Man* and some others. I was a big fan of these books, and I loved the fact that they had letters and commentary by the author. Leo Edwards was the only guy that did that. Maybe I remembered the warm, friendly feeling of those letters.

Roy: *When I came aboard in mid-'65, you were coming into the office only two or three days a week. Was it because it was getting too busy?*

Stan: That's a little bit of a story: A few years before that, I was doing so much writing and I couldn't finish it in the office, so I said to Martin, "I have to have one day a week off to get my writing done." So he said okay, and I took Wednesday off because it was right in the middle of the week and it broke it off into two two-day weeks.

Then, as I got more and more into writing, I said to Joan, "I'm gonna ask him for another day off." She said, "You can't do that! How can you have the nerve to ask for two days a week off and he's paying you a weekly salary?" Hey, the only thing he can do is say no. So I asked him, and he must have had a good golf game that day, and he said okay. I took off Tuesdays and Thursdays.

Then I still seemed to feel that I had too much writing to do,

so I said to Joan, "I'm going to ask him if I can take Monday, Wednesday, and Friday off!" She said, "Stan, I'm going to head for the hills! *Nobody* can ask for something like that!" I said, "Hey, what can I lose?" And he actually said okay! So there was a time when I came in Tuesdays and Thursdays.

The funny thing is that people still say to me, "Boy, you're lucky to stay home those days," and there's no way to explain that I'd rather be in the office! When I'm home, I'm working all the time; when I'm in the office, I'm talking to people, making phone calls, acting like a boss—being in the office is fun! Being at home, I'm sitting at the goddamned typewriter or, now, the computer and I'm working. But it still sounds to people like such a cushy deal.

Roy: *There were a couple of people who worked in the office in a vague editorial capacity in '65 before I came along. One of them was Larry Ivie. Was he working there as an assistant editor at the time?*

Stan: I remember his name—he wrote books, didn't he? But I really don't remember. I just recall the name.

Roy: *Now—about the famous "Marvel Writer's Test": Sol Brodsky and Flo Steinberg told me that you put an ad for writers in the* New York Times, *and had hundreds of people applying.*

Stan: It's news to me, but it sounds like something we might have done.

Above: Unpublished cover to the seventh issue of Stan's favorite comic book character, The Silver Surfer. Art by John & Sal Buscema. ©1998 Marvel Entertainment.

THING CAN'T MOVE

PARALYSIS GUN CONCEALED IN HAND

DOOM SEES HE'S TURNING INVISIBLE!

SUE RESPONSIBLE. DOOM BUMPS INTO THINGS.

Above: *The one extant page (of four) from the Marvel "Writer's Test," given out by the company to hopeful scribes. They were taken from "de-word ballooned" stats of Jack Kirby's art from* Fantastic Four Annual #2, *and writers were to create their own dialogue, á la the "Marvel Style."* ©1998 Marvel Entertainment. *[From the Archives (i.e., desk drawer) of Roy Thomas.]*

Roy: *Did you have to read a lot of the tests?*
Stan: I probably gave them to somebody else to read. I really don't remember.
Roy: *The reason I'm curious is that supposedly I was hired on the basis of taking this writer's test while I was working at DC.*
Stan: Then I must have been reading them.
Roy: *We met the next day after I turned it in. You offered me a job a few minutes later, but you never referred to the test then or at any other time, so I never knew if you actually read it or if I was hired because I was already working for Mort Weisinger over at DC. [laughs]*
Stan: I think I liked your personality.
Roy: *It was always strange to me: I went in there expecting to discuss this writing test and figured that I must have passed—but you never mentioned it! And I'm still waiting!*
Stan: *[laughs]* Maybe that's the case, Roy. I just don't remember.
Roy: *We're actually going to print one page of that test in* Comic Book Artist. *The test was four Jack Kirby pages from* Fantastic Four Annual #2....
Stan: Oh! When I wanted people to put dialogue over the pictures? That was a good idea!
Roy: *You had Sol or someone take out the dialogue. It was just black-and-white. Other people like Denny O'Neil and Gary Friedrich took it. But soon afterwards we stopped using it.*
Stan: That was a clever idea! I'm proud of me! *[laughs]* You know, I probably did read yours and most of the others, because

I know I hate to read scripts, but if it was just pictures with dialogue balloons, I could have read that very quickly, and chances are that I did read them all. And chances are that I'm a lousy judge, so I probably liked yours! *[laughs]*
Roy: *I was startled to learn in '65 that Marvel was just part of a parent company called Magazine Management. A lot of people from other departments went on to fame and fortune during Marvel's early days: [humorist/playwright] Bruce Jay Friedman, Mario Puzo, Ernest Tidyman (who created Shaft), and [gossip columnist] Rona Barrett. Do you remember when Puzo—before he came out with* The Godfather—*wanted to write for Marvel?*
Stan: Yeah. Either he came to me or I heard that he was kind of strapped for money and he would like to see if he could write a comic book. At any rate, I spoke to him and I gave him an assignment because I knew he was a good writer. He came back to me a few weeks later and he hadn't done the assignment. He said, "Stan, I didn't realize that writing comics was so hard! I could write a goddamned novel with all the work that it would take me to do this!" The next thing I knew, there was *The Godfather!*
Roy: *That was his third novel, but I imagine he could have been working on it at the time, so he eventually would have left us anyway. [laughs] I remember that when we started the Academy of Comic Book Arts in 1970-71, he sent a message to the first public meeting thanking Marvel Comics "for teaching my children to read when the public schools failed."*
Stan: Aw, gee, I wish I had a copy of that.
Roy: *I was sitting in the audience with Tom Wolfe at the time. I'd invited Wolfe because he was an idol of mine. So we had some nice heavy names for that first big public ACBA meeting.*
Stan: I would love the chance to start ACBA again. The industry could certainly use that. With all the contacts I now have in TV, if there were an ACBA, I'll bet I could get the awards ceremony to be televised once a year.
Roy: *Now that we wouldn't win anymore! [laughs] In the two weeks I worked for DC in '65, I learned they had an editorial meeting in which they were discussing the Marvel competition, because Marvel had begun to outsell DC in percentages. This was the second time—since EC had done it in the '50s—that Independent was distributing a comics company that was out-selling DC, percentage-wise. When did you begin to realize that Marvel was becoming a sensation?*
Stan: I would guess that (A) when I read the fan mail—would you believe that I read every damn letter! (Which is why I wear glasses now!)—and (B) Martin probably told me. I could tell how well we were doing by the letters where the kids would write, "You're our favorite magazines and we love these characters." Martin was very happy and proud about it and would tell me.
Roy: *In 1968 Marvel expanded. Every super-hero had his own title—Iron Man, Sub-Mariner, Captain America.*
Stan: I was drunk with power.
Roy: *And soon after that, there was a downturn in sales in general. Do you think there was an over-expansion?*
Stan: I don't even remember. Well, you were there long enough to know that sales have their ups and downs. Even the best books—*Fantastic Four, Spider-Man, Hulk, Thor*—some months they didn't sell as well as other months. The same went for *Superman, Batman.* Today the same goes for *Spawn,* which isn't selling now what it sold a year ago. They go up, they go down. It's hard for me to remember specifically any particular event or why it happened.
Roy: *You may recall that in 1971 Martin Goodman suddenly made the decision to jump the page count to 48 pages for 25¢. Then, after one glorious month of these big books, they were suddenly dropped back down to 32 pages for 20¢. I understand the motivation to give 50% off the cover price to the whole-salers, but I was wondering how you felt about this jumping around of page size.*
Stan: I had so little to do with that. The orders would just come

from Martin's office: This month the price would be this, or this month this is how many pages we had. My only job was to make sure somebody got good stories to fill those pages. I was never really consulted when they would raise the price. The only time I was consulted was when he wanted to put out the "treasury editions"—that may have been my idea. I think that I went to him once and said, "Why don't we put out a big book that people would notice?" But when he made these decisions, he made them all himself.

Roy: *I remember that one of the few times I met with Martin Goodman was when I was there with John Verpoorten [Marvel's production manager] and Goodman was talking about how suddenly we were going to cut all the books down in size and that DC was going to take a bath if they didn't follow suit right away—and they did take a bath, because they kept the giant-size books for a year and Marvel just murdered them. So it was a very smart move, but I remember him then saying, "Well, I'm sure that the artists and writers will like it better with the smaller books." And—this was the only time that I talked up to Mr. Goodman—I said, "Actually, we prefer the bigger books." And he just sort of stared at me blankly. That was the end of our conversation. [laughs]*

Stan: And almost the end of your job!

Roy: *[laughs] It probably was! I was polite, but once in a while you have to speak your mind.... You were writing less in the '70s, and that's the time you began working with [French New Wave film director] Alain Resnais on the film "The Monster Maker."*

Stan: That never was made. Y'know, we sold that screenplay, but it was never produced.

Roy: *You had another movie you worked on in the late '70s called "The Inmates." Have you ever thought about taking one or both of those properties and turning them into graphic novels?*

Stan: No, but I'm working on selling "The Inmates" as a movie now. It needs some revision, but I'm going to start showing it around. "The Monster Maker" would require so many changes that I just don't have the time. Maybe someday when I retire, which will probably be never.

Roy: *As we entered the '70s, the fans were writing in for us to do Tarzan and John Carter of Mars, Tolkien, Conan, and Doc Savage. All those properties were starting to be big in paperbacks in the late '60s. I remember us talking about Conan, and you had me write what turned out to be a two- or three-page memo to Martin Goodman to persuade him as to why we should seek the rights to a sword-and-sorcery hero. I've never been able to figure out why we didn't just make up a character!*

Stan: It was because of *you.* You were too persuasive and you wanted to do *Conan!* I was not a big *Conan* fan. I had heard of it, but I don't think that I ever read it. To show how little I know, I had that much confidence in you, and I figured that if Roy wants to do it that badly, well, let's try and do it!

Roy: *We originally tried to get the rights to Thongor by Lin Carter, because we didn't think we could afford Conan, but it worked out all right—certainly for me. [laughs]*

Stan: You were the guy who was totally responsible for doing *Conan* and for its success. That was one book that I had *nothing* to do with!

Roy: *I remember that you said that when I completed an issue that I thought was good, I should show it to you. So I gave you the make-ready of the fourth issue, which was "The Tower of the Elephant"—based on one of Howard's best stories—and you took it inside your office for a few minutes, brought it back, tossed it simply on my desk, and said, "Well, okay, that's it—not my kind of thing." I felt bad because that was a particular story in which Conan didn't do any rescuing or fighting at the end of the story.*

Stan: Maybe that's what I missed.

Roy: *If I had been making up the story, I wouldn't have done it that way, I'll admit.*

I was a little worried about that myself, but it turned out to be

quite popular. About 1970, ACBA was formed, and [DC publisher] Carmine Infantino and you were the official starters.

Stan: It was all my idea, but I knew that I needed some support. I wanted it to be like the Motion Picture Academy of Arts and Sciences, and I felt (and I feel this way to this day) that comic books are a great literary and art form that isn't appreciated enough in this country. I felt that why the hell shouldn't we have an *Academy of Comic Book Arts?* Even back then I felt that if we had an awards ceremony every year, we could probably get it on the radio and eventually, after we got a little more prestige, even have it tele-vised. I knew there were a lot of celebrities who were into comics, and that's all you need to get something on television—to get this actor or actress to serve as master of ceremonies. So I formed it and we were successful beyond my wildest dreams in the beginning, because every company joined and virtually every writer and artists joined.

Unfortunately, Neal Adams, whose work I respect greatly—he's one of the geniuses of the business—wanted to turn the damn thing into a union. At these meetings, Neal would get up and start talking about pay raises, benefits, and ownership for the artists. I remember saying to him and to the gathering in general, that he might well be right in everything he said, but this was the wrong forum for that sort of discussion. They don't discuss those matters in the Television Academy; that's the kind of stuff you discuss in a union meeting.

If Neal wanted to form a union, he should go ahead and do it, but the purpose of ACBA was to give our industry prestige, not to discuss the fact that artists don't have ownership or things like that. I was never able to convince him, and ACBA became divided into two camps, it seemed. I wasn't interested in starting a union, so I walked away from it. Neal was elected president, but it didn't last. The whole thing collapsed. I'm not saying this to put down Nal Adams, for most of the things that he was pitching were very worthwhile things, but, as I said, I just felt that he had picked the wrong forum. I think now it could be much more successful than ever before, because it's a bigger field and there are more celebrities involved.

I had done my best to build up Marvel, and as much as I may have contributed to Marvel's success with any stories, editing, or creating characters, I think equally as valuable was the advertising, promotion, publicity, and huckstering that I did, traveling around the country and talking about Marvel, trying to give it the right image. The reason I mention that is, *that* is what I wanted to do with ACBA; but I wanted to do it for the whole industry, not just for Marvel. That was the purpose. I wanted to make people feel that comic books are really great. I was very frustrated and disappointed that in

Above: *A Stan Lee/ Joanie Lee creation. Stan wrote this caption: "Our daughter, J.C., the actress/model with her blasé dog."*

some way I couldn't get everybody to have the same vision that I had for ACBA.

Roy: *The early '70s were a time when you started to move away from actively being a writer because of other things you had to do.*

Stan: Yeah, guys like Roy Thomas edged me out!

Roy: *[laughs] Right! I was so eager to do Spider-Man in those days! Much as I loved the character Spider-Man, what I wanted to do was Fantastic Four—though nowadays it would be great to write Spidey and get those royalties! The main reason I wrote Spider-Man #101-104 and Archie Goodwin wrote Fantastic Four was because you were working with Alain Resnais on The Monster Maker for about four months' worth of books. Did it feel odd to return to Spidey, F.F., and Thor after leaving them for four months and for the first time not writing any comics for a period of time?*

Stan: No. I think you can compare it to riding a bicycle; no matter how long you say away, you get on the bike and it's just like you never left it. For example, if I were to go back to writing a book now, I don't think that it would feel odd at all; my problem would be that I haven't carefully read the preceding issues, so I wouldn't know where the hell I was in the storyline. Or I might write a character in such a way that I think is the way to write him, but I wouldn't be aware that three other writers before me had changed the character totally, so I'm now writing it in the wrong way.

Roy: *So when you write the Spider-Man newspaper strip, you ignore what goes on in the comic books?*

Stan: Of course. I couldn't cope with that, because we do the newspaper strip so far in advance, and there's no way that I could make it compatible with the books—impossible.

Roy: *Another event in 1970 that had considerable impact at Marvel was Jack Kirby suddenly leaving. Do you remember his phone call?*

Stan: No. I know it must have happened, but I don't specifically recall it. I don't know who he called; it may not have been me. Maybe he didn't even call, but I just remember that at one point he just stopped working for me.

Roy: *I remember that he called, because you called us in and told us. In light of all that has happened since, do you think that the relationship could have been salvaged at some point?*

Stan: I think it certainly could have been salvaged if I knew what was bothering him. He never really told me, nor did Steve Ditko when he left. You can't salvage something if you don't know the cause.

Roy: *I remember the day that Steve quit, a few months after I began to work at Marvel. He just came in, dropped off some pages, and left. Sol Brodsky then told me he had suddenly quit. Sol had a memo on his desk to add $5.00 to Steve's page rate, a considerable raise at that time, so it certainly wasn't over money. He wandered off to do work for Charlton, which paid half of what Marvel was offering.*

Stan: As you know, I have the worst memory in the world, but maybe I knew why he left at the time. But right now, I absolutely cannot remember. The one thing I remember and felt bad about when Jack left, was that I had been thinking about—and maybe I even talked to him about it—that I wanted to make Jack my partner in a sense; I wanted him to be the art

director and I thought that he could serve in that function and I would serve as the editor. Maybe this was way earlier, but I was disappointed when he left because I always felt that Jack and I would be working there forever and doing everything.

Roy: *For some months when you became publisher, you needed someone to be art director, so Frank Giacoia came in [as "assistant art director"], and, very soon, John Romita succeeded him, becoming art director.*

Stan: But I wasn't thinking of Jack being art director because I would be leaving; I just thought that it would be great working with him in that capacity. I was serving as art director and thought that he could take it off my shoulders, so I could just worry about the stories. It probably wouldn't have worked out anyway, because I might have disagreed with him about things—not about his own work, but if we started critiquing other artists' work, Jack and I might have looked at it differently. So it might just be that I never could have worked with any art director who would function the way I did, because I guess no two people see anything the same.

Roy: *Also, with Jack being in California, there would have been a geographical problem. I have a memory that, sometime before Jack left, Jack called you up about some new ideas he had for characters. I don't think it went any further than that. Do you recall that at all? I was always curious if those were the same ideas that appeared a year or so later as The New Gods, and wondered if they could easily have ended up as Marvel characters.*

Stan: I don't know if he told me the ideas and I had said that I didn't like 'em! [laughs] I just can't remember.

Roy: *The last few months Jack was working for Marvel, he*

Right: *Marie Severin's incredibly detailed overview of the Marvel Bullpen, circa 1976. It appeared with ink wash as the cover of FOOM #16. Courtesy of the artist. ©1998 Marvel Entertainment.*

nded up doing the writing on a couple of series—Ka-Zar and he Inhumans. Did you invite him to write at that time?

Stan: I am probably the worst guy in the world for you to nterview! (A) I didn't realize he *had* written them; and (B) I can't emember if I invited him to or not. I don't think that I ever would ave specifically said, "Jack, I would like you to write," because I ever thought of Jack as a writer (but he was certainly a great lotter). Certainly 90% of the "Tales of Asgard" stories were ack's plots, and they were great! He knew more about Norse mythology than I ever did (or at least he enjoyed making it up!). I vas busy enough just putting in the copy after he drew it.

Roy: *I was always curious about those three buddies, Hogun, andral, and of course enormous Volstagg. Were those characters our idea or Jack's? That's one of those ideas that I could see ither you or Jack making up.*

Stan: I made those up. I specifically remember that I did them ecause I wanted a Falstaff-type guy, a guy like Errol Flynn, and hen I wanted a guy like Charles Bronson who was dire and loomy, riddled with angst. Those three were mine.

Roy: *When Marvel was acquired by Perfect Film, run by Martin ckerman—because of the Saturday Evening Post debacle, where hey dismantled the magazine, were you apprehensive about hat, or were you thinking mostly about the fact that now you'd e free to put out more books?*

Stan: I was just curious to see what was going to happen next. didn't know what was going to happen. It was the first time that ve were owned by a conglomerate and not by Martin Goodman, o it was a whole new experience for me. I was just hoping that I ould keep my job, probably—that was the thing I always worried

about! Then, of course, Ackerman left after a while and Sheldon Feinberg came in. There was something wrong with Perfect Film—I don't know what it was—but the stockholders or the bank or the board of directors got Martin Ackerman to resign and they put Sheldon Feinberg in his place. Feinberg changed the name of the company from Perfect Film to Cadence Industries, and then he was in charge for quite a while.

Roy: *Was it Feinberg's decision to make you President and Publisher?*

Stan: Yes. But I didn't stay *President* very long.

Roy: *Do you remember when we had problems during the Wage and Price Freeze during the Nixon administration, over the fact that we dropped down in size after one month of those giant-size 25¢ comic books? We had to put a slick, color, four-page insert in one issue of Fantastic Four; supposedly this was to make up for the fact that the Wage and Price Control Board had decided it was right on the cusp of whether we had, in a certain way, actually raised prices by charging 20¢ for 32 pages.*

Stan: How the hell do you remember that?

Roy: *Because I was the guy who had to write that insert! [laughs]*

Stan: That was what was so great about having you there; I let you worry about it. I don't even remember it.

Roy: *Do you still have the letter from the Department of Health, Education, and Welfare which prompted you to write the narcotics issues of Spider-Man?*

Stan: There used to be a scrapbook in the office, and if it's still around, the letter would be in there. I haven't seen it in a million years. I got this letter—I don't remember the exact wording—and they were concerned about drug use among kids. Since Marvel had such a great influence with young people, they thought it would be very commendable if we were to put out some sort of anti-drug message in our books.

I felt that the only way to do it was to make it a part of the story, and we made that three-parter of *Spider-Man*. I remember it contained one scene where a kid was going to jump off a roof and thought he could fly. My problem is that I know less about drugs than any living human being! I didn't know what kind of drug it was that would make you think you could fly! I don't think I named anything; I just said that he had "done" something.

Roy: *It was just a generic kind of drug. Just the same way we used to make up the names of countries. You made up Latveria.*

Stan: You're right! [*laughs*] Doesn't Latveria sound authentic?

Roy: *I take it that you didn't do a lot of research on drugs, then?*

Stan: I have never done research on anything in my life. Out here in Los Angeles, I work with and know so many screenwriters, and it amazes me the amount of research these guys do. I was going to do something about a prison, and I gave up the project because I realized I don't have any idea what the rituals are inside a prison and I just couldn't be bothered to look it up. But these guys would go and spend a week visiting a prison—even talking to the warden! I'm just no good at that.

Roy: *Back in 1965 I took a phone call at*

Above: *Joanie.*

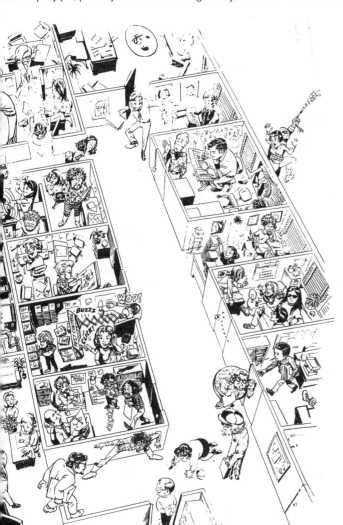

OBOY WATER!... AND ME A PISCES; JUST THE THING TO LIFT. MY SPIRITS!

Above: "*Howard Who?*" Frank Brunner's pencils to the splash page of Howard the Duck #1. Artwork ©1998 Frank Brunner. Howard the Duck ™ & ©1998 Marvel Entertainment.

the office sometime after 5:00 P.M. from somebody who asked me what you and Steve Ditko were on—because you had to be taking something in order to do those Dr. Strange stories with the fights. I said, "I don't think Stan or Steve do anything like that." (I wouldn't have admitted it if it had been true, of course.) Then he says, "It has to be, because I had a fight like that when I was high on mushrooms in Mexico City a couple of years ago! It was just like the one Dr. Strange had with Dormammu!"

Stan: It's just a testimony to Steve's ability to make things look real. I can't speak for Steve (who probably also was not on anything), but I never even smoked a marijuana cigarette. I never took anything.

Roy: After John Romita became too busy to draw or even lay out Spidey on a regular basis, you worked with Gil Kane and even Ross Andru. Do you have any thoughts about those artists?

Stan: They were great! Gil came first, and he was just terrific! And he was so *fast!* It was such a pleasure working with him, because he was fast. I missed John because I had such a great relationship with him—everything that John did I thought was perfect—but it really was a pleasure working with guys who were fast. I always loved Gil's stuff—very stylized, but very good.

Roy: My four issues of Amazing Spider-Man were with Gil. He and I had been friends ever since we had worked on Captain Marvel. We had a lot of fun together, too. You'll be glad to know I'm not going to ask you about who killed off Gwen Stacy. We'll skip that entirely, as we've had enough of that.

Stan: [laughs] It's funny, because obviously my memory is wrong. I think Gerry Conway has said that I told him to kill her off, but I don't remember saying that.

Roy: Actually, what he said was that evidently it was John

Romita's idea. All Gerry said is that we okayed it with you, but he never claimed that it was your idea. I don't think you would ever have come up with that idea.

Stan: The memory I have is him asking me how to write the thing, and I said, "Hey, it's your book, just keep it in character and write it." I took off, came back, and she was dead! I think he was quoted somewhere as asking me whether he could kill her off and I said yes. I don't remember that and can't believe I would have. The reason is not that I have an aversion to a character dying in a series, but that I always wanted her to marry Peter Parker. But even more than that, only a short time earlier we had killed off her father and I didn't want it to look like I had something against the Stacy family!

Roy: I do remember you agreeing to it. You probably felt that it was our ball—me as editor, and Gerry and John—and it was our job. I don't think you wanted to stand in the way, but you were never enthusiastic about the idea.

Stan: If I agreed to it, it was probably because I had my mind on something else. I was careless, because if I had really considered it, I would have said, "Roy, let's talk this over."

Roy: The final time you came back as a regular writer in the comics, after you spent those four months working with Alain Resnais.

Stan: Did I really take four months off?

Roy: Yeah. You wrote up to Spider-Man #100, which you ended by giving him four extra arms and tossed it to me, saying, "Take it, Roy." I was stuck with a six-armed Spider-Man for a couple of months! [laughs]

Stan: I thought *you* gave him the extra arms!

Roy: No, that was at the end of your story, so I can get out of that one! You were still involved editorially though, because this was right after the Code was liberalized, and you told us you wanted Spidey to fight a vampire. Gil and I were going to bring in Dracula, who was not yet a Marvel character, and you said, "No, I want a super-villain vampire." So we made up Morbius, the Living Vampire.

Stan: It worked out great.

Roy: Did you feel strongly at that time that the Code needed to be changed?

Stan: As far as I can remember—and I've told this to so many people, it might even be true—I never thought that the Code was much of a problem. The only problem we ever had with the Code was over foolish things, like the time in a western when we had a puff of smoke coming out of a gun and they said it was too violent. So we had to make the puff of smoke smaller. Silly things. But as far as ideas for stories or characters that we came up with, I almost never had a problem, so they didn't bother me. I think the biggest nuisance was that sometimes I had to go down and attend a meeting of the [CMAA] Board of Directors. I felt that I was killing an entire afternoon.

Roy: Do you think that there were any bad feelings on the part of the Code over the Spider-Man drug issues?

Stan: That was the only big issue that we had. I could understand them; they were like lawyers, people who take things literally and technically. The Code mentioned that you mustn't mention drugs and, according to their rules, they were right. So I didn't even get mad at them then. I said, "Screw it" and just took the Code seal off for those three issues. Then we went back to the Code again. I never thought about the Code when I was writing a story, because basically I never wanted to do anything that was to my mind too violent or too sexy. I was aware that young people were reading these books, and had there not been a Code I don't think that I would have done the stories any differently.

Roy: The only difference was that, technically, you could not do a vampire or werewolf story.

Stan: We couldn't do vampire stories?

Roy: No, they had been forbidden since the mid-'50s when the Code arrived. The Morbius story was done in the vein of just like any other super-villain—we even gave him primary costume colors of red and blue, just like Spider-Man. Very soon after that, we began the whole gamut of those creatures: Werewolf by Night, Man-Thing, Frankenstein. Many of these concepts flowed from you. Man-Thing was a sentence or two concept that you gave me for the first issue of Savage Tales.

Stan: That came after *Swamp Thing*, didn't it?

Roy: No, it came at the same time as the first one-shot "Swamp Thing" story, but before the regular series.

Stan: So we didn't copy it from *Swamp Thing*?

Roy: No, or vice versa. In fact, I had done a character a little earlier in The Hulk that was also a takeoff on the Heap character from the '40s comics. I had called it "The Shape," but you insisted that name sounded feminine, so you changed it to "The Glob."

Stan: It's funny that you mentioned The Heap, because when I did The Hulk, I had the Heap in mind when I made up the name. I thought "The Hulk" sounded like "The Heap" and I liked it.

Roy: The Heap was one of the great old characters; he's been copied more than most characters. Man-Thing ended up looking a lot like him. Do you remember how Savage Tales came about? I always got the impression that Goodman wasn't wild about doing black-&-white books. Were these something you pushed?

Stan: I wonder why I wanted to do black-&-white books. I did push them, but I can't remember why.

Roy: Well, there were the Warren books getting a share of the market that we weren't getting into, perhaps?

Stan: Were they cheaper to do?

Roy: Well, no color, so they were cheaper per page, certainly. They were also more expensive and we could, without the Code, go a little further. The first issue of Savage Tales had a little nudity in the Conan story and in your Ka-Zar story.

Stan: I was looking to grab older readers.

Roy: There was a little more violence, but nothing really salacious. I remember a story by Denny O'Neil and Gene Colan where, by the time the book came out, all the nudity had been covered up. We were feeling our way back and forth, because we didn't know exactly what we were doing. There were all sorts of distribution problems. There was a year between Savage Tales #1 and #2. Do you remember why that was?

Stan: No, but that seems to indicate a distribution problem.

Roy: I heard that we didn't get into Canada at all because somebody complained that it was salacious material, but I've never seen anything in writing about that. But I did get the impression that Martin Goodman was very happy to see Savage Tales die the first time.

Stan: Martin never had any interest in those books.

Roy: When Savage Tales came back, it quickly spun off The Savage Sword of Conan, and there were all those black-&-white books starting with Dracula Lives! that you heaped on my shoulders over a two-day period.

Stan: Well, you were good at it.

Roy: I was good at it because I got Marv Wolfman and other people to help a lot. This happened after you had become Publisher, and you used to always tell me that we needed to do these extra books to pay my salary. Except that I never noticed getting a big raise! [laughs]

One day you came in and said we were going to do a new book called Dracula Lives! which was about 60 pages of black-&-white material to fill. The next day you came in and said we're going to do a second black-&-white, too, because we can't fit non-vampire material in Dracula Lives! so we'll do Monsters Unleashed. I said that made sense, so I called in Marv, Gerry Conway, Len Wein, and we all got started on this. Then I came in the next day and you said, "Guess what?" I said, "Don't tell me, you have a third book to add." You said, "No, two more!" You wanted to do Vampire Tales—vampires that weren't Dracula—and Tales of the Zombie.

Stan: Didn't Bill Everett do that cover?

Roy: No, what happened was that, not too long before that, in the warehouse when we were doing one of our searches, I found this story from Menace that you and Bill had both signed—a 5- or 6-page wonderful zombie story from the 1950s.

Stan: That's the one that I remember.

Roy: The image on the splash page was one of the all-time great drawings of a zombie. I decided to make that the template of the title character, but you may have been thinking of that story, too, and just never mentioned it. I made up the name Simon Garth and turned it over to Steve Gerber, and it sort of went from there. So, in less than 48 hours, we suddenly had four gigantic books coming out and that didn't even count the Conan black-&-white!

Stan: I just wanted to make sure that we needed you.

Roy: It was a challenge. Some of the stories were good and some not so good, but all the mags lasted for a while—Savage

Above: *The above was published as an Op-Ed piece in the* New York Times *on the eve of the 1976 Presidential Elections between Gerald Ford and Jimmy Carter. Art by Johnny Romita, Sr., words by Stan Lee. ©1998 Marvel Entertainment.*

Above: Stan & Dan DeCarlo's syndicated strip, "Willie Lumpkin," about a smalltown mailman. Stan used the same name for his and Jack's postal worker in the Fantastic Four. Dan was the mainstay artist in Marvel's teen humor line. ©1998 Publishers Syndicate. [Courtesy of the Roy Thomas Collection.]

Below: Dan DeCarlo sketched this little sweetie on the back of the original art to the above Willie Lumpkin Sunday strip. There was also a date stamp of "February 11, 1961." Art ©1998 Dan DeCarlo. [Courtesy of the Roy Thomas Collection.]

Sword of Conan lasted for over 200 issues…. Next I wanted to ask you about a few people from that period. What's your main impression of Jim Steranko?

Stan: I loved him and was incredibly impressed by him. He was such a multi-talented guy. One of the most important things is to have a certain style, not only to be able to write or draw well but to do it with style and distinction. His style was so distinctive that he just seemed more hip, cooler, and more cutting-edge than any other artist at that time.

Roy: *This is the guy who walked in one day and told me that he had just come in from his fencing lesson. I don't know if that was hip or not, but it was cool.*

Stan: That happened probably after his magic show. He was a great guy who knew what he wanted and was very definite. He was the kind of guy who, after you got to know him, you were willing to give him a project and let him do it his way. I had a lot of confidence in him.

Roy: *After writing the first few SHIELD stories that he drew, I was happy to let him write them, as well, because he had his own ideas and I had other things to do. SHIELD was never a big seller, but it was one of the influential books. Steranko and Neal Adams were influential beyond their selling power.*

Stan: It was a big loss to us, and the whole business, when Jim decided to quit and do his magazine.

Roy: *Do you remember how Barry Smith got his job?*

Stan: No, but he had a *very* distinctive style and, at first, it took a little getting used to on my part when he developed into being so different from some of the other artists. He was more quietly illustrative. One thing I remember about Barry was a Dr. Strange story that he did with me. I was *so* pleasantly surprised at how well it turned out; when I had to sit and write the copy, it was so easy to write and it worked so well. I was very impressed and I think Barry is another guy who is very, very talented.

Roy: *The nice thing about people like Barry and Steranko is that they're not just artists, but real storytellers. They don't just draw a lot of pretty pictures. I've* never had much patience for artists who just draw very pretty because it's often either totally dull, like still photos, or else it's so illustrative that you practically have to connect the dots to tell a story.

Stan: That's one of the problems with some of the artists in the business today—they do nice, impressive individual pictures, but they don't have enough feeling for continuity—letting one picture run into another so that it tells a story.

Roy: *Another artist, whom I don't think you worked with, was Jim Starlin.*

Stan: There you go! There's another creative, stylized, very very talented guy. I was so impressed with that strip in *Epic* magazine, featuring that character with the long nose.

Roy: *How do you remember Herb Trimpe, with whom you worked for a long time on The Incredible Hulk?*

Stan: I liked Herb. He was a nice guy, dependable, with a style that was nice, simple, and clear. He told a story well. Herb was a pleasure. He was good.

Roy: *I had a very good time working with him on The Hulk after you. He's teaching now.*

Stan: If you speak with him, give him my best.

Roy: *Coming up from coloring, there was Marie Severin, with whom you worked on Dr. Strange.*

Stan: Marie is worth an entire interview just to talk about her. You talked about being multi-talented. She was great at humorous cartoons; she did *The Hulk* and all these serious strips; one of the best colorists in the business; she's a wonderful person with a great sense of humor; always cheerful and great to work with. She was also stylized; you could always recognize her work with that slight touch of cartooniness in the serious artwork that gave it a certain charm. I'm crazy about Marie.

Roy: *She and her brother John combined her style and his realism in Kull that are considered classics of the early '70s.*

Stan: Of course, you could do a whole interview about John, too; he is one of the real greats in the business.

Roy: *It must have been the money. [laughs] You also worked with Bill Everett over the years.*

Stan: Bill was great, and he was also very, very stylized. You could spot an Everett drawing, and he had his own way of telling stories. He was imaginative and talented, but the amazing thing was that he was very easy to work with. When I worked with him, there was no show of temperament at all. For a guy that talented, you would think he would have argued constantly—"No, Stan, I don't like that! Let's do it this way!"—but no, he was a joy to work with.

Roy: *Do you remember waking up one morning and realizing that Marvel had finally surpassed DC in total sales?*

Stan: I can't remember the exact moment I realized that, but I know it was very pleasant to hear it. I must admit that I expected it, Roy, so it didn't come as a surprise. I could tell by the fan mail we were getting, the write-ups we received in various newspapers and magazines—everything was Marvel and nobody was talking about DC. Just by talking to people myself when I went to conventions or lectures, I thought that we were outselling them before that became officially the case.

Roy: *I've heard that there was a great dropoff in female readers in the early '70s. We came up with three strips for which you made up the names and concepts:* Shanna the She-Devil, Night Nurse, *and* The Claws of the Cat. *Were we trying to woo the female readers back?*

Stan: Yes, and also to appeal to the male readers who liked looking at pretty girls. Unfortunately, we weren't able to draw the girls the way they're drawn now, because I think if we had been, our sales would have soared much more than they did!

Roy: *People know that I'm the one who assigned three women to write those books—Linda Fite (now Herb Trimpe's wife); my first wife Jeanie; and Phil Seuling's wife Carol—but I can't remember if that's something you suggested.*

Stan: You're so strong-willed, you wouldn't have taken my suggestion. I don't know! *[laughs]* If I had to guess, I'd say that it was your idea, because I don't think I was telling you who to use.

Roy: *Probably not. Of course, in some ways, I could have gotten more experienced writers, but I don't know if that would have helped the books, because the market didn't seem to be there at that time. We did everything we could. We got Marie Severin to draw* The Cat *and Wally Wood to ink; we got Steranko to do the covers to* Shanna.

Stan: The failure of *The Cat* was my biggest disappointment. I really thought that that would have worked.

Roy: *Strangely enough, the one that is collected now, for a reason I cannot figure out, is* Night Nurse, *by my ex-wife Jeanie and Winslow Mortimer.*

Stan: Martin Goodman always thought there was something inherently sexy about nurses. I could never get inside his thinking there.

Roy: *Considering the "men's-sweat" magazines he published with those ill-clad nurses, that's where it probably came from. Hadn't Timely done* Linda Carter, Student Nurse?

Stan: We even had *Nellie the Nurse,* a humor book.

Roy: *And* Tessie the Typist *and* Millie the Model, *my first assignment at Marvel.*

Stan: Not to mention *Hedy of Hollywood.*

Roy: *And probably your peak moment in comics,* Ziggy the Pig *and* Silly Seal.

Stan: Oh, that was our high point. *[laughs]* We peaked! That was with Al Jaffee.

Roy: *In the early '60s you had done that* Willie Lumpkin *newspaper strip. You used that name again for the mailman in* Fantastic Four.

Stan: That was just for fun. Mel Lazarus had done a strip called *Miss Peach,* which used not panels but one long panel instead. I liked that idea very much, so when Harold Anderson, the head of Publishers Syndicate, asked me to do a strip, I came up with *Barney's Beat,* which was about a New York City cop and all the characters on his patrol who he'd meet every day and there would be a gag. I did some samples with Dan DeCarlo, and I thought it was wonderful.

Harold said it was too "big city-ish" and they're not going to care for it in the small towns because they don't have cops on a beat out there. He wanted something that would appeal to the hinterland, something bucolic. He said, "You know what I want, Stan? I want a mailman! A friendly little mailman in a small town." I don't remember if I came up with the name Lumpkin or he did, but I hated it. I think I came up with the name as a joke and he said, "Yeah, that's it! Good idea!"

It was the one strip in the world I didn't think I was qualified to write, because I liked things that were hip and cutting-edge, cool and big city. I always wrote *Seinfeld* and that kind of thing. Here I'm writing about a mailman in a small town! Even though it was not my type of thing, it lasted for a couple of years. Unlike today, when I do the *Spider-Man* daily strip and never heard from the syndicate (I gotta call them a few times a year and say, "Are you guys aware that we're still doing this?"), in those days Harold Anderson passed on every gag, looked at every panel, and I

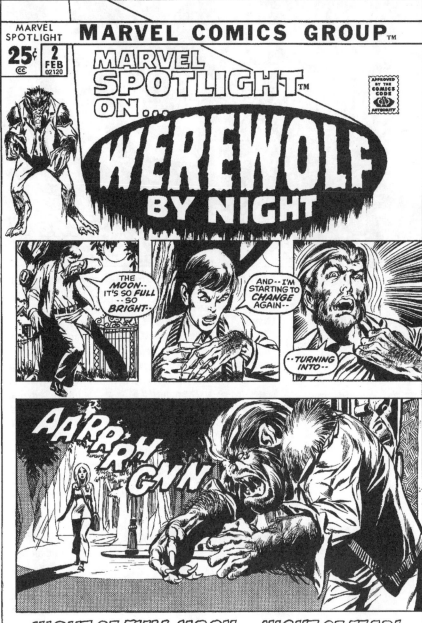

worked with him. He was a lovely man, but as an editor, he was a nightmare! *[laughs]*

Roy: *You said that you didn't stay President very long... just a few months, maybe a year.*

Stan: I found that I was expected to—and did—go to a lot of financial meetings where they would discuss costs and financial reports. We would have to come up with a five-year financial plan—things like that. I only stayed as President for a year—maybe less—because I would say to myself at those meetings, "What am I doing here? There must be a million people who could do this as well as or better than I." The thing that I enjoy the most and do the best is working on the stories, and I wasn't doing that! At some point I walked in to Feinberg and said, "I don't want to be President any more." I think I'm one of the few people who resigned the post of President. But I kept the title of Publisher, though I'm still not sure what a publisher's duties are!

Roy: *That's when Al Landau, not one of my favorite people, succeeded you as president of Marvel. His company, Trans World, had been selling Marvel's work in other countries.*

Stan: He came in because Martin knew him and dealt with him for years; they had been friendly. But then Martin and he had a falling out—I don't know. I always got along fine with Al. He

CONAN IN CHAINS-- BUT STILL CONAN!

"LAIR OF THE BEAST-MEN!" in CONAN THE BARBARIAN NO. 2... NOW ON SALE!

Above: *View askew. Having difficulty warming up to the commercial assignment of designing a Marvel house ad in 1970, Barry Windsor-Smith relied on an old art school exercise to get into it: He penciled the above ad for Conan #2 upside-down and, once satisfied, he inked it rightside-up. Conan ©1998 Conan Properties. ©1998 Marvel Entertainment.*

leaned on me a lot, so I helped him when he was President—he came to me for everything. I know that he wasn't all that popular. He died a few years ago.

Roy: *Al Landau was President a couple of years; then Jim Galton took over. The only time Al and I were on the same side (and it took me a minute to realize why) was when both of us wanted to get back one of the pages of story we had lost in our books. I wanted the page back just because I wanted it back, for better stories—and he wanted it because then his company Trans World could sell another page abroad. We had a community of interest only that once during the year or so he was there and I was Editor-in-Chief.*

I also remember when I was supposed to fly over to the Philippines and talk to the artists there. I would have had to spend 24 hours in the air, a day or so there when this revolution was going on, and then another 24 hours coming home. I remember you telling me that Al Landau didn't want me to go because it would have been too much like a vacation! [laughs] Some vacation! I was happy not to have to go!

Stan: *Al was a very strange guy.*

Roy: *Between my leaving in '74 and Jim Shooter's ascension in '77, a period of three years, there were four editors-in-chief, counting the three weeks of Gerry Conway: Len Wein, Marv Wolfman, Gerry, almost me again, and then Archie.*

Did that musical chairs of editors bother you?

Stan: Yeah. I wish that any one of those guys would have stayed for a while. But it didn't affect me that much; I just thought it didn't look good for the company—that we didn't know what we were doing. But they were all good. I was disappointed that Gerry didn't stay, because I always liked him and thought that he would do a good job.

Roy: *That's the only time the job didn't automatically go to the next person in line. I suggested bringing Gerry back from DC and thought that it would work out, but after three weeks he just couldn't handle it.*

Here's a question phrased by the CBA editor: "Arguably, the DC Comics under Carmine Infantino were art-driven—beautiful to look at, but maybe the art overwhelmed the storytelling. But Marvel seemed influenced by your legacy that, no matter how great the artwork, the story was paramount. Sales seemed to prove that out. What is it, do you think, that made Marvel the industry leader for the last quarter century?"

Stan: I would like to think that we had a good marriage of art and script. I think that the art has always been at least as important as the story. Because you can tell the best story in the world, but if the artwork is dull—it's like a movie: If the photography, acting, or directing is bad, you can have a great story but it's still not going to be a great movie. By the same token, you can have the best artwork and if the story isn't there, you're only going to appeal to people who like to look at nice drawings. To me, a comic strip should be a beautifully illustrated story, not just beautiful illustrations.

I would never say that the story itself is paramount; and as far as a style, I would think that one thing that made our work a little different from anyone else's is the fact that we tried to make our characters as real and believable as possible. Even though they were in fantasy stories, our formula always was, "What if somebody like this existed in the real world, and what would his or her life be like?"

We always tried to have dialogue that sounded as if real people might say it, and we always tried to give our characters different personalities so they weren't cut from the same mold. We tried to have each one talking differently from the others. But, getting back to the original statement, we never concentrated more on script than art, nor did we concentrate more on art than script. The two are indivisible; they had to work perfectly together.

Roy: *And now I have what Evans and Novak would call on their show, "The Big Question," which the editor requested me to ask you: Which is stronger, Thor or the Hulk?*

Stan: I would have to guess that Thor is stronger, only because he *is* a god and probably can't be killed. Again, I don't know how the guys have been writing him lately, but I thought of him as invulnerable. I would think that with his hammer and everything, he'd probably beat the Hulk. But what's interesting with the Hulk is, the more he fights and the more he's beaten, the stronger he gets, so maybe it would be a draw.

Roy: *It was really a facetious question—but, on the other hand, it's one of those things you could argue about forever. It's amazing that, after 25-30 years, people still think of that as the archetypal Marvel question.*

Stan: The thing I loved writing was having our heroes fight, and for me to figure a way to end the story without denigrating either one or making one seem stronger than the other. The best example of this was in one issue of *Daredevil*, where DD was fighting Sub-Mariner. Oh, I loved the way that story turned out! That was just so perfectly done. Daredevil was beaten, but he was just as heroic as Sub-Mariner.

Roy: *Thanks, Stan.*

Stan: Anytime, Roy. ⚡

Editor's Note: *Special thanks to Joanie and Stan for the timely loan of the photographs that illustrate this conversation.*

The Uncensored *Conan*

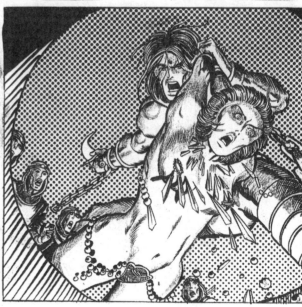

Sure, let poor Conan get whipped so the flesh is torn from him, but show some naked skin and, *yikes,* here comes the Code! Nine panels rejected for the semi-nudity from the pages from the story, "The Dweller in the Dark" (Conan #11). BWS inked these from his original pencils, and shared them with us. Artwork ©1998 BWS. Conan ©1998 Conan Properties.

The Heir Apparent

In deep with Marvel's Writer/Editor, Roy Thomas

Below: Thumbnail sketch for the splash page to Conan Annual #5, the last Conan story by Roy and Gil Kane. Our esteemed colleague, David "Hambone" Hamilton has amassed, over the decades, many thousands of photocopies of Gil's work (and the art of other greats), and we extend our thanks and gratitude to our pal for all of his very welcome help. Conan ©1998 Conan Properties.

Conducted by Jon B. Cooke

"Rascally" Roy Thomas, best known for his long writing stints on Conan the Barbarian *and* The Avengers, *also served as Stan Lee's top editorial assistant in the '60s, and became Marvel's editor-in-chief in 1972. Helming Marvel's "Phase Two," Roy served two years during a creatively rich and fertile period in Marvel's history, in which his participation is discussed below. This interview was conducted in three sessions via phone during May and June, 1998, and was copy-edited by Roy.*

Comic Book Artist: *When did you first realize that Marvel was really starting to grow?*

Roy Thomas: When I was working at DC for that week or two in 1965, I discovered management had an editorial meeting concerning the growing competition of Marvel (I, as a lowly peon, was not invited). Because both DC and Marvel were distributed by DC's Independent Distribution, DC had discovered that Marvel had basically started to outsell them in percentages. While Marvel had smaller print runs, their sales in percentage were better than DC, so Marvel was creeping up on them. Since that had happened before with Independent in the '50s with EC, they didn't like it at all. Up to that point, as a comics fan and publisher/editor of a fanzine, etc., I thought of DC as fairly solidly ensconced in the number one role and Marvel was this little company that wasn't as big as it used to be. I thought, "Well, okay, it's a little competition," but it just never occurred to me that DC would be worried. Still, Marvel only had a limited number of titles, though I didn't know at that time that they were limited by *contract*. In order to add any title, they had to kill something else. By '68, when Marvel went over to Curtis Circulation, that's when we really started to expand.

CBA: *Was Stan the one making creative decisions on books or was the publisher, Martin Goodman, heavily involved?*

Roy: Of course, I came along in 1965, so I can only reconstruct

these three or four years. I'm pretty convinced that it was Stan's idea to do *Fantastic Four* from the beginning. He may have specifically been told not to bring back Torch, Sub-Mariner and Captain America—after all, they had failed twice—but Stan was generating these ideas, with or without the help of Jack and Steve. It was coming from them, not Goodman. Martin just knew the *kind* of things that he wanted. Later on, Stan was always generating ideas for what the books would be, and I'm not aware of Martin ever saying, for instance, "Do a book about the Silver Surfer." It's not impossible that, when something particularly sold, he *could* have suggested something along those lines, but generally it was just Stan looking at the sales figures. But Martin would have a hand in there. He was a canny person who looked at those sales figures. Sometimes it could have been the confluence of the two of them. And it *was* Goodman who insisted we do a hero named Captain Marvel!

CBA: *In 1970, for instance, there was a wholesale revival of westerns—albeit they were mostly reprints—and, in very short order, there were a lot of cowboy books.*

Roy: I'm a little hazy on dates, but at that time, we were with Curtis and the whole lid had come off about how many titles Marvel could do. So, therefore, one more way to get space on the stands was to come out with more books. We could only put out so many books of original material with the limited personnel we had and still control the quality—just the sheer *production* of it. One easy thing was, if you thought there might be a little bit of a market (and since it was cheaper because, at that stage, we were paying *no* reprint money yet—and when we did a little later, it was only a couple bucks a page), we would come out with books just in order to crowd the market. You come out with a book and, okay, so it sells a couple hundred thousand copies even if it wasn't much of a hit, and suddenly Marvel was taking up more space on the stands. Curtis wanted more presence and more books, so we had to produce them the best we could, putting out whatever we could come up with—it was a case of sinking and swimming at the same time. It was not because we thought that westerns were the hottest thing. I can't imagine anything that would have happened then that would have made us to think that suddenly there was a big demand for cowboy stories. But we had a lot of inventory of cowboy stuff in the warehouses, so let's do a western reprint book or two and see what happens.

CBA: *Your work is very well remembered on* The Avengers.

Roy: By the aging few.

CBA: *Was there any relationship, in your mind, between* The Avengers *and the* Justice Society?

Roy: Terrifically, yes. Not in Stan's mind, of course, except that he created it in the same way. They both had the same basis behind them. In some ways *The Avengers* was really closer to Stan's answer to the *Justice League* than the *F.F.* It was a natural and, remember: Stan had been the editor of the "All-Winners Squad" even though he probably didn't recall it. Stan had originally done *The Avengers* with Thor, Iron Man, Captain America and the Hulk—characters who were solo stars or the next thing to it—and then he had this brilliant stroke to suddenly throw those guys away just to make it simpler to plot the stories, really. Stan

AVENGERS! YER COVER!

(ARGH! IT JUST OCCURED TO ME THAT I'VE LEFT NO ROOM FOR THE MASTHEAD, SO I'LL EXTEND THIS DRAWING SIDEWAYS, THEN PERHAPS AFTER INKING IT CAN BE REDUCED A LITTLE... O.K.?)

...just got to the point where he just didn't want to deal with keeping the continuity straight, so he said, "Here's Captain America and a bunch of secondary characters." Though the sales were pretty good anyway, my understanding is they actually went up with the new line-up.

By the time I got hold of *The Avengers*, that format was running out of steam—Jack wasn't on it anymore—and I immediately began to lay plans to bring back Thor and Iron Man. Stan made me take Captain America out (I brought in Hercules to replace Thor) and I was stuck with a bunch of minor leaguers. So I kept bringing back the heavy-hitters for an issue or two but Stan kept making me take them out. One day, with the issue by John Buscema that had The Collector [#51], suddenly I just went wholesale and brought all three back at the same time; I didn't ask Stan but just did it. I remember him looking at the cover and shrugging. He just accepted it by that point. I had always thought of *The Avengers* like the Justice Society, which is why I created a proto-Justice League in the book, Squadron Sinister (later, the Squadron Supreme).

CBA: *Did you seek out John Buscema to do the book?*

Roy: No, John was thrust upon me. John had done that "SHIELD" story and was working out okay, but Stan felt that he drew well, but needed to refine his style of storytelling by working over Kirby's layouts for a few issues to get away from the quiet things that he was doing. Here was a guy who was a nice draftsman, and suddenly Don Heck had to go on vacation, so Stan said, "Have Buscema do a couple issues of the book." So I did this plot that has the group sitting around the mansion, with Hercules absent-mindedly lifting some terrific weights, and John brought in the pencils (which had much more power than the finished inks). I looked at those pages and, except for a couple of guest appearances, Don Heck never came back to *The Avengers* again! [*laughs*] We gave Don something else to do because he was a good artist, of course.

CBA: *What's the "origin" of Conan?*

Roy: The first Robert E. Howard book that I ever bought was *Almuric,* which was published by Ace a year or so before the paperback *Conan.* I didn't read it but was attracted to it because it had a *John Carter of Mars* approach. So then Ace started coming out with all the *Conan* books and the one *Kull* paperback. They had the Frazetta and Krenkel covers. I was also interested in the title *King Kull* because that had been the name of a villain in *Captain Marvel* (which Otto Binder had named after Howard's character). So I took the first book (*Conan the Adventurer*) home and I thought it was going to be like *John Carter* or *Carson of Venus.* But it was just this savage guy running around, kidnapping a princess, and there was a little magic, so I just read ten pages of it and tossed it in the closet. I didn't pay attention to it for another couple of years, but we started getting letters from readers saying, "Bring in new stuff like *Conan,* Edgar Rice Burroughs, Tolkien, and *Doc Savage.*" We eventually went after all four of those and ending up doing everything except Tolkien (the estate didn't even want to talk to us).

We didn't initially go after *Conan* because we thought his popularity in all the paperbacks would have too high a price tag. So we went after Lin Carter's *Thongor* (which also had a Frazetta cover), but Lin's agent (probably because the money offered was so niggardly) stalled us. Lin kept telling us that his agent would be in touch with us, but the agent wouldn't respond. Finally, I just got annoyed, picked up the latest book, *Conan of Cimmeria,* and saw the address in there of this guy named Glenn Lord down in Texas listed as "literary agent" for the Howard estate. So I dropped him a line, and said, "Look—we don't have much money to offer you but I have the go-ahead to do a sword-and-sorcery comic from Goodman, so…" (Why we didn't create an entirely new character I'm not sure; maybe we felt like we wouldn't know how to do it exactly and perhaps we should seek out a property the readers were asking for.)

CBA: *Did you develop a feel immediately for the character?*

Roy: It took a couple of months, I think, for me *and* for Barry. Neither his drawing or my writing is anything to write home about—there are good things from both of us, but there are a lot of lines in the first issue that, a month later, I never would have used. And Barry's drawing improved enormously. But Barry had drawn better *Conan*-type stuff before and I think that he froze-up on the first issue. Remember, he was over in England at the time, so we couldn't talk. By the second issue, he was really starting to

Above: Rejected cover by Barry Smith to The Avengers #66. Check out the note by Barry Smith to the production department on the top margin. Art ©1998 Barry Windsor-Smith. The Avengers ©1998 Marvel Entertainment.

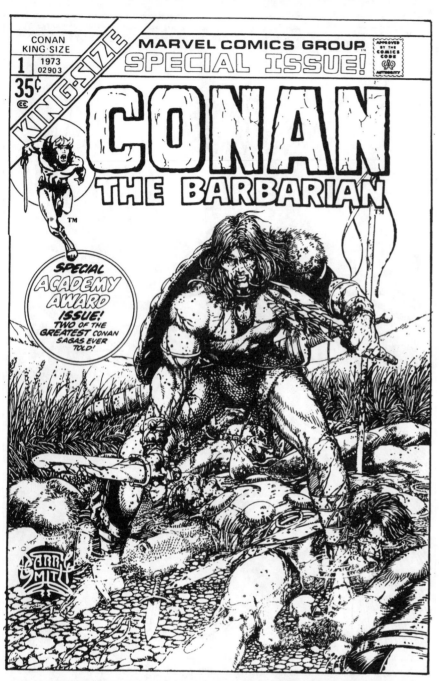

Above: *Barry Windsor-Smith's great cover to* Conan King-Size Special #1. Conan ©1998 Conan Properties.

Steranko at that stage. But that looked pretty good to us (Steranko had developed very quickly) and Barry developed in his own direction very well. I really did like the idea of giving him a book but, initially we needed John Buscema—he was the first choice—and it could've gone to Gil, but the trouble was Martin Goodman wanted somebody cheap. John had, in fact, read some of the books and was all ready to go for it. But suddenly Goodman said, "You can't hire a top artist because I want to recover the couple hundred bucks we have to pay for the rights." So all of the sudden, out goes John Buscema and the possibility of Gil Kane (who loved *Conan* a lot earlier than I did), and we had to get somebody else. Some people were pushing Bernie Wrightson at us, but that wasn't going to work out—I might have been more iffy, but Stan was right: Bernie wasn't quite ready. So we gave it to that kid in England, Barry, because he and I had been fooling around on a couple of sword-and-sorcery projects—that "Starr the Slayer" story and a couple of unpublished things outside Marvel—so he inherited *Conan* and ran with it.

CBA: *Did Stan suggest putting Thor in* Conan *to boost sales?*

Roy: Let's just say that it was a *strong* suggestion. We might have made him dressed more primitively but, yeah, Thor would've definitely been in there because we would've been trying to save a book we cared about. Sales started off good for the first issue, but for the next seven issues they kept going down. It was still Stan, as much as anyone, who saved it because he kept saying that he didn't want to use covers with animals on them—we had a tiger leaping at somebody; a giant spider—but he wanted more humanoid enemies.

CBA: *Were there statistics to back him up on that or was that just his inclination?*

Roy: There might be statistics, but a lot of it was just a feeling. Stan always had a problem relating to monsters if they're not a little humanoid. Even the monsters he had done with Jack and occasionally with Ditko; it's the humanoid ones that people remember—"Fin Fang Foom"—but the ones that were globs weren't remembered.

CBA: *Irwin Donenfeld felt that gorillas on DC's covers sold books. Did Stan have similar idiosyncrasies?*

Roy: He insisted that the logos on the comics be red, yellow or white. He didn't like it when Steranko used orange on *SHIELD,* for instance. A green or blue logo would be thrown out the window! He wanted them to stand out and was convinced that no other colors did the trick.

The most idiosyncratic situation we ran into in the early '70s was not Stan, but Martin Goodman's son, Chip, when he was briefly in charge of the company. It was a western cover and Chip sent back word that he wanted all the bad guys in the story inside and on the cover to be wearing animal masks. We asked why and he said, "I don't know. Maybe it'll sell better."

CBA: *Was Chip an asset to the company?*

Roy: He really wasn't in charge long enough to tell. I don't think that he knew a lot about comics, but he tried hard. One of the problems was just being Martin Goodman's son. I don't think that Martin respected Chip very much—he put Chip in charge but would treat him with less than benign contempt in front of other people. Martin was a little cruel sometimes. I forget who wrote it, but there's a story by one of the writers in the "men's sweat" division, that was written after he left the company, which was a thinly disguised version of Magazine Management. There was a Martin Goodman character who had two sons (which was apparently a true situation), one who dutifully stayed there and tried to help run the company but was abused constantly and called an idiot; the other just turned his back on the father and *that* was the son that the father worshiped and tried to get back. When that writer had wanted to come back to Magazine Management, he was afraid that Martin wouldn't let him, but Martin just thought it was funny as hell.

CBA: *The "men's sweat division"?!*

cook, and within two or three issues, he got really great. We got along and worked pretty well together. He needed the work over there in England. Now he tends to look down on the amount of money he was paid, but hey, nobody was twisting his arm and saying, "You gotta work with these rates." He wanted the work, and that was the most that we could afford. He had a lot of rough edges anyway—my God, the amount of letters we got complaining about the *X-Men* issue he drew on park benches!

CBA: *He actually drew the issue on park benches?*

Roy: Barry didn't have an apartment then, staying off and on with a couple of girls who were friends of his. I didn't know it at the time (I was married so I really couldn't put him up anyway) but discovered that later. When he drew that 15-page *X-Men* story [#53], which had some good touches but didn't come out too well, and he brought it in, I tried to tell him about some of the stuff that was "off." He stared at me quizzically and said, "You're kidding!" (Of course, within a year or two, if anyone had tried to tell him that it was a decent job, he would've thrown that person out the window!) He was defensive about his work because it had been done under adverse situations.

From the first, Stan and (later) I saw something really good in Barry but he needed a lot of work; he looked like the poor man's

GROO IN PARADISE

Roy: That was the name Harvey Kurtzman came up with in his *Jungle Book.* It wasn't a phrase used around there a lot. (If you want to read how Magazine Management was run, read *Jungle Book.*) By the early '70s, Martin was moving out and Stan somehow wrestled the company away from the control of Chip. (I don't know anything else about it because nobody ever told me this stuff. Apparently Stan, around this time, had a meeting at DC Comics about becoming Editor-in-Chief, and later when he told me, he said, "Yeah, and I would have taken you with me." But, hey, I might've decided to stay at Marvel and become editor sooner—but I would have probably gone because of my loyalty and feeling for Stan. It would've taken a heck of a lot to keep me. Overall, it was just as well that I didn't know these things, as I was usually knee-deep in comic book material, just looking up occasionally.)

CBA: *Were the mystery books a reaction to the success of DC's* House of Mystery?

Roy: Primarily—and of course the fact that if we were going do something new, we were going to have to go in different directions. DC was having some success with the genre and Stan, of course, had considerable success back in the '50s with the horror comics. It wasn't as if it was a totally new direction. But without the real horror, it was neither quite fish nor fowl. I was less than enthusiastic about some aspects of it, because I never was a big fan of that stuff. But that was the deal, so there we were and I discovered I had a lot of fun with a little freedom and worked with guys like Barry Smith and Gene Colan. The problem was that these guys were too valuable doing the major books so after a little while, you ended up with relatively minor people coming in to do the original stories in those books. That didn't work out quite as well and they never really caught on for Marvel the way they did for DC.

CBA: *How fast did you guys have to scramble when Goodman*

made the decision to go to the 25¢ size?

Roy: How fast can you get? [*laughs*] It was immediate. A few nice things came out of it: Archie Goodwin did a nice alternative world story in *Fantastic Four* and I did a *Hulk* story with Herb Trimpe that we threw in real fast about the Hulk in the middle of a mirage that was so well received that only a couple of years ago, they reprinted it as a "minor classic," which was funny because it was a desperate vignette that we tossed in because we had to come up with something *real* fast in seven or eight pages.

CBA: *After my brother and I started collecting Marvels around 1971, we naturally had to buy back issues, mostly at Phil Seuling's conventions. For the early '70s issues, we would always find copies that had colored ink smeared across the tops of the pages. I've been told that these were actually distributor returns and this method was to "destroy" them (though, of course, they ended up on dealer tables). Do you recall this happening?*

Roy: I don't remember seeing that particular method, but we all kind of knew that they were doing it. It wasn't something that I was involved with and anything that I could have done with it would have been taking my time away from the creative side of things. But I know that they did feel that there was a lot of dishonesty that went on with this kind of thing. They weren't even tearing off the covers sometimes and I'm surprised that they even bothered to smear it.

CBA: *What was the idea behind the Giant-Size books?*

Roy: You mean *Giant-Size Conan,* and everybody's favorite title, *Giant-Size Man-Thing*? It was just trying to squeeze some more income out of the most popular characters and maybe break out of the 32-page comic format. A couple of years before, we had those 25¢ annuals and specials but they had gone under because Martin Goodman changed plans. It was nice to have the quarter-lies but it was just a way to generate income.

CBA: *Steve Englehart and you seemed to seize the opportunity*

of the quarterly books and actually work out concepts for them. Steve developed an intricate, weaving storyline about the Celestial Madonna, and you specifically centered on Conan as King.

Roy: It was a better way for me to deal with the title rather than involve it in the continuity of the regular book. There was a little disagreement with Steve and me about the *Giant-Size Avengers* because I insisted on writing the first issue. Steve was not happy about this, but I looked at him incredulously and said, "Steve, I wrote this thing for *seventy* issues! Give me a break here. I think I've earned the right to do the first issue of *Giant-Size Avengers* if I want to." Steve didn't see things the same way and I can understand things from his viewpoint. I would have felt guilty if it would have been about royalties, but I didn't get a dime more than if I had been writing any other book. It was just a case of wanting to do the first issue because Steve was assured that he would then take over the quarterly. I gave Steve a lot of leeway when it came to his books. When he arrived and came up with the idea for that Avengers/Defenders war, I dragged my feet on it. Not because I thought it wasn't an excellent idea, but I was afraid that given sometimes the way production schedule went, a book would be occasionally delayed and come out in the wrong order. Eventually I gave in and it worked out very well, so I wasn't going to give Steve too much trouble for handling *The Avengers* however he wanted to—as long as he would keep it straight and on schedule.

CBA: *Were there often scheduling problems? Jungle Action skipped an issue and took four months to come out.*

Roy: That was the "Black Panther" and I know that Don

McGregor was always very slow with his plots, especially when he was also on staff. He was a very slow writer and found assignments difficult to get done on time. But we respected the integrity of his work and the effort that he put into it. If there was a delay, it may have been for that reason. It could be like pulling teeth to get a story out of him. But, like Stan earlier, I didn't really handle the day-to-day aspect of calling up the writers and artists to beat them up and get work out of them. Occasionally I had to get involved in that, but that mostly was left up to the production manager— who would have been John Verpoorten and, earlier, Sol Brodsky. John and the people in his department would take care of that and I would only occasionally have to call up and berate people if they were late, but that was only if it were an emergency.

CBA: *Don McGregor brought a new kind of writing, arguably, to comic books that was very adult and dealt with even domestic violence.*

Roy: Don's viewpoint was uniquely his. My feeling was that as long as they got in the story what Stan and I liked—action, emotion and all the elements we needed in a story—they basically served as unpaid *de facto* editors and, in return, they got a fair amount of freedom. If it didn't work out and the book got cancelled, the writer might or might not get a replacement book. If he went too far, I would try to catch it at the last minute and, if not, we'd say, "Hey, no more of this!" If I had any respect for their writing, I tried to give the guys a fair amount of freedom. Don was writing material that wasn't the way I would have written it (and not always the way I would have *wanted* to see it written), but I respected the fact that he was really putting himself out on the work. So, as long as it would sell, I gave him a fair amount of freedom. Over the long haul, his books weren't particularly successful sales-wise, but they didn't do that badly either. We didn't expect great sales from a book like the "Black Panther" series, and certainly not from "War of the Worlds" (which I had developed as an idea for a series though I never wrote it). By the time Don got a hold of "Killraven," he took off and made it his own. If I had done it, I would have done it a different way, but I wasn't the writer and didn't like the idea of the editor imposing his viewpoint that strongly on the writer for no good reason. I just let Don go and he took it in some interesting directions.

CBA: *After you left as editor-in-chief, there seemed to be an increased problem between writers and editors.*

Roy: Well, if a writer tries something different and the book isn't a great seller, he's much more vulnerable to an editor having *his* way. There's also the fact that Marv Wolfman and Len Wein (editors-in-chief after me, respectively) had originally developed working at DC and I don't think either was quite as devoted to letting the writers have quite as much leeway perhaps as Stan and I had. Maybe I was just non-directive and lazy! I don't know! (laughter) My feeling was that if you had a good writer, teach him a little bit here and there, and then let him go. I never taught anybody as much as Stan taught me, so maybe I should have directed more. But I felt that I lined up good writers with a lot of passion. When you look back, we always had our failures, but some of those failures—like Stan's *Silver Surfer*—were better in quality than the successes. Do I really think that Neal Adams and my *X-Men*, or Gene Colan and my *Dr. Strange*—both financial failures—were some of the best stuff that Marvel was publishing at the time? Of course I do. Steve Gerber's *Man-Thing* and *Howard the Duck*, Don's "War of the Worlds" and "Black Panther," Doug Moench's *Shang-Chi*, all had intensity and I wanted to let them go with that. It's not that I think that Marv and Len didn't want to do the same thing, but they seemed more willing to step in. Maybe they felt a little less secure because, after all, I had a particular relationship with Stan that was pretty firm and had worked under him, so I knew what he wanted. Marv and Len hadn't had that as much, even if they had worked editorially for a while, so they might have been more nervous about letting a writer of a not particularly successful book do something that they didn't feel comfortable with. They might have worried that they would be out there and get the limb sawed off. Then, of course, deadlines would intervene and I wouldn't be surprised if John Verpoorten wouldn't come in at times and hit them over the head and say, "Get this book out of here!" He did sometimes tend to treat Marv and Len as a couple of kids who had run amok in a candy store. (He would have liked to do it to me, too, but I sort of outranked him.) You can't say if Marv and Len weren't right or wrong, because it just got done and they obviously had the right to do that.

CBA: *Can an editor-in-chief be successful working on 52 regularly-scheduled books?*

Roy: You know that old story about carrying a baby calf? You just keep carrying it every day and it just keeps getting bigger and bigger, so eventually you're carrying a cow. That was me. I came along when there were 17 books on the schedule and then it started to grow. When I took it over, I didn't notice that I was carrying this cow, and once I put it down it would've been hell to pick it up again! So it was probably very hard for someone else to take it over, too. But I wonder about back in the '50s, when Atlas had 50 or 60 titles a month coming out, how many people had editorial authority other than Stan.

CBA: *That's a good point, because there were virtually no reprint books coming out then.*

Roy: I've heard Don Rico, a *Captain America* artist and friend, tell me he had some vague editorial status, but you never hear about anybody else doing that much editorially. There must have been traffic managers but they probably didn't have much more power—but there must have been *somebody*, because Stan couldn't have read all those scripts. And those books were much more difficult than the ones we were turning out, because they were filled with multiple seven- or eight-page stories. That's a *lot* more traffic. Those anthology books were a helluva lot more work. In our case, we just turned a lot of editorial responsibilities to the writers. It wasn't that an artist couldn't have done that, too, but it was my inclination because of my own experience *not* to turn the responsibilities over to an artist who would tell the writer what to do. I don't believe in that and don't to this day.

CBA: *Why?*

Roy: Oh, I'd have no hesitation if he were both an artist *and* a writer, like Starlin was. But I wanted *story men* guiding the book.

CBA: *When you got the job, did you feel like you were the heir apparent?*

Roy: I don't know. As far as writing major titles maybe, but as far as being editor, not really. Even when Stan quit writing for four months to work on a movie, I didn't really feel like an "heir apparent" because I knew that Stan was coming back. It was like being heir apparent of Zeus, because Zeus ain't going anywhere! [*laughs*] Zeus is immortal and, after all, Stan wasn't that old. I was in my early thirties and he was 50 or so, and I just didn't think of him as somebody who was likely to go away any time soon. I certainly wasn't going to think five, ten, 15 years down the line.

Other people told me that they had the same feeling about me; they were startled when I left in '74. Some people had not wanted to take the assistant editor job even though that was always the job that led to the editor-in-chiefship. In every case except Gerry Conway, the next person in line got the job—Marv, Len, Archie Goodwin, and eventually Jim Shooter. Some people passed it up because they were convinced I would never leave.

CBA: *When did you first hear about Atlas/Seaboard?*

Roy: Suddenly Martin Goodman was going to start a new company and Chip was in charge. They hired Larry Leiber, Stan's brother, as editor, so Larry had to come in and tell Stan, "No hard feelings but I have to go out and make a name for myself." Stan wished him good luck and was very gracious about it as far as I could tell, with never a lot of ill feeling. But there was a lot of ill feeling between Martin Goodman and Marvel (which had pushed

out his son), and Atlas was just a way of showing that he could do it again. But, unfortunately, the time wasn't quite right—they had a lot of titles but it never amounted to anything. It was a lot of sound and fury that never got off the ground.

CBA: *Did you take umbrage at the merciless swiping of characters—The Brute for the Hulk, Scorpion for Spider-Man?*

Roy: There was a little of that. They were just *so* close: They copied the look of the logo and so forth. Stan told me that he gave Martin full credit for calling our company "Marvel Comics" back in the '60s because Stan wanted to call it Atlas (because that had been the company's "name" for the longest period). But Stan said that Martin was right: You can't do nearly as much with the name Atlas as you can with Marvel. Martin had a lot of good instincts. He wouldn't have been around as long as he was if he hadn't. Atlas/Seaboard was an attempt to show that Martin could do Marvel Comics all over again and that he didn't need Stan Lee or Cadence. It was probably a combination of the time and trying to do so many books so fast—you can't do that many and make them good. If he'd started with one or two titles, he might have been able to build something. He offered me a chance to come over and said that he was committed to publishing for at least two years, but I just didn't believe him. So I wasn't about to consider quitting, and I just maintained a friendly relationship with Chip. They were offering higher rates than Marvel, throwing money at everybody, paying one and a half to two times Marvel's rate, so I did envy the guys who were getting higher rates than I was, but I was writing books that actually sold! It didn't last long. I *told* the guys to be careful about leaving since Marvel was not wild about Atlas. It wasn't a case of personal vengeance, but we

Above: *Ouch! Former colleagues Stan Lee and Roy Thomas receive some especially bitter satirical treatment from the "King", Jack Kirby, in the thinly veiled personas of "Funky Flashman" and "Houseroy." With Mike Royer's inks in the pages of Mister Miracle #6. Look for the black-&-white trade paperback collection of the complete Kirby run of MM coming this Fall, toned by our pal Jim Amash.* ©1998 DC Comics.

weren't going to try really hard to make a place for a writer or artist who wants to come back later. For the most part they went over there anyway and it didn't last so we luckily were able to get them back.

CBA: *Did you seek out minority writers to script* Luke Cage?

Roy: We would have if we could have found them. There were minority people applying occasionally as writers and artists, but they didn't quite work out. I think I had as much to do as anybody getting Billy Graham, a Black artist, to work on *Luke Cage* and "Black Panther." Don McGregor was a good choice for some of that material because he had quite a few Black friends and could relate quite well, but basically we were just trying to do good books. If we had had Black artists and writers who came in and were up to snuff, we would have snapped them up right away.

CBA: *Were you involved in the development of* Comix Book, *the black-&-white "underground" edited by Denis Kitchen?*

Roy: Not really. That was Stan and Denis. My one involvement was that I told Stan that (not just with me) it was going to cause some real resentment if you give these contributors total rights to their material—copyrights and everything else—if you won't do that for the people who work for you here. Denis has remarked that he knew that this was a problem. It wasn't that anybody was

out to get Denis or that book—I thought it was cute—but the problem was that it was one thing to just take over the writing of *Spider-Man*, but we had a lot of people making up new characters, myself included. And we weren't getting the tiniest little piece of them. We didn't care much for that aspect of it. Otherwise, I particularly loved Denis' covers. The material itself was, unfortunately, some of the weaker underground material. There was this attempt to do underground comix but because it was Marvel it somehow ended up being material that didn't have a lot of sex or violence or outrageousness. And if you take that out of underground comix, it's like chopping off Godzilla's legs; there's nothing left! I liked the experiment, but I just felt that there was such a difference between what we were doing that I never really felt comfortable with it.

CBA: *Were you involved in the creation of that fiction digest,* Haunt of Horror?

Roy: I put Gerry Conway in charge of that because he was someone who had written and sold real prose. Gerry put those couple of issues together pretty much all on his own. He got the artists to do pictures and got Harlan Ellison and others to submit stories. The only problem we had was that originally Stan felt that Marvel was going to own all the rights to that material, the same way it did with the comics. Gerry, who had a foot in the camps of both comics and science-fiction, kept having to say, "No, we can't do that, Stan! Nobody is going to write for us! You might be able to buy the artwork, but you can't do that with the writers. Nobody good is going to write for us if you have any other deal than First North American or, at the most, First World Rights." Gerry worked very hard at it and he won his point on that. It was an educational process for me, too, because I hadn't really any dealing with straight prose writing, but at least I understood what it was and was able to mediate a little bit. Officially I was the editor and could have stepped in at any time and dictated, but I left it almost entirely up to Gerry. I was just sorry that it wasn't more successful, but it was just another one of the many things that we were trying to do. It was either Stan's or Gerry's idea, but certainly wasn't mine.

CBA: *What's with all the monsters in the books? First came* Morbius.

Roy: The Code was changed and three minutes later, Stan tells me that he wants a vampire as the next villain in *Spider-Man*. By sheer coincidence, Stan had just written issue #100 and he turned the writing chores over to me so he could spend several months working on the film *The Monster Maker*. Gil and I were going to bring in Dracula (this was before the *Tomb of Dracula* book), but Stan said, "No, I don't want Dracula. I want a new character." We made up a more science-fictional kind of vampire in the same vein as Spidey's other villains like The Lizard. I remembered a movie in the '50s that was called *Atom-Age Vampire* or just *The Vampire*. It was about a guy who had a blood disease that made him go around drinking blood. I thought that was kind of neat; a science-fiction vampire. (Nowadays, that's done a lot but back then vampires were always the straight, classical vampires.) This guy was a little different; the same way that Michael Landon, in *I Was a Teenage Werewolf* was evolved into this creature by a psychologist! So, I came up with the general idea along with the name Morbius (totally forgetting that that was the name of the character that Walter Pidgeon played in *Forbidden Planet,* one of my favorite movies). It was a natural from the word "morbid" and related things. I worked with Gil, and we designed a costume in primary colors and I'm sure that Gil added a number of touches. It was a great collaboration and we had a good time with it.

CBA: *With "Ka-Zar" in* Astonishing Tales, *you and Jack Kirby had a rare collaboration.*

Roy: That was one of only two things I ever did with Jack. He had plotted that story (and I don't know if Stan had given him anything at all), and then he left Marvel. So I just inherited that story and dialogued it. If my name comes first, that's just because

that's the way we styled the credits then. It wasn't really a collaboration, as Jack was probably gone by the time I wrote it. I never talked to him about it.

CBA: *You worked on "Doctor Doom" with Wally Wood.*

Roy: It was fun for a couple of issues with the Doomsmith character. Wally and I didn't know each other terribly well, and I can't remember if Wally contributed substantially to the plot. The only thing I recall is after an issue or two, I became aware that Wally wasn't giving the art enough attention. We really wanted to see something that looked more like Wally Wood, but instead we ended up seeing *none* of Wally, because he just left! [*laughs*]

CBA: *What's the story with Man-Thing?*

Roy: That one I did take a credit on. Stan called me in when we were going to do *Savage Tales*, and he had a bunch of ideas for particular series. One of them was a Black character called M'Tumbu the Mighty (which evolved slowly under Denny O'Neil into the "Black Brother" story, which was totally different); and he had this idea for a character called Man-Thing. I wasn't too wild about it, because I thought it was just going to be confused with the Thing—these were the days before you had ten characters with similar names in the same company; I later even worried about having a character called Iron Fist—but if Stan wanted a Man-Thing, he got a Man-Thing! I don't know what he had in mind except the general idea of a guy in a swamp who gets some kind of powers from the swamp via a serum. He just had a two- or three-sentence idea like that. I always liked the character the Heap from the old *Airboy Comics,* but I don't believe Stan ever mentioned him. So I went and did a general plot, but I didn't want to write it, so I gave it to Gerry. That's what I always did with the horror/occult/mystery books: I'd make up an idea and lateral it off to Gerry Conway—Gerry was to me what I had been to Stan in some ways. Gerry wrote a full script because the artist, Gray Morrow, was uncomfortable working from a Marvel-style plot. So the three of us created the character. Gray did a really nice job and I remember that he used a guy I knew, Chester Grabowski, as a model for a villain in the story. I used to play poker with Chester at Phil Seuling's, and still think of that story when I run into him at conventions.

The weird thing is that while Gerry was writing the script, his roommate, Len Wein, was creating Swamp Thing for *House of Secrets,* a somewhat different character. But when Len created the continuing character a few months later, its origin was so similar to that of Man-Thing that Gerry tried to talk him into changing it. We felt that he was just going to stir up problems with such a close origin. But we let it go because we knew that Len hadn't really swiped it and, except for the origin, nothing was similar. They were both based on The Heap anyway, so what the hell. [*laughs*]

I had my own version of the Heap *earlier,* in an issue of *The Hulk*—that was a straight take-off, and I'm sure both Len and Gerry saw that, too. So, we all liked to do the Heap. So when Sol Brodsky went off to do Skywald and was looking for something to do, I said, "Why don't you bring back The Heap?" I was spreading The Heap all over the place! [*laughs*]

CBA: *What was the original concept for* Werewolf by Night: I, Werewolf?

Roy: Yes. I'd created *I, Werewolf.* It was an idea for a series to be narrated by the werewolf himself. It was basically *I Was A Teenage Werewolf* combined with *Spider-Man.* I have this foggy notion that Barry Smith and I may have discussed working on the strip together. I don't know if it had any connection with that unrealized team concept we worked on with Red Raven and Bucky, but it must have been around the same time, because we were looking for things to do together. Barry and I got along well and I liked his work. I understood that maybe he was going to work on it with me at one stage. Anyway, the only thing that Stan didn't like about my general concept was the title, I, Werewolf, and all I cared about was that it would be narrated first-person

because I wanted it to be different. I enjoyed what Gerry was doing with second-person narration in *Daredevil* so I wanted to try first-person and stretch comics just a little more than they had been for a while. As the credits for the first issue say, I had the general idea and my first wife Jeannie and I plotted the origin together. I remember we went to an auto show in the Coliseum in New York, and we got bored after 20 minutes (because I didn't even own a car!), so we just went outside, sat down on some monument or something, and plotted out the first issue because I was preoccupied and had to get it going. As usual, then it was Gerry Conway Time! I gave it to Gerry and he did everything else. He named him Jack Russell, after the terrier (which I didn't even realize 'til years later because I know so little about dogs), and made up the Darkhold—almost everything about it outside the general idea for the first strip.

CBA: *How did Mike Ploog become involved? Did you review portfolios of aspiring artists?*

Roy: Sometimes if they knew somebody who knew Stan, they might have a direct appointment. But I can't remember how Mike came in. Of course, he had worked as Will Eisner's assistant for a while, and that's where he developed that style. As soon as Stan and I saw it, our greedy little minds got working the same way we

Above: The top tier are uncensored panels of Conan #24 (the unforgettable "The Song of Red Sonja"—Barry's last work on the regular book), page 6. More uncensored panels of Conan appear on page 50. ©1998 Marvel Entertainment. Conan ©1998 Conan Properties.

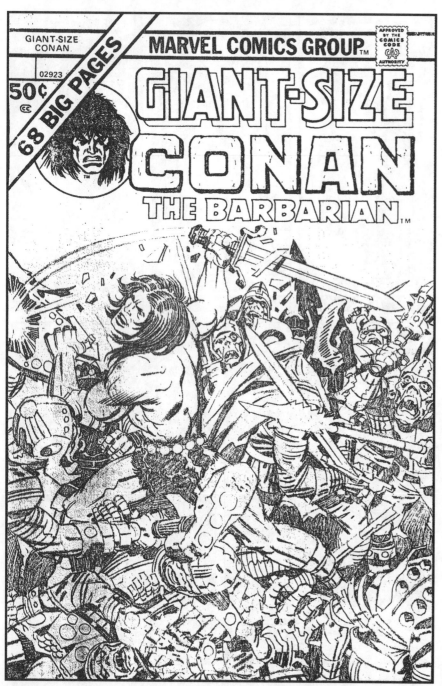

MARVEL COMICS GROUP™

GIANT-SIZE
CONAN

02923

GIANT-SIZE
CONAN
THE BARBARIAN™

68 BIG PAGES

50¢

Above: *Elric and our boy have at it in this, the unretouched pencils of Jack Kirby from his only assigned Conan job, Giant-Size Conan #5. Marvel's production department changed the Cimmerian's face in the published version. Conan ©1998 Conan Properties. Elric ©1998 Michael Moorcock.*

saw Sal Buscema drawing like his brother, or other artists drawing like Kirby. Naturally, we see these superficial aspects because we're trying to sell comic books, so we thought, "Hey, here's a guy who draws like Eisner," and we thought it was good stuff. Ploog and I were immediately going to work on a western together which I called "Tin Star," which was about a guy who lost his memory but had this tin star with a bullet hole through it, and he wandered around trying to find his identity. We maybe had three panels drawn before Stan yanked him off and put him on something else. He ended up doing *Werewolf, Man-Thing*—he always said, "You guys always get me to do the hairy creatures!" Maybe that was because he had a beard. I liked Mike. He was a big bear of a guy who was a lot of fun and laughed a lot.

The most fun we ever had was designing Ghost Rider. Strangely enough, that character wasn't based on Blazing Skull. I had made up a villain in *Daredevil* called Stuntmaster who had a motorcycle. He was not much of a character and Gary Friedrich wanted to make up a new motorcycle villain because he didn't like Stuntmaster any more than I did. (Gary had been writing the western *Ghost Rider*—Stan wouldn't let me write it because he said I was too important to the company to write a western, but I

really wanted to write it because I had always loved the character.) So Gary came to me and said that he had a weird idea for a villain in *Daredevil* called Ghost Rider who rides around on motorcycle. He didn't have too much more than that other than he was obviously a spectral-type character. I said that there was only one thing wrong with his idea, and Gary looked at me jaundiced (because, after all, we had known each other since he was in high school). I said, "It's too good to be a minor character in *Daredevil*. We should start him out in his own book." Gary's eyes widened and we talked it over. The only problem was that at that time Gary wasn't always coming into work every day he was supposed to. We made this appointment for Mike Ploog to come in and we three were going to talk it over and design the character. I don't think that Gary and I had talked at all on what Ghost Rider would look like. So Ploog shows up and Gary isn't there but we had to get going, so I told Mike that I really liked the leather jumpsuit that Elvis had worn in his so-called comeback special in 1968 (I have been a big Elvis fan since I first heard "Heartbreak Hotel" in '56). I said that his face was like a skull and that's all I mentioned. So Mike just started drawing and he put flames around the head. I said, "What's that?" He said, "I dunno, I just thought it would be neat if his head was on fire." The upshot is that we had the whole character designed right there, in 15 minutes or so. The next day, Gary comes in and looks at the sketch and says, "Yup. Just like I envisioned him!" [*laughs*]

CBA: *Whose idea was it for the "showcase" titles:* Marvel Spotlight, Marvel Feature, Marvel Premiere?

Roy: That was Stan's. I naturally got attuned right away because *Showcase* and *The Brave and the Bold* had been so influential on the material that I liked. Stan just liked the idea of doing something for an issue and then trying something else, forcing us to think of new ideas all of the time.

CBA: Red Wolf *is a character you obviously created in* The Avengers.

Roy: I described him visually with a wolf mask on his head. I designed him as a modern-day character in *The Avengers* because the American Indians had been in the news. There was Wounded Knee and I thought that it was time to go with a character who, though he was introduced as a villain, was really a hero. When it came time to do a regular *Red Wolf* book, I have this idea that Stan wanted to set it in the past as a western rather than what would have been the most logical thing to do, which was setting it in the present. (It's hard for me to imagine that it was my idea to set him in the past, but it may have been.) It just never worked out terribly well—none of the other westerns were doing that well, either.

CBA: *Did you offer the job of writing "Red Wolf" to your old friend Gardner Fox?*

Roy: Yeah. Gardner had dropped out of comics to pursue paperback book writing for a couple years after the debacle in the late '60s at DC. I can't recall if I offered him work in the meantime but I have the feeling that I did but he just didn't want to do it. Then at some stage, we ran into each other and he wanted to get back into it. I knew that it was going to be difficult because Gardner didn't write anything like what Stan or I was looking for, and yet, at the same time, I felt that this is one of a handful of people who, even if I had to rewrite every single word for years, was going to have a job in comics. I did a lot of rewriting on his material—Gardner would do the plotting and most of the words were his, so I would rearrange, write a few lines, and trim it down. But after three or four issues it wasn't really working, so when the book was discontinued I don't think Gardner was looking for anything else after those couple of issues of *Dr. Strange*. I think that he had the sense, without my saying so, that it really wasn't working out and he wasn't too interested anyway.

There was a sense among some of us that there were some people around that the field needed to keep busy. Bill Finger was one of them. Stan gave a job to Jerry Siegel (co-creator of

Superman), though he felt weird having Jerry working for him. But if Jerry was happy to take a low-level job, Stan said, "How can I *not* give Jerry Siegel a job?!" despite the fact that Stan didn't think much of the Mighty Comics that Jerry had written (though that wasn't personal or anything). Stan just felt that there were people like Jerry Siegel who, if they wanted a job in comics, somebody ought to keep them busy forever. Just like when we all looked for something for Bill Everett to do when he wasn't drawing for a period, when he became a colorist. George Roussos, who certainly could have kept working as an inker, became a colorist. We tried to find something for people to do; it was almost the opposite approach of now, when people are just looking for an excuse to toss you on the scrap heap as soon as possible.

CBA: *George is still there!*

Roy: Yup. George has outlasted us all!

CBA: *Barry Smith came in to work on* Avengers. *Was the plan for him to do two monthly books?*

Roy: I don't think that Barry could have ever done two books a month, but he may have wanted to do them. Remember that Stan had wanted Barry off *Conan* because he wanted Barry to do super-hero books and thought him too valuable, with *Conan* not selling well in the early days. That's why *Conan* was actually cancelled for one day on the basis of sales figures for #7, while I was home writing (as I did two or three days a week). I came back in the next day and got it put back on the schedule, because it was Stan who decided to kill the book rather than Martin Goodman. I said, "If you don't want Barry drawing the book because we need him for the super-hero books, we'll get another artist for *Conan,* but don't kill a book just to free up an artist!" But I knew that Barry didn't want to do super-heroes and I didn't think it would work anyway.

CBA: *Was the idea of* Dracula Lives!—*placing Dracula in different time periods—your concept?*

Roy: I'm not sure. It might have been. It's the kind of thing I would have done and I can't imagine that Stan got that involved in the details. But I'll bet it was one of Stan's concepts initially.

CBA: *John Romita told me that Martin Goodman was never really interested in pushing the black-&-white magazines?*

Roy: I don't think that he really liked the idea of *Savage Tales.* Goodman wanted to draw back the minute that things went wrong with *Savage Tales,* and I think that he was very happy to cancel it. Stan had pushed *Savage Tales.*

CBA: *Judging from Neal Adams and Len Wein's "Man-Thing" story inserted in* Astonishing Tales, *you did have a second issue of* Savage Tales *ready?*

Roy: Yes. There was that "Man-Thing" story, and a second "Conan" story by Barry called "The Dweller in the Dark" that appeared in *Conan* #12 as a 16-page story. We probably also had a "Ka-Zar" story prepared. "Black Brother" was not going to continue and I don't think they were going to continue "The Femizons." We were going ahead with it but there were always various problems with #1. There was a rumor that they couldn't get it into Canada; there was a rumor that a DC executive had called it "salacious material," which sabotaged it—but I never learned the truth of any of this stuff. I did hear that we never made it into Canada, maybe because it had a severed head on the cover! I never liked the fact that Conan was holding a severed head, and John Buscema had to bang out this rather rushed painting in a couple of days. (His cover for *Savage Tales* #2 was beautifully detailed, but the first was hurried.) It wasn't a gruesome cover—as Bill Gaines would say, "There's no blood on it!" There was some nudity inside but not much. There were a couple of panels of "The Frost Giant's Daughter" done in an art nouveau style, and there's a naked woman lying dead, face-down in muck in the Ka-Zar story (laughs), and a little wrestling around in Black Brother. There had been nudity in that one but I remember Stan had us cover it up.

CBA: *"Black Brother"?*

Roy: That was a story by Sergius O'Shaugnessey (which means Denny O'Neil) that was the result of the strangest episode I ever got into with Stan. Stan had this idea for "M'Tumbu the Mighty" which was set in Africa with a Black hero. I couldn't relate to it too well but I said, "The guy who should do this is Denny O'Neil." Now, somehow Stan and Denny were never even on the same plane when Denny had worked there briefly in 1965. Denny and I weren't close friends or anything but I always wanted to get him and Stan back together because I felt that these were two talented guys who are just different kind of writers. Maybe this project was something where Denny could do what he liked to do, and Stan would like it because he was looking for something different in *ST.* So the three of us got together to discuss this—I was there mostly as an observer—and Stan starts by telling his idea of M'Tumbu. Then Denny said, "That's right, Stan, but the real trouble with Africa is that White people keep going there and screwing it up." Then Stan would say what he wants, and then Denny would say what he was going to do, and I'm sitting there watching a ping pong game! The conversation ends, they shake hands, and Denny leaves. Fast forward a few weeks, the pages by Gene Colan arrive and Stan doesn't like the story. Maybe it looked kind of tame and Denny didn't use the name M'Tumbu, but I told Stan, "Denny sat right there and told you exactly what he was going to do." Stan shrugged and said, "Yeah, but when I tell a guy what I want him to do, if he wants to talk awhile, that's okay

"GREY GOD" GIANT BATTLES CONAN OVER GAL—

Blow up 2 pos— one for copy one for artist

Barry: PLAY UP GIRL (the one with breast—expos) all maybe ? WHAT?

y you don't want to ink it, send ck— RUSH is more than 45 $—

#3

Barry— pencil & ink for the phone bill

Above: *Cover design by Marie Severin for Conan #3. Note the comments regarding the transatlantic phone bill. Conan ©1998 Conan Properties.*

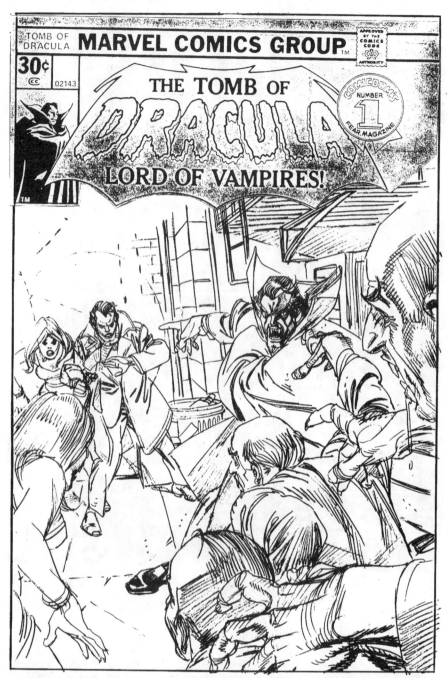

Above: *Gil Kane's pencils for the cover of* Tomb of Dracula #25. *Gil was one of Roy's favorite collaborators and cover artists.* ©1998 *Marvel Entertainment.*

trouble was that after the splash page, it's a very quiet beginning; basically Valeria rides into a glade, dismounts and stands around; until Conan joins her, nothing happens for two or three pages. Stan just thought that it was a very quiet beginning and I said, "Yes, that's why we have the symbolic splash page. But that's the story: it's beautiful and Barry and I want to adapt it straight." But Stan didn't like it too much. So when the sales figures for *Savage Tales* #2 came in—and they were *very* good—I proudly went into Stan's office and said, "Look, Stan, the book sold real well even though it had a quiet beginning." He just looked at me and grimaced, saying, "It would have sold even better if you'd had some action in it!" He was right; if I had been starting a story on my own, I would have not started that quietly for *ST* #2. With a title like *Savage Tales,* Stan wanted the stories nice and savage in the beginning, but I didn't feel like messing around with one of Robert E. Howard's better stories and a beautiful scene like that.

CBA: *Did you think that "Red Nails" was going to be that final collaboration between you and Barry?*

Roy: At the time, we talked about the possibility of doing some more work together. But with Barry, I was used to his quitting. This was about his third time around. First he quit *Conan* and Gil did two issues, then he quit the color comic after "Song of Red Sonja." He did do part of a "Bran Mak Morn" story later (which Tim Conrad finished). My idea with Barry was to take it as it comes, because you get out of Barry what you're going to get out of him, and if he says he's going to do it forever, you can't believe that; and if he's going to quit, you can't believe *that!* Who knows what any of us wants to do in a few months?

CBA: *Were you involved in the development of Howard the Duck?*

Roy: No, I was involved in *killing* him. Steve Gerber came up with this character that, he wrote, "vaguely resembles a duck." When I saw it, I thought it was cute, but I was a little worried— foolishly so—that it might detract from this horror book. So I told Steve to kill him off and get him out of there. We knew that he could bring Howard back even if the character was officially killed off. Steve wasn't too wild about it but he did it, but later on I realized that it was a crazy thing for me to do. So I offered Steve a spot in the *Arrghh!* comic I was putting together but by then he was using him in the *Man-Thing* giant books. Those issues of *Howard the Duck* sold well when Frank Brunner was drawing it, but somehow when Gene Colan took over, the sales just dropped.

CBA: *Where do you get off doing "Son of Satan"?*

Roy: Well, there's a story, as there usually is. Actually, I think I saved Marvel from itself with that one: We were doing all of this horror stuff, *Dracula* was reasonably popular, so the next step is, hey, if Dracula can do it, maybe Satan can, too! So Stan had this title, *The Mark of Satan,* and *that* was going to be the book with Satan as the villain. I just didn't feel comfortable with that idea. It's one thing to do Mephisto, but another to do Satan. I wasn't crazy about the idea but I very rarely refused a direct order from Stan—the one time I did, I quit! [*laughs*] So I just tried to talk him out of it and said, "You know, Satan is going to be a hard sell. Religious groups won't like it, but what if you had a character that was the son of Satan?" Stan said, "That's great. Let's do that, then." So I went off and did it (and only later realized that, several years earlier, Biljo White, the fan artist/publisher/editor of *Batmania,* had actually done a character called Son of Satan. It was pretty similar to what we had come up with, though Gary Friedrich and Herb Trimpe had as much to do with that as I, and they never saw the old fanzine). So I figure I saved Marvel Comics from having a book called *The Mark of Satan,* which I don't think would've done us any good in the long run.

CBA: *Were you involved in getting the Planet of the Apes license?*

Roy: Oh, yeah. DC was already doing *Kamandi,* which was influenced by that movie, and *Planet of the Apes* had the highest ratings of any movie on TV at that time. It turns out that the

with me." So obviously, the problem with these guys working together was they each said what they wanted to do, but neither one paid attention to the other. Yet again, I was trying to get Stan and Denny together, but they were on such different levels that they just didn't communicate. "Black Brother" was published but it was changed a lot and it was quietly decided that this character would never appear again. [*laughs*] I don't think that Denny was too happy about it in the long run. It's the only thing from *Savage Tales* #1 that was never reprinted.

Because there were so many leftover copies of *Savage Tales* that didn't sell, they had hundreds of them sitting around the office, all baled up. They kept telling us to take these things home! Gradually a stack here and there would be taken home and I ended up with maybe a hundred which I eventually used to finance my move to California.

CBA: *What was your reaction to receiving Barry's pencils for "Red Nails"?*

Roy: It was a step up from his previous work, and he had been moving along in that direction, so they were more advanced and beautiful. They were great. But Stan and I had different viewpoints on that story. When I showed him the finished version, he loved the artwork but wasn't too wild about the pacing. The

weather wasn't very good the night it premiered on TV, so everyone stayed home and watched *Planet of the Apes*. So it really wasn't this great phenomenon on TV that they were banking on with the subsequent TV series. I had a meeting with the licensing people and said, "We can't give a lot of money for this." They liked the idea of having a comic book, so the next thing we know, we're off and running. The real trouble started when George Tuska was drawing it.

CBA: *How so?*

Roy: We knew from the very beginning that we could not use Charlton Heston's likeness. So I told Tuska that and he came through for us. As usual, we were running a little bit late and we hadn't had a chance to get the book approved by the studio. We sent it out there but they hadn't done anything about it yet. It was just sitting there, so Stan told me to talk to the lawyer and do what he says. I spoke to our attorney and he says, "Send the book out—it'll be okay." So I did. Then we got this letter from 20th Century-Fox which said that one or two faces of the handsome hero looked too much like Heston and they weren't going to take a chance of having Heston sue them. They said we had to change it, but the material was already printed—so we had to destroy an entire section of the magazine and reprint it. They made the guy a blond with a moustache or something; they did whatever they could and it *never* looked liked Charlton Heston in a single panel to begin with! It cost a *lot* of money and, boy, was I lucky that I was covered by talking to the lawyer like they told me to. The funny thing is that the *Planet of the Apes* magazine never sold worth a damn! They had nothing but disaster with that book! In fact, somebody lost their job (after I was gone) because somebody stuck the same month date on the cover of two separate issues; so one had a shelf life of three minutes!

CBA: Spidey Super Stories. *Was that Stan's project?*

Roy: The Electric Company people came to us and said that they wanted to do a comic. I got my wife, Jean, to write it and she did a good job. It wasn't a big seller but was a prestige book to be associated with the Children's Television Workshop. It's just

unfortunate that there wasn't much of a market for kids.

If there was one thing that I felt I knew, it was balloon placement so that the eye is led from one to another. I was helping Jeannie to set up the pages, and was happy the way it was turning out (because, after all, we never had more than two balloons in a panel for *Spidey Super Stories,* anyway). But The Electric Company had their eye-movement-monitoring machine and said, "We take kids in here and they read *this* way." I said, "Well, I've been writing comics for years and I don't think your machine is right." So we would go around and around about balloon placement. Of all the weird things to be arguing about!

CBA: Bill Everett's tenure on Sub-Mariner, *the character that he created—were you involved in getting him back that comic?*

Roy: I don't know. He was just as likely to have gone to Stan to get that. But if Stan hadn't given him permission, I would've. Everybody up there who was an editor was a sucker for Bill Everett. Even Martin Goodman, who didn't have a lot of sentimental streaks, would forgive Bill anything and when someone would say that Bill's making a comeback, Goodman would just chuckle and say, "Bill is always making a comeback!" Everybody just had a soft-spot for Bill. They knew that he was a little too dissipated and that he smoked too much (which is probably what killed him more than anything), drank too much by his own admission, and goofed off a lot. But he was such a talented guy and there was just something about him that you liked. You'd give him a million tries. His last *Sub-Mariner* run didn't sell that well but he had some nice moments in that book, bringing in Namorita, a character that was totally ruined by later people.

CBA: *What's the story behind* Marvelmania?

Roy: I remember there was this guy named Steve—an energetic young man who seemed to really love Marvel. He was the hustler-type and—before that, there had been so many weird deals, like the time Chip Goodman told Stan that he had to go out to lunch with somebody because Chip had accidentally sold exclusive rights to something or other to two different people; things like that. We felt that we didn't have the right kind of projects and

Above: *Two of BWS & Roy Thomas' "dailies" for the fictional* Mandro the Barbarian *comic strip, used in Oliver Stone's 1981 film,* The Hand. *(Yes, that* Oliver Stone.*) Art ©1998 BWS.*

Above: Gil Kane's breakdowns to Marvel Premiere #2, pg. 2. Roy intended for Warlock to be martyred and then resurrected, a la Infinity Man/Forever People, by trading places with his four disciples. Art ©1998 Gil Kane. Warlock ©1998 Marvel.

mania organization; it *was* manic—manic-depressive. It had a lot of good intentions and a lot of ambition but somehow the guy just didn't have the expertise to put it together or the capital to give it what it needed. I just cooperated as best I could, and when the chance to sing on the Carnegie Hall stage came up, I said what the hell, you don't get a chance to do *that* every day. He did get some good people to appear: Chick Chorea, the jazz musician played; Tom Wolfe recited something I wrote; Rene Auberjonois, Will Jordan and Chuck McCann performed; but he couldn't quite pull it off and eventually Marvelmania just withered away.

CBA: *You and Stan seemed to attract the attention of some pretty mainstream and popular writers. For instance, how did you become connected with Tom Wolfe?*

Roy: I just loved Tom's stuff when I started reading it in the *New York Herald-Tribune* when I first moved to the city. I loved the New Journalism (and while Denny O'Neil was the real journalist, the only time I impressed him was when I brought Tom to the first ACBA meeting in early '71). Wolfe's book, *Electric Kool-Aid Acid Test,* had a lot of references to Marvel—to Dr. Strange and the Purple Dimension—so I contacted him by mail and asked him for permission to use him in an issue of *Dr. Strange.* He gave me permission, so I threw him into a few panels, and he wrote me this wonderful letter after the comic was published that for the next couple of years the most-asked question in his college lectures was how did he ever become a character in *Dr. Strange!* I was just amazed that we were able to use him! It was another thing I did to bring Marvel into the mainstream to attract older readers. Tom wasn't a dyed-in-wool Marvel reader but he had the connection through his book. Later, he gave me permission to use him in a *Hulk* comic based on *Radical Chic.* I just maintained contact with him during those brief years.

CBA: *With Marvel reaching out to the mainstream, how come a decent movie featuring Marvel characters has yet to be made?*

Roy: They just never managed to get hooked-up with the right people. One of the reasons was that Warner eventually ended up buying DC and, whatever flaws it may have, Warner is a class operation. Marvel was always just waiting for someone to come in and offer some money. When Marvel finally was bought by a movie company, it ended up being New World Cinema, which had its own problems. It just never quite worked out.

CBA: *Were you surprised at the similarities with "Star Wars" and some of Kirby and Stan's concepts?*

Roy: I don't know if George Lucas ever quite admitted it, but I got the impression in my conversations with him that there was a little influence there. I first had dinner with George about six months before I started to write the *Star Wars* comic. Ed Summer, who owned the Supersnipe Art Emporium (where George was evidently a silent partner), knew George from film school. The three of us went out to dinner in New York and I was impressed with him because he was the director of *American Graffiti,* one of my favorite movies. That's where I heard my first reference to a movie to be called *The Star Wars,* with a hero called either Luke Skywalker or Luke Starkiller. I didn't pay too much attention to it though they were talking about it. Months later, Ed brought George's right-hand man, Charles Lippincott, to ask me to talk Marvel into doing *Star Wars* which Marvel had evidently already turned down. They got me interested so I could convince Marvel to reconsider.

CBA: *Was it a fight to make Marvel change their mind?*

Roy: Not that much, once I went in there, because I assumed I was going to lose. After all, they had already rejected the idea but I said that we were getting the license to a big movie from a big studio virtually for free. We weren't going to pay anything— science-fiction didn't have a history of selling. (Martin Goodman always had his three things that he wouldn't allow to be used: Rockets, ray-guns and robots. When he saw all those elements in a "Starhawks" story we were preparing, he cancelled the book, *Marvel Super-Heroes!*) I did have some fights: a very nice, talented man, circulation director Ed Shukin was really down on the

Steve had this idea to become the face of Marvel to the media through *Marvelmania* magazine, and branch out into a million different directions.

CBA: *Did the Merry Marvel Marching Society just become too big to handle in-house?*

Roy: Stan's idea was for this tiny club that promoted the magazines but Stan didn't have the expertise or desire to handle a big publicity thing. And nobody would come along to do it properly. First, there was that almost animation-less animation show, and Marvel felt like it needed something more. So, Steve showed up and he seemed the answer to our prayers. He had a million plans for stuff to do—wallpaper, everything I suppose—and the only things to bear fruit were the *Marvelmania* magazine and the January 5, 1972 "A Marvel-ous Evening with Stan Lee." It was a sell-out (maybe in every sense of the word) and Steve really hustled to get that together, yet it never seemed to properly come together. For example, he got this whole show together and yet the sound equipment wasn't working properly when Barry, Herb Trimpe, the drummer (who was supposed to be Gary Friedrich but he was stuck in a snowstorm) and I, as singer, tried to perform our prearranged banter; the lighting wasn't rehearsed; and the show just sort of limped along. It was indicative of the whole Marvel-

134

Star Wars project—probably one of his few errors—and he kept wanting to cancel it. He asked me if I could do the adaptation in one or two issues to get it out of the way and not lose money on it. So I said if he wanted to have somebody else do it, I'll drop out; but if I was doing it, it had to be five-six issues. It was Lucas and Lippincott who wanted Chaykin to do it.

CBA: *So George was following comics that closely?*

Roy: I think that they were influenced by some of Chaykin's science-fiction work, "Iron Wolf." And George was a big fan of Jack Kirby's work.

The first time I saw "Star Wars" was a rough cut in George's private screening room in February 1977, about three months before the movie opened. He flew me, Chaykin, and Steve Leialoha out to California. We saw the movie, which didn't have the special effects inserted yet, but World War II dogfight footage; lines drawn to show the ray-gun blasts; Darth Vader had a Scottish accent; and it had a whole different crawl at the beginning. That crawl was used in the comic book and fans would write in, "How dare you have a different crawl!" But we prepared the comic four months before the film's release. That was part of the deal: They would give us the license practically for free, but wanted two to three issues out before the film's release because, contrary to popular legend, there was almost no advance publicity.

CBA: *Obviously you had faith in the film, but did you feel it would become that big?*

Roy: If it came together, I thought it was going to be a real good movie. Even sitting there, watching a rough cut without the music on a smaller screen, it was really an experience to see that oft-imitated opening sequence for the first time—when this big ship is being chased by a *huge* ship. That sets the tone for the movie that it's on a vast scale, and you have to be impressed by that. You could just see that a lot of thought had gone into the story.

I never really got into what the hell was going on in the story. Up in my apartment, when Charlie Lippincott was telling me all these names—Luke Skywalker, the planet Tatooine, C3PO, R2D2, Obi-wan Kenobi, Chewbacca, Han Solo—and flashing Ralph McQuarrie drawings, my mind was just overwhelmed! I couldn't tell what was going on! All I knew was that, when he flipped over a drawing of the "Cantina Sequence," it had the look of *Planet Stories,* a pulp magazine which I loved as a kid. It was space opera and by the space Cantina sequence, I was sold. So I went in and turned around Marvel's decision.

CBA: *Was Al Landau the right man for the job of Marvel's President as far as you were concerned?*

Roy: I just know that we never agreed on anything, but maybe I wasn't the right guy to be editor-in-chief either, so I can't really judge how good his decisions were. We didn't get along personally and we were never, except once or twice, on the same side of any single argument.

CBA: *What kind of arguments would you have?*

Roy: We just had different attitudes about dealing with creators. Even though I had always accepted the situation when I came in—work for hire, etc.—I thought that we should try to do more for the creators. Stan and I wanted to give the original artwork back to the artists, even though we weren't the first company to do it (nor the last). Stan wanted to get employees pension benefits and make our comic book company seem more like a real business. I don't think that Landau had any appreciation for that because all of these things cost money.

CBA: *Why did Landau leave?*

Roy: I really don't know because by that time I was gone. I know that Landau was why I left! [*laughs*] He was one of the reasons I was dissatisfied with the job. He cancelled my trip to the Phillipines because he felt it was a plum for me; like I wanted to fly there for one day! Because I was Editor-in-Chief, Stan would try to maintain a kind of benevolent neutrality and let me fight it out with Landau, so that was a problem too because that would always be an unequal fight. I was Editor-in-Chief but that was not

the job then that it would become in the next few years when Stan got more withdrawn. When I had the job, Stan still acted in the same capacity as Editor-in-Chief. The position would gradually grow until Jim Shooter assumed the role as the most powerful Editor-in-Chief. I was more like Perry White than some executive editor. That was a part of the frustration: To the rank and file, I was management and yet, quite often, I was on their side but I couldn't express it because of my position.

CBA: *In the early '70s, Jack Kirby came out with a real scathing satire of Stan and you, with "Funky Flashman and Houseroy."*

Roy: Most satires have some accuracy to them. If you're going to satirize a relationship, at the core is something real and it may get distorted to the point that it doesn't depict the true relationship. Jack was living out of Manhattan and rarely coming in—the last few years all the way out in California—so he wasn't seeing us from close at hand. What he saw was me (or somebody else if I wasn't there) as a flunkie, and what the hell, I was and anybody in that job would have been one too.

CBA: *So you don't see it as such an attack on you personally, but your position?*

Roy: I didn't see it as particularly personal because the relation-

Above: *How's this for an art team? Barry Windsor-Smith pencils with Neal Adams' inks. Neal kinda gets lost in this rare turn, huh? Your guess is as good as ours on what this was drawn for. Art ©1998 BWS and Neal Adams. [Courtesy of the Michael Thibodeaux Collection.]*

ship between me and Stan wasn't totally unlike that but that's only to the extent that you consider Jack's picture of Stan accurate. My character, Houseroy, was only there as a cipher, somebody to talk to, to be a toadie, and eventually abandoned by Flashman. It was kind of mean-spirited and warped out of recognition. I did love the name Houseroy, which was cute, but it hurt to some degree. But I realized that Jack didn't know what he was talking about and was just putting me in to fit the role. Besides, I was a sympathetic character because I get sacrificed!

CBA: *When Jack came back in the '70s, do you think he got a fair shake from the editorial staff? There was some talk of disparaging remarks written on xeroxes of his art taped to walls.*

Above: *As seen on pgs. 148-149, here's another Barry Windsor-Smith pencil page featuring an unrealized super-hero team of Bucky, Red Raven, and Quicksilver proposed by Roy and BWS in the late '60s, but never got off the ground. Art ©2000 BWS. Bucky, Quicksilver, Red Raven ©2000 Marvel Characters, Inc.*

Roy: I never saw any of that. Some doubted whether he should be writing these books. When Stan asked me what I thought of Jack coming back (he didn't name specific names, but Stan knew that there were people who were not wild about Jack returning), I said, "First, I think it's great; you should have Jack back under any circumstances. Second, don't let him write." Even though Jack had written good material back to the '40s and up to *The New Gods,* I didn't think it was going to work out from a sales viewpoint if he wrote. I didn't think the readers would like it, but Stan said, "Part of the deal is that he is going to write." I thought that it was still better to have Jack back, even if he wrote, than not at all. Stan said that's how he felt and, though the decision was made anyway, he was glad to have me confirm it.

CBA: *When we say "writing," we're saying dialoguing, right?*

Roy: Yeah, because everybody knew that Jack plotted. When I was going to do the *Fantastic Four* in the mid-'70s, I offered Jack plotting credit with his name first, but he just didn't want to do it. He said that he would do it if I did a panel-by-panel breakdown for him, but I thought that was ridiculous. Doing that, we'd have had such a closed-off kind of relationship, it wasn't worth doing. So I dropped the idea. Doing a panel-by-panel breakdown, I might as well get Rich Buckler or Sal Buscema to draw *like* Kirby. If you didn't get Jack's mind, his drawing didn't make too much difference by then because by then, everybody drew like him anyway! What you needed was Jack's thinking and enthusiasm.

CBA: *Why did you quit as editor-in-chief?*

Roy: First of all, the reason I quit was *not* the reason I quit; it was the excuse. I pretty much covered the specifics in *The Comics Journal* interview in the early '80s. It just got to the point where I really wasn't enjoying the job enough. I had to come to the office

five days a week, after doing it for two or three days a week for several years; just the hassle of being a part of management and not being a part. After a couple of years, I had had it, so all I needed was an excuse. In the meantime, because Stan was feeling caught between the internal disputes of Landau and me (which basically amounted to whether I was or wasn't a company man; to which the answer was increasingly "no," not a good situation for the editor-in-chief), a situation arose where I was asked to do something I just refused to do. Stan and I just agreed to part company on a pretty friendly basis. There was no hostility and Stan felt my memo expressing my refusal should be considered my letter of resignation. I said, "Sure, okay." My thoughts immediately flashed to quitting the company entirely, but we got very friendly, and discussed making me a writer/editor. It was as friendly a parting as could be, that let Stan out of a bad situation because he was caught in between a real animosity between Landau and me.

After I quit, my first wife, Jean, put it very well when she said, "I always knew that you wouldn't keep that job too long and that you didn't really like it." I said, "Why's that?" because I hadn't really said a lot about my discontent other than the usual grumbling. "Well, you had that little office with a window for two years, but you never put up any pictures or do anything to personalize it. It was always like you were just getting ready to move out." I suppose that's true and I guess I never really felt that I fit in there. I just wanted to get back to the creative side of comics. I never really thought about succeeding Stan at all; it just wasn't in my purview but all of the sudden it happened. I never really thought, "Hey, I'm going to be in charge of this place when Stan leaves," because one didn't think about Stan (only in his forties) as leaving anytime soon. So when it happened, I liked and didn't like certain aspects of the job, but eventually it got to be too much. I didn't like dealing with the business and advertising people and they didn't like me too much either, so it was just time to leave.

I've always felt that I was ruined for the job by Joseph Heller. Heller is my favorite living author (and he'll be my favorite when he dies) and I love his various works, especially *Catch-22.* About the second time I read that, I realized, as much as anything, the book is about bureaucracies and society in general. It's not really a war novel at all, except incidentally. I suddenly started seeing myself at Marvel, especially after I became editor-in-chief, as being all of the characters in that novel. I'd see myself as Major Major, trying to avoid seeing people (I would keep inviting Doug Moench up to the office when I thought I would have the time, but he would finally just go home); the whole Byzantine intrigues of the office; the bizarre ironies of that book made me realize that I really wanted to be Yossarian and set off on a raft for Sweden.

I can't even begin to say how strongly reading *Catch-22* made me unfit to be editor-in-chief of Marvel Comics, even though a year and a half later I was offered the job again and was all ready to go back in!

CBA: *In a perfect world, if you didn't have to deal with the problems of being management, would you do it again?*

Roy: Sitting in front of a monitor and just typing is kind of lonely and cold. I liked the office setting and the interaction. Sure, I'd do it again. Especially if it meant working with Stan again—because, despite the fact that I've tried to cover the good, the bad, and the ugly about those days in this interview, working with and for Stan Lee was one of the greatest experiences of my life. I feel very lucky, not just because I've had a career in comic books for almost exactly a third of a century, but because I spent so much of that career working closely with a bunch of greatly talented artists and writers, and particularly with Stan. When 99% of the guys now ranked as "top ten" writers or artists by *Wizard* magazine are gone and forgotten, Stan Lee's influence—like that of Jack Kirby and Will Eisner and a bare handful of other people—will still be being felt in the comics field. ⚡

"The Mutant Blackhawks"
The Real Origin of the New X-Men

Editor's Note: *Al Landau, hired to replace a dissatisfied Stan Lee as Marvel's President, knew his business and that was international business. Sometime in 1974, he came up with possibly his only vaguely creative contribution to Marvel Comics, one that had a profoundly profitable impact on the company. But let's—in typical CBA style—have the participants relate it. First up, Roy in his talk with Stan:*

Roy Thomas: Al Landau did do one great thing for Marvel.
Stan Lee: What was that?
Roy: It was he who suggested in 1974, not too long before I stepped down as Editor-in-Chief, that if we had a comic book that featured heroes from the various countries where Marvel sold its pages, we could probably do really well with it. I said, "Hey, what if we brought back the X-Men, with a guy from Canada, etc.?" Again, I suspect he was thinking as much of his other company Trans World as anything. Still it was a good idea… So you have to give Al credit for that, at least in part.

Next, a word with Mike Friedrich:

CBA: *Were you involved in the creation of the new X-Men?*
Mike Friedrich: There's actually quite a story there: I met Dave Cockrum in the lobby at DC when he had just left the Navy. He was showing his portfolio to DC and, I think, from showing that portfolio is how he got the job doing the "Legion of Super-Heroes."

Afterwards I stayed in touch with him and, sometime in 1972, he showed me his idea for the *New X-Men* that he described as a reworking of the old Blackhawk idea. I set up a lunch meeting with Dave and Roy Thomas for him to show the stuff to Roy. I remember very clearly where it was — two or three blocks from Marvel was the General Motors building and in the first floor there was a restaurant that had a classic automobile theme to it. Roy liked that place a lot. We ate, and showed Dave's work. Roy liked the idea and said he would try to talk Stan into doing it with the idea that I would be the writer of it. It took a long time before that approval came down, and at this point, I had moved back to California. As I remember the story, Roy had stopped being the editor-in-chief and Len Wein had become the new editor-in-chief and Len, somehow or other, got involved with Dave and assigned himself to be the writer of the first issue. I had a conversation with Roy about this recently. He doesn't remember any of this.

CBA: *But he did recall that you were at the birth of this idea?*
Mike: It may be because I reminded him. Len and I have never talked about it. We see each other a couple times a year but that's one of the things that Len and I have never talked about. It was always a little bit of a sore point with me because I thought I got gypped out of a really fun series.
CBA: *Who came up with idea for an international group?*
Mike: That was Dave's concept from the beginning. The characters that were introduced in that first issue were all Dave's he had showed me and I showed to Roy. There were minor modifications, as I recall, but all of the characters were there. I don't know who had the idea that one of the characters got killed right off but the whole international thing was Dave's idea.

CBA: *Did you make any contributions to the concept?*
Mike: No. I didn't add anything to the concept and didn't get involved in it at all.

Finally, we talk to Dave Cockrum:

CBA: *Mike Friedrich told me a story that back in 1972 you had an idea for an international team book that eventually turned into the new X-Men. Is that true?*
Dave Cockrum: It wasn't my idea. Roy brought up the idea that he wanted to do a new X-Men book but he was talking about approaching it as "Mutant Blackhawks." That was Roy's suggestion when he took us to a fancy restaurant, telling us to order whatever we wanted—he had a hamburger. That was Roy's proposal: He wanted them international and to operate out of a secret base. Part of the rationale, as I understand it, was that Marvel was looking for foreign markets. And then, ultimately, we picked a bunch of nationalities whose countries weren't liable to buy the book! It never wound up fitting that proposal anyway.
CBA: *After that, how long you go to work on the proposal?*
Dave: I had gone home and started designing some characters, but for some reason, there was a pause in the development, and they just "hung fire" for months. When it came back, Mike Friedrich wasn't involved any more but Len Wein was. I had drawn up a number of characters: The original Black female in the group was to have been called The Black Cat. She had Storm's costume but without the cape, and a cat-like haircut with tufts for ears. Her power was that she could turn into a humanoid cat or a tabby. She wore a collar with a bell on it. When we came back to the project, after the hiatus, all of a sudden all of these other female cat characters had sprung up—Tigra, The Cat, Pantha—so I figured that we'd better overhaul this one! She wound up getting white hair, the cape, and becoming Storm.
CBA: *Where did Nightcrawler come from?*
Dave: When I was still a fan and in the Navy, my first wife and I were living on Guam in a house in the boonies (which was infested with roaches and rats). There was a terrible storm going on overhead, we had no lights, it was noisy and loud and raining like hell with thunder and lightning. To keep ourselves occupied and keeping ourselves from being scared to death, we sat around making up characters. We made up this duo, a guy I called the Intruder (a cross between the Punisher and Batman, with a chrome skull and black jumpsuit) and his demon sidekick, Nightcrawler. The original concept was a lot different in that Nightcrawler would howl at the moon, run up the sides of buildings and do all kinds of weird sh*t. He really was a demon who had screwed up on a mission from Hell and, rather than go back and face punishment, he hung around up here with this do-gooder. So he was considerably overhauled when he wound up in the X-Men. ⚡

Above: Gil Kane & Dave Cockrum's cover to the one that started it all—for better or worse! Giant-Size X-Men #1. Be here next issue for an indepth look at Neal Adams and the X-Men! First look at an abandoned X-Men graphic novel, and more! ©1998 Marvel Entertainment.

William Blake Everett

A Conversation with the Great Cartoonist's Daughter

Conducted by Mike Friedrich

Wendy Everett is the daughter of Bill Everett, creator of Sub-Mariner and one of Marvel's greatest artists. She lives in San Francisco and was interviewed by Mike Friedrich, Bill's friend, former Marvel scribe, and artist representative. This conversation took place after lunch in a San Francisco restaurant on June 20, 1998.

Mike Friedrich: *Did you go into the Marvel office with your dad often?*

Wendy Everett: I did. "Often" is relative, since when you're a kid, it's a full time job going to school. But I got to go into New York City a lot.

Mike: *When would this be?*

Wendy: From 1952 to probably 1960, the last year that he worked for Marvel.

Mike: *Did he work in the bullpen or at home?*

Wendy: Both. He had an office at home—he always had one. Even if he was going to New York—which he did a couple of times a week—he always still worked at home.

Mike: *I know this is a big topic, but can you describe what it felt like?*

Wendy: The artists lived a pretty wild life. After you called me to set up this interview, I went back and reread some of articles that have profiled my dad over time. I was reading these pieces and there was very little distinction between the fancifulness of how they perceived their lives and their work. This is a great example: I'm reading a several page interview with my dad and someone is asking him about the origin of Daredevil. They asked Dad if he created any other characters. He said, "Yes, I did." And he named such-and-such character and in his regular, daily life, his name was Bob Blake. So the interviewer asks, "How did you come up with that?" Either the reporter made this up or my father—which is much more likely—in a slightly baldfaced way, said, "Well, I named him after my brother, Robert, and William Blake, because Blake was a relative." Well, William Blake was a relative; my father's name is William Blake Everett and was descended from Blake. But I'm sitting there, saying *"Uncle Bob*? I have no '*Uncle Bob*'!"

Mike: *"I don't remember an Uncle Bob…"* [laughs]

Wendy: There *was* no Uncle Bob. Nice try! You read it and think, "Ohh, isn't that charming! Totally charming!" It was just "what they did."

It was almost as if he came back from the grave! I was waiting for one of these "gotchas!" I'm sitting there thinking that this is a national publication and this guy says the character was named for his brother Bob! As a kid, it makes you question your own reality, because your reality is not exactly in sync with theirs.

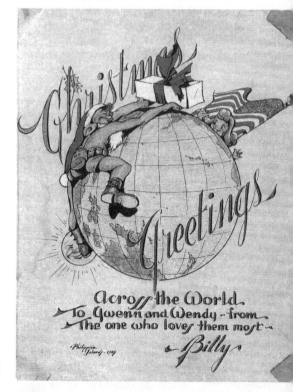

Mike: *Do you think being related to William Blake influenced your dad?*

Wendy: It did. One of the things that you know well but that people outside the industry don't understand is that the people who wrote and drew comics *knew* mythology, and *knew* the historical characters. They had read the classics. All of those characters, that we as kids were just kind of reading just to be entertained, had this great mythological background. It's true (as anything can be true that my father ever thought or said), that the Sub-Mariner was based on the "Rime of the Ancient Mariner" by Samuel Coleridge. He *had* read Coleridge and this background gave the characters a very erudite wholeness.

Mike: *As a kid, was it cool that your dad did comics?*

Wendy: As a kid it doesn't matter. When you're six, seven, eight, nine, ten, it didn't matter what anybody's father does. You don't know if he's a doctor or a lawyer—you're worried about Cub Scouts. But, as you might recall (knowing the history backwards and forwards), Timely was close to being blacklisted by the PTA. We were in an interesting situation. I would come home after school and sit with my dad. He had a studio set up at home, with a drawing board, taboret, and all his supplies. I'd sit there and watch him draw. At the same time, I heard the PTA call up my mother to get her to sign petitions banning all comic books. So my parents didn't exactly advertise that he worked for the business that the PTA had blacklisted.

And I was indifferent one way or another. I didn't spend a lot of time reading comics. The way that they were drawn back then was on these huge white boards and my father taught me how to letter. (This is probably stuff that Stan never needs to know

bout.) I was good. My dad would do the pencils and say, "Okay, want you to letter." I'm eight… and nine… and ten. [*laughter*]

Mike: *Do you remember what kind of comics they were?*

Wendy: The *Sub-Mariner* comics. Some of them were war and horror stories. I can't quite remember when *Namora* came out but it may have been about that time. My dad would always be under deadlines and almost never made them. My parents were very social and partied quite a lot. My father came from a 300-year-old New England family. Everett, Massachusetts, is named after his great grandfather, who was also a president of Harvard University and became governor of Massachusetts. This guy grew up very privileged. My parents got a $20,000 inheritance when one of his uncles died. They spent the entire thing in one weekend. It was very wild. So he never got anything done on time and, of course, Stan or Martin Goodman would call him up, and hammer him. We would have to get out nine days of work in two days. It was not this great family bonding but that I could do lettering fairly quickly! [*laughs*] We had a really great, terrific time. I would just stand there and watch him draw and then go off and do something. There was never any "Gee, Daddy's working so we can't go in there." It was always, "Hey, what are you doing?" In that regard, he really liked having us around.

Mike: *Did he bring comics home, other than the ones he did?*

Wendy: He probably did. I was a pretty avid reader but I wasn't a big comic book reader. When you see them being done, you don't necessarily want to see them again just because they're in color. The important thing was the story. I loved to *read* read, but we always had comics around and they weren't a big deal. It was just life.

Mike: *Were there people that he knew from work that he met socially at the house?*

Wendy: He was more part of a suburban commute. We lived in northern New Jersey and occasionally went over to John Severin's house because John was married and had kids—the cutest little kids that were about my brothers' ages. Marie would come over and we would do things with them. But my parents had their own social set of friends who weren't related to work. Once every three weeks, he went into New York to deliver work and would take me with him. Once it was delivered and the pressure was off, everybody would either go to Schrafft's or the Algonquin, and he'd take me along. That started when I was about eight years old.

Mike: *Who did you meet at this point?*

Wendy: There was John and Marie, Johnny Romita, Stan, and whoever else was there at that time. Marie was the only woman then so I particularly remember her. John Severin was really a sweet guy or at least sweet to me. I'd go and they'd drink all afternoon, keep buying me Shirley Temples. I'd take a book and sit in the Algonquin while they caroused, drank and told stories.

Mike: *Were they telling comic book stories or…?*

Wendy: Everything. They blurred the boundaries. They lived their work: They created new characters. One of the fun things would be when my dad would sit and talk to me about characters. I very clearly remember Daredevil. The two of us talked about what should happen to him, what should his tragic flaw be, and how should he get it. Whether he should be a doctor or not (I think he ended up being a lawyer). Should he be blind or not. I was always legally blind, but corrected. Because I'd never been able to see well, I have a very finely attuned sense of

hearing and sound. So when someone comes down the hall, I know who it is. We took that and played with it. There were no boundaries between work and life; everything that happened got incorporated into the work—all of the time.

Mike: *Were you aware why he didn't continue with Daredevil? You spend all that time coming up with that one character and then that's it, he's off the book after one issue.*

Wendy: Again, when you're that age, you're pretty involved with your own life. The way that it was presented in the family was that he was offered a job to be the art director for Norcross Greeting Cards. So it was more that he was going to do something else. It didn't seem strange. Another one of the things about being the kid of an artist—and one that is so prolific and talented—is that he'd create art for us all of the time. When I was young and went to camp, every week he would send me one of those old Manila postcards and draw these *fabulous* cartoons that would depict what happened at home that week. So one would have a swimming pool with my brothers in it, and he'd put the dog in the middle. You know, *no one* in camp ever got anything like that and, of course, because they were postcards, everyone else at camp got to read it before I did.

Every time there was a birthday, Mother's Day, or other celebration, he would create a big card. It wasn't just that the artwork was good; it was the writer in him, as well. He would create a funny story just out of some "nothing" thing that happened at home and make it into some unbelievable creation! So for him to go and be the art director for a big greeting card company made perfect sense because that's what he did. I assumed that either Martin or Stan fired him, even though I never exactly knew, and he went and he got another job. He was not the least bit suited to be in a business environment. But no, it never dawned on me to consider why he didn't continue with *Daredevil*.

Mike: *There was that tragic time in 1957 when everyone got fired at Marvel overnight. I think your dad was part of that process. How much of that do you recall?*

Wendy: Not very much. They always landed on their feet. They were all a part of the Marvel Bullpen but they were also freelancers. It was a kind of loose association. They usually found the money to survive. My dad was so thoughtless about money. He grew up

continued on page 161

All the photos and drawings illustrating the following two articles appear courtesy of Bill Everett's only daughter, Wendy. They arrived (with the much-appreciated help of Mike Friedrich) without comment, but speak volumes as to the sort of sentimental, playful and affectionate man Bill must have been. Our enormous gratitude to Wendy for sharing such intensely personal affects. We hope this tribute goes some way in expressing our love for the man and his work. All material ©1998 Wendy Everett.

A Friend of Bill

Talking to Mike Friedrich about Not-So-"Wild" Bill Everett

Conducted by Jon B. Cooke

Mike Friedrich is probably best known for his work at DC during the late '60s and early '70s, but he also wrote prolifically for Marvel from 1972-75. He also created Star*Reach, the "above ground" comic book line, and currently is an artists' representative under the same name. Mike was interviewed in May 1998 via telephone.

Comic Book Artist: *When did you first meet Bill Everett?*

Mike Friedrich: I believe it was in either 1968 or 1969 in New York City. Bill knew Dave Kahler, who I roomed with on the Upper West Side during my summer breaks from college. Dave had this basement apartment, piled to the ceiling with old newspapers (he swore that some day he was going to tear the comic strips from them).

I remember that Bill came to New York for one of Phil Seuling's July 4th conventions. Bill had just started inking "Nick Fury" over Steranko's pencils. Steranko had announced this at the convention. Bill must have known Dave somehow because he crashed at the apartment during the con and there's where I met him. A year later he came and shared the apartment with Kahler. They had the place together for a couple of years, so I roomed with the two of them for the summers of '69 and '70.

When I graduated from college in 1971, Bill had his own apartment and the two of us decided to get one together in the Upper East Side at 81st and Second. Bill was very active in Alcoholics Anonymous at this time, and he met a woman who became his girlfriend and I got kicked out. [*laughter*]

So then I would visit regularly. By the summer of 1972, I moved back to California, and by the fall Bill had gotten sick. He had an operation, and it killed him.

CBA: *He died during the operation?*

Mike: I think what happened is that he had a heart attack and was in bed. I know that he was sick and not doing well, when I came to visit him in January 1973. I knew that he was dying at this point. And he went in for this operation and died in the hospital. I was told that it wasn't the drinking that killed him; it was the smoking. His lungs failed. Bill was a very heavy smoker the entire time I knew him.

CBA: *The ravages of drinking and smoking weakened him?*

Mike: Oh, yeah. He was not that old—at least, it seems to me now! [*laughs*] I wasn't conscious that Bill was a physically weak person when I knew him. The psychological damage was much more significant. His self-confidence in his own work was nil. There were all these young guys, my age, trying to convince Bill that he was still a really good artist—I remember Steve Gerber trying to pump him up and Steve wound up writing Bill's *Sub-Mariner* stories—and I remember looking at Bill's stuff and I really liked it. I thought that there was still something there that was fun to look at.

For some reason, at that time Stan had a problem with Bill's artwork (and I now don't remember what the problem was, but it certainly didn't look like Jack Kirby's or John Buscema's work) but Bill couldn't draw any other way than the way he drew. Nonetheless, Marvel took care of him and kept him busy. As long as Bill could meet his deadlines, Marvel kept him working. Martin Goodman paid his health insurance policy which was good all the way to the end. They went out of their way to treat him right.

CBA: *Creatively, Bill had a pretty unique status at Marvel as writer/artist/inker on his short run of '70s Sub-Mariners.*

Mike: Very few people at Marvel did that. Steranko did it and that was about it.

CBA: *As a kid, I saw Bill as refreshing and original. His death hit me like a ton of bricks when I was 14 years old; it was the first time I dealt with death in my hobby, and I was an enormous fan of that Sub-Mariner work.*

Mike: Bill was the first grown-up friend of mine that died and it was tough for me as well.

CBA: *What was Bill working on when you knew him?*

Mike: Bill was inking *Thor* over Kirby's pencils and working on *Millie the Model*, inking over Stan Goldberg. There was a brief period when I did background effects inking for Bill on some of those Thor pages. Kirby did all these weird little background effects and I'd fill in the blacks on 'em. (It wasn't actually inking but filling in the blacks.) That was my one and only work as a professional artist.

CBA: *[laughs] What did Bill think of Jack's work?*

Mike: Bill was always complaining about it because it made no sense. It had this internal logic so the only thing Bill could do was ink what was there. It may have made sense in and of itself, but he said these are not real people; not real perspective. So Bill just tried to give it whatever he could, but he didn't say that it was great stuff. It was a job to him. At this point, his personal self-esteem was very low and I think he felt that this was the only work that he could get, and he was happy to have it. It's not that he hated it—he was at least being an artist and getting paid for it.

CBA: *He did "Dr. Strange" for a while and did "Sub-Mariner" and "Hulk" in Tales to Astonish. He would seem to come and go.*

Mike: He was constantly working through that whole time for Marvel. I think he did a lot of *Patsy Walker* stuff. He inked the *Thor* material fairly straight through. I don't remember the other work that well, but he certainly was working to whatever capacity he had. They kept him busy.

CBA: *When he was doing his own penciling and inking, was there a time when it was difficult to meet his deadlines?*

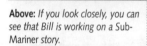

Above: *If you look closely, you can see that Bill is working on a Sub-Mariner story.*

For the uninitiated: *Check out Bill's short but glorious run on the '70s Sub-Mariner for a very inexpensive peek at his charming stories. Many issues between #50-60 have his writing, pencils & inks.*

Mike: Not that I'm aware of. I know that it was very difficult for him creatively—he had a very hard time getting into it. He said that it was very slow and he didn't like the results. I think that he did do two or three issues of *Sub-Mariner* before he got ill, pencils and inks, monthly—pretty damn good in my book.

The deadline problem he had was earlier because of his drinking. That was the reason that he never continued with *Daredevil* after drawing the first issue. He was unreliable when he was drinking.

CBA: *Did he ever discuss his earlier days at Timely?*

Mike: A bit. He told a version of a story that Steranko had in his *History of Comics* of there being this deadline of this massive weekend where everybody had gotten into one room—like 12 people doing a 64-page comic between a Friday and a Monday. It was not consistent with the version that Steranko printed. (His daughter, Wendy, would tell me that Bill would tell stories that wouldn't make sense all of the time. She remembers him talking about his brother Bob only he didn't have a brother Bob!)

He told me this story of creating Sub-Mariner when a publisher told him that Burgos had created this fire guy and we want something else to go after Superman. Bill said, "Fire and water," and came up with Sub-Mariner. He said, in the late '60s, that he didn't realize how much of an angry young man *he* was in the '40s, and when he read his stuff later he could see that Sub-Mariner was himself as a very upset young man. He expressed that anger through these stories. That's about as close as he got. I didn't get a lot of stories from him. He generally said that he didn't remember much of it and that the drinking had taken all the memories away.

CBA: *Did you two get along?*

Mike: We were very good friends, which is why we agreed to get an apartment together.

CBA: *What was Bill like?*

Mike: For me at that age (20-22), the thing about him was that he was just very accepting. He was very easy to get along with, not very demanding, cooperative—we kept the place clean and we cooked; all the stuff that you need to do when you don't have a helluva lot of money. But we didn't go out often, though we would occasionally go out for a bite to eat together at a coffee shop. He worked during the day and had AA meetings about three nights a week. Occasionally he would see friends from there. I went to one of his AA meetings over near Columbus Circle and it reminded me of the encounter groups I was in during college, so it seemed like old home week to me. I got right into it, and it was my introduction to 12-Step programs. That was interesting.

In retrospect, the fact I was interested in his life at AA and the fact that I went to that meeting must have impressed him.

CBA: *Bill was very active in AA. Was he a sponsor?*

Mike: I presume so. He said that he needed it for himself, absolutely, and he credits AA with turning him around. He met a lot of friends from there and, apparently I'm told, that at the funeral service, there were more AA people than comic book people. It was a pretty large turnout. The comics people were impressed that there were all of these total strangers.

CBA: *You don't think that he fully appreciated his own work?*

Mike: No. One of the very sad things was there wasn't anything that I could tell him to make him feel good about his own stuff.

CBA: *Do you think he always had this feeling?*

Mike: I couldn't tell you that. He dismissed fans. The opinions of fans to him were non-meaningful. These were kids so what did they know? Fans were fans. He remembered being a movie fan and he felt that as a professional, fans didn't mean anything.

CBA: *When you started living with him, Bill was in AA?*

Mike: Yes. He must have already been in the program by the time I met him.

CBA: *Did he credit any incident when the moment of clarity came for him to join AA?*

Mike: I have a vague memory of Bill talking about being on this gigantic bender and waking up three days later and he said, "That's it. I've hit bottom." But I couldn't put a time or place to it. I don't remember why he realized he'd hit bottom and why he didn't just keep drinking. He did talk about somebody who told him that AA was something that he needed to do.

CBA: *Were you interested in the lives of people who had long histories in comic books?*

Mike: Personally, no. I had a very high sense of my own self importance at the time—probably still do—and I was happy to meet these people as equals, fellow professionals. At that time, it was very hard for me to be a fan. I would be a fan of the stuff I liked but it was harder for me to be awed by the people who did the stuff.

And there was a huge generation gap at this point. I had a very difficult time talking to any grown-ups who were 20 years older. That's why Bill was very unique for me. So I didn't really get into trying to track down old history. It was later on when I got interested. Later on, I regretted the fact that I had those opportunities and hadn't done much with them.

CBA: *Was Roy Thomas pushing for Bill to do Sub-Mariner?*

Mike: Absolutely. He definitely was and, if anything, it was probably Roy's opinion that would have swayed Stan to go along with it, even though Stan might have thought that Bill's style was out of date. I can understand Stan's position—I didn't think that Stan was wrong, in this sense as Bill's style *was* an old style—but I *liked* the style. But I wasn't a 12-year-old reading comics, I was a grown-up. What was my opinion worth? [*laughs*] 💀

The Mark of Kane

An Interview with Marvel's Cover Man, Gil Kane

Comic Book Artist: *You sporadically did work for Marvel in the '60s but by 1970 they seemed to be your major source of income.*

Gil Kane: Yes. I had been doing work on and off for Marvel and they called me in to do *Captain Marvel*. *Captain Marvel* was killed after a few issues, I did some DC work for Joe Orlando. Then I got a call from John Romita, who wanted to leave as penciler of *Spider-Man* because it was becoming too much for him. He never wanted to be a full time penciler he wanted the *ex-officio* art director job as Stan's "fixer-upper" in the beginning. He had a little office and later became the art director.

CBA: *Marie Severin worked as his lieutenant, so to speak?*

Gil: Marie worked on staff; she penciled, she fixed up, she did covers, and things like that. But John was the chief fixer-upper, but he didn't layout covers for anybody else. Everyone did their own covers. What John did, and what Stan wanted him to do, was the promotion drawings on Spider-Man and the other characters. Stan liked John Romita's work better than John Buscema, and thought Romita drew the most beautiful women. (Stan told me that I was making the Hulk too ugly, but I said I was just copying Jack's look — which was Boris Karloff. He said, "No, no. Why can't he be nice looking?" And Marie took over the strip and made him nice-looking.)

CBA: *So Stan didn't give you enough work when you were there briefly in the '60s?*

Gil: I had never left DC when I first worked for Marvel. Things would just finish up at Marvel and I was not one of Stan's favorite artists. The only reason I got *Spider-Man* was because Romita left the book. Once I started to do *Spider-Man*, Stan started to move up in the company, and Roy Thomas became the editor, so I found my place in the starry sky. Then I started doing a million covers and I did a million strips with Roy. I did "Gulliver Jones," jungle stuff, covers, all the fill-in books, but the only regular strips I did were *Spider-Man* and *Warlock*. I had to leave those books because they would want me on the covers which paid more and were easier for me to do.

CBA: *Were you involved in the plotting of the* Spider-Man *drug issues?*

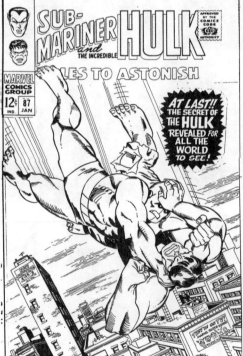

Above: *Gil's memorable run on The Hulk in* Tales to Astonish *was cut short because Stan thought Gil's Greenskin too ugly. ©1998 Marvel Entertainment.*

Gil: I was involved in the plotting but the idea of doing the drug issues wasn't my idea. As usual, the idea came from Stan. Then, when it came to actually structuring the story, the plot that you'd get from Stan was a couple of lines of conversation after which you'd have to flesh-out an entire story. You'd bring it in and he would say, "Jesus, I don't care too much for the way you did this character; he doesn't have any real strength." He held you responsible for the plotting. That's why Jack deserved a lot of the credit because he made up most of those characters and most of the plotting. When Stan would get those pages for the first time, they were all penciled with instructions written on the sides of the page as to what the characters were saying. What he did was to put in the dialogue. But, on the other hand, the quality of that sort of mock-irreverence, that was Stan. It was the balancing element.

Stan could be a good collaborator, but soon he had completely moved on.

CBA: *You arrived pretty much when Jack left in 1970.*

Gil: Actually, I started in '66 and was there on and off all through that period, so I saw Jack regularly. Then, by the time Jack left, I was a regular doing all the work that they could give me. I was still doing some occasional work for DC—*Green Lantern, The Hawk and the Dove*—because I was desperately in need of money. I had just gotten a divorce and had a studio so money was just going out like crazy. I was just doing *every-thing* that I could handle, so I was putting out more work than anybody (except *maybe* John Buscema). I did work for Tower, Gold Key, everybody; I worked all the time, seven days a week. I got to the point when I was just penciling to do three to four pages a day; when I was inking for myself, I could pencil seven pages in a day, and ink three to four pages without too much trouble. But once I inked seven pages in one day on a 37-page Conan story!

CBA: *There have been some incredible estimates of the amount of covers you did for Marvel…*

Gil: I was told by David Hamilton that I had done 800 covers for Marvel in the '70s. The majority of the covers were inked by others like John Severin, Bill Everett, and others. They always allowed me to ink my own western covers and, at first, I wasn't that great with the inking, but then I caught the hang of it. I think I turned out the *best* western cover I ever did; it's Kid Colt lying in a ditch of water, with his hand scooping the water up to his face —but in the water you can see the reflection of a gunman with a gun pointed at Kid. I was drawing like a son of a bitch in those days! I was practicing every frigging day—I practiced from photographs, plaster casts I had, models and other artists. I would take that day's newspaper and copy all the photographs; I got to the point where I could draw like a whiz.

Whenever I would have a period when Marvel wouldn't come through with a script because the writer was a couple of days late, I would call up Joe Orlando and see if he had work. Usually he would let me write one of my own and very often he would even let me ink it, so I was very happy with him.

CBA: *I've only recently been seeking out those Marvel western reprint books because of the astonishing work by you on the covers. What* horses!

Gil: After a while, I really laid into it! I was so sure of my drawing and close to the top of my form. I actually reached my peak immediately after that when I came to California and started doing animation. Through that Marvel period, I was really going. I did the *Starhawks* strip and the Sunday *Tarzan* page. I used to do the *Tarzan* page in one day, and after awhile it ran down. I structured the first episode and they didn't like my syntax so I called in Archie Goodwin to do the scripting. But it was my story based on Kipling's *Captains Courageous,* taking a spoiled kid who gets lost in the jungle and Tarzan teaches him to be unselfish and a good scout. The *Starhawks* daily was the equivalent in size to a comics page and that took me four days.

CBA: *You've called Roy Thomas a "perfect collaborator"?*

Gil: Yes. He was non-competitive when it came to structuring the material. If I had an idea for something—and I usually did—that was strong enough, we would usually go with it. That's the way we worked. The whole business of "Amazing-Man" was because I always kept bringing the character up because I never forgot that damned thing! Roy knew the character too, so we based so many strips on "Amazing-Man." So much came out of that. For instance, we decided to do a *King Kong* story under the guise of a *Spider-Man* comic; we put Jack Palance in as Morbius, the Living Vampire, and I have to say that we had a lot of fun. It was an absolute pleasure working with Roy.

I can't remember why I left *Spider-Man* after drawing it for well over a year, but something happened and Romita came back. Later I worked with Stan and it was not a good collaboration because he was very unhappy with me, though I don't know why. I thought I built up a nice style of my own on *Spider-Man*.

CBA: *Did you collaborate on the death of Gwen Stacy?*

Gil: I collaborated but it wasn't my idea. They had already wanted to kill her when I was assigned the material — my first Spider-Man job when I was called back.

CBA: *You were replaced by Ross Andru on the strip. When I was a kid, I couldn't see how good he was but many artists, including you, have gushed about how good his pencils were.*

Gil: He was a sensational artist! He only had a problem that was a characteristic of his work (nobody's perfect): His figures never seemed to move gracefully. Everything was so beautifully designed and so well drawn, but I never felt that he had a natural feeling for romantic action. But he didn't make any mistakes! I used to look at his stuff and it just boggled my mind how good he was! I still feel that way.

CBA: *Did you like Bill Everett's work?*

Gil: I liked Everett's work in the early days. In the later days, I thought he was an excellent inker; as a matter of fact, I thought that Bill's inking on Jack Kirby was the best inking that Jack ever got when he was at Marvel. Those *Thor* books were just beautifully inked, and he kept *all* of Jack's essence. At the same time, he beautifully finished everything up. I hated Vince Colletta's inks and never cared much for Joe Sinnott's inks.

CBA: *What did you think of Colletta's inks on your work?*

Gil: Vinnie used to erase anything that wouldn't allow him to finish by 12 noon. He would erase backgrounds, figures, anything, because he knew at noon, he was through for the day. He started at 6 A.M., worked until 12, *through.* Then he would come into the city and do his other business. The best inkers that I ever had were Dan Adkins, Wally Wood, and Kevin Nowlan.

CBA: *Did you like Neal Adams' inks?*

Gil: Of course, but he would transform the material! He would improve it to the point where all I was doing was little layouts for him. Neal had such facility and was such a supple artist. He was not only fast, but drew better than anyone, and he also had superb experience. He had done a lot of work in commercial advertising, learning how to adapt his stuff. I used to work same-size as the original paper, at first, *on* the paper, big. Then I'd take a piece of newsprint, same-size as the 10" x 15" page, and I would pencil on that first. So I would have a clean page when I would start to tighten up on a lightbox. Then I saw what Neal was doing; he was breaking down little thumbnails and could break down a whole story in one day! I learned by example from Neal. It expedited my work *enormously* and I also had more control over the page. I still mostly work that way.

CBA: *Weren't you involved with bringing Conan to comics?*

Gil: I was supposed to do *Conan* as a sister book to *His Name Is… Savage* in 1967. The guy who I thought owned the rights to it was my next door neighbor—his name was Marty Greenberg and he had a little publishing house, Gnome Press. He published all the Conan books and I got copies. I believed that he owned the rights to Conan but he didn't. I tracked down the agent, who lived in Levitown, called him up, went to his house and he gave

Above: *We had hoped to feature Gil's favorite cover from his '70s Marvel work, a Kid Colt Outlaw piece, but we just couldn't locate it at presstime—when we find it, we promise to run it! In the meantime, indulge Ye Ed and allow him to feature his favorite Kane cover from those days; a collaboration with the great Ralph Reese, who inked this cover to Iron Man #46. (Anyone have the original art to this puppy?) One estimate of Gil's output for Marvel ranges at over 800 covers! Yow! ©1998 Marvel Entertainment.*

do; there was a million crowds, a millions riots and everything. One was inked by Ralph Reese and the other by Dan Adkins. They both turned out pretty well. But it was *hard!* I felt that I was working on *Prince Valiant* material! I couldn't do three or four pages a day on that stuff so I gave it up after two issues and came back to covers, because they paid the same! I just couldn't do it fast enough though I was given it to be the regular artist. I was always in need of money, but *Conan* lowered my income! Then Buscema took it over.

CBA: *Did you like Barry's stuff?*

Gil: Yes. I was surprised how good it was when it started to show up. The longer he did it, the less I liked it, but his storytelling was always good.

CBA: *What was the concept for Warlock?*

Gil: We wanted to do a strip with religious connotations. Warlock's whole stance and everything about him was godlike. But somewhere in there was "Amazing-Man," using some aspect of the historia and persona for that. And it turned out pretty well. The best of the jobs was one where there was a giant pig, a warthog. (That was the first time in my life, when I was at a convention, that Rich Buckler — who usually ducked his head when he saw me because he was lifting Kirby's, Neal's and my stuff cold — actually gave me a compliment! He came up to me and said, "That warthog material was the best you ever did.") Dan Adkins did a sensational job of inking. The nicest part was that he retained the pencils. So I just loved it.

CBA: *Iron Fist?*

Gil: That *was* Amazing-Man. It was about a guy from a monastery in Tibet going through the same tests. I think I only did the first issue because Roy and I would only do first issues.

CBA: *Did you ever have the desire to follow-through with Warlock?*

Gil: I made a bad mistake: I didn't stick with any one character but was an opportunist, just jumping to the next best opportunity. I missed the chance of being identified with a character, whether *Spider-Man, Conan,* or any of those features, like I held on to *Green Lantern.* Every time there was a new opportunity, I would jump. The covers paid more than anything else, so I would jump to the covers. The only thing is that nobody collects covers and you have a million guys who are connected to *X-Men,* connected to *Spider-Man,* and locked-in. If I think about all of the characters I did, and had put in two or three years on each one, I would have had a following. When people recall me, it's always from *Green Lantern.*

CBA: *But didn't you jump around to sustain some interest in the work?*

Gil: No, it was just the money, my boy. I was under pressure, divorced, re-married and I needed money. It took me ten years to get out of debt. Through that period I was the workingest guy in comics. And, in fact, when I came out to California, I became the workingest guy out in the studios. They always knew that if they wanted stuff done overnight, they called me. That was the most money I ever made in my life through that period. And I also did the best work I ever did in my life.

CBA: *Did you go into the Marvel bullpen to work?*

Gil: No. I would come in and, in one morning, Roy and I would plot 25 covers. I would go home and do 'em, come back at the end of the week and that was it. Once in a while I would take a break and do a book for them.

CBA: *You did five covers in a* day?

Gil: Yeah. Sometimes I would do five cover pencils in a day. It wasn't great stuff. [*laughs*] But I managed to get a couple of nice covers out of that batch, though I would also do a lot of stinkers.

CBA: *Did you design the overall Marvel cover look in the early '70s, with a block for the illustration and copy across the bottom?*

Gil: I designed some of the stuff but they kept switching the formats on me. I know that I made contributions toward the look of the covers but they would then just keep on developing it. Two

me a cardboard box that was about three foot square. It had all of the extant work of Robert E. Howard; all of the scripts he wrote that existed — the entire estate! I read letters from C.L. Moore, H.P. Lovecraft, Conan stories, and I became totally familiar with the Conan material. There were Conan sea stories, Conan pirate stories, and I read *everything.* I kept that box for nine months and I thought maybe he died. But, one day, I got a fateful call from his wife asking me to bring the box back as he was quite ill and needed the material to sell. So the agent died and Glenn Lord, who was just a fan, lived in Texas and the bank got in touch with him and made him the agent.

CBA: *So you saw the comic book possibilities of Conan?*

Gil: Immediately. I wanted to do it as the second book to *Savage.* In fact, that's how I sold *Blackmark.* I gave them samples of the type of material I could offer; I did romance, and they liked the Conan-type stuff the best. So I did *Blackmark* which was in the tradition.

CBA: *Did you try out for the Marvel adaptation of Conan?*

Gil: I was supposed to be the artist on it but was unable to do it. So they got a hold of Barry Smith. He did maybe 15, 16 issues. I took over with #17 and did two issues. They were *very* hard to

...months later I would see that they're not doing the white border all around
...ut something else.

CBA: *Did you feel that you were called in as the answer to Kirby?*

Gil: John Buscema was their big, strong guy to take on Kirby material and I
...was the guy who took on everything else. I did all the covers — Buscema
...hardly did any covers — and I did books… John Verpoorten (who was the
...production head and one of the nicest guys in the world) would just feed
...me, feed me, feed me! After a while, Roy left to go out to Hollywood and
...Len Wein came in. But once Roy went, the structure started to become a
...little shaky because nobody had the authority that Roy had. Roy took that
...ob and he became the head. Stan had jumped to being publisher, so Roy
...ran the comic books with a strong hand. He was very authoritative. But
...after that, I couldn't depend on the consistency of Roy's viewpoint any
...more. There was inconsistent attitudes, modifications because of pressure
...that they would succumb to, so I started taking some work at DC. Then I
...got the newspaper strips and stopped doing comic books altogether.

CBA: *You were one of the few major artists who seemed to appreciate
Kirby's DC work at the time, judging from your essay in that Harvard
...ournal [reprinted in* The Jack Kirby Collector #20 *in edited form], so you
...were reading his work.*

Gil: Everybody thought Jack's writing stunk, but I thought it was very
...good. The only trouble with him is that he needed a very strong editor but
...he didn't get one. His ideas were all very good but each issue he would
...nvent brand new characters and ultimately the place was flooded with
...3,000 brand new characters and you couldn't tell sh*t from Shinola because
...there were so many! There was a lack of real order to the material, with the
...focus shifting and jumping. That's what he needed editing for—not to write,
...ut to direct the writing. Stan was very successful at it. We used to go out
...to lunch, and Jack would say about Stan, "I'm going to break this guy! I'm
...gonna do some work for someone else! I'm gonna start a new company! I
...'m gonna see this guy run out of business!" And then we'd come into the
...office and Stan would say, "Jack, I need you to change something." And
...ack would comply without question. That's the way it *was,* and don't let
...anyone bullsh*t you about anything else.

CBA: *I always felt that it was the rage within which came out in
...his work.*

Gil: Because he was repressed. He was not a confronter, and all of that
...epression was just backed-up!

CBA: *When you and Roy got together on* Warlock, *did you specifically
...eize upon Kirby's characters and take them a step farther?*

Gil: You want to know what one of our inspirations was? Fawcett's
Captain Marvel was one of Roy's favorite characters. He wanted a Captain
Marvel type costume and what we got was red and yellow, the whole
Captain Marvel look, lightning bolt and all. Somehow I came through with the religious angle, with the character floating in space.

CBA: *What was your favorite experience working at Marvel in the '70s?*

Gil: It was working with Roy. I enjoyed *Spider-Man, Captain Marvel* and the early *Warlock.* 🗲

Editor's Note: *Look for an extensive, in-depth interview with Gil about his entire career, Jack Kirby, and the "art" of comics in
...he next issue of our sister publication* The Jack Kirby Collector *(#21) on sale in September! Who says this isn't the TwoMorrows Age
...f Hyperbolic Declaration!*

Alias Barry Windsor-Smith

Interview with Storyteller & *Conan* Artist: BWS

Conducted by Jon B. Cooke

The following interview was conducted via electronic mail in May, 1998, and it features a wry storyteller in a playful mood. Enormous thanks go to Barry, Alex Bialy and the Windsor-Smith Studio for their exhaustive efforts in attaining this interview and the art that illustrates much of this issue.

Comic Book Artist: *When did you develop your interest in comic books and the art form?*

Barry Windsor-Smith: I have been interested in all forms of graphic art since childhood. At the same time I was copying Wally Wood cartoons from *Mad* magazine I also copying Leonardo Da Vinci. I perceived little difference between what is called fine art and what is considered otherwise, and in fact, since the Sistine Chapel ceiling is now so clean and bright I suggest you might notice the strong facial link between Michelangelo's figures and colors with those of the best of super-hero comics art, Jack Kirby for instance.

CBA: *Did you gravitate towards the American imports over the British weeklies?*

Barry: Yes, once they started being imported into Britain as ballast for American cargo ships. That was the early '60s, I believe. Before that it was just black-&-white reprints of American material and the English so-called funny comics. I was never much of a fan of the British stuff although I enjoyed *Marvelman* for a while. *Desperate Dan* was so particularly British in his manifest brutishness (rather like Monty Python's "Mr. Gumby") that one couldn't help but identify with him somehow.

CBA: *Any favorite British cartoonists, such as Frank Bellamy?*

Above: Sample page Barry sent to Marvel in 1968. An encouraging letter from Linda Fite (Stan's then-assistant/writer/future Herb Trimpe wife) prompted Barry to fly to the U.S. with friend Steve "BoJefferies Saga" Parkhouse and camp out at Marvel's door. Artwork ©1998 BWS. Captain America ©1998 Marvel Entertainment.

Barry: I was quite awestruck by Bellamy, his "Heros the Spartan" was simply magnificent. I was never particularly influenced by him, however. Britain had a clutch of exceptionally gifted comics artists during the '50s and '60s but the subject matter of the strips often disinterested me. I liked "Dan Dare" and Heros, I think that's all. I named the lead male character in my "Young Gods "series Heros in homage to Bellamy.

CBA: *Do you remember your first Kirby comic?*

Barry: Yes, distinctly. *The Double Life of Private Strong*, which, incidentally, I had misremembered for years as *The Private Life of Double Strong.* Although some other hand was evident on the cover's main figure, it was the background figures, and more-so, the vignette film-strip-like drawings by Kirby that framed the cover that caught my eye: I'd never seen figure drawing like that before, dynamic, fluid, highly romanticized. Kirby stunned me with that first issue's interior work.

CBA: *You obviously have an affinity for the work of Jack Kirby from your "Kirby-esque" drawing style when you arrived at Marvel to your dedication to the King in the series "Young Gods." What was it about his work that grabbed you?*

Barry: As above, really. But as Kirby continued to evolve into the major conceptualist he was in the mid-sixties, with his drawings of figures and fantastic buildings and machines coming to such a breathtaking peak of knowledge, assurity and sheer visionary power, utterly unequaled by anybody as yet, the question might be better rendered as "What *wasn't* it about Kirby that grabbed me?"

Kirby's only drawback was his simplistic and naive scripting style, and I believe an intelligent, in-depth study is well overdue on this most blatant of discrepancies in an otherwise genius-level creative energy.

CBA: *Did you seek out Marvel because of Jack's work?*

Barry: Yes. Marvel was my only interest because of Kirby's work.

CBA: *Did you submit material by mail to Marvel or basically show up at their doorstep?*

Barry: Both. I sent material first, and based solely upon a pleasant return note from Stan's assistant Linda Fite, my pal and me were at Marvel's doorstep in the blink of an eye. That was the summer of 1968.

CBA: *Herb Trimpe mentioned that he remembers you virtually living out of a suitcase during your initial stay at Marvel. What were impressions of New York at that young age?*

Barry: Terrifying, to be frank. The summer of '68 was a time of considerable unrest in many urban areas in the States. We saw homeless people laying in the street unaided, we saw policemen in riot gear beating up groups of Black kids. A building we stayed at for a few days was blown to bits a short while after we left because there was an illicit bomb factory in the basement. And yes we lived out of suitcases—sometimes, without money, we went without food or water for days in stifling 90 degrees-and-up heat.

CBA: *Did you aspire to live in America?*

Barry: After my above allusions it is bound to bring a laugh if I say "yes," but the fact is, despite the poverty and misery of those days in 1968, yes—I had every intention of living in the States. I needed to be physically free of my roots, that I might start afresh and explore my own visions in a new and thoroughly different environment.

CBA: *What was your first break at Marvel? I recall a* Western Gunfighters *story.*

Barry: "Half Breed," I believe it was. My first work was *X-Men* #53. Then it might've been "Half Breed," then a *SHIELD* book.

CBA: *Can you give a brief chronology of your output at Marvel?*

Barry: Well, heck—whaddaya think I'm doing here? Cutting *sushi*?

CBA: Daredevil? The Avengers?

Barry: I think *Daredevil* (the Starr Saxon story that, bizarre as it may seem, has some cult following somewhere) came next. I pretty much just made that up as I went along, giving Roy Thomas a taste of what was to come in later years with *Conan*. I think I started *The Avengers* after the US government told me to get out of the country. I believe I drew those books in London, circa 1969.

CBA: *Were you seeking a regular book? Were you able to pitch your work to Stan Lee?*

Barry: There was no pitching required, really— Stan loved my stuff because although it was pretty amateur and klutzy, it had the essence of Jack Kirby about it, and that was what sold Marvel Comics in those days. Stan wanted every "penciler" in his employ to draw like Jack—not necessarily copy him, I must point out, because that has been misconstrued for too long—but, rather, to adapt from Kirby's dynamism and dramatic staging.

Many pencilers pretty much had their own personal styles wrecked by Stan's insistence in this matter. It was horrid watching Don Heck—a perfectly adept illustrator of everyday things and occurrences—struggle to create a dynamism in his work that simply was not a part of his natural capabilities. Herb Trimpe, John Romita Sr., and others were all twisted away from their own natural proclivities to adapt to the Kirby style—disastrously affecting their own artistic vision or needs. I doubt whether Stan pushed Steve Ditko to be more like Kirby because, after all, Ditko's style was already dramatic in its staging and pacing. If Stan had insisted that Herb Trimpe, for instance, should draw more like Ditko, I don't think Herb would have felt so buggered about by Stan's need for a "Company Style."

In my case there was no problem—I had an *idée fixe* that comics were Kirby and, in so drawing a comic, I drew it, to the best of my young abilities, as if I was Jack Kirby. However, if during that same period I chose to draw, say, a tree that I admired in some park somewhere, I would draw it in the correct and well observed manner that my brilliant drawing instructors had taught me at Art School. Real drawing was academic, but comics was Kirby.

CBA: *Are you satisfied looking over your work from that time?*

Barry: No, not at all. I have no sense of satisfaction about practically anything I've ever done. I perceive those very old works as mere vehicles to move from one challenge to the next, in terms of learning my craft, though at the time of their creation I had no self-perception beyond a powerful instinct to always move forward. I was really just a young guy with a lot of talent—I was a natural who wanted to do as much and learn as much as possibly can be done in one lifetime. I still feel exactly the same way.

CBA: *Did you work in the Bullpen with regularity? Do you recall what the atmosphere was like? Any anecdotes or memories of Marie Severin, John Verpoorten, Herb Trimpe, Frank Giacoia, Bill Everett, Gil Kane, and other office "regulars"?*

Barry: I worked there on occasion. The offices were no bigger than an average NYC apartment. Areas were sectioned off—the Bullpen itself could hold four people sort-of comfortably, with liberal deodorant use. Stan had the only office with a door. The atmosphere was quite merry most of the time. Marie was a constant source of laughs with her wonderful cartoons of all of us. I remember one afternoon in the late summer of '68, the radio was playing the Beatles' latest song and as it came into the long, chanting coda one by one each person began singing along— Herb, John Romita, Morrie Kuromoto, Tony Mortarello, Marie and a few others—all singing at the top of their lungs, "Naaa—NaNa, NaNaNaNaaa—Hey Ju-u-ude..." It was wonderful, gave me chills of pleasure.

CBA: *Did you meet Jack Kirby? Did he look over your work?*

Barry: I met Jack only once and it was during that first year. It's an old cliché, I know, but I was really surprised that I, at 18 years, was taller than The King. I had envisioned him as a physical giant

as well as a creative one. He was a lovely man, thoughtful and considerate, and although he could obviously see that I was imitating his style, in my own less than skillful way, he was not the least put out by it and simply said, "You've got some strong design here, Stan likes that." I have always regretted not knowing Jack better. I've had a few chances, over the years, to approach him and take of his time, but I always stayed away, not wanting to bother him. I guess I thought he was going to live forever and I'd just catch up with him one day in the future. I was mistaken about that. I used to be a neighbor to John Lennon and Yoko; I'd see them around just like I'd see any other neighbor but I never approached him (even though I knew that he liked my work) because I had the same imaginary sense that I had with Kirby; that we'd get together eventually, naturally, somehow. I was wrong about John, too.

CBA: *I recall through reading the Bullpen Bulletin pages in 1969 that you were suddenly back in England for a period. Did you have a work visa?*

Barry: I worked all of 1968 without a work permit. The government got pissed about that. It took several years to secure the proper papers and I returned to the States in 1971, I believe.

CBA: *Do you recall the circumstances surrounding Jack Kirby's 1970 departure from Marvel? Do you think that overall Jack was treated fairly by the company? What was your reaction to the King's leave?*

Barry: No, I was in England at the time of Jack's resignation. I recall Roy Thomas' letter to me beginning, "There's no way to say this but straight: Jack Kirby has left Marvel." Obviously Jack's

THE SUMMONS! SPLASH!

Above and next page: *A super-hero team of Bucky, Red Raven, and Quicksilver was proposed by Roy Thomas and BWS in the late '60s, but never got off the ground. Here are the first three pages of Barry's pencils from the pitch. Art ©1998 BWS. Bucky, Cap, Thor ©1998 Marvel Entertainment.*

departure was cataclysmic to Stan and Marvel as a publishing entity. It affected me in no way whatsoever, I just wished him well. As to being treated fairly by the company that he co-created, I'm not privy to the internal goings on that existed between Jack and Marvel management, but I would hazard a guess that if Jack was less of a romantic and more of a business man, he could have had anything he wanted from Marvel. Hindsight is so easy, but if Jack had hired a smart lawyer to do business with Marvel at the time that Jack felt the urge to split the "House of Ideas," it's a pretty good shot that Jack could have written his own ticket. But then again, if Kirby had more of a head for business, he probably wouldn't have been the genius artist we have all benefited from. There's a tragedy of some considerable proportion right there, know what I mean?

CBA: *How do you recall the development of Conan as a comic series?*

Barry: It's pretty well documented by Roy Thomas and others who dwell upon such things. Roy's historical materials tell the tale fairly accurately, as far as I know.

CBA: *It has been oft-mentioned that you were put on the Conan book because (due to the outlay of funds to pay for the*

licensing agreement) *you were less expensive per page than John Buscema or Gil Kane. Is this true?*

Barry: Yes, I believe so. Though, interestingly or not, the fee Marvel paid to Glenn Lord for the *Conan* rights was pitiably small in those days. As an adjunct to the licensing fee situation, though, I believe that Stan wasn't wholly behind the idea of a *Conan* comic and, if I recall, he was against putting an important artist on a book that was probably going to tank. Obviously, I was not considered an important artist at that period.

CBA: *Did you have any previous affinity for the character before you started working on* Conan?

Barry: Yes and no. Roy had sent me all of the Lancer paperbacks some months prior to our beginning the first issue, so my prior affinity was merely months old but, as it happens, that made my perceptions energetic and fresh because I was utterly hooked by Howard's writing style. "The Tower of the Elephant," in particular, was a real head trip, to use the vernacular of the time.

CBA: *Were you satisfied with the selection of inkers during your run on* Conan?

Barry: Well… y'know, it was a crap shoot always. I really don't know who chose Frank Giacoia for that one book, but the likelihood is that it was a last-minute decision because Dan Adkins had screwed up some deadline or other. Dan was certainly my favorite inker at that period because he meticulously followed my every line, but he was hopeless at controlling his time in relation to deadlines. Sal Buscema was serviceable and competent, I suppose, but he would often slick over my more sensitive mannerisms.

CBA: *Can you describe the collaborating process you had with Roy Thomas?*

Barry: Sure—he created everything and told me what to draw, everybody knows that.

CBA: *In very short order, your drawing style matured from Kirby-pastiche to a more romantic, illustrative technique. Were you becoming exposed to Beardsley, Raphael, Pyle, Wyeth, et al. for instance? Did you begin to develop more of a taste for illustrating over sequential storytelling at the time?*

Barry: No, that's not the least the case, and I can't imagine how you include Beardsley and Raphael in the same sentence without such a qualification as "As diverse as…"

I had always been influenced by so-called fine artists, even including some illustrators such as Pyle or Wyeth, but in the '60s I had not made the connection that to create comics didn't wholly mean to create Kirby. It is not as if my love of Kirby waned at all, rather, I allowed my other influences to come to the fore, and that brought about the many turning points in my work that seem so evident today but, frankly, I was not fully aware of at the time. Some observer somewhere said in print that I was responsible for bringing Romantic art to American comics. I believe that is quite correct (and that's why I self-servingly re-quote it here), but it was not an intentional program on my part but, rather, it was simply my need to break the chains of conformity. *Conan*, being non-super-hero and non-Marvel universe, just happened to be the right vehicle to create havoc with the old order, the *status quo* and its flabby trappings. I harnessed all sorts of influences in that series— some not even noticed or acknowledged. But it's like Bob Dylan answered in some long ago interview that asked who his influences were: "Open your eyes and your ears and you're influenced, man." Or Marlon Brando replying to the question, "What are you against?" with, "Whatcha got?"

CBA: *There were some fill-in issues featuring a reprint of "The Frost Giant's Daughter" and Gil Kane's work. Did you actually quit the book for brief intervals?*

Barry: Yes—this was the beginning times of my dissatisfaction with the way Marvel was running the railroad. I was in dissent and there was friction.

CBA: *Were you satisfied with that story from Savage Tales #1, "The Frost Giant's Daughter"? Was it finished entirely in pencil?*

Barry: No, not all—I inked it myself. You must be thinking of the latter pages of "Hawks from the Sea', which was printed from not-too-keen copies of my finished pencil drawings. That came about because of the aforementioned Dan Adkins' deadline problems: It was a choice of getting Verpoorten, Giacoia, Trimpe and Romita to hack black ink through those pages in a matter of days or go with pencil drawings. My pencil work was quite finished in those days (had to be because I never knew what inker I'd end up with) so we went with printing from pencil. It looked pretty lousy even though I tried to beef up some lines on the copies and I deliberately toned the color vocabulary down to pastels so as to not obliterate what little line work remained in the copies. Comic book printing in those days was deplorable, to say the least.

CBA: *For a few issues before your departure you had a number of assists from fellow artists. Were deadlines becoming a problem?*

Barry: Technically those weren't assists to me, rather they were assists to Dan Adkins and his inking coterie. It was an experiment that failed utterly—that being that to catch up on the heat of the deadlines, I'd do a book, every now and then, in breakdowns only and Dan and his studio would finish the work "in my style." Needless to say, this didn't quite work out in the end. I've never looked at that particular issue since it was published.

CBA: *Did you prepare "The Song of Red Sonja" as a fare-thee-well to the color book?*

Barry: I knew it was my last book of the series. Push had come to shove and I hated everything about Marvel Comics' policies toward their creators. Once again Dan Adkins was slated to ink the work (he had just done an excellent job on the previous story, "Black Hound of Vengeance"), but I decided that I wasn't going to risk the possibility of a screw-up on this, my final *Conan*. I inked it myself whilst I was back in London for some months—it is inked entirely with a Mont Blanc fountain pen and I wrecked the pen in the process. I have been complimented over and over again for "Sonja"'s color work yet, as it happened, I had photo-copied the artwork just slightly smaller than the correct size for the hand-separators we used in those days and, as a result, the separators could not trace my work onto the film as usual. They had to "eyeball" the placements of the color and simply could not

follow the intricate patterns I had created with the use of white and black as color entities unto themselves. The result was not bad and hard won by the crew of separators but, unfortunately, the multi-toned flesh passages, that became a bit of a trade-mark for me, were never reproduced at all.

CBA: *Did you ever have any interest to do work for DC?*

Barry: In one of my tantrums over some aesthetic mistreatment or other at Marvel, I decided to check out DC. I sat with a DC executive in his office, and he asked me what was wrong at Marvel. I think at that time I had some sort of upset over the printing of my coloring, so I told him that. He then told me in the most hyperbolic fashion imaginable, how "Just last week…" he had reamed out one of his printers for getting a yellow tone (or something) wrong. The executive described how he had ordered the printer to be at his office in the morning, dammit! Then, he said, "I had him on th' *carpet!* I had th' son-of-a-bitch on th' goddamn *carpet!* And he *begged* me to keep his job!"

Throughout this outrageously ridiculous piece of opera, I kept saying to meself, "Y'know, Stan's not such a bad ol' fart after all… Wonder how ol' Herb's doing… Gee, I miss those nutcases in the Bullpen." That executive totally turned me off of working at DC.

That was thirty years ago—today I'm involved with two, maybe three important projects with the modern DC and I feel quite happy about that. Paul Levitz has been a thorough gentleman in all my dealings with him.

CBA: *How would you assess your experience at Marvel?*

Barry: Concisely—a learning one.

CBA: *What was the level of editorial interference? Did you feel any constraints?*

Barry: The better I got at what I was doing, the more constraints sprung up like weeds. Come to think of it I guess they were always there but as one grows one must challenge the old order or you're not really growing. I outgrew the Marvel style quickly, in just a matter of a few years.

CBA: *Was Marvel going in a direction that interested you in the early '70s? Did you have any interest in other Marvel books?*

Barry: I was losing interest in all comic books, Marvel in particular, I guess, because I was right there in the thick of it. With Kirby gone and Stan decreasing his script output and with a change of style in both story and art that I perceived as a backward step rather than an advance of merit, I felt that I couldn't tolerate the whole scene anymore. I was becoming more and more disillusioned and, independent of whom ever else claims to have coined the phrase, I started referring to Marvel as "The House of Idea."

CBA: *Did you collaborate with Stan for that issue of "Doctor Strange" [Marvel Premiere #3] or did he dialogue your story after you completed the pencils?*

Barry: No, "collaborate" isn't the word. Not only did Stan dialogue the story after I had created it but, marvel of marvels, he ignored my plot and wrote another story entirely over my staging. Remarkable feat, actually. It wasn't until many years later that I realized that Stan's grafted-on title "As The World Spins Madly"

Lower left: Page 2 of "The Summons." **Above:** Page 3. Art ©1998 BWS. Bucky ©1998 Marvel Entertainment.

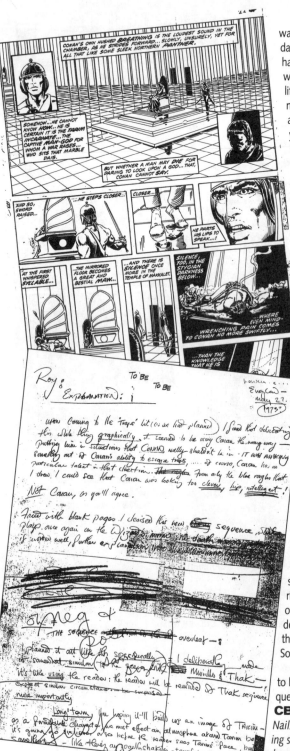

Above: *Evidence of the intense collaboration between BWS and Roy in developing Conan. The above pages are actually the front and back of pg. 22 of Conan #20, and features an explanation by Barry to Roy on why he deviated from the original plot. Barry felt the barbarian's entrance as first conceived was, "too clever, hip, intelligent!"; attributes not usually associated with our hero, eh? ©1998 Marvel Entertainment. Conan ©1998 Conan Properties*

was a spin (as it were) on the title of a daytime soap-opera. I've always hated that sort of thing, y'know, where some ass-wipe comics writer lifts the title of a film or a famous novel thinking he's being cool or allusory to another art form, y'know. That sort of stuff is so immature and, wouldn't cha know it? Stan pulled it on me and I didn't even know it at the time.

CBA: *Are you satisfied with your short tenure on The Avengers?*

Barry: I can't really remember my *Avengers* stuff, to be honest. I recall the nightmare of drawing the 100th issue, though—all those bloody characters that I didn't give tuppence about. That was another disaster in the inking department. Although, if I recall correctly, the one and only Joe Sinnott did a couple of pages over mere layouts and, as always, Joe was wonderfully rich and detailed.

CBA: *"Red Nails" is, in my opinion, your best work from that era. How long did it take you to complete that incredibly detailed work? Were you satisfied with the final production?*

Barry: Oh, God—! "Red Nails"! How many time can I use the term "nightmare" in one interview? I should grab a thesaurus right now, right? How long did it take? Oh, only forever. Detail—? What detail—? There was detail in that thing? Where're my pills—? Somebody get me a doctor.

No, I'm fine. It's okay—I just need to breathe. S'okay. What was the question?

CBA: *The second chapter of "Red Nails" showed a departure in your inking style from the delicate, finely rendered line to a more spotted, bold approach? Was this experimentation or the demands of the deadline?*

Barry: Deadline—? There was a deadline? What do you mean "spotted'? Am I alright? Where's my medicine?

CBA: *Why did you leave Marvel?*

Barry: Did I leave Marvel? When? What time is it? Hello?

CBA: *Your work on Conan has been reprinted an untold number of times. Have you received compensation for the reissues? Any frustrations over their dealings with creatives?*

Barry: No. I loved every single second of every single minute I spent in the Marvel Universe. Compensation for reprints—? Why isn't anybody getting my bloody medicine—? Do I have to do everything around here?

CBA: *Did you feel driven from comics or did you simply aspire to more creative freedom and independence when you established Gorblimey?*

Barry: I needed to be free of constraints and policies that were imposed by the dictates of creating entertainment for children. If Marvel (and the other comics companies) had grown up and out of its own immaturity and spread to new avenues of expression as it filled its coffers out of repeating itself over and over ad nauseum, the comics industry would be a wholly different medium today that could embrace, and perhaps even influence, the world at large in all its many-faceted and textured complexities. But, *No-o-o!* It's still the same old, same old. Just older, not to mention in the way, too.

CBA: *I'll be honest and tell you that while I have long admired your pacing and abilities to sequence a story (never mind the pure artistry of your line work) I never was aware of your superior writing ability until Barry Windsor-Smith: Storyteller came along. Your flair for dialogue is among the best in the field and your characterizations are compelling and realistic. Did you aspire to write way back when at Marvel?*

Barry: I was always plotting my own stories right from the beginning. *X-Men* #53 I just made up, The Daredevil/Starr Saxon stories were stream-of-consciousness fabrications of mine. To give the scripter some clue as to what was going on, I would write my own dialogue on the edge of the pages. Some scripters would use my dialogue, others would willfully ignore it. In either case I was never paid or credited for the work. Some of the more amusing dialogue in *Conan* came from me, Jenna telling Conan he looks like a yak with that dumb helmet he used to wear; the slow-dawn on Conan's face as he realizes he gotten involved with a wizard again. "Sorcery? No one said aught of sorcery [when I signed on for this war]!" Roy was good at picking up the better stuff and letting others go.

Largely, I think, the reason for my earlier reticence to become my own writer was a gullible acceptance of the chain-gang system of creating American super-hero comics—y'know, "he's the inker" and "he's the writer" thing. The workload had to be sub-divided in order to get the material out every month, so if you hook into that sort of thing you're pretty much a part of a chain, no matter what you might imagine yourself to be otherwise. In later years, like the '70s and '80s, when I'd do this or that fill-in issue for some title or other, it was horribly evident that my storytelling and artwork were existing, and operating, on an entirely different level from that of the continuing series itself and my fill-ins became anomalies in the stream. It was around that period that I concluded that if I wished to continue moving forward in the realm of the comics arts I'd better take control of the entire palette—stop fiddling about like I'd done for years and get some serious work done. Thus was born BWS the writer. But, you must realize that it is not simply a matter of getting all the words in the right order (as some Python skit asserted), it's largely about *staging* and allowing characters to have their own personalities invested into the stories. This sort of procedure, in itself, is a trick-and-a-half and I don't advise people to try it at home, but once one is over those annoying little details of actually creating a character that has his or her own life independent of what somebody like me has to say about it, the rest is pretty much, as they say, a walk in the park.

That last sentence—? I was lying big time!

CBA: *Is Axus a "grown up" Conan?*

Barry: Almost. He's a Conan for grown-ups, if you get my drift. Howard's character was hopelessly without humor, of course, and Axus is the very soul of dry wit and befuddled perspectives. As with almost all of my characters they are, in some form or other, extensions of myself (even the girls), and it's not unknown that, at times, the Windsor-Smith Studio more resembles the Ram and the Peacock tavern than an art studio.

CBA: *What next for Barry Windsor-Smith?*

Barry: Never did get that medicine I asked for. ⚡

In 1995 Barry Windsor-Smith returned to Conan one last time to celebrate the 25th Anniversary of the publication of **Conan The Barbarian** #1.

Written and drawn by Windsor-Smith and produced by his own Studio, Barry's revival of the character was an artistic triumph one could hardly have guessed at in the long ago days of Zukala's Daughter or the Elric adaptations.

The story was called **The Dark God** and featured Rune, the vampire creature Barry co-created for the Ultraverse line. This Special Edition, Silver Anniversary comic book was grievously marred, however, by some of the worst reproduction ever seen in modern times. The beautifully colored pages looked like cheap xeroxes and the drawings themselves were obscured.

In these four pages we present a collage, created by BWS himself from panels of **The Dark God**, that tenders the artist's work in good ol' -- can't go wrong -- **black and white**.

BWS

HI, EVERYONE. TODAY, AS MY GUEST, I'M HAPPY TO HAVE THE *ORIGINAL* NOMAD--NO, *NOT* THAT GUY WHO CAN'T SEEM TO EVER FIND A *SITTER*--BUT YOU FOLKS PROBABLY KNOW HIM *BETTER* AS STEVE ROGERS!

UH, HELLO, FRED. SAY, *WHY* ARE YOU WEARING THAT *OTHER* COSTUME OF MINE?..

BECAUSE, BACK IN 1974, WHEN YOU *ABDICATED*, *ANYBODY* COULD'VE SUITED UP AND TAKEN ON THE ROLE OF CAPTAIN AMERICA--*EVEN* A YOUNGER, FITTER AND...*ahem, SLIMMER* VERSION OF *MOI*. HEY, A PRO THIRD BASEMAN GAVE IT A SHOT --SO DID A BIKER. OF COURSE, THEIR CRIME-BUSTING CAREERS LASTED ALL OF A *PAGE* APIECE, BUT--

AND THEN THERE WAS..*choke.. ROSCOE. POOR, *NAIVE* ROSCOE..*snif...

OH, YEAH. THAT *KID* FROM YOUR *GYM* WHO TRIED TO *REPLACE* YOU...

YOU WOULDN'T THINK THE KID COULD FOOL ANYONE IN THAT OUT-FIT, BUT HE *FOOLED* THE RED SKULL! THE SKULL WAS SO *INCENSED* WHEN HE REALIZED THE TRUTH THAT HE *SLAUGHTERED* THE BOY. THAT'S WHEN I HADDA PUT THE FLAG SUIT BACK ON TO AVENGE THE POOR LAD. PEOPLE THINK I'M STILL RACKED WITH *GUILT* ABOUT THE *BUCKY* THING, BUT IT'S *REALLY* ROSCOE THAT KEEPS ME UP NIGHTS! *POOR, NAIVE...snif... DEAD* ROSCOE.

UM, MAYBE YOU SHOULD *EXPLAIN* TO LATECOMERS *HOW* YOU CAME TO TAKE UP THE GUISE OF *NOMAD*, THE MAN WITHOUT A COUNTRY?.

Whew! THAT'S A WHOLE 'NOTHER STORY. WELL, IT ALL STARTED WHEN THE FALCON, PROFESSOR X, CYCLOPS, MARVEL GIRL, S.H.I.E.L.D. AND I WERE WAGING A LONG-RUNNING BATTLE WITH *THE SECRET EMPIRE*. WHO, HIDING BEHIND AN ORGANIZATION CALLED *THE COMMITTEE TO REGAIN AMERICA'S PRINCIPLES*, WERE IN FACT ATTEMPTING TO *SUBJUGATE* THIS COUNTRY.

EVEN *WITHOUT* THE SUB-MARINER, THINGS WERE GOING ALONG JUST SWIM-MINGLY, AS WE GOOD GUYS WERE PUTTING THE *KIBOSH* ON THE FORCES OF EVIL DURING OUR FINAL, CLIMAC-TIC BATTLE IN OUR NATION'S CAPITAL--THAT IS, *UNTIL* THE MALEVOLENT MASKED MASTERMIND KNOWN TO US ONLY AS *NUMBER ONE* SNEAKILY SLIPPED AWAY AND *INTO* THE WHITE HOUSE..

NOT FOR THE TOUR, I TAKE IT?..

BELIEVE ME, HE *DIDN'T* NEED THE TOUR. I HAD HIM *CORNERED* IN THE OVAL OFFICE WHEN I MANAGED TO *PULL HIS HOOD OFF!* I WAS SO UTTERLY *SHOCKED* BY WHAT I SAW--*WHO* I SAW --THAT I JUST STOOD BY *HELPLESSLY* AS HE PULLED A *GUN* AND COMMITTED *SUICIDE*.

... ..*NIXON*?

SORRY, BUT I'M STILL NOT AT LIBERTY TO SAY. HOWEVER, DO YOU RECALL THAT FAMOUS *CAMPAIGN SLOGAN?..

YOU MEAN, "NIXON'S THE ONE"?

YOU SAID IT, *NOT* ME.

Geez, AND I THOUGHT THE WATERGATE SCAN-DAL IN *OUR* UNIVERSE WAS ROUGH!?..

Brrr. YOU SEE SOME-THING LIKE *THAT* AND YOU WANNA FLEE THE COUNTRY. I JUST *HADDA* GET OUTTA THE RED, WHITE AND BLUE.

SO *THAT'S* WHEN YOU BECAME NOMAD?

ACTUALLY, I JUST *LOUNGED* AROUND FOR A COUPLE OF ISSUES, SPENT SOME *QUALITY TIME* WITH *SHARON*. THE FALCON TOOK *CENTER STAGE*, WHICH WAS JUST FINE WITH *ME*. I'D RETIRED, AFTER ALL.

THAT'S WHEN *HAWK-EYE* SHOWS UP, WEARING THIS GOOFY "*GOLDEN ARCHER*" GET-UP-- MAYBE HE WAS BUCKING FOR AN *ENDORSEMENT DEAL* FROM *McDONALDS* OR SOMETHING, I DON'T KNOW--AND CONVINCES ME THAT, WHILE *CAPTAIN AMERICA* MAY'VE BEEN IN *STORAGE*, THERE WAS *NO REASON* MY SKILLS NEEDED TO BE.

NOMAD WAS BORN!

VOILA.

I DON'T MIND TELLING YOU THAT THAT *ENTIRE* SEQUENCE, FROM THE FIRST STIRRINGS OF THE SECRET EMPIRE IN "CAPTAIN AMERICA" #170 UP THROUGH THE RED SKULL'S ESCAPE IN #186 (SURPRISINGLY, NOMAD WAS FEATURED *ONLY* IN ISSUES 180-183) ARE AMONG MY *VERY* FAVORITE COMICS OF *ALL* TIME. FEATUR-ING *GOOD*, SOLID ARTWORK BY *SAL BUSCEMA* AND *FRANK ROBBINS* (AS WELL AS ONE ISSUE BY *HERB TRIMPE*) THIS STORYLINE SCORED BIG WITH ME *PRIMARILY* DUE TO THE *MULTILEVELED* SCRIPTING OF *STEVE ENGLEHART*.

..*Sigh*. STEVE WAS *GREAT*, WASN'T HE?

MAYBE *YOUSE* THINK SO..

--BUT I SURE AIN'T HIS *BIGGEST FAN!*

R-ROSCOE?

AZRAEL REPLACES *BATMAN*, GETS HIS *OWN BOOK*. *JIM RHODES* TAKES OVER FER *IRON MAN*, SAME THING. *ARTEMIS, STEEL, ERIC MASTER-SON*--AFTA DA FILL-IN GIGS, DEY ALL GOT DA GLORY. *ME?* ALL DIS BROOKLYN BOY GETS IS *DEAD*--AN' I WAS DA *FOIST!* IT AIN'T FAIR, I TELLS YA...

SON, I NEVER WANTED--

AW, *PIPE DOWN*. "RACKED WID GUILT" MY *BUTT*. I AIN'T *NEVER* READ A *SINGLE* REMORSEFUL THOT BALLOON IN NEARLY A QUARTER CENTURY, SO DON'T TRY SELLIN' ME *DAT BOLOGNA*, CUZ I AIN'T BUYIN'!

DA ONLY THING *YOU* REGRET IS DAT *JACK MONROE* GOT HIS *OWN SERIES* PRANCIN' AROUND IN DAT OUTFIT O' YERS, DRAGGIN' DAT *BABY* O' HIS WID HIM!!

ROSCOE, BE FAIR. I THINK WE *ALL* REGRET THAT!?.

..HOWCOME *BUCKY* NEVER HAUNTS *ME*...

The Man Called Ploog
Bronco-busting to Eisner to *Frankenstein*

Conducted by Jon B. Cooke

By his own admission, Mike Ploog, the artist who seemed to come out of nowhere into Marvel, has not done many interviews. I knew nothing about him other than I liked his work, that he was born in Minnesota, and (I had learned an hour before I called him) that he worked for the great Will Eisner, creator of the Spirit. What I didn't expect was the rollicking good time and laughter! Getting to know Mike is like finding a long-lost buddy; he's, well, cool. This interview, transcribed by John Morrow, was conducted via phone on May 31, 1998.

Above and below:
Character sketches for Mike's glorious rendition of Victor Frankenstein's misbegotten boy, the Monster. Certainly one of Marvel's best horror titles, don'tcha think?. ©1998 Marvel Entertainment.

Comic Book Artist: *You were born in Minnesota. You weren't much of a comics fan as a kid?*
Mike Ploog: Not really. Being a farm kid, we didn't get to town much. Usually the comic books they did sell were *Donald Duck.* The only one I kinda got wrapped up in was the old *Roy Rogers* comic book; I wanted to be a cowboy, that was my big aim in life. That was it other than the Sunday funnies; I was crazy about Al Capp. In my teens I moved to my grandmother's house, and she had a whole basement full of old comics, and I discovered Kirby and the *Boy Commandos.* I flipped over that.
CBA: *Did you key into Kirby's style right off?*
Mike: I never got into his style, but I loved the *Boy Commandos.* But I never keyed into a style because I never thought about being an artist. I doodled and drew, but I never took it seriously.
CBA: *When did you enter the service?*
Mike: When I was seventeen; a little early, due to circumstances. My mother signed me in, and I went in for four years initially. When my reenlistment came up, I really didn't know what I was going to do. I had spent three of those four years on the Marine Corps rodeo team; I had it made. [*laughter*] Being born on a farm, I was always into that kind of thing. I was a bareback bronco rider and a Brahma bull rider—I'm starting to feel it now. [*laughs*] Toward the end of my great military career, I spent some time overseas, working on *Leatherneck* magazine. I did a little bit of writing, a little bit of photography, a little bit of artwork, a little of everything.
CBA: *When did you start developing your drawing abilities?*
Mike: When I was at *Leatherneck,* I was doing some drawing. I just decided I'd had it with the Marine Corps after ten years. I figured I'd give art a shot, so when I got out I drew up a portfolio. I'd literally draw up the portfolio the night before for whoever I was going to see the next day, thinking, "This is what they want to see." Relatively quickly, I went to work for Filmation doing the *Batman & Superman* series, about 1969. I started off doing cleanup work for other artists.

I did cleanup for one season, and then I was doing layout work for *Batman & Superman* for one season. The following season I went to work for Hanna-Barbera. I was doing things like *Autocat & Motormouse* and *Whacky Races.* I worked on the first *Scooby-Doo* pilot; nothing spectacular, though. Layout is what happens between storyboarding and actual animation; you're literally composing the scenes. You're more or less designing the background, putting the characters into it so they'll look like they're actually walking on the surface. It was okay; it was a salary, y'know? It was a way of making a living without sitting on a tractor. I had very few aspirations, because I didn't know where anything I was doing was going to take me.
CBA: *How'd you get involved with PS Magazine?*
Mike: Will Eisner started that magazine; he was the creator of it way back in 1940. He came up with the idea and started the magazine. The ten years I spent in the Marine Corps, I spent taking a look at that crazy magazine. It was brilliant; I loved it. I copied stuff out of it continuously, never even thinking I'd ever work for Will. I didn't even know who Will Eisner was; I wasn't a comic book fan as a kid. So when I got a call from Will, it was just another name. When he said *"PS Magazine,"* I thought, "I can do that."
CBA: *How'd you get the call from Will?*
Mike: I was working for Hanna-Barbera, and the guy in the room with me belonged to the National Cartoonist's Society. He got a flyer Will had put out, looking for an assistant. He looked at it and said, "Ploog, this looks like your stuff." I looked at it and said, "It *is* my stuff." [*laughter*] I called Will, and two days later he was in L.A. and interviewed me. We met at the Beverly Hills Hotel. The following week I went to work for him.
CBA: *When you hooked up with Will, did you move east?*
Mike: Yeah, the following weekend. I was a bachelor then. I just packed my bag—I don't think I had any belongings—and moved to New York. Most terrifying experience of my life. [*laughter*] I stayed at the Washington Hotel, down by Greenwich Village. That was a nightmare; the first night I moved in, a rock group came in and stayed there. They were up and down the halls all night long, drunker than skunks. I really thought I was going to kill one of them that night. [*laughter*]
CBA: *How was it working on PS Magazine?*
Mike: I enjoyed it. It was something I was very familiar with, stuff I'd dealt with a lot in my military career. It was really easy. I was doing character stuff; all of the stuff Will had done earlier. I was doing the gags.

It was a clever magazine, and it took somebody like Will to actually think of doing something like that, and then actually pulling it off. Will has got a real talent for taking something really complex, and turning into the simplest form, to where the average G.I. can understand, or the average guy on the street, or the average kid.
CBA: *Was it tough working for Will? Was he a taskmaster?*
Mike: Well, he was. One of his biggest gripes was when he would hire somebody, and two or three years later the guy would leave and become world famous. [*laughter*] It really pissed him off. [*laughter*] He would go out of his way not to teach you anything. [*laughter*] You had to watch him to learn, but I don't think he wanted to teach anybody anything, because as soon as they

ot good enough, they left him.

I love Will; he's a dear, dear old friend. He's been an enormous influence on my work both in comics and film.

CBA: *Who did you get together with to get the PS contract?*

Mike: It was Will and I. I was going in and picking it up by myself, and Will was going to be my shadow. He and I were going to be partners, but I was actually going to hold the contract. That didn't work out for beans! [*laughter*] For one, Will's smarter than I am; smart as a whip, ol' Will! [*laughter*] Part of his character is, if he can get the edge, he'll take it. [*laughter*] A damn good poker player. I let it go, and then Murphy Anderson picked it up.

CBA: *When you first burst upon the scene in comic books, you had a style very reminiscent of Will's work. Did you start developing that style through osmosis, just being around him?*

Mike: It was very difficult for me, because I hadn't done that much work. I really didn't know what a "style" meant. When Will saw my work, he said, "This guy can adapt to what I'm doing easily." Obviously whatever I had, it was adaptable to him. I could emulate Will right down to a pinpoint on an occasion. I never felt it was a style. When I left Will, whenever I was insecure about something, I'd probably fall back on it. But it was basically what was there was there. I'm sure from working with Will, it developed in that direction.

CBA: *Not only did it resemble Will, but it also had humor.*

Mike: With Will, I did an awful lot of the gag writing. I'd get an article, and I had to come up with the gag that was going to fit the big piece of machinery or something. I love humor; I don't take much of anything seriously. That's probably why I've lasted as long as I have in the film industry.

CBA: *Did you start thinking about writing then?*

Mike: I didn't know how to write. I could do a gag, but to string a story together—I didn't have a clue. It wasn't until I actually got into comics that I realized stringing a story together was not all that difficult. With most of the people I worked with, we'd talk about the premise of the story over the phone. We'd come up with the gag, and I'd put the gag on page fifteen, and work my way backwards to page one, then get together with the writer again to figure out how to end it.

CBA: *You'd actually do page fifteen first?*

Mike: Oh yeah, because the gag was the point that you had to get to, and you didn't know how many pages it would take to pull it across. I'd work my way to the front, and work my way to the back. Sometimes it was just rough thumbnails, but often I'd just sit down and start drawing. In those days you didn't have time to do thumbnails. I love it when these guys talk about sitting down and doing a complete book in thumbnails. I would've starved to death if I were doing that. [*laughter*]

CBA: *When did you start getting an independent yearning working for Will?*

Mike: Actually, it was out of necessity. I was living in New York, and there were no animation studios I could fall back on. People like Ben Oda, who was doing our lettering, and Wally Wood, who was hanging around the place, suggested I get into comics. Ben took me over to Warren. I did two or three stories for him. That was the first work I did.

CBA: *How was that?*

Mike: [*laughter*] Have you ever met Jim? Well, then you know. [*laughter*] Actually, Jim and I got on great. He was the cheapest man I ever worked for, and he was full of sh*t. Two-thirds of Jim—and he's not all that big—is sh*t. [*laughter*] But we got on, 'cause I'm full of sh*t myself. [*laughter*] He's was kind of taken by the fact that I was this ex-Marine, and all that macho crap. We got to be decent friends. But he was cheap! [*laughter*] I think I was making $23 a page for those black-&-white books.

One time, I'd just picked up a freelance check from Murphy [Anderson], and I had $500 worth of $50 bills in my pocket. I walked into Jim Warren's office, and I'd just finished a monster

story about a flaming hand that somebody turned into a candle. I said, "Jim, I busted my ass on this thing. I've got to have more money." He said, "How much more you want?" I said, "Let's make it an even $50 a page." Jim had just returned from lunch with Bill Dubay. He called Bill into his office. Jim looked at me and said, "$50 is a lot of money. I betcha we don't even have $50 between the three of us." Well, Dubay was broke; he probably bought Jim's lunch. Jim had about a buck on him. "How much do you have, Ploog? If you got $50 on you, I'll give you that page rate." So I began to pull $50 bills out of my pocket, one at a time, and he gave me the page rate. Thought it was the funniest thing he ever saw. He thought it was a set-up, like I had instigated it.

I think that was the last book I did for him. [*laughter*]

CBA: *Where'd you go from Warren?*

Mike: I'd done up a western, and I took it in to Marvel. They looked at it and said, "No way. We don't do books that look like this." But I'd met Roy Thomas there, and I went on home, trying to figure out what I was going to do next. A couple of days later, they called me up and said, "How'd you like to do monsters?" Obviously they'd seen what I'd done for Jim, because I'd done some werewolf stuff. I said, "Sure, I'll do anything." I couldn't

Above and below: Before and after. Mike's take on the Hunchback of Notré Dame is futzed with by the Marvel production department. Hunchy is much more scary with a knife, yes? ©1998 Marvel Entertainment.

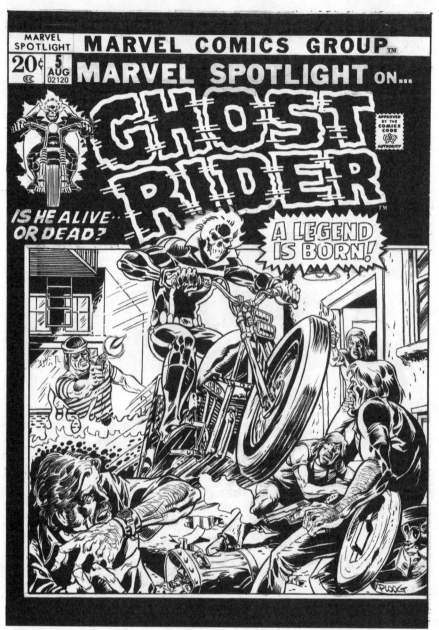

MARVEL COMICS GROUP

20¢ 5 AUG CC 02120

MARVEL SPOTLIGHT ON...

GHOST RIDER

IS HE ALIVE... OR DEAD?

A LEGEND IS BORN!

Above: *Shake that money thang, Johnny Blaze! This property, created by Gary Friedrich and Mike Ploog, made a couple of bucks for Marvel earlier this decade. When he agreed to draw the book, Mike thought he would finally get to do a western! ©1998 Marvel Entertainment.*

draw super-heroes; I had no heart for super-heroes.

CBA: *Was "Werewolf By Night" the first thing you did for Marvel?*

Mike: Yeah. I thought it was going to be a very short-lived thing for me. It was really hard work; I was drawing things I was not accustomed to drawing, like cars and chairs and things like that [*laughter*]—things I'd never drawn before in my life. I thought this would be a great learning period, and they'll get wise to me real fast, and I'll be off this job. Well, I just kept doing it and doing it, and they didn't tell me to stop. [*laughter*]

CBA: *What did you think of the comic book industry when you got into it?*

Mike: Marvel Comics at that time was magical. There was magic around that place. John Verpoorten took me under his wing; God love the great big giant. Everybody there were great people.

CBA: *Did you work "Marvel Method"? Did you co-plot these stories?*

Mike: Oh yeah. I think most people did. When I was doing *Man-Thing,* poor Steve Gerber was going through every crisis of life known to man! [*laughter*] He was like an insect; every day, somebody was trying to kill him! [*laughter*] I loved him; he'd call me up with this, [*whispering*] "Mike, I can't talk right now. I'll get back to you later." And I'm thinking, "Steve, why'd you call me in

the first place?!" [*laughter*] I'd say, "Okay Steve, what are we doing this month?" "Oh Mike, I can't think now. My wife just le me," or "I just shot myself in the foot." He had everything wron, with him. Steve and I worked this very strange method; it was wonderful. Then I'd have people like Gerry Conway come in and say, "I don't like the ending." I didn't even have a beginning! [*laughter*]

CBA: *So you'd get very loose plots?*

Mike: Yeah. I didn't mind that. It got to where I preferred working from a loose plot. What I really enjoyed was coming up with the gag. Sometimes, the sillier the gags were, the easier it was to plot the story.

CBA: *You did some great stories with Gerber on* Man-Thing.

Mike: Steve really is a bit of a genius. But genius comes in very strange forms. With Steve, it was not only strange, it was very deceptive. My favorite one was the clown story. That was a goofy one where we really didn't know what the hell we were gonna do. Just over the phone came the ghost of the dead clown; we milked it for three books.

CBA: *Do you remember how "Ghost Rider" came about?*

Mike: That was a Roy Thomas idea. Roy asked me if I wanted to do "Ghost Rider." I thought, "Yeah! Horses! Get me away from these city scenes!" [*laughter*] It wasn't until two or three weeks later they called up and said, "Can you do some drawings of costumes and the motorcycle?" This was the first I'd heard about a motorcycle. So off I went; I did a bunch of drawings for the character, and off I went.

CBA: *You came up with the idea for the blazing skull?*

Mike: Yeah, the blazing skull, the… I tell you, it was a rip-off of the old western one.

CBA: Ghost Rider *brought in some good income for Marvel over the years. Did it ever bug you that you didn't have a piece of that?*

Mike: No. Stuff like that doesn't bother me. I just felt fortunate I was working at the time. Marvel gave me a lot of good breaks. I was doing three books a month, because I needed the money.

CBA: *How many pages did you do a day?*

Mike: I didn't; I worked nights. When I was doing "Ghost Rider," I was doing *Werewolf By Night,* and I was starting the *Frankenstein* book, and covers to boot. I was doing all three a month, and I inked the first couple of *Frankensteins.*

CBA: *Did you deliver your work by hand?*

Mike: Yeah, I lived in New Jersey. Once a month I'd go into New York. I couldn't afford to go in more often because each time my car would be towed away.

CBA: *Did you hang out in the bullpen for any length of time?*

Mike: Not so much. Vinnie Colletta had a studio where I used to go over and do my changes. It was pretty busy up there, and there were a lot of stars, and I didn't feel like I was one of them. I always felt like a poor cousin. They didn't make me feel that way, it was my own mentality.

CBA: *Did you go to comic conventions?*

Mike: No, I stayed away from them. I went to one, and that was enough to turn me off of ever going to them again. In the past few years I've gone to a few. To me it really was a job.

CBA: *You must've been aware from some of the fan mail that people really enjoyed your work.*

Mike: I did, but I didn't understand it. I was always amazed when I met someone who had actually read one of my books. I'd spent ten years in the Marine Corps, and I was just making a living. I can remember many times I'd be walking through Marvel, delivering pages, and people'd come up and say, "I saw that last issue; that's great!?" And my opinion of that person would drop enormously. [*laughter*] I felt like I really wasn't an artist; I was just faking my way through this thing. It wasn't until later years that I realized how good I really did have it, and how wonderfully supportive those people really were.

CBA: *It always seemed to me you didn't want to stay long in*

...mics. You had a great deal of output for a period of time, and
...en it got sparse, and then you were gone. I got the sense that
...u weren't happy with comics.

Mike: It wasn't that I wasn't happy with them. I literally didn't
...el like I was a good enough artist to compete with the quality of
...ork that was being done at that particular time. I really felt I had
...ore to learn. I drifted back to film because I could hide in film,
...know? I still had a lot of work to do, and I didn't feel like I was
...oing to get it done in comics. I felt like I was getting into a rut,
...nd I was doing the same kind of stuff over and over again.

CBA: *Did you have any concepts yourself you wanted to do?
...ny story or character ideas?*

Mike: Not really, because most of the books I was doing were
...retty fulfilling in themselves. I was a great fan of horror films. It
...as just a fluke that I fell into it. I watched every horror film ever
...ade. I liked the melodrama, because the melodrama has a smile
...it. It's the same kind of timing that humor is. You can sit there
...nd kind of make fun of yourself. I really enjoyed that.

CBA: *As the monster material started to wane, did you just...*

Mike: For instance, they wanted to bring Frankenstein up to the
...Oth century, and have him battle in the streets of New York with
...pider-Man, and I just couldn't do that. To me, I felt it was disre-
...pectful to the poor monster. [*laughter*] That's when I left
...rankenstein. Then they gave me *Planet of the Apes,* which I got
...big kick out of in the beginning. We had a lot of good stories;
...oug Moench is a brilliant writer, and we had some real good
...aterial.

CBA: *That stuff was great. Wasn't some of that reproduced
...traight from you pencils?*

Mike: Yeah, the majority of it was. But the material started get-
...ng weak.

CBA: *Did you get any interference from 20th Century-Fox
...bout that?*

Mike: No, nothing.

CBA: *You also worked on a revamp of* Kull the Conqueror. *Did
...ou feel an affinity for the barbarian material?*

Mike: Not the barbarian material so much as the fantasy. I had
...ind of a secret love affair with fantasy. When we did *Kull,* the
...rst few issues dealt with a lot of fantasy, and I really enjoyed the
...ell out of them. Just this invincible, half-naked man doesn't
...ppeal to me all that much. But the fact that it was dealing with
...an against nature, and man alone against masses, I really
...njoyed that.

CBA: *Did you have any favorite writers you worked with?*

Mike: I was really fortunate; I had good writers. I think Doug
...Moench and I really connected well. We'd speak over the phone
...nd do our plotting, and we really had to work closely together.
...Vorking with Doug was a good experience because it gave me a
...ttle bit more of an idea what story structure was. We were work-
...ng with larger stories and larger pieces.

CBA: *In a weaker moment, did you ever do any tryout pages
...or a super-hero title?*

Mike: Never did. I cannot recall ever sitting down and drawing
...super-hero. It's not because I dislike them that much; I was just
...always so busy doing what I was doing, I couldn't imagine doing
...omething on a lark. On a day when I didn't have anything to do,
...was down at the bar playing pool with the boys.

CBA: *You really started drawing as a novice, and came into it
...and picked it up really fast.*

Mike: I had to! Can you imagine the fear, walking into Marvel
...Comics with pages under your arm that you had just faked your
...way through the night before? I didn't have a clue what I was
...doing. The Marvel office was a scary place for me, with people
...ike Barry Smith wandering around. [*laughter*] You're walking
...through there, just hoping nobody says anything so you don't
...have to look up, y'know? [*laughter*]

CBA: *But your work held its own.*

Mike: But you don't know that when you're doing it. [*laughter*]

I was terrified. I remember when someone introduced me to
Bernie Wrightson. I looked at him and thought, "Geez, he's
younger than I am. This guy's a genius," but I couldn't look him in
the face. [*laughter*] Today, Bernie and I are the best of buddies.
But that's human nature; I was older and I had a lot of experience,
but as an artist I was a novice, a kid.

CBA: *I seen your recent work; you're better than ever.*

Mike: I'm not saying it to blow my own whistle: What I do now
comes so much easier. I thinks it's self-confidence, and maturity as
an artist. One of the things Will Eisner gave me was the instinct to
see as an artist. It's a hard thing to explain: One day you just start
looking at things as an artist. As time goes by, everything you see
you see as blocks, shapes, forms, colors, hues. After years you
know what you want to see on that blank canvas and you just
instinctively know how to achieve it. Everything is automatically
on the paper. There's no longer any terror of that blank sheet of
paper. It's a welcome friend.

By the time I began the *Frankenstein* series, I had learned a lot.
Storytelling became easier and my artwork was beginning to come
into its own.

CBA: *Would you consider your* Frankenstein *material the
height of your color comics work?*

Mike: I really enjoyed doing *Frankenstein,* because I related to
that naive monster wandering around a world he had no knowledge of—an outsider seeing everything through the eyes of a
child. That took me right back to my childhood, being a farm kid,
moving to Burbank, California in the middle of the hot rods and
the swinging '50s.

CBA: *Did your Marine Corps experience help you or hinder
you in comics?*

Mike: It helped me throughout my whole life. There's no trading personal experience for anything. Just getting into a fight...
unless somebody's punched you in the mouth, it's pretty hard to
make a convincing fight sequence. Living is a very strange thing;
you can't help but learn something from it. [*laughter*]

CBA: *What made you leave Marvel?*

Mike: I had a disagreement with Jim Shooter. I had moved to a
farm in Minnesota, and agreed to do a hand-colored *Weirdworld*
story. Marvel backed out of the deal after I had started. I can't
remember the details, but it doesn't matter. I think I was ready to

KULL THE DESTROYER

MARVEL COMICS GROUP™

APPROVED BY THE COMICS CODE AUTHORITY

20¢ 11 NOV 02446

FROM THE CREATOR OF CONAN!

KULL THE DESTROYER

BY THIS AXE I RULE!

BEGINNING: A PULSE-POUNDING NEW CHAPTER IN THE STARTLING SAGA OF THE MAN CALLED KULL!

PLOOG

--AND WAIT TILL YOU SEE THE SHOCK ENDING TO THIS STORY OF STORIES!

Above: *If there was any consolation over the decision to take the superb art team of Marie & Johnny Severin off Kull, it was the arrival of Mike Ploog doing his great stuff. ©2000 Marvel Characters, Inc.*

Right inset: *Not to forget his great work on Frankenstein, here's Mike's cover to the second issue. ©2000 Marvel Characters, Inc.*

move on. Marvel and I were both changing. I finished off a black-&-white *Kull* book that was my last comic for many years.

CBA: *When you went to Hollywood, is it true you worked on "Ghostbusters"?*

Mike: Yeah. I did post-production. All that stuff you saw on cereal boxes are my paintings.

CBA: *Did you work with Ralph Bakshi?*

Mike: Yeah, I did three movies with Bakshi. I did *Wizards, Lord of the Rings,* and I worked on a thing called *Hey, Good Lookin'.* I don't know what the story was on that one, but Ralph likes to do that. He likes to keep the story away from everyone, including the audience. [*laughter*]

I enjoyed the hell out of working with Ralph, even though we fought like cats and dogs. Part of working with Ralph was the fight, because everything was a fight. He's an individual; quite a character, and even to this day, almost every six months, I get a call from him.

CBA: *Do you enjoy working in animation?*

Mike: Animation is tedious. Film as a whole is tedious. It takes too long; especially animation. You work on a concept for two or three years and, by the time it's finished, it's

already history before anybody sees it. But it beats working for a living. [*laughter*]

CBA: *We all have a price. [laughter]*

Mike: Yeah, and mine isn't all that high! (*laughter*)

CBA: *What movies did you work on?*

Mike: I've done like forty of them—storyboarding, design work. I was the production designer on Michael Jackson's *Moonwalker.* I was designer on *Little Shop of Horrors.* I enjoyed that; I was working with Frank Oz, and I'd done a lot of work with the Muppet people. Frank is the Gentleman of Motion Pictures. That was his first movie, and he walked into the art department and said, "Okay guys, I want to let you know right now: Family comes first, movie comes second." That's the way it is with Frank. He was a jewel to work with.

CBA: *Did you do any work for Jim Henson?*

Mike: I worked on *Dark Crystal, Labyrinth,* and *Return to Oz.* There was a TV series I worked on called *The Storyteller.* I've done a lot of work with the Henson organization.

CBA: *So you gravitate toward fantasy material.*

Mike: Yeah, I like that kind of material. It's easy to do. There's nothing worse than working in the story department and not being able to relate to the story. But on the other side, I worked on *The Unbearable Lightness of Being.* [*laughter*]

CBA: *Did you work closely with Kevin Eastman when you did your* Santa Claus *book?*

Mike: Actually, I didn't do it for Kevin at all. I did it when I was living in England, and the original publisher was in Paris. We just sold it to him. That was a labor of love. I worked on in-between movies, and it took me about two years all together.

CBA: *Do you have any similar projects planned for the future?*

Mike: Yeah, actually, I'm really looking forward to getting out of the movie business altogether, and moving back to England and doing nothing but comics, even though the future of comics is a grey area right now. I have a deep-felt desire to be a storyteller again and I think I can walk in there and look Bernie in the eye now. [*laughter*]

CBA: *Once you got into comics, did you become a fan of others' art yourself? Did you hang out with the guys?*

Mike: I did in a sense. I respected their talents but I knew nothing about comics. I remember sitting in a cafe called Friar Tuck's, across from DC Comics, with a group of artists. Sitting next to me was a total stranger. He had been introduced to me as a big wig at DC Comics. His name was Carmine Infantino. Everybody

FRANKENSTEIN

MARVEL COMICS GROUP

20¢ 2 MAR 02105

THE MONSTER OF FRANKENSTEIN

PLOOG

MEET THE BRIDE OF THE MONSTER!

as chatting and drawing on the table cloth. Suddenly this executive next to me picks
up a ball point pen and begins to draw on the table cloth. I was impressed; imagine
an executive that can draw! I attempted to pay him a compliment, and said, "I'll be a
son of a gun! You can draw too!" [*laughter*] He glared at me, and you could have
fried eggs on his cheeks. I don't think he said a word, just glared at me as if to say,
"What do you mean, I can draw??" I looked around the table at a lot of blank, wide-
eyed faces. And, with a further display of ignorance, I added, "Yeah, now if worst
comes to worst, you could do that for a living." My memory is a bit vague about
what happened next but I never worked for DC Comics.

CBA: *What was John Verpoorten like?*

Mike: He was magic. When he died, I wept for him. He was this gentle giant, and I
really loved him

CBA: *Did the office change when he left?*

Mike: The changes began before Big John died. Stan had become more of a figure-
head in the company, and I always felt that a lot of integrity went out the window
about that time. After Verpoorten, there was a lot of shuffling around. I don't remember who became what but it seemed everybody became something. Comics were
attempting to become big business. All I remember was that Johnny Romita became
art director, and he kept reinking my pages with the wrong side of the brush, which
used to piss me off. He should really know the hairy end goes in the ink.

CBA: *Did you get to talk to Stan at all?*

Mike: Oh, yeah. He had an awful pretty secretary, Holly Resnicoff, who in a weak
moment married me. She soon regained consciousness and thought better of it.
Stan was a big part of that office and he took pride in being a major contributor to
what was known as the bullpen.

CBA: *Did you do work for Atlas Seaboard?*

Mike: I did a couple of stories for their black-&-whites. One of them I've never
seen in print; it was this Artful Dodger story, but it was in more modern times. I
wrote it and illustrated it.

CBA: *Overall, how would you rate your experience at Marvel?*

Mike: They were great years; I'd do them again, any day, but I'd want to do
them with the same bunch of guys. I'd want to do them with John Verpoorten, and
Gary Friedrich. I never met anybody that could outdrink me until I met Gary.
[*laughter*] I think the last time I saw him we were both sleeping on John
Verpoorten's floor. (*laughter*) ⬢

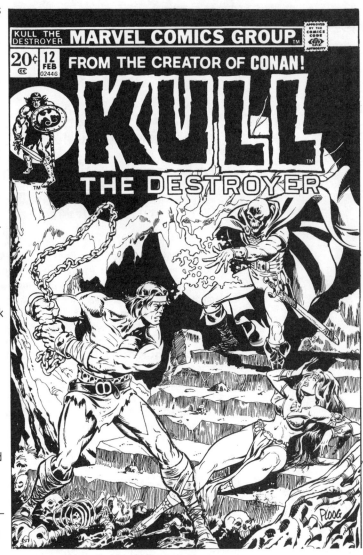

Right: Courtesy of art collector Victor Lim is this unaltered Mike Ploog cover for Kull the
Destroyer *#12. The printed version featured a pasted-up John Romita Sr. face on our hero king.
©2000 Marvel Characters, Inc. Kull ©2000 The Estate of Robert E. Howard.*

William Blake Everett

continued from pg. 139

with it so he didn't have much sense about it—I was reading
through some articles, and the writer described a period in 1939-
40 when they had first started in comics. My dad was broke and
didn't have any money. I thought that he was probably the only
person at Marvel who grew up with gazillions. He didn't have any
money and didn't particularly care.

I read how he had to work all weekend to get a comic out by
Tuesday so he could eat. That was how he lived and that was
how we lived in our house. He'd come home on Friday night after
Stan had paid him, and he'd stand in the living room and take
these hundred dollar bills and throw them around the room and
catch them. That was pretty much how he felt about money.
[*laughs*] Is that how it should be when you're a kid? No. It doesn't
make for a very stable household. [*laughs*]

Mike: *He is, of course, associated primarily with the* Sub-
Mariner. *There was, in the '50s, that TV show,* Sea Hunt, *with
Lloyd Bridges that had a lot of the same elements. Did he ever
talk about that?*

Wendy: We had television from 1950 on so I guess in some
ways TV was an extension of work. But I never saw the connection between the two. I don't think he made that connection. The
Sub-Mariner was an integral part of my whole life. That's different
than everything else—as if Sub-Mariner was the core and everything else was around it until Daredevil. I think that if he'd been in
a position to continue, Daredevil would've probably taken the
Sub-Mariner's place. My dad loved the Sub-Mariner and loved the

concept of it—he loved creating the stories. The good and evil,
the retribution for the genocide motif is what he loved to develop.
I'd come in and say, "What're you drawing?" He didn't exactly
write the story and then illustrate it—it didn't go that
way. It was, "I think I've got an idea and I have to
get this thing out by Friday or Stan's going to kill me.
I'll just make it up as I go along; I've got to turn in
ten pages because I get paid by the page." It was
not very well planned. He'd say, "What comes to
mind?" And we'd think out loud and he'd go back
and change something.

Mike: *How much of your dad was the Sub-
Mariner? Do you think there was a lot of identifi-
cation with the character?*

Wendy: I don't, but that's not to say that he
didn't. I know who my dad was and I know who
the Sub-Mariner is. It may have been who my
father aspired to be in some way, but I don't think
so.

Mike: *He told me in the late '60s that when he
looked back at the early '40s, what he saw was a
very angry young man that he later
recognized as himself. Though he said at the
time he wasn't conscious of it and was just doing the work.*

Wendy: My guess is that what he said is accurate. My father
was a charming, intelligent, immensely talented—and
complicated—human being. I loved him enormously and
miss him to this day. ⬢

Starlin's Cosmic Books

Talking to Jim about Adam Warlock and Mar-Vel

Conducted by Jon B. Cooke

Jim Starlin was another creative bolt out of the blue when he arrived at Marvel. In short order, he took Captain Marvel into a new cosmic direction while unloading new concepts wholesale on the readership. He capped the era by taking Warlock into a more sophisticated direction and then killing him. Jim was interviewed via phone on May 25, 1998, and he copy-edited the final transcript (which was transcribed by John Morrow).

Comic Book Artist: *Let's talk about your fan days. How'd you get involved in comics?*

Jim Starlin: Comics were about the only art you could get in Detroit in those days, and it was an artistic outlet that was different. My dad worked at Chrysler, and he used to bring home tracing paper and pencils that he would liberate from the drafting room. I would learn to draw the comic books, tracing off *Superman* and *Batman.* That's how I got started.

When I was in the Navy, I was drawing for fanzines. At the same time, I was sending stuff off to Marvel and DC. I sent in maybe a half dozen "Hulk" stories while I was away. They were pretty amateurish drawings, but I was getting better each time. They were never good enough to get published. One time I got a real kick because they said they had shown some of it to Herb Trimpe, who was the artist on *The Hulk* at that point.

CBA: *How'd you get involved doing Dr. Weird?*

Jim: He was from one of those fanzines. Al Milgrom and I were friends way back in high school, and he knew about all this fan stuff. I did one whole book of Dr. Weird, maybe four or five stories.

CBA: *How did you learn about comics art? Did you seek out advice on what pen to use, and that type of thing?*

Jim: I didn't know anything when I came here! I was lucky they were hiring as many people as they were at that point. Comics were going through a boom; Marvel was beginning to put out something like 56 books a month from 16 books a month. They were basically hiring anybody who could hold a pencil.

CBA: *When did you first become exposed to Marvel?*

Jim: I was reading them back when they were the monster books: "Fin Fang Foom," this dragon running around with a pair of swim shorts on. That was the first time I became aware of them.

CBA: *Did you recognize Kirby's style at the time?*

Jim: Yeah, he was always my favorite, him and Ditko. They were the foundations of what I

STARLIN & 90

was going to become as a cartoonist. I became aware of them before any other comic artists.

CBA: *Who's your greater influence: Kirby or Ditko?*

Jim: That's a tough one, because so much of what I got from Ditko was his head. Steve had a style that was completely different than anybody else in the industry. *Spider-Man* and "Dr. Strange" are completely divorced from the rest of the Marvel Universe in so many ways, just because of his influence on them. Compositionally, I was more influence by Kirby, but the spirit was more Ditko.

CBA: *You seemed to stylistically embrace them both.*

Jim: Yeah, my four big influences at that point were those two, Joe Kubert, and Carmine Infantino. Those were the ones I though were the best, and my structure came from those four places.

CBA: *What was your first professional sale?*

Jim: It was a couple of two-page stories for Joe Orlando; something about a butterfly, a witch, and a cauldron. I figured at that point I might as well come out to New York and give it a shot. Then at Marvel, it was a six-page love story. Gary Friedrich wrote it

Then I became the art director up at Marvel; I'm serious! They didn't have an art director at that point. This was just before Fran Giacoia started up. I started doing cover layouts up there; at first I was $10 for every one I sketched up. I wasn't good enough to be drawing comics at that point, but with basic outlines I was terrific. I'd take them in to Stan, and he would hop on his desk and really pose out how he wanted these things to look. One out of ten times he'd then get back into his seat and sit on his glasses! [*laughter*] He used to frustrate me because nothing was ever perfect the first time around. You always had to come back and do it again. But working for him, he was so wild that you just couldn't help having a good time.

CBA: *Was it a control thing with Stan?*

Jim: No, I don't think so. I think he really had a vision of what things should be like, and it was still his vision at that point.

CBA: *Was it more often than not seeking a Kirby-kind of look?*

Jim: He'd never say "Draw it like Kirby" but what he would describe to you would be a Kirby drawing. He would get up there and pose it all out for you. It always had that sort of dynamic feel

CBA: *Do you remember particular favorite cover layouts today?*

Jim: Some stick to mind. I did the layout for the first Valkyrie cover on *The Defenders.* She's on horseback; I think it's *Defenders* #4. It was one of the early ones, and I thought Sal Buscema did a beautiful job with it.

CBA: *You started in 1972. How long was it before you were doing stories, like* Iron Man?

Jim: My apprenticeship up there couldn't have lasted more than two or three months. It was changing that quickly. They were pulling people out of retirement who hadn't worked in 15 years. They grabbed Wayne Boring, and I don't think he'd drawn a book in a decade. Roy talked him into coming back because they need books filled up.

CBA: *What was the office like?*

Jim: One big room with a bunch of dividers, with two little offices at the back; a larger one for Stan, and a smaller one for

Roy Thomas, who was the new editor up there. Everybody else had cubicles. Marie was there; Herb wasn't there too often, he was freelance by the time I got up there. It started filling up with people. George Roussos was starting up there about that time. He sort of took over for Marie, who was in charge of the coloring for a long time.

CBA: *Were you actively lobbying to get a strip? Was there a strip you had your eye on?*

Jim: I wanted to do *The Hulk,* but Herb had that locked up. Starting off you get whatever they have available. They weren't going to give me the *Fantastic Four.* George Tuska got sick or something, so they needed fill-in issues of *Iron Man.* That's how I ended up doing two of those. The second job I did with Steve Gerber, and they were talking about having us do it regularly, but then Stan saw it and fired us both! He hated it!

CBA: *Didn't you also sneak in an issue of* Daredevil?

Jim: There were some pages that got used later on; there were four pages, the origin of Moondragon. I think that was through Mike Friedrich, who was writing *Daredevil* at that time, and we sandwiched those pages in; or maybe it was Gerber.

CBA: *When you came upon the scene, you seemed to have enormous, big ideas that you seemed to have been thinking about for quite a while. Were you considering these concepts for some time before you did them?*

Jim: No, most of the time it was flying by the seat of my pants from month to month.

CBA: *It seemed you really built off the cosmic foundation Kirby laid at Marvel; you were one of the few artists able to tap into that.*

Jim: Jack's *Thors* were his most impressive to me, where he got out there in the stars and stuff like that. As soon as I got to Marvel, I wanted to do cosmic stuff.

CBA: *In that "Blood Brothers" story in* Iron Man, *you started to introduce concepts that you later exploited fully in* Captain Marvel. *Were you developing a whole mythology of sorts?*

Jim: That was the one exception where there was some long term back plotting, on Thanos. Kirby had done the *New Gods,* which I thought was terrific. He was over at DC at the time. I came up with some things that were inspired by that. You'd think Thanos was inspired by Darkseid, but that wasn't the case when I showed up. In my first Thanos drawings, if he looked like anybody, it was Metron. I had all these different gods and things I wanted to do, which eventually became Thanos and the Titans. Roy took one look at the guy in the Metron-like chair and said, "Beef him up! If you're going to steal one of the New Gods, at least rip off Darkseid, the really good one!" So okay, I beefed him up, threw him in the story, and he worked much better that way.

I loved the *New Gods,* and they came and went, out like a light. I always felt that was such a shame.

CBA: *So you were pitching the idea to Roy?*

Jim: No, they asked me if I wanted to do *Captain Marvel* with Mike Friedrich. Mike and I were two of five comic guys who were sharing an apartment out in Staten Island; Bill Dubay, Steve Skeates, Mike Friedrich for a while, and later on Al Milgrom came from Detroit and replaced Mike. It was a strange group.

CBA: *How many pages could you do in a day?*

Jim: Back then I was doing about two pages of pencils a day. Mostly it was Milgrom and Dan Green inking.

CBA: *Where were you going with* Captain Marvel?

Jim: At the time there was this TV series called Kung Fu; it was about this martial artist in the old West being enlightened through discipline and training. I decided I wanted to do something like that on a space level. That's basically where *Captain Marvel* started going; it was about to be cancelled, so they said, "Do whatever you want with it." And we saved it; I was surprised.

CBA: *You had some pretty major characters coming out of the woodwork: Mentor and Eros...*

Jim: I brought in most of what would become half the cast of

the *Silver Surfer* TV-cartoon show.

CBA: *This seemed to be well thought out, with everything connected. Dr. Weird resembled Drax the Destroyer. Warlock was connected with Him, who was connected with the High Evolutionary. You had this really cool cosmic continuity going on. Were you thinking in that Marvel mode of trying to connect elements?*

Jim: No. I'd redesigned Dr. Weird, and when I did Drax , I thought, "Gee, that's such a nice design, why waste it?"

CBA: *Was there a connection with the Golden Age Destroyer?*

Jim: I knew it was there; there was also a Destroyer in *Thor* at the time. Roy gave it the name Drax. There had been many Destroyers at Marvel; I didn't think one more was going to clutter things up too much. [*laughter*]

CBA: *Did you have ambitions to spin off characters, and create your own sub-universe?*

Jim: I would like to have done it, but it was always so much trouble working with Marvel. They were always changing owners, editorial. During the time I worked from *Captain Marvel* up to *Warlock,* the editors I went through were Stan Lee, Roy Thomas, Len Wein, Marv Wolfman, and finally Archie Goodwin near the end. Every time I turned around there was somebody new to

Above: Adam meets the enemy, and he is hisself! Starlin gets Ditkoesque in the writing as well! Go Ayn Rand! From Warlock #11. ©1998 DC Comics

work with, and the owners were changing even more often. The richer the owners got, the stranger it was working up there. There was a spell there when I was working on the Epic books when I suddenly stopped getting paid; my vouchers disappeared. Like any office, there are times when things get out of control. A lot of times I was working on new projects up there, and those were the ones always getting screwed up clerically.

CBA: *When did you realize it was nearing time to leave? Was it as early as the interference creatively on Captain Marvel?*

Jim: There was a little bit of that. I needed a change by the time I got done with the Thanos thing, and I probably would have moved off the book anyhow, but there was some friction about changing the inker on me at the last moment without letting me know. Klaus Jansen was supposed to do the next book, and all of a sudden Jack Abel was on it. I liked Jack and I liked Jack's work, but they should have told me. There was some hard feelings on that, but it was also time to move on.

CBA: *Did you wrap up the Thanos saga like you wanted to?*

Jim: The Captain Marvel/Thanos stuff settled out just about where I wanted it to. The sales on the book were going up, so I could've run that out until they went down again. But I wanted to do something different.

CBA: *In a sense, would you say that by the end of your run on* Captain Marvel, *your Captain Marvel died?*

Jim: After I got done with it, Englehart and Milgrom did a nice run on it, but Archie, who was the editor up there later, told me that after that Marvel had no idea what to do with the character. So when I did the *Death of Captain Marvel*, I think I just wanted to connect it up, rather than say nothing else mattered. He did have a life, and we made reference to the latter series, even the Doug Moench stuff which didn't work too well, as far as I was concerned.

CBA: *Did you keep your eye on the book after you left it?*

Jim: Yeah. That was my first mistake! Now when I get off a series I tend to not look at it for a while. It was hard seeing where it was going. Even when I liked the stories, like with Englehart and Milgrom, there were things I wished they hadn't done. It's just your baby, and you can't help yourself.

CBA: *Whose idea was it to do the* Death of Captain Marvel?

Jim: Jim Shooter. He said, "We don't know what to do with this character; we haven't for a long time. Kill him off so we can bring somebody else back as it." I went, "Sure." I had no idea what I was going to do with it.

CBA: *He died in a very unMarvel-like way, a very human way.*

Jim: I had about five different plots I kept playing with. The first few plots he died in an explosion, but we'd been there, done that. My dad was suffering from cancer during that period and finally died, and after an appropriate period, it occurred to me that's how Captain Marvel should go out. In some ways, it was a means for me to work out my dad's death, doing that story.

CBA: *It was the first Epic graphic novel. Was it a good deal?*

Jim: It turned out to be a great deal. It was one of the first books Marvel gave royalties on. That was pretty unheard of at that time. We were setting up a whole bunch of contracts at that point; this was at the same time as *Dreadstar*. I had stopped working for Marvel for a while, and I was coming back.

CBA: *What came after* Captain Marvel?

Jim: "Warlock." There was also a few issues of the Thing team-up book [*Marvel Two-In-One*].

CBA: *Were you happy with the Sinnott inks on that?*

Jim: Well, I gave him really light breakdowns, and he did what he wanted to on them. They're not my favorite comics, but they're nice professional jobs. He was inking *Fantastic Four* over Buscema at that time, so it looked like the *FF*, which is what they wanted.

CBA: *Did you want to continue along in the cosmic vein, and is that why you did "Warlock"? Did you lobby for "Warlock"?*

Jim: No, I'd quit Marvel and I went out to California for a week or two to hang out with some friends. I came back and Roy asked me what I wanted to do. I'd thought about it the night before, and I said, "How about letting me do 'Warlock'?" That night I went home and started drawing it. It was as simple as that.

CBA: *Were there concepts you wanted to expand upon that you'd started in* Captain Marvel?

Jim: No, "Warlock" was a different head. "Warlock" was me working out my parochial school upbringing. [*laughter*] I went to Catholic grade school; I have to admit the nuns taught me how to think, but a more sadistic bunch of gals you'd never want to find. This was a lot of working out my anger at those years.

CBA: *Did you take a lot of heat about similarities between Thanos and Darkseid?*

Jim: No, once we got going, the only similarity between them was their size. There was a whole different head to these two guys. I don't think anyone ever mixed them up, or anything like that. They were both schemers, but Thanos was more scheming on an individual level, whereas Darkseid had his grand games that never reached fruition because the comic books got cancelled before the stories ended.

CBA: *What do you remember about when Kirby returned to Marvel in the mid-'70s?*

Jim: That was such a disheartening thing. I hadn't been working up at Marvel at that point, and he had come back recently. I guess he didn't want to do the old characters he had done, like *Fantastic Four*. He was doing things like *Devil Dinosaur* and *Eternals*. The editorial staff up at Marvel had no respect for what he was doing. I came into the office, and I remember being heartbroken, walking through this office. All these editors had things on their walls making fun of Jack's books. They'd cut out things, saying "Stupidest Comic of the Year." It was all really tasteless and dumb, and terribly disrespectful to the guy who had created this company they were working for. The part that blew me away the most was that this entire editorial office was just littered with stuff disparaging the guy who founded the company these guys were working for. He created all the characters these guys were editing. It was a very strange period.

CBA: *Do you think it was a problem overall hiring fans as editors? Did it created a lack of diversity of the books?*

Jim: They were the only people you could hire at the prices they were paying for editors. Especially after the royalties came into the situation, anybody who knew how to do it could make more money doing it. A lot of your editors were wanna-be writers. Archie Goodwin just died recently, and Archie was the pinnacle of what an editor should be. The art of what an editor should be doing has been lost completely, as far as I can see. I've talked to editors who have told me straight out that no one has ever put the lettering directly on a comic book page in the history of Marvel Comics; it's all been done by computers. [*laughter*] Their history of what they do goes back only two years or so.

CBA: *Were you able to run the course of* Warlock *the way you wanted?*

Jim: Pretty much. I remember there were some scraps along the way with some coloring things, and stuff like that. I was getting hit by the Comics Code a lot on *Warlock* at the beginning. There was a scene in the first issue where these guys are being tortured; one of them's being dipped into burning oil. The Code made us change it but the office only changed the black plate, so when it was published the guy was still dipping into the vat of oil in the coloring. It just didn't have any black lines around it any longer. It was rather funny. After that, I had a page in the first issue where a bunch of demons were attacking Warlock; they had bare bottoms, and in the next issue's flashback sequence we literally reprinted the same drawings that had passed in the first issue, and the Code made us go back and put little diapers on all the demons.

CBA: *It must've seemed ludicrous at times.*

Jim: It did. I had no desire to do exploding heads back then. [*laughter*] I was always pretty much able to do what I wanted. It got harder as the years went on. In the early years, Roy was the only editor. Most of the time, these books got done and were gone. Other than proofreading, there was no heavy editorial control.

CBA: *Was it difficult to come to the realization that all these heartfelt concepts you came up with were being appropriated by the company completely, and you had no hand in their future, or the profits thereof?*

Jim: Along this time, every time I took off, nobody touched the stuff. I took off for a while, and Thanos was a stone statue, and nobody bothered with him until I came back. Jim Shooter kept them off it for a long time, and just said, "When Starlin wants to come back, he'll do these." Now, they just recently had Thanos fighting Ka-Zar in a recent Marvel comic book. [*laughter*]

CBA: *I got the feeling that DC during the early 1970s was a very art-driven company, not that focused on the storytelling. Marvel had the storytellers, but it seemed at times the artist didn't matter; you could throw George Tuska on a book, then Sal Buscema could come on, and it was still chugging along. But you were an anomaly at Marvel; you were an all-around creator. You created all these concepts. Did you feel that writing was king? Why didn't you dialogue your own books?*

Jim: I didn't go too long without dialoguing my own books. I think we went only three issues with Mike Friedrich scripting *Captain Marvel,* and then I took it over. Steve Englehart later came along and finished off the last two issues for me. I wasn't happy with my writing at that point, and I voluntarily gave it up. I wanted to take a break, and I wanted to work with him again. He was a good writer; it was a way of learning. He and I and Alan Weiss used to hang around a lot together, so besides working together, we were also friends. That was a very close collaboration.

CBA: *Did you give story ideas for Steve to use in other books?*

Jim: We would talk over ideas, but I would never help him plot his books. There was a spell where we were all talking about God over a weekend up in Rutland, Vermont. The month that followed, *Dr. Strange* had God in it, *Captain Marvel* had God in it; different versions going in different directions, but it all stemmed from that same weekend.

CBA: *Did you have ambitions at Marvel? Did you look at Kirby's position at DC as editor/writer/artist as something to strive for?*

Jim: I always figured "editorial" meant you had to be up at the office, and I never wanted to do that. I liked setting my own hours; I was happy with what I was doing. What I did want was

an editor who had no control. I wanted somebody to proof for me, and do the letters pages.

CBA: *When you're writing your own stuff as an artist, do you still do it "Marvel style"?*

Jim: Back then I used to draw it and then write it. Even today I still sit down and do the same thumbnails I did back then on loose leaf paper.

CBA: *Did you ever work full script?*

Jim: Yeah, most of the stuff I did at DC was full script; all the *Batman* stuff, everything I ever did with Bernie Wrightson. With *DC Presents,* usually I sat down and talked with whoever the scripter was, but I plotted every one of them.

CBA: *What are the attributes of a good editor?*

Jim: A good editor will give you help when you ask for it; doesn't micro-manage what you're doing; trusts you to tell the story. You always need somebody to be looking over your shoulder, just to catch your mistakes; on a proofreading level if nothing else, you always need an editor. They place where the ads go, they take care of the letters page.

CBA: *Would you characterize Roy as a hands-on editor?*

Jim: No, Roy was really loose. He was good at that point; he'd

continued on pg. 169

Above: Sharks in Space! Jim Starlin page from Warlock #14. ©2000 Marvel Characters, Inc.

Steve Englehart & Soul

The Celestial Madonna, Nixon, and God

Conducted by Bob Brodsky

Steve Englehart accomplished a lot during his five years writing for Marvel Comics in the early 1970s. In his stories, after all, Dr. Strange met God, the Avengers fought the Defenders, and Captain America watched as a scandal-torn President Nixon blew his brains out in the Oval Office.

Englehart originally pursued a career as an artist. By 1970 he was assisting Neal Adams, and doing background work for Bob Oksner at DC. In 1971 he landed in the Marvel Bullpen, where he turned a chance writing assignment into a remarkable career.

Englehart's approach to writing is based as much on his degree in Psychology as it is on his affection for the heroes of the Marvel Universe. He delivered complex plots and sub-plots, shaping the characters over time, from what they were to what he envisioned they could become. His organic approach to characterization was perfectly suited to the Marvel "soap opera." His characters had soul, and readers could feel it.

The son of a newspaper journalist, Englehart grew up in Kentucky and Indiana, but has been a Bay Area resident for 25 years. We spoke with him by telephone from his Oakland home last May. "Stainless" Steve is direct, and intense. Our conversation nicely illustrates why he was a major contributor to the success of Marvel Phase Two.

Above: *Certainly a highpoint of Steve's Cap run was the revelation of a '50s Cap. Here's a page from* Captain America *#154. ©1998 Marvel Entertainment.*

CBA: *Where you a Marvel fan growing up?*
Steve: I was too old to have read Marvel growing up. As a kid, Walt Disney, DC super-hero comics and "Dick Tracy" were favorites of mine. In terms of super-heroes, it was Superman, Batman; that stuff.

I outgrew comics at around the age of 14. Specifically, I remember reading a *Superboy* comic and somebody wrote in to the letters column asking, "Why doesn't Superboy fight the Commies?" The answer was, "He's not interested in political matters." I thought, "This doesn't make any sense, this doesn't sound real to me," so I outgrew them.

During my freshman year of college in 1965, a friend said, "You've got to take a look at this." It was a Ditko *Spider-Man,* and I liked it. I bought three months' worth of all the Marvel books at a little newsstand in town. So I not only met the characters for the first time, but I really got the full force of the soap opera and the ongoing relationships between all those characters. That sucked me in.
CBA: *How did you make the leap from being Neal Adams' assistant to a writer at Marvel?*
Steve: I was doing freelance art, and not much of it. The great thing about comics in those days was that it was small community located almost entirely inside New York. As soon as you joined comics, you had 300 friends. One of the guys I got to know was

Gary Friedrich, who was a writer and an assistant editor at Marvel. In the summer of '71, Gary called and said, "I'm looking for somebody to sit in on my job at Marvel for six weeks while I go to Missouri. It would just be proofreading and art correction, low-level stuff."

At the end of six weeks, Gary decided that he liked it in Missouri, and was going to see if he could make a go of it living there. So I was asked if I wanted to keep the job and I said I would because I had gotten to enjoy it by that point. Not too long after that, Gary sent back a six-page Al Hewitson-plotted story for *Where Monsters Dwell* that he didn't feel like writing. I was asked to write it and they liked what I wrote.

Marvel at the time was a bullpen. There were probably no more than 15 of us in the office. I really enjoyed sitting next to Johnny Romita, Herb Trimpe, Roy Thomas, and Stan Lee, and a half dozen other people. A couple of days after I wrote the Hewitson story, Roy asked me to write the Beast in *Amazing Adventures*. Roy liked my work on that and after a couple of months he asked me to write *Captain America* and *The Avengers*. In the space of four months, I went from not being a writer to writing five books for Marvel.
CBA: *What was your initial approach to the books?*
Steve: The books were what you made of them. When I took over *Captain America*, it was about to be cancelled. Six months after I began on the book, it was Marvel's top-selling book. I believe in my characters. If I write them, I try to get inside their heads. When I took over *Captain America*, my approach was to say, "If this guy really existed, if he'd gone into that lab in 1941 and had come out and lived through World War II, had been frozen and was living in the 1970s now, who would he really be?"
CBA: *Your first Beast story had great narrative and a crisp plot. I thought it was a superb debut.*
Steve: Thank you. It must have been okay, because they gave me more work.
CBA: *Were you intimidated graduating from the Beast to, by the end of 1972, handling* The Avengers, Captain America, Doc Savage, *and* The Defenders?
Steve: No. That felt comfortable. It wasn't until the next year, when I went to six books, that it felt uncomfortable. There was no reason not to do it.
CBA: *Was it your idea to expand The Defenders to include Silver Surfer, Valkyrie?*
Steve: When Stan retired as active editor, the one commandment he left was that he wanted to be the only one to write the Silver Surfer. It was possible to go and say, "I've got a really good idea, can I do a couple issues with the Surfer?" But in general, the Surfer was not supposed to be part of any ongoing deal. Roy had done a couple of issues of *The Hulk* with the Surfer and the Sub-Mariner, and people liked it. That was the genesis of the Defenders. But he had to take the Surfer out, and put Dr. Strange in.

When I was doing it, I thought I'd like to put the Surfer in for a few issues because he does work well with those characters. So the Surfer got involved. I think Valkyrie was my idea. She was a Roy character from *The Avengers*. I thought, "The team needs a woman, she's a butt-head, she'll play off these guys." You don't want wimps hanging out with the Sub-Mariner and the Hulk. I felt like I knew what to do on *The Defenders*. I knew how to develop them, and make them cool and so forth.

CBA: *You seemed to solve the problem of finding them powerful enough opponents, by centering most of it on Doc Strange and the supernatural.*

Steve: Yeah. Dr. Strange had an interesting group of villains. If I wanted to use Hulk villains, they were already being used in *The Hulk.* And Sub-Mariner also had his own book. But Dr. Strange, I think that was in-between his books. I was the only one who had to deal with Dr. Strange, so I had access to all those villains.

CBA: *Did you or Roy originally plot the "phony Cap" series?*

Steve: It was Roy's idea. He said to me, "It would be cool to have a '50s, right-wing guy—now you take it and run with it." The actual story was mine, the idea was his.

CBA: *Had the continuity problem bothered you?*

Steve: I think that was a Roy thing; he was big on continuity. I was able to read a lot of those '50s *Captain America* stories. A lot of the stuff that I did came from saying, "Okay, all this is true, what can I use from it? How can I build a story out of these facts?" In any event, I tried to make all that '50s stuff fit into the Marvel Universe.

CBA: *You had to do a lot of explaining, but that was irrelevant by the time the reader got to that point, because you'd done such a masterful job of moving the story. I think that ultimately your version of Captain America was about a good man's disillusionment. It really began right there with the phony Cap. You gave Cap a personality. You made him more of a human being. Your writing itself was very warm, very personal.*

Steve: I liked him. I did not share his patriotic sensibilities. He wanted to volunteer for the Army, I didn't want to get anywhere near the Army, but I had no choice. But I never condescended to him. Here was this guy, he was a 1940s guy, and he was living in the 1970s. To me, that was a major component of what that book was supposed to be about. Once you start saying, "Okay, he's real," then everything sort of flows out of that.

CBA: *Why did you revisit the Steranko-era Hydra stories in* Avengers *and not in your* Captain America?

Steve: When I took over Avengers, I already had Captain America. Roy handed me a completely-drawn George Tuska story, and said, "Stan plotted this for an inventory issue and never used it. You can use it in either *Captain America* or *The Avengers,* but you have to do something with it." I decided to build an Avengers story around it.

CBA: *I thought it worked pretty well. It resolved another continuity question, the matter of Cap's secret identity. Do you have any favorite Avengers, Steve?*

Steve: Vision and (Scarlet) Witch, and Mantis. Mantis because I created her and just because I really liked her. I thought she was really cool. But I've always had a real soft spot in my heart for Vision and Witch. I think a lot of people have. I liked everybody else, but my favorites would probably be those three.

CBA: *For me, 1973 was your pivotal year. You wrote numerous titles including* Cap, Avengers *and new projects like* Master of Kung Fu, Luke Cage *and* Dr. Strange. *'73 was also the year of the* Avengers/Defenders *crossover. Had anything changed for you that lead to your creative explosion that year?*

Steve: No, I think it was just continuous. Marvel gave me a place to stand and I started doing what I did.

CBA: *Do you think you realized your potential in 1973?*

Steve: Yeah, with their encouragement. Nobody told me, "You can't do this." In fact, they said, "How can you make this cooler than it ever was?" I just took whatever skills and interests I had and applied it. I just kept doing what I did.

CBA: *Did you request Luke Cage, or was he assigned to you?*

Steve: I think he was assigned to me. Archie Goodwin had started that off. That was an interesting book.

CBA: *Were you satisfied with your Cage work?*

Steve: Pretty much. I wouldn't say it was as memorable as *Cap* or *Avengers.* I loved the Luke Cage vs. Dr. Doom storyline.

CBA: *I really remember your villains in the series; they were very oddball—kind of Chester Gould-ish.*

Steve: Yeah, exactly. I loved *Dick Tracy* as a kid and Cage, the way Archie had set him up, wasn't really fighting super-villains, *per se.* He was fighting Dick Tracy-kind of bad guys, and I also tried to do that. With characters like Black Mariah and Señor Suerté, I tried to figure out urban variations on the whole thing.

CBA: *Any thoughts on* The Hulk? *You wrote the title throughout 1973.*

Steve: I had a good time with that. Herb Trimpe and I were both in the office, and we'd work out the stories together. That was fun. Again, I was following Archie and he had done a masterful job.

CBA: *Was your* Hulk *run a conscious tribute to early '60s Marvel? You gave the book an anachronistic, Cold War flavor, and introduced one-shot exotic-named villains like Aquon and Zzzax that reminded me of Marvel's "Fin Fang Foom"-era monster stories.*

Steve: Well, there was no conscious tribute on my mind. I just was looking for guys strong enough to fight the Hulk. I always come at it from the characters and I was more interested in the relationships between Bruce, Betty, Talbot, and "Thunderbolt" Ross than the villains who came in to give the stories a context. I

Above: *Frank Brunner's pencils for Doctor Strange #4, page 22. CBA hopes to interview Frank for our upcoming "Marvel Age: Phase II" special issue. Art ©1998 Frank Brunner Dr. Strange ©1998 Marvel Entertainment.*

Above: *Mike Ploog's Marvel Premiere #6 cover before it was altered. Note the repositioning of the woman from recline to defense. Art ©1998 Mike Ploog. Dr. Strange ©1998 Marvel Entertainment.*

think that's pretty much true for any of my books. Roy once told me that when he wrote *The Avengers,* he would think out the super-villain in the plot and then he'd figure out what Wanda and the Vision were going to do. I always figured out what Wanda and the Vision were going to do and *then* added the super-villain.

CBA: *The Avengers/Defenders crossover is my best memory of the summer of '73. Did Gardner Fox's JLA/JSA stories inspire you?*

Steve: Not in any significant sense. I had read and enjoyed the Gardner Fox stories, but that was a very different sort of thing. The whole Julie Schwartz/Gardner Fox vibe was so different from what Marvel had been doing, going back to the Human Torch and the Sub-Mariner in the '40s. Crossovers had been done at Marvel many times. I just wanted to bring my two groups together.

CBA: *The crossover was a very memorable event for a lot of fans. I've always been amazed by how much you were able to do, and how smoothly the books played off each other.*

Steve: Well, you don't know what you can do until you do it, so you just go for it.

CBA: *Did the end of the Vietnam War inspire your creation of Mantis, a half-Vietnamese character?*

Steve: I think that's why she was Vietnamese. I wanted to do a Kung Fu character. I decided to go with an Asian character and Vietnam was in the news.

CBA: *Right. On the Swordsman, I thought it was neat the way you avoided the obvious by giving him thought balloons that showed the reader he was sincere about reforming. You didn't make us guess "Is he or isn't he?" Did you view him as a tragic character?*

Steve: Definitely; from the beginning. My original idea was that Mantis was going to come in and just be a *femme fatale.* She was going to seduce every male Avenger and cause problems among the group members. The Swordsman was always set up to be a loser in this situation. But her seduction of the Vision seemed to work so well that I stopped at that point. Over time, she turned from being a cheap slut into the Celestial Madonna.

CBA: *You planned for her to become the Celestial Madonna?*

Steve: No, that all just developed as it went. She was just there to be a seductress, and then the whole thing just grew out of her relationships. As people interacted, things happened. Every writer talks about characters coming alive and writing themselves, and Mantis pretty much did just that.

CBA: *Was it difficult for you having to carry on with the book after completing the epic Mantis series?*

Steve: Yeah, but that's part of the game. After Mantis, I was able to look around in the rubble, so to speak, and I decided to bring back the Beast and Patsy Walker. I didn't get to do everything that I wanted to do with those characters and I got the chance to continue them on.

CBA: *Moving over to* Dr. Strange, *you basically turned it back into a counterculture book. Frank Brunner and you were incredible together. Was it liberating working with a guy more your age, more experimental, after working with a lot of traditional people?*

Steve: Yeah, I guess so. I hadn't really thought about it in those terms, but Frank and I were good friends. We co-produced the book together. Every two months, before we both moved to California, I would go to his place in New York City or he would come to my place in Connecticut. We would discuss the things that we each wanted to see happen in the book that month. We would have dinner, and spend the night marrying our different versions together.

CBA: *Your treatment of Dr. Strange in his own series was very different from how you portrayed him in* The Defenders.

Steve: When I wrote him in *The Defenders,* he was just a super-hero who had magical schticks. When I started writing him as himself, I thought if I'm going to write about a magician, I really ought to learn something about magic. So I started studying tarot and astrology, and as I learned things there I was feeding them back into the book. So Strange, for me, became a way of imparting mystical knowledge that I was picking up elsewhere.

CBA: *Was inheriting* Captain Marvel *from Jim Starlin difficult?*

Steve: That was interesting because Jim and I were friends. He came to me two or three issues before he left the book and said that he didn't feel that he really could write well enough to do those issues, and would I do them? I think Jim asked me because he really wanted to learn about being a writer. So I was doing the characters and, when Jim left, I just slipped into the book. There were three or four issues at the beginning of my run with Al Milgrom that I consider to be up there with my best stuff.

Now, of course, however he learned it, Jim's a great writer.

CBA: *Let's move over to a book that was amazing—*Captain America. *Let's pick up with 1973 and move through to 1975, the final year of your run. Your introduction of Peggy Carter, Sharon's older sister and Cap's long-lost lover from World War II created an interesting triangle. What was your motivation there?*

Steve: My introduction of Peggy was an attempt to link the generations by introducing somebody who knew Cap in a previous existence. The fact that she's the sister of the girl that he's in love with now, created even more possibilities in the storyline.

CBA: *Was Dave Cox, the heroic conscientious objector, a surrogate for you?*

Steve: In a sense. I've got both of my arms, but I wanted to do a heroic conscientious objector, because you weren't likely to see it anyplace else. It wasn't that I was a *heroic* conscientious objector, but I was a conscientious objector, so I understood what that entailed. I threw him in to speak to that point.

CBA: *Were you a Watergate buff?*

Steve: Oh, yeah, a lot of us were. I really saw the whole thing unfolding like a novel. Watergate fascinated me and naturally it occurred to me that Captain America had to react to this. How could this be going on with Captain America ignoring it? So, we took this turn where Cap decided to give up being Captain America, which was unheard of. I had a lot of fun with that. Everybody sort of assumed that Cap would be gone for an issue or two, maybe four issues, but he was gone for a long time. Doing the book month after month without him—you talk about challenges, that was a challenge. I loved every minute of it. I would think, "How can I keep this going without Captain America in it?" My answer led to the Nomad, Roscoe, and all this stuff, which went where no comic had ever gone before. That was total Marvel in those days: "Just go for it."

CBA: *Had you thought about making Nomad permanent?*

Steve: No. I thought long and hard about who Captain America would be if he weren't Captain America, but I couldn't imagine Steve Rogers being the Nomad for the rest of his life. It would have taken something as dramatic as the Red Skull returning, or whatever, to get him to come around, but I think in his heart of hearts Steve wanted it all to work out somehow so he could still be Captain America.

CBA: *You've talked about having a lot of creative freedom at Marvel. Did your off-panel Nixon suicide in* Cap #175 *meet with their resistance?*

Steve: No.

CBA: *He was still President when that was published.*

Steve: Right. I think I got to that and said, "If I say that it's Nixon, I might run into trouble." So, I just kept it all off panel. It was self-censorship. I just assumed it was better to keep a low profile for something like that. I knew my story wasn't going to bring down the Republic, but it wasn't nearly as easy to trash the President and walk away from it as it is today. Yet, I was very clear that the President had trashed himself and deserved this sort of fate. I just decided to do it off-panel.

CBA: *Why did you leave Marvel in 1976?*

Steve: Professional run-in with the editor-in-chief.

CBA: *Why does your '70s Marvel work still stand up so well?*

Steve: Somehow I just had the affinity and ability for doing that work. Maybe it was my dad's genes, or whatever. I just did it. 🌀

Above: *More Brunner's pencils from Doctor Strange #4. Art ©2000 Frank Brunner. Dr. Strange ©2000 Marvel Characters, Inc.*

Jim Starlin

continued from pg. 165

have his monthly meeting, and talk a little bit, but if things were going right, he'd leave you alone. I'd meet with him mostly in his office individually, but every two or three months he'd have a group meeting of all the writers or all the artists. It wasn't that many people back then, so we could all fit into his office. Usually it was stressing storytelling; that was the big thing everybody had to keep coming back to, being able to tell the story. It made them the popular house that they were.

CBA: *Did Stan look at your work while you were working on* Captain Marvel *and* Warlock?

Jim: Shortly after I was working on *Captain Marvel,* he went out to California to sell movie rights. That was pretty much the last time he was involved in the office, to be honest. We'd see each other occasionally at a convention and he'd say, "This is nice." I don't know if he actually saw any of it, to tell you the truth. I remember him coming back to the office, trying to figure out who the hell Howard the Duck was. He disconnected pretty well, despite the fact that his name was on the books for a long time.

CBA: *Were you able to retrieve your art during this time?*

Jim: They started returning artwork about the time I started doing *Captain Marvel,* so yeah, I was able to get most of the artwork back. I saved a lot of it for a long time; later on I sold some.

CBA: *Did you get close with any other artists at the time?*

Jim: I rented space up at Continuity for a while. I got tight with Alan Weiss, Chaykin; Brunner and I were close for a while. Bernie and I got very close over the years. Ploog and I were pretty chummy back then.

CBA: *Do you have a particular fondness for the material you worked on in the '70s?*

Jim: Yeah. When I decided I was going to come back and do more comic book stuff, I went to Marvel to see about getting a hold of Thanos again. That was my first inclination. That didn't happen, but I still think Thanos is my favorite character, bar none.

CBA: *Overall, how would you characterize the time? You seemed to progress very rapidly.*

Jim: Everybody was trying new things, so if you got into that group, you flew. It's not like it is now; the editorial control now is just frightening, stifling. Now I can understand why all these guys ran off and started Image.

That's what I'm going to go do. I've tried the stuff with DC and Marvel, and I've got an idea that I'm going to self-publish. It'll probably start off black-&-white, but I can't see working under these... it just doesn't work for me anymore. 🌀

Below: *A rare take on The Hulk by Jim Starlin in this collaboration with Bill DuBay. Jim was a cover designer when he first arrived at Marvel in the early '70s. ©2000 Marvel Characters, Inc.*

"That Kid from Out West!"

Alan Weiss talks about his rootin', tootin' times in '70s comics

Right inset: From a tribute to Jack Abel, here's a Weiss panel featuring young Alan and his brother Howard reading comics. The one-page strip will be featured in TwoMorrow's autobiographical anthology, Streetwise. Courtesy of the artist. ©2000 Alan Weiss.

Below: Courtesy of the artist, here's Alan Weiss ready to saddle-up in a recent photo.

Conducted by Jon B. Cooke
Transcribed by Jon B. Knutson

We're including an interview with Alan Weiss because, for one thing, he's one of those few artists from the '70s who was perfectly at home drawing for the Big Two, DC Comics and Marvel—or at Warren, National Lampoon, Esquire, and Atlas/Seaboard, for that matter!—and for another, we think his artwork is simply superb. As enthusiastic today about comics as when he first entered the field in 1970 or so, Alan proves to be a highly entertaining interview, giving insight to some legendary stories of the past and enriching us with ones previously unheard. The artist was interviewed via phone on March 9, 2000, and he copyedited the final transcript.

Comic Book Artist: *There's very little on you written in the historical record.*
Alan Weiss: I'm that mysterious, "Who the hell is he?" guy.
CBA: *I think you first appeared rather early in Silver Age fandom, in the letter column of Fantastic Four #3.*
Alan: I was there. I didn't know who the artist of *FF* was at the time, and I think that's what the letter was about. Remember, they didn't credit the jobs quite yet, and I was commenting on the very first issue. "I think your book will be very successful." Stan wrote something like, "What do you think we are now, chopped liver?" [*laughs*] They'd just come out of being Atlas Comics. I thought it was pretty brash for them to be calling *FF* "The World's Greatest Comics Magazine." [*laughs*] "Yeah, prove it, sucker—where's your cape?" [*laughter*]
CBA: *You were born in Las Vegas?*
Alan: No, Chicago, but from age seven on, I lived in Las Vegas.
CBA: *Remember your first comics?*
Alan: Soon after I got to Vegas. There are some earlier, vague memories of looking at a *Lone Ranger* comic book, or perhaps *Superman,* because I used to watch him on TV, and I must have started drawing even that early.

CBA: *Your brother Howard is older or younger?*
Alan: Younger.
CBA: *Did you both draw together?*
Alan: Yeah, we did. I have another brother, Curtis, who's younger than Howard, but it was mostly Howard and I that drew together. My dad, while never a professional, was a hell of an artist and a fine painter, and he knew a lot. He directed us in terms of the fundamentals, the basics. One time, he drove us out to the local newspaper, and we got the end of a giant roll of newsprint, right off the machines, because when they got to the end, they couldn't use them anymore, but it was enough paper for us for three years. I'd made the decision relatively early that I wanted to have my own style, and the way to do that was to learn real anatomy rather than just drawing versions of other people's drawings, so that's what we did. Fortunately, this was before I discovered girls, or else I never would've put in the work, I'll tell you that right now.
CBA: *[laughs] So, did you seek out the Bridgeman and Burne Hogarth anatomy books?*
Alan: You bet. Bridgeman, Loomis, Hogarth, and just about everyone else. We learned the Latin names for the muscles really early on, long before I took any courses in anatomy, and certainly before I did any life drawing.
CBA: *Was your ultimate goal to do super-hero comics, per se?*
Alan: Yeah, sure! Well, certainly comics. Super-heroes were my favorite thing, but I liked all different kinds of genres. Give me sword-&-sorcery or the *Hercules* comics being done at the time. I was following the movies, and even then, I always liked cowboy movies and Western stuff.
CBA: *You were introduced to fandom through the letter pages?*
Alan: Yeah, I saw the letter from Roy Thomas in *Justice League of America* that mentioned *Alter-Ego,* and they printed the address, so I sent for it. That was the beginning in finding this whole other weird world by mail. I did a lot of fanzine work in those days, and that's how I discovered the old characters, as I'd never seen any of the '40s comics at all. It was a real delight that at the exact same time, some of the old heroes were coming back into the Marvel books. I was learning about their previous history in the '40s, like my favorite, Sub-Mariner, and Captain America, of course. My uncle used to tell me about reading those books when he was a kid.
CBA: *What was it about Sub-Mariner?*
Alan: I missed the fourth issue of *FF* with Namor's revival, and I was frantic to get hold of it. So, I wrote to Marvel—because I was just a little kid, and I didn't know what they did and didn't do—and asked, "Do you guys have any extra books, because I sure want one, and I'd be glad to pay for it." Well, the very day I bought the fifth

issue, FF #4 arrived in the mail from Flo Steinberg, with a little note that said, "Here you go—we happened to have an extra, but don't worry about it." So, I got to read them back-to-back, "The Sub-Mariner Returns" plus Subby's team-up with Dr. Doom, and that was it for me. I was *gone!* Those two issues blew my mind, and I loved that artwork—and there's something about Subby… I mean, he is such an absurd idea in so many ways, a guy dressed in a swimsuit. But he had a kind of alien nobility about him, an elfin-looking eeriness, with that weird head and the eyebrows, pointy ears, and really, the stupid idea of the wings on his feet… stupid, but cool, like comic books are supposed to be! [*laughter*] I have this concept that I haven't been able to do in print yet about how he can fly with those little, tiny wings… it's a real great pseudo-scientific explanation… but if you go by straight physics, I don't think so. [*laughter*]

CBA: *Did you seek out the Golden Age issues?*

Alan: I did eventually send for a few of the earlier issues from the guys who were hawking old comics at the time. I ended up getting some of the ones from the '50s.

CBA: *The Bill Everetts?*

Alan: Yeah, actually that was some of Everett's best work. In fact, I think it was some of John Romita's best work on *Captain America,* too, when John was doing nice, tall figures. Those books were really special. At the same time, I found a couple of Mac Raboy *Captain Marvel, Jr.*s—Raboy's right out of Alex Raymond, and that was my favorite stuff. Fortunately, my father encouraged me. He was more into fine arts, but he wasn't a snob, so he loved good animation and illustration, and he certainly loved *Prince Valiant* and *The Spirit.* He remembered *The Spirit* from the newspaper insert, the cinematic quality of it. It was great to have a father that well-rounded.

CBA: *Was your father from Chicago?*

Alan: He was originally from New York, and then lived in Chicago for many years before going out to Las Vegas. He worked at various jobs in the gaming industry; but my grandfather—his father—had been a gambler always, back to the old speakeasy days in New York and Chicago. "Silent Max" had the connections, so he was there when Vegas was first starting up. Casinos used to hire him to not only shill, but also to keep an eye on everybody else, because he could spot the cheaters. It was just kind of a cool thing. So, both my father and his brother followed him out to Vegas. I was real sick as a kid, with very bad asthma, so they thought it would be a good idea for us to be in a warm, dry climate.

CBA:
Was growing up in Las Vegas like one would imagine—provocative?

Alan: I don't know if it's like what you'd imagine! "Nobody lives there, do they?" [*laughter*] You know, we were kids, didn't go near the gambling. We just got to sort of enjoy the fringe benefits of it, the pretty lights and the food. Mainly, as kids, we had desert two blocks away from anywhere you were at that time, so you could run around, chase lizards, and play cowboys. It was just really a great place! Of course, when we first landed, I was very disappointed. "Where are all the horses? What are these taxicabs doing here?" I was a little kid, I thought it was going to be like a Western movie. I had no idea we were actually going into the modern West. I thought we were just going to ride horses from then on, there wouldn't be any cars…

CBA: *The Wayback Machine. [laughs]*

Alan: But it's an amazing place. Everybody dwells on just the strip or the downtown area, but 40 miles in one direction you've got the world's largest man-made lake, with that fantastic dam across the Colorado River, and a few miles in the other direction, you're up in the mountains, where you can ski in the Winter. Every time I'd go back there, I'd have friends come through, and it was great to take them out of the city… like Steve Englehart. We'd go up to Pine Creek and spend a day going around checking out the petroglyphs, you know, and making up stories. Vegas is really beautiful, but it's become so huge and congested compared to what it was—about 50 times larger than what it was back then, and a whole lot more pollution—but it's still a great town. It really is the adult Disneyland, if you can take that as a compliment. [*laughter*] My brothers are still there. I went to school there, UNLV. "Tumbleweed Tech," it was called back then.

CBA: *Did you make a conscious decision then that you were going to be a comic book artist at a certain stage?*

Alan: It's the kind of decision you make in stages. You say, "I'd like to do this, but I don't know if it's really a practical thing," so you think, "Maybe I'll become a medical artist," or "Maybe something in design." None of them quite got to the level of reality, but I worked for both newspapers in town, working my way, proverbially, through college, so….

CBA: *What were you doing?*

Alan: Artwork. Different kinds of things, some for the paper, some

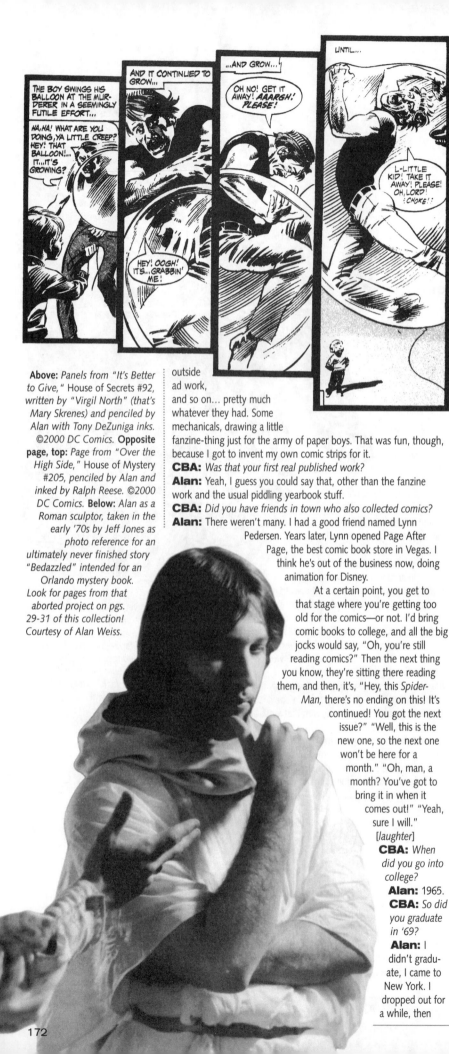

Comic panels:

THE BOY SWINGS HIS BALLOON AT THE MURDERER IN A SEEMINGLY FUTILE EFFORT...

HA, HA! WHAT ARE YOU DOING, YA LITTLE CREEP? HEY! THAT BALLOON!... IT...IT'S GROWING?

HEY! OOGH! IT'S...GRABBIN' ME!

AND IT CONTINUED TO GROW...

OH NO! GET IT AWAY! AARGH! PLEASE!

...AND GROW...

UNTIL....

L-LITTLE KID! TAKE IT AWAY! PLEASE! OH, LORD! CHOKE!

Above: *Panels from "It's Better to Give," House of Secrets #92, written by "Virgil North" (that's Mary Skrenes) and penciled by Alan with Tony DeZuniga inks. ©2000 DC Comics.* **Opposite page, top:** *Page from "Over the High Side," House of Mystery #205, penciled by Alan and inked by Ralph Reese. ©2000 DC Comics.* **Below:** *Alan as a Roman sculptor, taken in the early '70s by Jeff Jones as photo reference for an ultimately never finished story "Bedazzled" intended for an Orlando mystery book. Look for pages from that aborted project on pgs. 29-31 of this collection! Courtesy of Alan Weiss.*

outside ad work, and so on… pretty much whatever they had. Some mechanicals, drawing a little fanzine-thing just for the army of paper boys. That was fun, though, because I got to invent my own comic strips for it.

CBA: *Was that your first real published work?*

Alan: Yeah, I guess you could say that, other than the fanzine work and the usual piddling yearbook stuff.

CBA: *Did you have friends in town who also collected comics?*

Alan: There weren't many. I had a good friend named Lynn Pedersen. Years later, Lynn opened Page After Page, the best comic book store in Vegas. I think he's out of the business now, doing animation for Disney.

At a certain point, you get to that stage where you're getting too old for the comics—or not. I'd bring comic books to college, and all the big jocks would say, "Oh, you're still reading comics?" Then the next thing you know, they're sitting there reading them, and then, it's, "Hey, this *Spider-Man*, there's no ending on this! It's continued! You got the next issue?" "Well, this is the new one, so the next one won't be here for a month." "Oh, man, a month? You've got to bring it in when it comes out!" "Yeah, sure I will." [laughter]

CBA: *When did you go into college?*

Alan: 1965.

CBA: *So did you graduate in '69?*

Alan: I didn't graduate, I came to New York. I dropped out for a while, then

went back. At a certain point, it felt like it was getting too repetitious, and I wasn't really making headway. I wasn't making any decisions, and couldn't see what the future was going to be. So I figured, go to New York, take a shot, find out if you are or aren't good enough, and if not, you can always come back home, finish college, and make new plans. That didn't happen.

CBA: *Going back to your fanzine days a little bit: Was mail like a magical thing for you? Were you always looking forward to correspondence and the latest fanzines?*

Alan: Oh, it was—finding these people who were interested in what you were interested in. It was like Christmas every day in some ways! Of course, I went through the usual sequence of subscribing to the comics, and they would arrive two weeks before they came to the stores, except they were folded in half—that drives collectors crazy! You didn't want it folded in half, for God's sake! [laughter] So I had a year's worth of subscriptions for a while, and that was fun. Most of the guys who did the fanzines were the same age, and there were some older folks who remembered the books from when they originally came out. Fanzines were the first place you could have any kind of intellectual contact with the present-day creators of the comics—a little interview with Steve Ditko, like that. I started up these long-distance relationships with guys who I eventually met in New York—Rich Buckler, Jim Starlin, Roy Thomas.

CBA: *You had a lot of published work in fanzines?*

Alan: Well, I don't know if it's a lot, it was a certain amount.

CBA: *Well, there was Star-Studded Comics, for instance.*

Alan: I did work before *Star-Studded*. I think the first black-&-white ink work was for Bill Spicer's *Fantasy Illustrated*. I don't think I even knew you inked with a brush yet, I'm trying to do it all in pen, some of them must've been lettering pens—who the hell knew? I don't think I saw an original page until I went to visit Ronn Foss in California one spring, and he had those giant DC originals—huge pages. He had some Kubert Hawkman pages that'd take your breath away.

CBA: *When you visited Ronn: Was that before college?*

Alan: It was probably still in high school, yeah. I was doing black-&-white work during the college years—17, 18, 19 years old. *Star-Studded* was one of the main ones, but there were a few others. I did Dr. Weird, and I did some of my first original characters for them. I did two Westerns, as a matter of fact—nobody was doing Western fanzine work, nobody cared about that.

CBA: *"Boy, You Sure Don't Look Like a Hero"?*

Alan: Yeah, and "The Battle of Credibility Gap." [laughter] Which featured the same character.

CBA: *And you wrote them!*

Alan: Yes, and then, I did a character of my own called Dragonfly.

CBA: *What kind of character was he?*

Alan: He was an insect-based character! [laughter] I wanted to do some version, some cross between Spider-Man and the old Fly, from Harvey, so there were some different bits with him. He had kind of a nice outfit. They just reprinted one of those in *Fandom's Finest Comics*.

CBA: *Yeah, that's actually where I saw the Western strip.*

Alan: It was pretty accurately costumed, I'll tell you. I was doing my research back then. I wanted to show the difference between the real old West and the Hollywood West. That was the point and the purpose.

CBA: *I'm surprised, for early work, to see it really has your idiosyncratic style. The posturing of the characters is very identifiable as Alan Weiss! You were developing a distinct style relatively early.*

Alan: Well, it was mostly from trying to extrapolate from reality—which also includes films and magazines—but there's also the level of your own aesthetic, of how you feel it in your own body, in your own makeup, and how you relate to those emotions. I really wanted to get facial expressions. I would sit there with the yearbook and draw everybody, to try to get them both realistically and in caricature—even the really hard stuff, meaning the irregular features or the soft features, the things you wouldn't necessarily go right to for a comic strip character, because they're not exaggerated. If you can get the racial differences without exaggerating them, get the logical flavor and feel for the three-dimensionality of it, that's the real challenge. You're trying to put in your artwork what you like

bout other guys' artwork, but you're just trying to do your own
ersion of it.

CBA: *When you say that you were particularly attracted to any
pecific styles, was it Alex Raymond?*

Alan: Well, I hadn't seen Raymond's work until later, when those
eprint *Flash Gordon* books came out. Of course, I fell in love with it,
s I had with Hal Foster's *Prince Valiant.* As a young kid, I had a little
mannequin who I'd named Kirby Kane Kubert, the three K's, because
hey were my three favorite guys in comics, at least names that I
new. I came in after the ECs, which is a damned shame, but when I
aw Al Williamson, I went crazy! I didn't discover him until his *Flash
Gordon* comics in about '67, '68, remember?

CBA: *Beautiful stuff.*

Alan: Yeah, those will ruin you! You can't go back to that flat DC
tyle after looking at Al, you know? "How are you going to keep
em down on the farm after they've seen Al Williamson?" [*laughter*]
Williamson, Reed Crandall—holy sh*t, Reed Crandall!—and Alex
oth, doing those beautiful wash drawings, and on and on… my
God, John Severin, Russ Heath—I'd seen Heath's work in those
Warren war mags… and those washes by Gene Colan—how about
hose, right? Things were revving up into the '60s, and it seemed like
omic books were taking on this whole new kind of life and majesty
nd interest. I was more interested in the more illustrative type art, of
ourse, but I liked cartooning, and when the Harvey *Spirit* reprints
ame out, I said, "Oh, this is great, because this is like Wally Wood in
Mad magazine!" Of course, that's putting the cart before the horse,
nce Woody was inspired by Eisner, but I loved those *Spirit* stories so
much. I still want to do one. I had a small taste when I got involved
with that *Spirit Jam* that came out in about '80.

CBA: *So, going to New York was specifically to go to the comic
ook publishers and try to seek work?*

Alan: Yes, I went to the Seuling convention in the summer of
968. I had my trusty little sample case, and went to the Big Two. I'd
ent work to various people and got my rep with a number of pink
ejection slips, but I would've been in the next issue of *Web of
Horror,* if there'd been a next issue.

CBA: *The fourth issue?*

Alan: Right, the one Bernie Wrightson and Bruce Jones were
utting together. It was a weird situation. You couldn't get past the
aiting room at Marvel, really, even when it was a small place. But
he scene at DC was a better story. I went up there, and they had
his receptionist named Carol Fein, who had a real thick New York
ccent, which of course sounded a lot thicker to me then. I'm there
ith my partner—Scott Bell, a fine artist and a good friend I'd
ollaborated with on a lot of the fanzine work—and she took our
tuff in, came back out, and says, [*mimicking a New York accent*]
Carmine says that these are not quite up to professional standards
t this time, but good luck, and feel free to try us again." And I'd
ome 3,000 miles for this! I managed to ask, "Why not? Why aren't
hey good enough?" Of course, she didn't know, so she says, "Let
e take a minute." She goes back in, she comes out with Dick
iordano, the greatest thing that could ever happen. So Dick—being
he guy he was—took us back to the snack room, and sat with us
or, I swear, it must've been two hours! To this day, I can remember
pecifically what he said… how to consider the whole page as a
omposition, and to vary the weights, and think about things on
rids… it was just the most wonderful, friendly thing to do. I stayed
contact with Dick.

So, I came back to New York for the convention the next year.
ich Buckler and I had gotten fairly close, because we felt we were
t a similar level of development, and right about that time, the first
racks were opening for new guys to get in. Now, Neal Adams and
m Steranko were already there—and I consider them to be a two-
an wave of their own of new ideas, new thoughts and new styles.
ernie Wrightson was the first one of our generation really, to get in,
ith "Nightmaster"—I think because Williamson didn't want to do it,
nd he recommended Bernie. Barry Smith came in soon after.
nyhow, after the convention, Buckler gave me a call and said,
Listen, I'm in New York, getting some work, and you're as good as
e, so I think the key is to be here so you can turn the corrections
round overnight." Simple as that! So I said, "Okay, Rich, I'll be
here in two weeks." I didn't know how I was going to do it at the

time, because I didn't have a dime, but I figured if I didn't make up
some date—it could be six months to two years—I'd never go. So, I
lit an artificial fire, and it worked. It was good. I'd met Neal Adams at
the previous summer's convention, so I was staying in contact with
him, and Giordano said, "Well, Jim Warren owes me a couple of
favors, so I can get something going for you over there,"
so that's how I got started at Warren. We did some
filler pages, sometimes just single-page stories or
ad pages, things like that. I was working with
Neal, assisting and even penciling, and he'd pay
out of his pocket. It was just a really special time
back then. So, little by

Below: *Panel detail of an early
Weiss job—both drawn and
written by the artist—from his
story, "Lair of the Horned Man,"
Eerie #34, 1971. ©2000 the
respective copyright holder.*

Above: *Penciled page by Alan Weiss of a real early Marvel job (1972) from an unpublished Rawhide Kid story. That's Rawhide meeting Billy the Kid. Courtesy of the artist. Art ©2000 Alan Weiss. Rawhide Kid ©2000 Marvel Characters, Inc.*

Opposite page, bottom: *Splash from 1972's Sub-Mariner #54 back-up story, one of Alan's first Marvel jobs. Pencils and inks by Alan, script by Mike Friedrich. Courtesy of the artist. ©2000 Marvel Characters, Inc.*

little, a couple of us sneaked in, and then a couple more. Buckler was doing work, Howie—oh, excuse me—*Howard* Chaykin came in soon after that, Jim Starlin came in… that was the story. Kirby left Marvel about that time, so some of his features were open.

CBA: *Did you immediately join a community of like-minded young artists?*

Alan: Well, we pretty much knew each other though the various fanzines and the conventions, and then a little bit later, it turned out that so many of us just happened to be living in almost the same part of town. There was that great little artists' community, so to speak, in the 70s and 80s on the Upper West Side. In one building, Jeff and Weezie Jones were on the sixth floor, and two floors above were Wrightson and Kaluta, and then later on, I moved in with them, and when Kaluta moved out, it was just Bernie and me for the last year or two. Barry Smith was in that neighborhood, and so were Frank Brunner, Archie Goodwin. Jeff and Weezie had these get-togethers on the first Friday of every month, and whoever was in town would come to 135 79th Street. Since it was Friday, people would be turning in jobs, or picking up checks, or doing whatever the hell they were doing, so it was convenient. Vaughn Bodé would come after delivering his job to *Cavalier*. Gray Morrow would be there, Williamson if he was in town. It was just priceless… Roy Thomas and

of course, Marv Wolfman, Len Wein, and that gang.

CBA: *Roy Krenkel, Wally Wood?*

Alan: Absolutely. Krenkel, and many times Woody, sure. Larry Hama.

CBA: *Larry Hama, straight out of the service?*

Alan: Yeah, fresh out of the service, full of stories, and they were all hilarious. He's a really good storyteller. Just sitting here, talking about it, I'm thinking of some of the weirdest stuff that happened at those things, I just don't know if I want to tell you! [*laughter*] We were so nuts in those days! Chaykin was completely crazy, Steve Mitchell and Alan Kupperberg were just really still teenagers, we weren't much older… Dan Green used to be up there, as I recall.

CBA: *Did you feel like you were living in unprecedented, magical times? You guys developed your talents so quickly. I look at Bernie's work in '68, then in '72, and it's night and day, just a grand progression of talent—and you came in, and your work just adapted very quickly and excelled.*

Alan: If I could tell you the difference between trying to learn it, back in Nevada, and learning in the first six months in town—it would've taken six *years* to learn any other way, because you're *there!* I could just go over to Neal's place, and look at what he's doing. Of course, there was a certain level of competition, but it was just to try and be as good as the guy next to you!

CBA: *Did you try to top each other?*

Alan: I really don't think it was that. We each had our specialties… what, you're going to try and top Wrightson in horror? That's just not the way it works. I'll tell you, especially among that small group—we wanted to be the new EC guys. We wanted to be the new illustrators in the comic books, to do both. See, for me, I'd love Kirby, but the abstraction… I just loved what the reality looks like. So, I didn't want a photographic, still feel, but if there was a way to get Kirby's animation, and draw it realistically—or at least render it somewhat realistically—that, for me, was the way to go. So, when Neal Adams hit, I said, "There it is! *That's* the blend! He knows how, he's not afraid to exaggerate, but then he renders it realistically so it's perfectly believable, and it looks solid." Of course I wanted some grace as well, that's Al Williamson's influence. I wanted accuracy in terms of costuming and historical flavor and feel—that's Crandall, Severin, and Heath. My God, these guys… they're magic! It's one thing to look at the work, but if you're drawing, and trying to understand what it takes to get to that level, these guys become all the *more* magical.

CBA: *So when you saw Neal Adams' work, did you say, "Yes! This is what I'm trying to achieve with my work"?*

Alan: Pretty much. I'd been following his *Ben Casey* strips while I was working at the Las Vegas newspaper, and I just loved the feel of reality there. And then, I used to think, "Geez, if this guy was doing some comic books… "—BLAMMO!—the next Summer, first he drew those couple of war books, and then… Deadman. With Batman and Deadman, that was it, boy, look out! That was about as good as you need. You could obviously tell he loved comic books, you could tell he appreciated what had come before him, but then he was adding a whole other dimension to it. He loved Kubert, loved Kirby, certainly loved all the *Mad* magazine guys, but he brought a new take.

On the other side of it, on the graphics and layout side, you had Steranko coming in, with his cinematic style. And Gray Morrow… he's technically of the EC school, he just missed the ECs. But Gray, my God, he's just brilliant! He really understands so much about the reality of things. There were guys drawing romance books that had an extra flavor, it was fantastic.

We really felt we were some kind of parallel of those few guys, those excellent EC artists—or at least we were aiming for it. The Fleagle Boys, right? Williamson, Torres, Krenkel—those guys used to go and sword fight in the park, and we used to do that. We lived on 79th, right near the Museum of Natural History, we'd throw the Frisbee and climb the trees, and Wrightson would sing the theme from Robin Hood… or break into his Bela Lugosi or Boris Karloff voice… or Daffy Duck!

Neal was the guy that got us all in. He was our big brother. He literally was our protector, a guy who would pay you out of his pocket so you could eat and stay in town another couple of weeks. That was the very early, early days, before Continuity was even officially formed. We used to go up to his house and eat meals, and play with his kids, and it was really something.

CBA: *Were you guys seeking to try to go into Marvel and try to change it your way, hoping to make it more open?*

Alan: Not so much change it; we just wanted to do our own thing, and Marvel was very resistant to that at the beginning. They had a house style and wanted a certain level of conformity. It was pretty much, "Look like Kirby—if you want to look a little like Ditko, that's okay, too." They wanted those real, big, round shoulders. That's one of the reasons Wrightson didn't get the *Conan* book, because his stuff had too many lines on it, and his Conan wasn't hugely muscular enough for their taste. At first, they asked Wrightson to ink *Conan*—I saw some of the samples he inked over Smith—but I believe Bernie inked about two-thirds of the page and said, "Hmph, not for me!"

CBA: *You and Bernie were pretty tight.*

Alan: Well, we were living together at that time.

CBA: *Your first break was at Warren.*

Alan: There were only two or three. I got to write them, as well, and that was good, considering that it was my first break. We were always trying to break in to Marvel or DC. Warren wasn't bad, and there were a few other lesser black-&-white companies along the way there. I was doing a job for Skywald, a story I wrote, when I got the call to do some samples for "El Diablo." I literally took that Skywald page, threw it off the board to the other side of the room, and started on those samples that night. [*laughter*]

CBA: *Joe Orlando called you?*

Alan: Yeah. I was That Kid from Out West! "He can do cowboys, he can do horses." [*laughter*] Wrightson would always say, "Here, Al, you do my horses, mine just look like big dogs." [*laughter*]

CBA: *Did you do a lot of animal drawings?*

Alan: They say a horse is one of the most difficult animals to draw, but it's such a beautiful, dynamic, balanced machine—come on, you've got to believe in God when you see humans and horses in actual motion! It's just too wonderful. So, yeah, but for instance, there was a job for Orlando for *House of Mystery* [#205], which Joe offered to Wrightson first, because he knew how some of these things would work: If one of us couldn't do it, maybe one of the other guys could.

CBA: *"Ask your roommate." [laughs]*

Alan: The story had to do with a motorcycle gang. He said, "Bernie, are you good at drawing motorcycles?" Wrightson said, "No, I can't do it." So, he asks Mike, "Well, how about you, Kaluta? Motorcycles? You know anything about motorcycles?" Mike says, "No, I don't want to… " So he says, "Okay, what about you?" I said, "Motorcycles? Sure!" I'd never drawn one in my life, I figured I'd go buy a magazine or two and figure it out—and I got Ralph Reese to ink that, too, and Ralph is really good on mechanical stuff. That was a fun job, I enjoyed that. Ralph put on the back of one guy's jacket, in the studs, "Alan's Angels." [*laughter*] I hadn't penciled that. Ralph inks with a precision that is beyond mere mortal men. He could get into a concentration that was really phenomenal.

CBA: *Ralph got his start with Woody?*

Alan: Yeah, he was one of Woody's guys, and he has a very unique sense of humor, too. I guess we all have our angles, but Ralph was *something*, I'll tell ya.

CBA: *He didn't seem to stay in mainstream comics too long.*

Alan: No, not really, but then again, in some ways, he was kind of like me. He'd go away and come back. You'd see him doing the Byron Preiss project, *One-Year Affair,* which is a brilliant piece of work. Or how about his piece in Flo Steinberg's book, *Big Apple Comix*?

CBA: *That was a great job.*

Alan: That job Reese and Adams did is absolutely… well, the whole book is a classic.

CBA: *Oh, that was that dual story, right?*

Alan: Yeah, "Over and Under." Wasn't that fantastic? And you had Herb Trimpe in there, you had a little Archie Goodwin job…

CBA: *You had Stu Schwartzberg, you had Marie Severin, the most eclectic crew, with the Woody cover.*

Alan: And Ralph's back cover. We had some great meetings to put this book together over at Flo Steinberg's place, down in the Village. What a group! Can you imagine just a punk kid like me working with

guys like these in the same book? Wally Wood, for God's sakes! And I got to write, pencil and ink my own story. It was about this kid that comes from the West to New York City to be an artist! [*laughter*] I was really getting my brushwork together. At that point, the Filipinos had already gotten into the business—Nestor Redondo, Alfredo Alcala, and Rudy Nebres. I just thought their brushwork was exquisite, and I was trying to nail my own version of that style in some way. I think a lot of it comes out on that job. I'm trying to get Flo to do a 25th Anniversary Second Issue. She said, "Oh my God, I can't go through that now!" [*laughter*] Flo's still at Marvel. She's great.

I believe it was Larry Todd who coined the phrase "ground-level comics," an overground approach to underground comics. With no holds barred, nothing restrained, creator-owned, all that. There were a few experiments along those lines that were successful. I just think the single best one was *Big Apple*.

CBA: *Were you involved in ACBA at all?*

Alan: Yeah. I was there at the initial meetings. At one point, Neal wanted me to get involved at some sort of administrative level, but I didn't want to do that—it's just not my cup of tea. I also felt it would

Above: Subby pencil study by Alan. Art ©2000 Alan Weiss. Sub-Mariner ©2000 Marvel Characters, Inc.

A MIGHTY MARVEL MINI-CLASSIC!

NAMOR THE FIRST, PRINCE OF ATLANTIS, BATTLES "THE MER-MUTANTS!"

WHEN IT CAME TIME FOR *ACTION* I PROVED I WAS---

AS GOOD AS ANY MAN!

As Told To: HOLLI RESNICOFF *Illustrated by:* ALAN WEISS *Edited by:* STAN LEE

CHEER UP LAURA! YOUR BROTHER AND I ARE ONLY GOING CAMPING FOR THE **WEEKEND.**

ANYWAY, YOU **KNOW** YOU WOULDN'T **ENJOY** IT! CAMPING IS TOO **ROUGH** FOR GIRLS!

YOU THINK **SO,** DO YOU...?

WHY DON'T YOU GIVE ME A CHANCE TO MAKE UP MY **OWN** MIND, DAVID?

HEY, YOU REALLY **ARE** BUGGED! I DIDN'T **REALIZE---**

WELL, **OKAY--** IF YOU THINK YOU CAN **HANDLE** IT!

THERE'S ONLY **ONE** WAY TO FIND OUT---

---AND **BESIDES,** WHO WOULD YOU RATHER HAVE **LIGHT YOUR CAMP- FIRE**--TED OR ME---?

Above: *Splash page from* Our Love #16, *penciled and inked by Alan in 1971. Courtesy of the artist. ©2000 Marvel Characters, Inc.*

be more valuable to be more connected with my peers, the free-lancers at large. I'm sure you've heard the stories about the meetings of a bunch of freelancers who can't get along or agree on anything. [*laughter*] That's a little bit of an oversimplification, but there were a lot of obstacles. Still and all, it was quite a big thing, a very positive move for its time. It would be harder to put together something like that now, since there are so many more people involved in the business and so many of them don't live in or around New York. Back then, it was a very insular society, and most of the people had access to or lived somewhere in the Manhattan area. A lot of those meetings were just terrific, especially afterwards,

Right inset: *Alan, along with Tom Palmer, helped Neal Adams ink The Avengers #96. We're not exactly sure if Alan inked this panel detail from that issue but everyone involved did a spectacular job on the entire story! Courtesy of Tom Palmer. ©2000 Marvel Characters, Inc.*

when you'd go out and party, it was amazing. But I remember some kind of bitter stuff. There was some controversy about whether the writers were entitled to keep any of the artwork, and things like that.

CBA: *Actually, Roy Thomas implemented that policy at Marvel for a period of time.*

Alan: He did, and that's what led to—at least in my mind—the famous Craig Russell story.

CBA: *What was that?*

Alan: Craig peeled off the pasted-up word balloons off the artwork, put them in an envelope, and sent them to the writer! [*laughter*]

CBA: *I thought Craig told me, "I didn't do it, Jim Starlin did it!"*

Alan: It sure could've been Jim, [*laughter*] but I heard it was Craig. See, if you say it's Jim, I'd believe it in a minute, but if you say Craig, I'd say, "Oh, geez! Mild-mannered Craig Russell?"

CBA: *One would think it takes a long time to achieve the kind of results you did with your art. Were you prolific at all? What was your general rate? Could you have had a regular book every month, and been able to meet the deadlines of a 20-page book?*

Alan: Sure, I could have, but I didn't really want to at the time. Sustaining that pace can really get to be a grind with that deadline looming *all* the time. It's hard to keep the quality consistent under that constant pressure. I mean, how many times have you seen a book looking real detailed, then by the third issue, it looks like somebody else drew it? Some of us didn't want to do a regular book as much as we wanted to go for variety. That would have been an extension of the EC experience, where you'd do a science-fiction story, then some historical period story, then a horror, or a war, or a romance.

CBA: *So working not just for one publisher, but for a lot of publishers. It was a much wider field then.*

Alan: That's right, sure. Plus there were different formats available to work in. There were also the half-books, so those stories were a different length, as well. Sometimes if I do a whole book of one character, it feels like more than just one issue. I'm trying to vary the angles on the heads and the lighting and the expressions so that it's more of an experience than just knocking out a homogenous look. Also I got into doing layouts. I can do layouts as fast as just about anybody. But after a certain point I didn't want to do layouts anymore because mine were as tight as a lot of guys' pencils—I've heard that said, so I'm not making this up.

CBA: *Were you offered a regular assignment?*

Alan: Oh yeah, lots. I turned most of them down.

CBA: *You inked Neal Adams on some* Avengers. *Was that you just showing up, being available? I think you're highly underrated as one of Adams' best inkers, maybe because you didn't ink a great deal of work.*

Alan: No, I didn't do a whole lot of inking on Neal's work. It would've been nice to do more. There was a point there where the first two guys of our generation that he asked were Wrightson and me. He got Wrightson to ink a page or two of that *Green Lantern.*

CBA: *A whole issue, actually, right.*

Alan: Well, it started with a page or two in a previous issue. Then, the whole Kaluta issue, right, with the Kaloota machine. I inked the splash on that job. I can remember to this day what Neal said about it, and I'll never do that again on a background!

So, yeah, it was quite a privilege to be trusted with it. Neal knew I loved the line variation he got, and I think he felt that I could understand the construction, because I myself was taking that approach. You know, Neal had taken me into the famous Art-O-Graph room during one of these early jaunts to New York, one of the first two trips before I even got in the business. He sat me down, and very honestly asked, "How do you want to do this?" What he meant was, "Do you want to do it right? Do you want to do it photographically and realistically, or do you want to cartoon?" And he was honest enough to tell me—to warn me—that if I wanted to come at it as an illustrator, it was going to be a harder road, and a higher hill to climb. I told him, "Well, I just want to do it like you, like Gray, Williamson… these are the guys that excite me most, who are producing the most intelligent, complete work." He was testing me, he wanted to find out if I'd be tough enough. He knew, walking into Marvel, they'd say, "Oh, no, get rid of this rendering, we want these guys to be bigger."

CBA: *Kirby, Kirby, Kirby!*

Alan: "Make it bigger." So, that was a good thing.

CBA: *How do you take that in retrospect now? Was he right?*

Alan: He was absolutely right; but I don't think I made the wrong decision either. It was a little tougher. I mean, look: I don't want to make it sound like it was a martyrdom of any kind, because it was wonderful. At that time, it was a privilege and a joy to get through the front door and work for the company that was one of the main reasons you came to town. Before we knew anything about the business, we were just drawing artwork, boy! [*laughter*] When we all got in, we thought, "Uh-oh, The Big Time! Look out!" [*laughter*] See, Wrightson and Mike Kaluta were not interested in doing super-heroes at all, they really wanted to do mood stories, horror stories, science-fiction. I didn't care; I liked the super-heroes, and I liked the cowboys. I wanted to do *Classics Illustrated*, for God's sake! Give me some period stuff! I never really did much war, but I liked that genre, and it was so much fun to get involved with some of the romance books too. Not too many, but I co-wrote some with Mary Skrenes, and one of my own.

CBA: *Was this for Dick Giordano?*

Alan: This was for Dorothy Woolfolk at DC.

CBA: *What was she like?*

Alan: [*laughs*] You know, when you ask me these questions, my brain just explodes in thoughts that I haven't had in a long time. I seem to recall that Dorothy used to have little crush-like flirtations with the younger artists, even if some of us looked a little strange, you know—some of us had hair that was a little long, some of us might have beards, even. [*laughter*] At that point, I always had my cowboy boots on, and hell, Frank Brunner, the first time he went into DC, wearing a buckskin jacket with long blond hair, they said, "It's Tomahawk!" [*laughter*] But Dorothy, she was all right, she was a sweetie. Mary Skrenes was writing stories for her. I could be wrong, but Mary might've been the only female writing romance stories, or any other kind of stories, for that matter—certainly the only female writing horror stories. That's why she had to have a male pseudonym, "Virgil North." We co-wrote the first full-length job I drew, for DC, for *House of Secrets* [#92]—that issue also included first Swamp Thing story. It was in the back and was about a little kid and a bum. Tony DeZuniga inked my pencils on that, but Mary and I wrote that together.

CBA: *So you met Mary when she was working for Dorothy?*

Alan: No, Mary and I were college pals. She came to New York from Vegas with me the first time, and we also had another friend from Vegas who lived in town here.

CBA: *Did she have any interest in comics?*

Alan: Only because I had told her there were some exciting new things going on, and one thing led to another, she came to that convention, she met a couple of people. She was always interested in writing, so it just sort of fell into place. I don't think she had set out to do it, but she ended up doing a considerable amount of work with a lot of different people. She was also quite a muse to a lot of guys!

CBA: *What kind of person was she?*

Alan: She is a delight! She's a tough gal—beautiful, lithe, but she can handle herself in a conversation and handle herself on the street. She could drink and swear with the boys, you know? Everybody was in love with her, and she was just a great spirit. She was always welcome to hang with the guys.

CBA: *She was obviously one of the few women who were*

involved professionally with you guys, right?

Alan: Yes, that's true. Even before Weezie Jones got involved in the game. The only other women were those who got in much earlier—Ramona Fradon, Marie Severin—and that's about it. A few women were in maybe the administrative or the mechanical side, right? I think Dorothy was certainly the only editor back then, and that was because her husband, Bill Woolfolk, was her *entreé*.

CBA: *Actually, Dorothy goes back to Fawcett. Her maiden name was Rubichek. So, yeah, she goes back.*

Alan: I remember a few times Dorothy would come out for a drink with the younger guys after work at the old Abbey Tavern, across the

Above: Claws of the Cat page penciled by Alan and inked by Frank McLaughlin—the book was co-penciled by Alan and Jim Starlin, both featured as characters in the top panel (no, no—the people with the facial hair, dummy!). ©2000 Marvel Characters, Inc. Below: The Darknight Detective meets Alan Weiss in the legendary Rutland Halloween story, "Night of the Reaper," Batman #237. Pencils by Neal Adams, inks by Dick Giordano. Courtesy of Alan. ©2000 DC Comics.

Alan: That's the difference between drawing purely mechanically and having a feel for it, and you extend that out to how you perceive how Errol Flynn moves, how Bruce Lee moves, how a dancer moves…

CBA: *There came a point where this culture actually was realized within the comics themselves to some degree. There was a Batman story, "Night of the Reaper," which took place in Rutland, Vermont. You were there in Rutland, right?*

Alan: Yeah, I was there two years in a row. The first year was the year that the comic book was based on.

CBA: *What was your memory of that? Was it just being spooked out in the woods?*

Alan: Oh, no, the whole thing was so magical. We knew from fanzines we knew they had this Halloween parade and party. But it was small-time until it started to integrate into the comics. A whole bunch of us went up there, and they had the costume party in this house in the woods, it looked like a haunted house with this big belfry with a red light in it. It was Halloween, and there was a full moon, the whole thing. At one point, Bernie, Denny O'Neil, and I were walking back to the house through the woods, and Wrightson told an axe-murderer type of story, just to try and scare us. Now, we're adults, but still, we're in the deep, dark, black woods, and it had one of those "boogey-boogey" punchlines, where he'd jump or you or something. O'Neil got a kick out of that, and he wrote the *Batman* story.

CBA: *And Bernie, Mary Skrenes, Gerry Conway, and you were all prominently featured as characters in the story.*

Alan: Right… my character almost gets killed! But to me, the real kicker was what happened the next year. We had the actual printed

street from DC when it was up on Third Avenue. Guys like Steve Mitchell and Alan Kupperberg worked at DC in production, and they have a lot of stories about that generation of folks: Murray Boltinoff, Jack Adler, Sol Harrison.

So sure, there were times up at DC… I remember late Friday nights. Everybody's gone, most of the lights are off, we're jamming on a job with Neal Adams—in fact, I think it was an *Avengers* job, but we were doing it up at DC. [*laughter*] Kupperberg was doing Zip-A-Tones and filling in blacks, I was inking a little bit, Mitchell was there. Afterwards, we're playing Neal's patented version of Hide-n-Seek, which was Gorilla—if you got caught by the gorilla, he'd pick you up and slam you down on a desk or something. [*laughter*]

CBA: *Was Neal the gorilla?*

Alan: Well, it varied, but it was just… gosh, *DC*. I mean, we were kids, and here we were in the place where they made the comic books that we grew up on, and we're stalking each other up and down empty dark halls in the middle of the night, [*laughter*] but it was in one of those sessions that I came up with the phrase *the kinetic aesthetic*, the way of drawing along the lines of how you feel your body move, and the weights and the balance, and the extension. I was in a room with Len Wein once, and my back was turned to him, and he threw my coat at me and said, "Think fast!" I swung around to catch it, and he said, "You did that just like you would draw a guy doing that!" [*laughter*] So I came up with a name for that, the kinetic aesthetic.

CBA: *You are what you do. [laughter]*

...omic book with us when we went back there the following year. So ...m at the parade—and everybody up there's seen the comic book— ...nd at a certain point, this guy comes up to me, dressed just like the ...illain in the comic book, the Grim Reaper, and he has a real scythe! [*laughter*] He has a mask on—I had no idea who this guy was—and ...e comes up, points at me, and says, "I know you," and I say, "Oh, ...y God, it's him!" So, I'm young and brash, and I say, "Hey! I'll tell ...ou what, sucker. I'll meet you on the dam tonight at midnight, and I ...on't bring Batman this time." [*laughter*] So that was the running ...ke, and word got around.

CBA: *There's going to be a rumble in Rutland!*

Alan: After the parade, there was an all-night party. There were all ...orts of things happening, just sequence after sequence of great ...tuff, a lot of dancing and running around. At a certain point, Jim ...tarlin, Steve Englehart, and I think Allen Milgrom and myself took ...ff to go to the dam, and the whole damn party eventually follows ...s. We go across the dam below it, walk across the rocks across the ...ver, so we are on the far side of the dam, and the rest of the party ...on the other side. A full moon is hanging directly over this dam, ...he trees are forming deep black shadows, and there's this black sil- ...ouette of this big haunted house over on the other side with a red ...ght in the belfry, and we're joking and shouting and yelling into ...pace there… and this Grim Reaper shows up! Now it's starting to ...et more real.

So, on the other side of the dam, are some guys I know and I ...ke from the business. But they aren't very… hedonistically inclined, ...hall we say? So, at one point, I remember one of them ...aying, "Oh my God, they're drunk, they're stoned! He's gonna hurt ...imself, he's gonna kill himself!" I remember thinking to myself, "What a fool! How could he possibly think I'd do anything to jeopardize the miraculous vehicle for my consciousness that is this body…!" But I'm telling you, on top of that, Jon, imagine: I look across this dam, and there's just the light of the moon, and here's this guy standing there. Now, the dam doesn't look like it does in the story, it's not as grandiose for one thing, but on one side, the water was almost up to the level of the dam itself, within six inches. On the other side, there was a drop-off to rocks, which is still about 12 feet, it looks higher standing on it. It is enough of a drop to where you could break a leg, or if you land on your head, you'd be pretty messed up. I'm wearing my Eisenhower short jacket and probably bell-bottom jeans, cowboy boots always. My guys, Englehart and Starlin, are yelling, "Go get him, Al! You're our boy, go get him!" [*laughter*]

So, I step out on the dam, and you hear rumblings in the distance from the crowd on the other side, and I'm process- ing this in about four different dimensions. Now, this guy's on the other side, so we start walking towards each other, and we meet in the middle—and you hear some hoots and some calls from each side… and here you are, it's become performance art, and your friends and acquaintances, the best young people in the comic book business, are your audience. So, I'm think- ing to myself, "Okay, well, this is cool. Once we get into the middle, what are we going to do?" Well, he's got this real scythe. I have no idea what he's saying to me, but I'm joking with him, old-time stuff, like "Your shoelace is untied," sh*t like that. I think, "The guy is not really a homicidal maniac, and he's not really gonna kill me out here, and he's not really

gonna slice me in half with that scythe." At that point, this guy takes a swing with the scythe, and he splashes it into the water, and the water splashes up on me…. *a real wake-up call!* At that point, I'm saying, "I have no idea who it is behind this mask!" Probably some- body I've never met, but I don't know what he is! Now, I'm thinking, "Hmmm… but I can't back up." [*laughter*] "I'm not gonna back up on the dam on Halloween! Sh*t!" I step back a couple of steps, I whip off the jacket and wrap it around one arm, like you do in a knife fight, big deal, and I'm realizing, "This is surrealism, Alan—here you are in your own life as a comic book artist, you appeared in this *exact scene* in a comic book, now you're taking that to the next dimensional layer." So it was just this fantastic rush, can you imagine? So, I just say, "F*ck it, this guy's really not gonna kill me, if I start advancing towards him, he has no choice." So I just do it, on a wing and a prayer. I start walking towards him, if he isn't gonna kill me, he has to back up. So, I back this guy up to the other side of the dam, and at the point of doing so, I hear this cheer rise from the woods! You want to talk about a "Top of the world, ma!" moment! I look up, there's the full moon, I'm thinking, "All I need here is a little Erich Wolfgang Korngold theme music, and this is a perfect picture." So, I'm telling you, nothing could have brought me down for the rest of that night. [*laughter*]

That was only the beginning! Skrenes and I adventure around town, we meet the guy dressed as the Grim Reaper, we go to his house—that's a whole other adventure! Later on, there is Indian wrestling going on in the party itself—Neal Adams-style, where you

Above: Page from "Castle of the Undead," written by Roy Thomas and penciled by Alan, with Crusty Bunkers inks (mostly by Neal Adams). Solomon Kane meets Dracula from Dracula Lives #3. Courtesy of Alan Weiss. ©2000 Marvel Characters, Inc. Solomon Kane ©2000 Robert E. Howard Estate. Opposite page: Two pages from 1971's Batman #237, the classic "Night of the Reaper" tale written by Denny O'Neil, inspired by Bernie Wrightson, and refined by Harlan Ellison, with Neal Adams (pencils) and Dick Giordano (inks) art. Featured as characters are real-life comics creators Alan Weiss, Bernie, Mary Skrenes, and Gerry Conway. Courtesy of Alan Weiss. ©2000 DC Comics. Left inset: Panel detail of Weiss' Solomon Kane from Dracula Lives #3 (1973). Pencils by Alan, inks by Neal Adams. Courtesy of Alan Weiss. ©2000 Marvel Characters, Inc. Solomon Kane ©2000 Robert E. Howard Estate.

stand with your feet on a line, clasp one hand, and try and push or pull the other guy until he moves one foot off the line. It's balance as well as strength. Neal used to do that with all of us to prove he could kick anybody's ass, and when he'd win, he'd toss you across the room. I was the only guy who could beat him—not out of strength, but because I have long arms and a decent center of gravity—so if I could keep him from pulling me back from beyond my point of gravity, gradually pulling my arm across my chest, and I'd get him. He'd just take one little one step back, and that's the difference. So, we were Indian wrestling, and along came this big, Vermont lumberjack. I thought, "I must be insane to Indian-wrestle this guy," but I beat him! I remember Milgrom saying, "You guys were so low, your knuckles were brushing the floor." That's how bent the knees were.

It was such an incredible night, and it was Halloween! Talk about feeling like, "Wow, what a great time, what a great business, we're in comic books!" Of course, this could give the impression that we were partying all the time, and that was certainly hardly the case, but….

CBA: *You had to work.*

Alan: Yeah, sure we did! And we worked hard, but we managed to have fun. Wrightson had all his lizards and snake cages in there between us. At one point, after Kaluta left, we painted the place. He

said, "I've got this plan to paint the place orange and blue." I said, "You're out of your mind, that's going to look garish and ridiculous!" He said, "No, no, it's gonna work. Trust me!" Well, it did, because we had all these black cases, black file cabinets, and glass terrariums in the middle, where the drawing boards were, the ceiling was blue and the walls behind it were orange. It looked better than it sounds, [*laughter*] but what it looked like to me was the inside of a toy box, and that's what the apartment got nicknamed, The Toy Box, or The All-Night Freak Show. Since all the other freelancers knew we worked at night, they would just drop in at all hours. If they were in town to see a Broadway show or were working late on a job, people would show up, and sometimes they'd be there until dawn, and we'd go walking in Riverside Park at daybreak. There's this big Civil War monument in the 90s in Riverside Park, and it's got columns and it looks like it could be from John Carter of Mars, drawn by Roy Krenkel. In fact, Kaluta and Wrightson used to

call it the Krenkel Monument. To this day, I still think of it as the Krenkel Monument… "Yes, there goes the 6:10 to Barsoom… " [*laughter*] and it's right over the Hudson River. It's beautiful architecture, just a great place to hang around.

We used to go out for snacks in the middle of the night, up Broadway, and you want to talk about running into horror stories? This was gritty New York in the 1970s. Bernie didn't like the realities, but he liked the fantasy! I dug the reality. For me, coming to New York was a dream of getting to the place where all those dark alleys were, film noir in reality, whereas I'd just come from Las Vegas, which was a different kind of fantasy-land, everything was bright, brand-new and shiny-clean.

CBA: *There's something to your work that you seem to seek out enormous diversity in race. You drew women who were certainly no typical comic book women, and I always perceived a level of humanity to your work, a humanism that was very intriguing.*

Alan: Oh, I love to hear that, because I was certainly trying to go away from the norm, and go for some of my preferences, and most for the variety of it.

CBA: *Yeah, you had black characters who looked like real black people, I mean, there wasn't a stereotypicality to their depictions. There was a villainess, Deadly Nightshade, that comes to mind. She was a… I don't know, disco princess teeny-bopper… you know? Didn't she even have platforms?*

Alan: She had big black boots, with the high heels. I went completely bananas inking those leather boots. And Englehart and I portrayed her as a little girl. She's this terrible, scary villainess, with the personality of this little girl, this flirtatious teenager.

CBA: *And you had her hair up in a bun, which visually seemed to*

indicate that there was a little girl quality to her.

Alan: I also tried to get it in the posing, the expressions, in the little things. You know, there's a story about that *Captain America* book. Englehart and I always wanted to work together on something or other, that was one of the main times we got to do it, that and a later *Kung Fu.* I had this idea: I'd love to do Captain America fighting pirates—swashbuckling is another genre I really liked. Wouldn't it be fun if Cap was fighting modern-day pirates… but they were still *dressed* Long John Silver-style, because their base was an off-shore gambling ship that, as its cover, was a replica of a pirate ship? I just had this visual of Captain America swinging around in the rigging, like Errol Flynn or Burt Lancaster. So we thought, "Great, we can do this, this'll be easy, it'll be terrific, and we haven't seen Captain America do this before," and we took it into Roy. He said, "Nope! Pirates don't sell." *BLAM!* That's that. "Well, okay, what's selling these days?" "Well, monsters seem to be hot." So I look at Englehart, he looks at me. I said, "Steve, werewolves?" He said, "Okay." *[laughter]* Then I said, "Well, if I'm going to do this prison full of werewolves, I'm going to try to make them all look different." Great idea, and then the more you think about it, the more of a pain in the ass it is to actually do.

CBA: *You've got your Pekingese werewolf… [laughs]*

Alan: Oh, yeah, and how about Deadly Nightshade's little pet guy Sparky? *[laughter]* I even had a very effeminate-looking werewolf, he's got curly hair. I remember Roy said, "All right, I'll let it go through this time, but after this, take it easy on the leather ladies." Now having said that, fast-forward 15 or so years later when everybody was wearing stuff like that.

CBA: *Yeah, so it was atypical of Marvel. You were putting characterization in the most minor of characters, giving them personality and life.*

Alan: The way I felt about it was, let's try to make it all special, so there's really nothing that's cast away, or just faked and hacked out. The first time I spoke with Gray Morrow, after Neal introduced me, I was trying not to be too ridiculously fawning, but I said, "You know, I just love the fact that you go past most artists in terms of the research. Real costumes, real weapons, and a variety of them—everybody in a Western isn't just carrying the same old Colt Peacemaker." And Gray, in his typical way, would just raise his eyebrow as if it was nothing, and say, "Well… that's the fun!"

You know, some of my favorite stories hinge on, "Well, that's

the fun." The first full job I did for Marvel was a *Sub-Mariner* back-up, in an issue drawn by Bill Everett. Mike Friedrich wrote it, and I drew and inked. I was really proud of those undersea hybrid characters, especially the mermaid. There was the shark head, the hammerhead guy, and the octopus guy. I even tried to figure out new ways to split the panels to make them look like undersea caverns. This is a story that Wrightson relates in *A Look Back*—Bernie said, "Yeah, Al worked all night on this mermaid, and he did a beautiful job, and he came in the Bullpen and the older artists jumped all over him for it, saying, 'Oh, yeah, of course, you're a

Above: *Page from* Deadly Hands of Kung Fu *#2. Pencils by Alan, inks by Allen Milgrom, and script by Steve Englehart. That's Milgrom, Weiss, Englehart, and Starlin in the background of the third panel! Courtesy of Alan Weiss. ©2000 Marvel Characters, Inc. Fu Manchu ©2000 Sax Rohmer Estate.*

John Romita. Gil Kane is in the office that day. Now Gil has some pointed opinions about the younger artists and what he considers their overuse of rendering; and I get a talking-to from Gil Kane, a lecture. He's pacing back and forth, orating about masturbatory rendering. Here, we want to be illustrators, and we are trying to utilize the rendering for the sake of a hyper-reality. But what they are saying is, "This just takes too long! That's the main reason we don't do it! It costs money!" Of course, at that age, we are just doing the best we can, and speed and finances are a secondary consideration! [*laughter*] There was a radio interview with Kaluta where he said, "I don't know how we survived, sometimes I wonder how the hell we ate!" You know, he would work for God knows how long on an eight-page story, until he thought it was done! He'd do tons more research than you ever had to do, because *that was the fun!*

So I'm sitting there—and here's one of my three earliest favorite artists telling me I'm doing it wrong! Oh, sh*t! He's saying, "Well, m'boy…" and proceeds to list all things I *shouldn't* be doing. Then John Romita chimes in with his story—"Yeah, once I did this romance job for Stan, and I put in the feathering"—they have different words for feathering, sometimes if they are denigrating it, they'd just call it "hay"—"and I did all this illustrative linework, and when I came in the other artists collared me at the elevator saying, 'Are you out of your mind? Now he's going to want us all to do that! How are we going to make a living?'" So they were all pissed off at John, because it was going to cost them time and money. So, Romita's telling me this story, further discouragement, and I'm thinking, "I can't, I'm not going to open my mouth to *Gil Kane,*" not at that time—I was 21, 22 years old!

Here's Herb Trimpe, the guy with this relatively cartoony style, right? The least amount of rendering, just nice, big, thick Marvel lines, right? And I didn't know Herb, but his certainly wasn't the style of artwork I was trying to do. I'll never forget this, he's playing with little toy cars—sort of absent-mindedly running this little car he is holding in one hand around the drawing board—very mild mannered. Herb is the one guy who has an encouraging word, and he says, simply this: "I don't know, I think you ought to just do it the way you want to do it!" Just like that. It was the best thing that could've happened, you know? It was just so right! It was really wonderful, it lifted my spirits, and I've been grateful to Herb ever since. Let me tell ya, if I hadn't been the biggest Herb Trimpe fan before that day, I sure as hell have been ever since! [*laughter*] He's a

Above: *Marvel calendar piece, 1980, penciled by Alan and inked by Joe Rubenstein. Courtesy of Alan Weiss. ©2000 Marvel Characters, Inc.* **Below:** *Alan's Kiss character sketches for a proposed 1977 animation project. Next time we promise we'll talk to Alan about his and Steve Gerber's best-selling Kiss Marvel Super Special! ©2000 the respective copyright holder.*

hippie, and you don't have to do this stuff fast, I guess you don't care if you make any money.'" That's Bernie's memory of it, but here's the real story:

I bring that job in. I have to finish a panel up there, and this is a big deal, you know? It's the first Marvel job I get to both pencil and ink, and it is the Sub-Mariner, my favorite character. I am trying to really express my vision of him and make him look real, but more than real, and very noble, because I loved the John Buscema *Sub-Mariner*s. So, that day, I'm in this little cubicle with Herb Trimpe and

GENE LION MANE EFFECT

DEMONIC TONGUE LEAR

CAT type cuddly

PAUL - Aggressive Pout

ACE - ALWAYS DREAMY

terrific artist, he's as good as anyone ever has been—did you ever see Savage Tales in the '80s? Herb wrote and drew this post-apocalyptic flying strip—you've got to see this! It's the best Herb Trimpe artwork you've ever seen in your life. It's real high-contrast, illustrative… beautiful.

CBA: *Did you read Herb's article in The New York Times?*

Alan: Oh, I read that, that just broke my heart. Yeah, that really hurt, because… that story's become all too common these days. Herb deserved a lot better from the industry—and he's not the only one. Fortunately, that story had a happy ending. Herb's okay, it's Marvel's loss.

CBA: *You had the opportunity to work in a different field, in advertising, which is obviously much more lucrative and varying.*

Alan: Neal brought a bunch of us in to advertising work through Continuity and his own work. I learned everything I knew about advertising work from Neal—storyboards, comps and animatics. I started out assisting him, and then he let me move up a little, do a little penciling. When I came back from California, I got into splitting my time between advertising work and comics. To me, the comics work was much more important and most enjoyable.

Later on, after working with Neal, I worked with Jim Sherman for a while, and I did some work out of Studio 23 with a bunch of guys that included Ralph Reese, Joe Barney, and Joe Desposito. Carl Potts had a couple of clients that he would get his comic book pals to do storyboards for. Sometimes they'd call in three or four of us for four days running to do an entire campaign. We'd do all-nighters, and then we might not hear from them for a bit, so then I'd go back and work on comics. For me, this was really, in its way, the best of both worlds. It wasn't this incredible grind for a relatively small amount of money. But it also wasn't the way to stardom, I'll tell you that. The way to stardom is frequency and visibility. [*laughter*]

CBA: *And ownership?*

Alan: Well, for ownership, I would do it! That was part of the decision, too, if I was going to go through that much of a grind, I'd like to do it as an investment in some future, rather than just being the 895th guy to draw Batman. There's nothing wrong with that, depending on where you are when it happens. Don't forget, this was before the big royalties kicked in. Look, I still never quite got my shot at Superman, and there's no question I'd still like to, but I did this Batman Elseworlds Western graphic novel a couple of years back, *The Blue and Gray and the Bat.* It was my concept, and I co-plotted with Elliott Maggin. Okay, so I was number 896, but I had a great time.

Elliot's a good friend and a terrific writer. Again, I don't think he's as well-appreciated as he ought to be. He's not the only one. Cary Bates is terrific. Remember Cary's book *Video Jack?* I drew a pirate segment for him. Cary and I also did a story for *Secret Origins*, the origin of Captain Atom, and it was the old Charlton Steve Ditko Captain Atom… I *loved* the chain-mail. I did another *Secret Origins*, Johnny Thunder, with Elliott. It was a beautifully-written, solid little 38-pager. That was fun, and that kind of led in to working on the Batman thing with Elliott, who was a big Abraham Lincoln fan, and he took direct quotes and inserted them into within the narrative.

CBA: *You did one mean Sub-Mariner, a great Captain America, but there was one character that is somewhat identified with you. You drew Robert E. Howard's Solomon Kane for a couple of stories.*

Alan: Yeah. I loved that character. That character was introduced to me by Bernie Wrightson. I'd read *Conan* before I got to New York, but I'd never seen *Solomon Kane.* He said, "Oh, you've *got* to read these!" And he pulled out one of the paperbacks with a Jeff Jones painting on the cover, and he says, "This guy is right up your alley, because you like to do those tall, wiry-muscled guys," and he was right on the money! So, I was really glad to have gotten the chance to kind of be, in essence, the signature artist on it. The first one was drawn by Ralph Reese, but I did ghost several pages of that job.

CBA: *In pencil?*

Alan: Yeah. I believe Ralph inked that job, he probably did. But I loved the idea of that character, and I really think I made a real connection with him… Here's this guy, this religious Puritan, swordsman, swashbuckler. "Yeah, okay, I'm going to rationalize my skewering people by the fact that I'm doing it for the Lord." [*laughter*] They were mysterious, really gritty stories. So, again, while I might've done

a total of three or four stories, it feels like a lot more, because I was so into that character. I did research on the Matchlock rifle he had, I was really working with the leather textures of the boots, and trying to get the right angle of that hat. I suppose Solomon Kane really could've become a signature character for me, my Swamp Thing or Shadow, but there weren't really enough of them. The same goes for Pellucidar.

CBA: *Did Joe Orlando approach you for that?*

Alan: No. The Burroughs line-up went like this—Joe Kubert was doing *Tarzan,* Frank Thorne drew *Korak,* Murphy Anderson had "John Carter of Mars." Orlando had Kaluta on "Carson of Venus," and he'd signed Wrightson for "Pellucidar." Again, I hadn't read *Pellucidar,* but I had the books because of the Frazetta covers, so I said, "Well, my roommate's going to be drawing this strip, I should at least pay him the respect of reading the books." So I read the first four of 'em, and it's a good thing, too, because about the time I was finishing up, Wrightson had done the first Swamp Thing story around that time—not to digress, but I worked on that, too; a couple of us did. I penciled most of the female heads, and I think I drew a head or two of Bernie's, with the long hair and the round glasses.

CBA: *Was the main female character based on Weezie?*

Alan: Weezie Jones, absolutely. So around the time he would've

Above: Page from Shazam! #34, featuring Alan's Raboy-esque version of Captain Marvel, Jr.! Pencils by Weiss, inks by Joe Rubenstein. Courtesy of Alan Weiss. ©2000 DC Comics.

Above: *Page from* What If? #37 *X-Men story featuring The Beast, written and penciled by Alan, inked by Jim Sherman, from 1982. Courtesy of the Alan Weiss. ©2000 Marvel Characters, Inc.*

what got the gig. It was Bernie's intention to do Roy Krenkel as Abner Perry, which couldn't be more perfect, because not only was Roy a wonderful Burroughs artist, but a delightful curmudgeon as well. We all loved him. So I wanted to follow through on that Bernie had taken a bunch of Polaroid shots of Krenkel, so he gave them me, so I worked from that reference.

I did the character samples on Vellum overlay-type sheets, inked with Pentel felt tips. Orlando loved the look of the inking, he thought it was very unique, and he said, "Why don't you ink the book this way?" I said, "Well, do you think it'll reproduce all right?" He says, "Oh, yeah, the way our reproduction is now, it'll be just fine, no problem." So, that's how I did the first installment, and when I saw it printed, I just about died, because half the linework dropped out. It looked broken, it looked sketchy, and the originals did not look like that. I felt, "This is my first series thing, oh, my God, everybody's going to think this is what it's *supposed* to look like!" I felt awful about it, so I made sure on the next one to just *ink the sh*t out of it,* you know? I took out the brush and really went to work. I was much happier with the second one. After that, as the dreaded deadline doom descended, we got the Crusty Bunkers on the inks. #3 was among the first jobs the Crusty Bunkers worked on.

CBA: *Were you a Crusty Bunker?*

Alan: You bet, one of the charter members! [*laughter*] I'm a charter Bunker! Yeah, it was Neal's name.

CBA: *Did the name come from working on* Swords of Sorcery?

Alan: You mean Chaykin's thing?

CBA: *I think that was the first job. Were you called the Crusty Bunkers because you guys were doing basically swashbuckling on the first story?*

Alan: No, no, no. Crusty Bucklers? Swashbunkers? The name "Crusty Bunkers" has nothing to do with swashbucklers at all; it was a phrase that Neal's used with his kids. It was like calling somebody a name that really wasn't dirty.

CBA: [*laughs*] "You crusty bunker!"

Alan: "You crappy bastard"? No, "You crusty bunker"! It didn't really mean anything, it just sounded good, you know? So he adapted it as a name. I think at one point, before it was even "The Crusty Bunkers," it was just "Crusty Bunker," singular—but that's all it was. Neal just threw that name on it. We liked it. It sounded tough, abrasive, and a little bit rebellious, right?

CBA: *Yeah, sounds like pirates to me! So you worked on 'Pellucidar,' and then you worked over at Marvel for a time. You were basically back and forth?*

started on "Pellucidar," they decided to do Swamp Thing as a series. Given the choice, of course, he preferred to do horror. So, that left "Pellucidar" up in the air. I used to hang around Orlando's office, and he had the covers of the books he edited up on the wall, and I didn't want to say anything outright—I would just kind of hang around and look up there and say, "Yeah, Burroughs' stuff, I really like it." At one point, he said, "*What?!? What do you want?!?! What?!?*" I said, "Well, you know, this 'Pellucidar' thing, Bernie's not going to do it." "Nope. Gil Kane's going to do it." That's *it*, nothing more to be said, Gil Kane's going to do it, he's got it, I've got no chance. So I walked away. A couple of weeks later, I get this call from Orlando, and he says, "Uh... Gil Kane can't do this thing, what do you know about 'Pellucidar'?" I said, "Oh! The Thipdars and the Mahars and Hoo-Hahs," whatever the hell. [*laughter*] So, he said, "Okay, do me up a couple of sketches." So I did samples, and that's

Alan: I was freelancing for both Marvel and DC and other companies as well. I did some humor stuff. I did some work for Lampoon. Did you ever see that *Esquire* thing? Jeff Jones, Barry Smith, Bernie Wrightson, Mike Ploog, and I invented characters for this short feature—we were "the new artists of the '70s." Bernie did "Redneck," this flying super-hero. Mike Ploog did a "Spirit" kind of a guy, but I think he was black, it was really nice. Barry Smith did some sort of super-soldier, Jeff Jones did an out-of-body soul/spirit thing, Egyptian... what was mine? Oh, yeah! [*laughs*] Geez! He was called "The Incredible Phizgink." He was the most insane, mundane, and something else that rhymes with that... inane, mundane, insane, that's it. [*laughter*] He was just this surrealistic hero who could return lost time in bio-degradable containers. [*laughter*] He fought against such villains as Plastic Patsy and Captain Apathy. It was vaguely political satire, weird, bizarre. He had sparklers on his helmet. I don't

ven know where the idea came om now, but it was a lot of un.

CBA: *You told me a story bout the creation of Shang-Chi.*

Alan: Yeah, but Englehart idn't tell the whole story [*in Everybody Was Kung Fu Vatchin'," CBA #7*]. In fact, he orgot the punch line! Englehart alked about the use of the Bell elephone Building for Shang-hi. Well, this was a night that our of us prowl all night around own—as a matter of fact, it's he very night before the day I as to leave New York to go to egas, and I don't know if I'll be ack or when. So, we just have his all-night incredible prowl nd adventure in the streets… e mentions there were guys vorking in the street with big rc lights, with welding torches hat cast these gigantic shad-ws? That's exactly true, it was a henomenal sight—middle of he night, quiet, no traffic, and ve're watching these giant hapes in shadow moving on the kyscrapers, on the buildings. It's owntown, so it's older build-gs, not as high as midtown kyscrapers. There's a huge, big onstruction site that we go into nd we're climbing on all the big gs and construction tools—they re all shut down, but we're limbing on everything that ight. We go down to the World rade Center, which is still under onstruction, but we get in here—I don't know how, we st kind of walk past everybody. t one point, we go to this big kyscraper with no windows! It oks like this big monolith. It oks like something out of eorge Pal's *The Time Machine* hat the future Morlocks would onstruct…no windows! Two penings out of a building that nust be 30 stories high, with our kind of separate pods. They ook almost like giant meer-chaum pipes on each side, we on't know what they were. Ve're trying to figure out, What the hell kind of building an this be with no windows?" Ve go walking all around it, ooking for an entrance or some-hing, and we finally get to a doorway, and it's the Bell Telephone uilding. It looks like the wall to the door is eight feet, then there is he door, then on the other side, there is eight feet of thickness. By ow, we're attracting the attention of the rent-a-cops. It's the middle f the night, and there's these four hippie types running around! What the hell are they up to?

CBA: *"Are they Weathermen?" [laughs]*

Alan: [*laughs*] You know, of course, that's the last thing we are. It's ist, "Oh, what a great idea! How about we have the Sub-Mariner ome in." "Oh, no, what about Captain America… " So this guard comes out, and he ascertains that we're completely harmless, and friendly, and he needs somebody to talk to, because it's lonely up there—no way is anyone breaking into this building! [*laughter*] He is from the Burns Detective Agency—I'll never forget this, the guy has a Spanish accent—and he is explaining why the building has no win-dows, because it's where the transatlantic cables come in, so it's atom bomb-proof! So, they can keep the telephone lines humming even if the rest of New York is reduced to ashes around it! [*laughter*] And the people inside can stay alive, until the radiation filters through those little apertures that we saw, right? So we think this is pretty

Above: *1986 cover illustration for Steelgrip Starkey and his All Purpose Power Tool. Pencils by Alan, inks by Jim Sherman. Courtesy of and ©2000 Alan Weiss.*

interesting, and we're thinking maybe we can do something with this at some point down the line. But here's the punch line: Englehart says to him, "Well, tell me, sir, what does the Burns Detective Agency manual advise as tactics during a nuclear holocaust?" [*laughs*] So the guy says, "Well, I don't know what the detective agency say, but I've always heard that you should bend down and put your head between your knees." And Starlin says, "Yeah, and kiss your sweet ass good-bye!" [*laughter*]. We work our way down to South Ferry, one of my favorite parts of the island. Battery Park is

where my story from *Big Apple Comix* is set—where that big eagle is, facing the Statue of Liberty in the harbor. That's the point where you really feel like you're on an island. In fact, if you're standing exactly at the edge there, you can almost believe the whole island is a ship. We get there by dawn, watch the sun come up, you know? So, that was an incredible way to send me off.

CBA: *Then you moved to California.*
Alan: Well, I didn't know yet I'd be settling in California for some years. I spent most of the next year back in Vegas. Englehart came through, and we scouted California together. Steve fell in love with it, and he's lived there ever since. A bit later, Starlin and Brunner came out too. We all ended up in the Bay Area. Tom Orzechowski and Mike Friedrich were there as well. For awhile, Starlin, Brunner and I shared Studio Zero, a basement… hence the name.

CBA: *Did you have any exposure to the undergrounds while you were in the Bay Area?*
Alan: Absolutely, lots. We got to know a lot of those guys. We were interested in owning our

own creations like they all did. At one point we were approached by *Rolling Stone* to produce a comics insert feature, all creator-owned characters. We were really excited about it! Wow—a chance to do something outside of any editorial policy or censorship—but the whole thing turned sour fast. *Rolling Stone* wasn't really interested in any innovative concepts. They wanted super-heroes in glitter bands! So *that* thing never happened—and of course there were the many dead-end adventures with various hippie entrepreneurs who were all going to create the newest, most futuristic, hip, creator friendly comics company…but ended up blowing any capital on announcement party favors. [*laughter*]

CBA: *So after a few years, you returned to New York City?*
Alan: Well, I'd headed back out West to back off from the comics for awhile, to refresh and reprioritize, so to speak. You know, there are some elements of the business end of the comics business that can tend to really grind down your original love and youthful enthusiasm for the medium. So while I was out there I spent a little less time doing comics and a lot more time exploring, researching, and experiencing…you know, real "meaning of life" stuff.
CBA: *And did you find the answer?*
Alan: Maybe not *the* answer, but *my* answers—enough to recapture my enthusiasm for comics, and then some. It was during that time I began concentrating on creating some original characters and concepts of my own. Since then, I've had deals with four or five companies for several of these strips, but for one reason or another the only ones that have actually seen print so far are *Steelgrip Starkey and his All Purpose Power Tool* for Marvel's Epic line, and *War Dancer* for Defiant. I was developing and producing four more of my properties for Broadway Comics' creator-owned line when the company folded.

So after a short stint in animation down in Hollywood, I decided to go back to the East Coast. Jim Starlin was down there, working with Ralph Bakshi. "Wait for me in Vegas for a week or two and

we'll drive back together. Well, that trip turned into a minor odyssey! Lots of adventures. There was this guy I'd done an X-rated Solomon Kane illustration for use in his fanzine. Well, this jerk wouldn't return the original. I couldn't reach him by phone or mail so I was helpless—but that October, Starlin and I showed up at his house in Missouri. I had all these angry plans…" Yeah, if he won't give it up we'll grab him, tie him up, and keep him in a motel room till he…" "Hold it," says Starlin. "Calm down. We can't do that. This is not our home state, and if we go kidnapping people they may not realize we're the good guys!" Instead, Jim pretended to be an art dealer/buyer to case his place and see where the art was. Then he came out to get me, to bring me in as his partner. The guy froze in mid-introduction! I think he peed his pants! So I got that piece back.

CBA: *[laughs] When you got back to New York, you worked for both DC and Marvel?*

Alan: Mostly Marvel for awhile. A few stories for DC—Flash, Atom, Supergirl… I did a lot of inventory issues and *Fanfare* jobs for Allen Milgrom, because they were on extended deadlines and they'd just schedule them as fill-ins whenever they needed one. That way I got a crack at lots of my favorite Marvel characters— Quicksilver and the Inhumans, The X-Men, Iron Man, Power Man/Iron Fist, John Carter of Mars, The Avengers, Silver Surfer, Dr. Strange—a Western—and, of course, the Subby, my favorite.

CBA: *You also did Captain Marvel for DC. It was a real surprise to see your work on Shazam!, of all things. Did you clue into Mac Raboy very strongly?*

Alan: Well, the main reason I wanted that gig was because it featured Marvel Jr., and I loved Raboy's work so much. Captain Nazi was in it, too. Joe Rubenstein did some really nice inks on that job. As a kid, I'd never seen Captain Marvel. My first exposure to the character was Wally Wood's "Superduperman" strip in a *Mad* reprint, so when I finally saw a copy of *Whiz Comics*, I was really disappointed in that flat outline coloring book Marvel had. Sure, that style has a charm of its own, but it wasn't what I expected. Raboy's Marvel Jr., though… *that* was the stuff! So when I got my shot at Captain Marvel, I added a little Woody-style lighting to the guy to add a bit of dimension, and gave him that Fred MacMurray face. That was a lot of fun. A few years later I proposed a redo on another ex-Fawcett character, Bulletman. Another case of "close but no cigar" at DC. They were gonna do it, then they weren't, then they were, but of course they didn't. I thought I had a nice angle on a relatively ridiculous character, and I actually got to use it later in *War Dancer*, where Bulletman became Billy Ballistic and the Bullet Babes.

CBA: *How do you assess those times? Did they form you?*

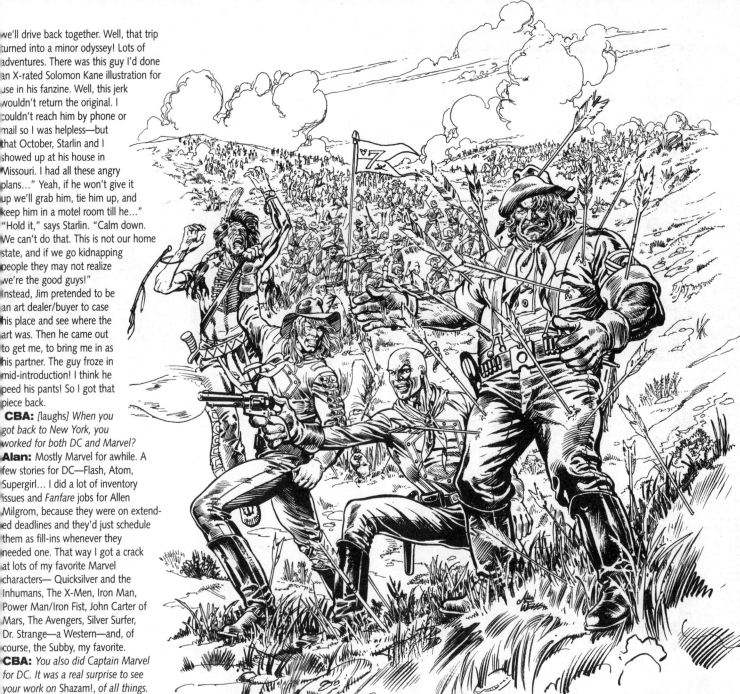

Alan: They either formed me… or de-formed me. Sure! In every way. The New York experience, especially my early years, was like coming to this amazing gritty real-life Oz, the place where it's all done, where it's always been done. It was a big risk too, because that's where the toughest competition was. So if you can make it there… you know how the song goes.

Drawing comical books for a living—what a surrealistic thing! See, to the average "read-'em-when-I-was-a-kid" type of person, a comic book is just a comic book—but to those of us who love them, they're still an extraordinary dimensional doorway. I don't want to wax too fantastical about it, but look: an idealistic viewpoint is what keeps you relatively sane and fresh, so you're still having fun. So even after kicking around…and *being* kicked around… this biz for a stretch, there are those of us who, far from being burnt out, feel they're at the top of their form, the peak of their powers —and that's just how I feel.

Above: *Alan penciled and inked this extraordinary pin-up of Archer and Armstrong at Little Big Horn for Valiant in 1992. Courtesy of the artist.* Art ©2000 Alan Weiss. Archer and Armstrong ©2000 Barry Windsor-Smith.

Editor's note: *We sincerely look forward to talking with Alan again about later aspects of his career, and we thank the artist and his wife, Pauline, for their herculean efforts in supplying us with art and extensive copy-editing. We hope you enjoyed reading this talk as much as ye ed did conducting it.*

Bernie Wrightson Portfolio

AND THE OTHER, THE ONE OF SHUFFLING BODY AND STUMBLING MIND, MAKES HIS WAY TO A MORE CONVENTIONAL HOME...

"CALLED ME FOOL BUT THEY DIDN'T KNOW I DID FIND A WAY TO HAVE FUN...FUN EVERY NIGHT..."

HE ENTERS HIS HOUSE AND THE VAST MATRIX OF COMPLICATED CHEMICAL APPARATUS SPARKS A VESTIGE OF MENTAL...

HE FINDS THE FERMENTED CONCOCTION IN OBVIOUS VIEW WHERE HE LEFT IT THE NIGHT BEFORE -- THE ANTIDOTE TO THE POTION WHICH HAS RENDERED HIM THE MINDLESS BRUTE HE NOW IS...

LIQUID FIRE SEARS HIS THROAT, HIS STOMACH... AND OVERCOME BY A PAROXYSM OF INSENSATE RAGE, HE SMASHES THE BEAKER...

THE EFFECT OF THE ACRID-SMELLING FLUID TAKES HOLD IN RAPID STAGES OF CONVULSIVE CELL REVERBERATIONS... AND HE TRANSFORMS...

...CHANGES, REVERTS BACK TO HIS NORMAL SELF...FOR UNLIKE THE SUPERNATURAL VAMPIRE, THE ASPECT OF THIS MAN'S EVIL IS ATTRIBUTABLE TO A RATIONAL, SCIENTIFIC, EXPLANATION...

"M-MUST GET SOME SLEEP..."

Opposite page: *Unidentified late-'60s/early-'70s page.* ©2000 Bernie Wrightson.

Left: *Cover layout.* ©2000 Bernie Wrightson.

Below right: *Swamp Thing illustration. Swamp Thing ©2000 DC Comics. Art ©2000 Bernie Wrightson.*

Below left: *Pencil layout for the Plop! story, "Molded in Evil." Art ©2000 Bernie Wrightson*

Right: *Daredevil by Alan Weiss (pencils) and Bernie (inks). Art ©2000 Alan Weiss & Bernie Wrightson. Daredevil ©2000 Marvel Characters, Inc.*

1980s X-Men poster art by Neal Adams.
Courtesy of the artist. ©2000
Marvel Characters, Inc.

The Adams Impact
Celebrating Our Featured Artist and His Stint at Marvel Comics

As we were coming down to the wire on putting *Comic Book Artist* #2 to bed, rushing to get the issue ready for the San Diego Comic Con, we were faced with the prospect of announcing what's coming up in issue #3. The plan was originally to feature "Empire of Horror: The Warren Publishing Story" as the subject for our third edition, but we had virtually no specific material on hand to promote in the *Previews* solicitation (due the same day we had to finish *CBA* #2). Somehow—and I can't remember the exact chronology—I found myself on the phone late on that Sunday night chatting with Kris (Adams) Stone, Neal's daughter and manager of Continuity Associates, and she offered *CBA* use of two incredible works by Neal: An (oddly) unused X-Men wraparound cover and six pages of an unpublished X-Men graphic novel. Well, needless to say, as a fax of the cover art came out of our machine, the probability of a "Neal Adams: The Marvel Years" issue became very real. (That moment—as this extraordinary image was transmitted between facsimile machines—won't be forgotten by this editor for some time to come.) Very special thanks to Neal, Kris, Cory (who again—under crushing a deadline—colored our cover to perfection), Jason, Zeea, Josh, Marilyn, and all the fine people at Continuity Associates. (Because of their efforts we were able to have proofs of our cover available for inspection at the San Diego Con, certainly the hit at our booth.)

To make this issue a reality, we next had to line up our pal Arlen Schumer, undoubtedly the world's biggest Adams fan—author of the bestselling "Neal Adams: The DC Years" issue of *Comic Book Marketplace* [#40, reprinted in #56] and one-time Continuity employee—to helm this companion issue, using his interviewing skills and design magic to bring this issue to light. Arlen is a *big* DC fan, so it took some work wearing him down to focus on the Marvel stuff but, as the talk and layout reveal, he put in great enthusiasm and (yet again) has achieved seminal work.

Arlen and I traveled down to Continuity's New York studio and spent a number of hours interviewing Neal about his Marvel experiences. While I just sat back and soaked in Neal and Arlen's conversation, I could see that a great issue was coming together and all of my questions were being answered… except two.

As the duo took a breather, I asked Neal, "Why are you giving *CBA* this great piece of art for our cover? What's the story?"

Neal said that he originally drew it as a wraparound cover for the *X-Men Visionaries 2: The Neal Adams Collection* trade paperback that was released in 1996, compiling the entire Adams/Thomas run of *X-Men*. "One of the reasons I offered you guys use of the cover, was that Marvel vignetted these characters—not even using Xavier's face—and cutting out the rest." It seems some freelance art director had different thoughts about Neal's submitted piece.

Neal was "terribly upset" with the published cover. "There's no worse color for comic books than eggshell blue [the most prominent color on the cover]… Look at the reproduction inside. The way this thing happened was they called me and said, 'We're going to reprint this stuff.' And I said, 'I'd kinda like to have the black-&-whites to retouch them—we're in the '90s now. Can I rework the pages just a little bit?' They said, 'We've already started work on it.' I said, 'Okay. How about I art direct the color?' They said, 'Sure, we'll send you over some of these proofs.' I know what *that* means, so I said, "Okay, I'll do the cover." So I did it and they vignetted it, and the rest just disappeared! How much can one sabotage by good intentions?"

Holding up the *CBA* #3 cover proof and the *X-Men* collection, Neal said, "I submitted this and I got that. How would that make you feel? So *Comic Book Artist* gets the cover."

Thank you, Neal.

As for our special Artist Showcase, six pages of an unpubbed X-Men graphic novel, Neal answered my second query:

"In the early '80s, I got a call from Jim Shooter and he said, 'Do you have any problem working for Marvel?' I said, 'No.' He said, 'I've got a graphic novel I would like you to do.' I said, 'I would love to do it but let me let you know ahead of time just so you know, Jim—I've sort of taken this stand against work-made-for-hire, but it's not hard to write a contract that's not work-made-for-hire. And you can take everything; it's not a problem. So you know that going in.'

"He said, 'Yeah, that's not a problem.' I said, 'Well, as long as you understand that, I'm fine. No problem; I'll be glad to do it.' Of course, everybody was surprised; I never said no.

"Jim said, 'Let me send you the outline,' which I think he wrote. So I read it and talked to him afterwards, and I said, 'The outline's a little loose; can I have flexibility to play with it?' (something I always ask when I get a new job). And he said, 'Sure.'

"I said, 'How's the contract coming?' He said, 'We're working on it but you can get started if you want to.' I said, 'Fine.'

"The result is what I did. I called a couple of weeks later and he said, 'I can't put the contract together. I can't do it.' And I don't know why. So they gave the project to Brent Anderson [*God Loves, Man Kills*]. I said to Jim, 'I've already done some pages.' He said, 'What can I say?' [laughs] So I guess I sent him Xeroxes of the pages and said, 'Maybe some other time.'

"These were the pages that were done and never paid for."

The Adams generosity continues. For a peek at the never-before-seen X-Men graphic novel pages, please turn to page 45 to see a bit of what could have been….

Above: *Can you believe that Neal submitted the cover art of this issue to Marvel originally for use as the cover art to X-Men Visionaries 2: The Neal Adams Collection and Marvel came up with the above, severely revised (and over-designed, methinks) finished piece? Go figure. ©1998 Marvel Entertainment.*

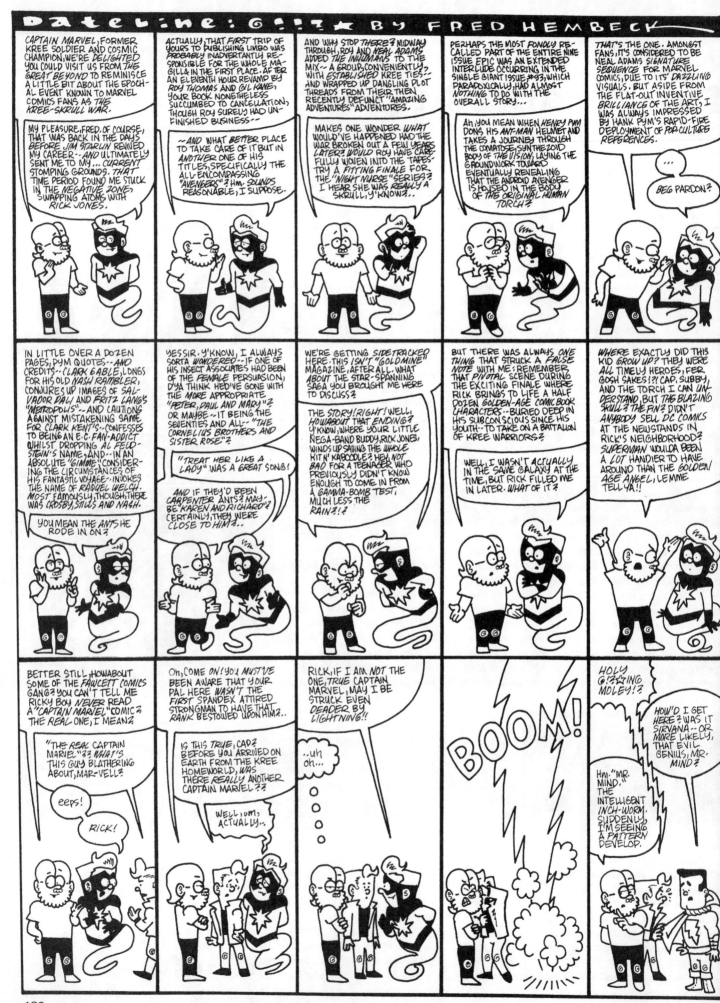

NEAL ADAMS
The Marvel Years

Interview
by Arlen Schumer

In the 1960s, I was a DC Comics fan: the Weisinger Superman line, Julius Schwartz's sci-fi super-heroes, and, of course, Batman (the debut of the '66 TV series was a seminal event in my childhood). Marvel didn't appeal to me; they seemed too complicated, too busy-looking (too many words!) compared to the somewhat banal simplicity of DC's line.

My brother, though, was a Marvelite and devotee of Jack Kirby. I was a fan of newcomer Neal Adams, who had every DC follower excited by his work on "Deadman." We would argue endlessly about who was "better," and daydream about company crossovers, like what if Kirby went to DC, or Adams worked at Marvel. In those days, it was unheard of for any artist to be working for more than one company at a time (we didn't know then that Marvel's new "Sub-Mariner" artist, Adam Austin, was DC's war artist Gene Colan, or that Marvel's "Mickey Demeo" was a pseudonym for DC's Mike Esposito!). It was a shock when DC stalwart Gil Kane drew a few issues of "The Hulk" in 1967, but nothing prepared us for that day in 1969 when Neal Adams began drawing the **X-Men!**

The **X-Men**? According to my brother, the title had been going downhill ever since Kirby stopped drawing it years earlier, and, save for a few recent issues drawn by the great Jim Steranko and new kid on the block Barry Smith (then a Kirby clone), the title was all but forgotten and destined for discontinuation. Suffice to say, even my diehard brother became an Adams believer because of his breathtaking **X-Men** work.

Back then, I was too enamored by what Adams was doing at DC with **Batman** and **Green Lantern/Green Arrow** to notice what a body of incredible work—in addition to his **X-Men**—Adams was compiling at Marvel. Doing this interview as a follow-up to "Neal Adams: The DC Years" was an eye-opening experience for a self-styled Adams expert like myself, as revelations of the breadth of his storytelling achievements came to light.

Just as his Batman became the modern standard, influencing Frank Miller years later to do **The Dark Knight Returns,** which in turn influenced the movie portrayals, making Batman DC's franchise character, so too did Adams' **X-Men,** with far less fanfare, go on to become the new model of the characters, influencing a new generation of Marvel artists and writers to create their versions of the X-Men based on his, which became the cornerstone of Marvel's hegemony in the '80s (and "spawned" Image's super-hero line). So one might argue Adams' Batman and X-Men are the twin pillars upon which today's DC and Marvel rest.

Like his contemporary Steranko, Adams' relatively small body of Marvel work stands in direct converse proportion to its enormous influence. So I was not surprised by Neal's answer to my first question, "Why did you go to Marvel Comics?"

[The following interview was conducted in two sessions during September and October 1998 and was transcribed by John Morrow and Jon B. Cooke.]

Above: Portrait of Neal Adams from the 1970 Comic Art Convention Program book.

AND INTRODUCING PENCILING WIZAR OF: NEAL ADAM

Arlen Schumer: *Why did you go to Marvel Comics?*

Neal Adams: I was inspired to come to Marvel to a great degree by Jim Steranko. He dropped in to DC's offices months before and caught me there—I was there nearly every day—and after we had a good-humored yuck over my "Hey, it's a Jim Steranko effect" panel in "Deadman," [*Strange Adventures #216*] he described the Marvel style to me: Basically, they just let you free to do whatever you wanted to do, and you just went ahead and did it. If you did it wrong they'd correct you, but he hadn't been corrected along the way, so he was pretty happy; Stan had given him *carte blanche* to do anything he wanted to do storywise, within certa boundaries.

It seemed to me to be a wonderful way to do comics. Certainly, coming from DC Comics, there was nothing at DC that even resembled what happened at Marvel Comics. We wrote scripts, w wrote descriptions, we wrote balloons, and the artist was expected to fit them into the pictures.

Arlen: *What'd you think of Steranko?*

Neal: I thought Steranko's stuff was fantastic, and Steranko did a very similar thing that I did but within *his* style. Maybe what I did put the exclamation mark on what Steranko did, or mayb I just took it another way.

Arlen: *It was about a year after Steranko did h SHIELD epics; did the competitor in you see thes works and say, in a sense, "How can I top what Steranko did at Marvel?"*

Neal: Not really. Part of what I did was say, "I like this Marvel style; it's a little scary. I wonder what I would do with it if I had it available to me?" I didn't know what I could do; when I cam from comic strips into comic books, I felt a tremendous amount of freedom—so much so tha I never turned back to illustration, which I was headed for. I felt this freedom and I thought it wa wonderful. The next step in this freedom would b the Marvel style.

Arlen: *Was the discontinuation of "Deadman" the impetus to go to Marvel?*

Neal: I'm sure that it wasn't. I was happy with the "Deadman" stories but at the end, I was writing, penciling *and* inking the book. After "Deadman," others inked and most often others wrote with rare exception which I enjoyed, but I did feel the need to be "the storyteller" and the "Marvel Style" presented that opportunity.

Arlen: *Had you talked to Stan before this meeting? Did he know of you because of the splash you were making at DC?*

Neal: When I went over to see Stan, I didn't go over to get the *X-Men;* I didn't know what was going to happen and whether he would pick me up. I had no idea.When I went in to meet him, h told me that he was glad I came over and he

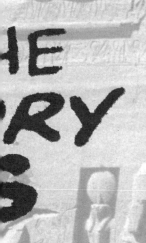

wanted me to do something for Marvel. One of the reasons was that "Deadman" was the only DC Comic that the Marvel guys read. So he asked what title did I want to do. I said, "Well, I'm sure there are titles I can't do." And he said, "No, you can do any title you want."

Arlen: *He would have given you any title? At the time, Kirby was still there and, other than his titles, you had the pick of anything?*

Neal: Yeah, but I don't necessarily think he meant it, though he certainly was generous in his approach. I said, "Tell me what your worst selling title is." And he said, of course, *X-Men.* Werner Roth had done the story just before me; they were giving it to anybody who would wander in. They gave the job to Barry Smith (and of his story, I would say the job he did on it was not his best); they gave the job to Steranko, but it was dribbling down. Not that I want to insult anybody but it didn't seem that anybody was giving it much attention at the time. So I said I'd love to do it.

Arlen: *You did it only because it was a loser? You had no affinity for the characters?*

Neal: Not at all.

Arlen: *You were reading the books?*

Neal: Sure, I read all the Marvel and DC books at the time; I read everything. I had no idea what I would do with the *X-Men.* I just knew that I had this pile of stuff that nobody seemed to care about. Perhaps intentionally because nobody cared about them, I could remold them. So the process was to remold them from the core that Jack had begun.

Arlen: *Looking back on it now, if you had your druthers, what would you have drawn?*

Neal: Whatever their lowest seller was. Stan asked me why I would do that and I said, "If I do the *X-Men,* your worst selling title, would you pay that much attention to it?" He said, "No, you can do what you want." So I said that's probably a pretty good reason for me to want to do it. He said, "I'll tell you what: I'll make you a deal. You do *X-Men* for two issues—or however many issues you're going to do—and after that you do a good selling title like *The Avengers.*" So I said, "Fine, I'll do that." And that was the deal between Stan and I.

Stan then said, "How do you want to be known at Marvel? Do you want us to give you a different name?" I said, "No, my name will be just fine." So Stan said, "Well, you know, here at Marvel we don't like people working for the other company." I said, "Well, I guess you can't let me do the *X-Men.*" But Stan said, "No, no, no. That's fine. It's not a problem." I said, "Good." And he said, "Hey, how about I give you a nickname? How do you feel about 'Nefarious Neal?'" I said, "Well, if you feel like doing that, I guess it's okay. I'm not really prone to nicknames; I never had one, but if that's what you'd like to do." So I agreed to do the *X-Men.*

Arlen: *Your working at Marvel represents the whole break-down in that pseudonym game, where for instance, Gene Colan*

was Adam Austin.

Neal: There were so many things that were wrong in comic books that had nothing to do with conscious efforts to be bad—but it's almost like going to another country where they haven't discovered fire and they're eating raw meat. So you teach them to cook meat and they don't necessarily like it at first but after a while they find that their digestive systems work a little bit better with it.

It was sort of the same way in comic books; the things they were doing wrong would have been so evident to somebody from advertising or book publishing—any of these worlds outside of comic books—but comics were so insulated, they didn't know they were wrong; they didn't know that they were backward and foolish. So, for me, it was perhaps an adventure in breaking these rules down but at the same time it was my day-to-day existence. It wasn't like "I'm going on this adventure to break down this rule"; it was more "I think I should try to do this and see what happens and maybe I'll get something else out of it."

My motives weren't so clear, but certainly that little piece stuck in the back of my head when I went to ask Stan if I could do a book for Marvel. I had seen those altered names of artists in the Marvel books, and felt that passing back and forth from Marvel and DC would be good for creators. And I didn't like the way creators were treated in general.

Arlen: *Didn't Gil Kane do it about a year-and-a-half before you, in 1967 when he went to Marvel to do the "Hulk" for Stan Lee?*

Neal: Oddly enough, it seemed when Gil Kane went to Marvel and used the name "Gil Kane" that, for whatever reason, there wasn't a significance to it; perhaps it became clear that Gil was "changing companies"! Somehow when I went, it seemed to make a statement.

I'm not saying that going back and forth to Marvel and giving my name was my goal. It just seemed it was silly to hide it; I guess because of whatever position I held in the comic book field, my going and being so overt about it, and being so comfortable and willing to talk about it—which of course I did— had more of an impact.

Above: *Oft-printed but still impressive rejected cover design (X-Men #56) by Neal Adams for his first Marvel comic book job. Neal says, "I did this cover and handed it in. Stan took it to [Marvel publisher Martin] Goodman and afterwards, Stan called me in, saying, 'I really have to reject the cover, but if it were up to me, I would say go with it. But I'm told we can't do it because the figures obliterate the logo.' I said, 'Stan, when it's colored, the figures aren't going to obliterate the logo.' He said, 'Well, it's just not acceptable. You'll have to do it over or I can get someone else to do it.' I said, 'No, no, Stan, I'll do it.' I thought, they're going to kill the book in two issues, and they're worried if anyone can identify the logo because of sales! If you obliterate the logo and make it hard to read, you might actually pick up sales! That's not a thing I could argue, so I did the cover over because you can't argue past a certain line." ©1998 Marvel Entertainment.*

something to say about that.

So Roy and I went to a coffee shop nearby, and I asked him about it. He basically said that he had worked only on that one previous book, and I asked him where the story was going. He told me that Cyclops' brother was kidnapped by this guy in an Egyptian costume, and they were in a museum, and it might have something to do with blackmail; Roy wasn't altogether sure what Werner was going to do with it and what was going to happen; he didn't quite know where this was going to go. So I said, "Why don't I just wing it and find someplace for it to go; we'll take off from there."

Arlen: *You mean you didn't know where you were going?*

Neal: No. I usually hit the ground running anyway, and if you do a Marvel book, nobody hands you a plot. There was no written plot. So what you do first is what you're secure in doing, setting the scene.

I had been to the Metropolitan Museum of Art and had seen an exhibit on the Aswan High Dam that the Egyptians had moved from the Lower Nile Valley floor to the upper tier of land, so this incredible sculpture would not be destroyed. I had magazines, photographs and brochures from that and I thought, "Jesus, this is an incredible place." I said to myself, since this is a pharaoh, why don't I just go to Egypt and start my story with the X-Men trying to rescue the brother not in some museum, but in Egypt, at the Aswan High Dam?

The first thing I did was trace a photograph of the Dam to give me a solid lock into reality and I worked off of that. I try to give everything I work on a sense of authenticity so when you look at it, you believe it.

Now what was I going to do? The next thing, to make a little time for myself to start to think, let's have a fight! I'm at Marvel! Let's have a fight! The Pharaoh threatens them, and suddenly these guys in Egyptian costumes start a fight. By the time I get through this— all of the X-Men are doing something with their powers, before anything else happens. That gave me a couple of days; in that time I worked out what was going to happen for the rest of the story, and I was able to put it down and send it to Roy.

Arlen: *You were literally making it up as you were going.*

Neal: What I did was take the pieces from the previous story that didn't seem to go anywhere and just reformed them so they would go somewhere. I remember even talking to Roy, saying, "Why is this guy kidnapping Cyclops' brother?" And Roy said, "I don't think we really worked that out." Y'know, if they had cancelled that book after that issue, nobody would've ever known.

I had a second conversation with Roy and said, "Y'know, if Scott Summers has mutant abilities there's a certain logic that says his brother would have mutant abilities. Can I take that and weave that into the story?" Roy said, "Sure, go ahead."

I thought, if I suck off the power from Alex and the Living

Above: Sequence from X-Men #57. Neal said, "[This is] an experiment. I looked to see what is the greatest dimension on a comic book page that I could make somebody fall from. I realized it wasn't from the top to the bottom of the page, it was diagonally on the comic book page. I also realized that because of the way I set up the previous page, I couldn't just have the fall take place immediately on the first page. So it actually gave me the excuse to use the diagonal to make another panel precede it, where the Beast gets knocked off the window and then we use the full page to have the drop taking place, and sock your eye back up to the top of the page. If I were doing it today, I possibly would reverse this page, so I would have this last panel down in the lower right-hand corner." ©1998 Marvel Entertainment

Arlen: *So you agree to do the X-Men for Stan; then what happened?*

Neal: I was hit with a surprise: The extra thing Stan threw in was that Roy Thomas was the writer. I had no idea who Roy was; I'd never heard of him. It came to me as a surprise. I asked Stan if I could work Marvel style, and just go ahead and do the books and Roy would dialogue them. Stan said that was fine with him, except Roy was the writer and he might have

haraoh takes it, what does he do with it? What character do I make him into? I don't think I got to that problem until later in the book.

Arlen: *At what point while drawing X-Men #56 did you do the cover?*

Neal: Near the end. I didn't know where I was going with this character to be perfectly honest. I knew that I wanted him to be sucking this power off. But I still had a page or two to go before I had to figure that out. Near the end of the book I realized I could turn him into the character on the cover.

Arlen: *So you're working true Marvel style; you're telling the story and Roy's dialoguing it?*

Neal: You must understand where Roy was at this point: Roy knew the book was going to be cancelled. He really hadn't made a lot of plans as to where he was going to go with the story. Nor did he understand whatever my capabilities were or whether it would be an interesting relationship or whether I would just be doing one or two issues and that would be the end of it. It was our first date. So I suspect he really didn't put a lot of energy into what was going to happen. We were going to pull it out of the crapper or we weren't.

Arlen: *In all these issues you're just credited as artist or penciler; it doesn't say "By Roy Thomas and Neal Adams," it says "Roy Thomas, Writer" and "Neal Adams, Artist." I think this is part of the misconception that these are Roy's stories, and à la DC, you "just" drew them, yet these were your stories that Roy dialogued.*

Neal: Yes, but I must say this. It's never really arisen as a question until it's become part of some kind of history. We just did the stories. I was the storyteller but I had one of the best associates you could have.

I'm one of those lucky people who got to work with my favorite writers. At DC I got to work with Denny, and at Marvel I got to work with Roy, arguably the two best writers in comics in those days.

Arlen: *What about Stan Lee?*

Neal: I think Stan's personality was very melodramatic. Even when Stan spoke, it was quite melodramatic. Every book that Stan did was melodramatic. But there are times in comic books that you don't want to be melodramatic. There are times you want to be scientific, there are times you want to be conversational, times you want to be clever, or cute, or whatever it is. For me, I appreciate more the greater variety a writer can bring to the work, and that's what Roy brought to the work.

Roy crafted the flow of words so that they blew apart everything that had been done with group super-heroes right up to that day. There was no end to the way he would handle dialogue; the way he would approach the subject matter. When I had the Sentinels fly into the sun to destroy themselves, he basically described the sun in very dry terms, and said finally in the end that the arrival of the Sentinels would make the smallest of ripples. It was very, very beautifully and cleverly done. Stan would either say, "Well, there's no need for words on this," [laughter] or "Excelsior," or come up with a very passionate description.

Not that I want to criticize Stan, but I feel that Roy has a very fan outlook; he knows all the little things that we all know. He remembers all this crap that we all have stored away in our

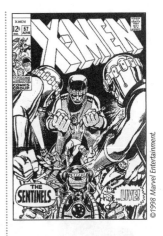

Below left: *Panel from X-Men #58, pg. 5.* **Below right:** *Neal's thumbnail of the same panel. Neal explains, "This was kind of an experimental drawing. I was looking to make an action sequence, looking to bundle up a figure and make it bulky like a block, and put everything inside of the figure. Normally if you do a blow, you have the fist or kick or whatever go outside of the figure and stretch it. I thought, 'That's the way everybody does it. I wonder if it's possible to use dimensionality?' I had the thing come toward us, and impact the blocky figure within itself, and not allow anything to come out, and still get across power. To some extent, the sketch is more successful than the finished piece. The blockiness is there more in the sketch than it is in the finished piece."*

heads, and nothing gets by him. Roy has it in him to find these things, to craft them. Roy took his craft and gave another level to understand it on. Sometimes the level was totally different than what was there, and then, almost like a whiplash, came back and succeeded in enhancing the drawing, which is very hard to do; but if you take your time and are skilled enough, you can do it—and Roy did. For me, Roy made me know that I could move forward with confidence, that I could go just as crazy as I wanted with this comic book and he'd be equal to the task. You have no idea how that buoys a partnership.

Because once Roy got to believe in me, we could sit and throw ideas back and forth. They were not necessarily story ideas but Roy, again, had this font of knowledge that he could throw at me. We would have these conversations and they never would really be involved with the story, but when I would walk away from them, I would feel that I had enough information to put these pieces together.

I drew the stories, I handed them in to Roy, and he made sure that I made notes on the sides of the pages. As he explained to me, "Unless I know what's coming up at the end of the story, I don't know how to write the stuff early on." So I would have to kind of add notes to describe what was coming up, and where we were going. I would call Roy about the rules and what he was concerned about and what he wanted to have

happen. But essentially I was doing something that I considered to be a very personal experiment in how to tell a story with this group of characters, hold them together and mold them through the story.

Arlen: *But the fact that you conceived and told these stories on paper, that is the act of "writing" that is not given enough credit. Because the Marvel Style developed the way it did, artists like you, Steve Ditko, Kirby, were not given enough credit for "writing."*

Neal: Based on what you're saying, I've spent a lot of time writing. If anybody cares to look it up, they can find the stuff I've written from *The Spectre* on down, and they can make their own judgment and decide what they want. The thing to remember is whether or not I wrote something or didn't, plotted or I didn't, I was smart enough to get the best writers to work with me. [laughs] So I must have known something. Most people who knew me knew what was going on at the time, and most people who knew the Marvel style knew what was going on.

But essentially, it was never a question; we weren't sitting down, splitting hairs about who was writing, who was drawing, who was telling a story. You have to understand that we were collaborators and the half that I didn't do, Roy did. And the half that he didn't do, I did. And that's all I care about. It was an adventure, and we were on the adventure together.

Arlen: *How did it feel while you were working Marvel style and also working at DC from traditional full script? Once you got the taste of this freedom and expansion, were you feeling like it was hard to go back to the full scripts?*

Neal: No, what was so good about it was that one was a relief from the other. One I had to follow the script, and I enjoyed the pleasure of following the script and solving those problems; the other I could just kick out and do basically whatever I wanted, within a certain range.

I think I can make an analogy that will make this more clear. The artist of a comic book is like the director of a film. There are times the director can sit down and write out the film the way he wants it, before it's filmed. If he's not a standard writer, he might then call in a writer, and say, "This is what I want it to be; can you write the script?" If the writer is a skilled writer, he can then add whatever his contribution would be to the outline the

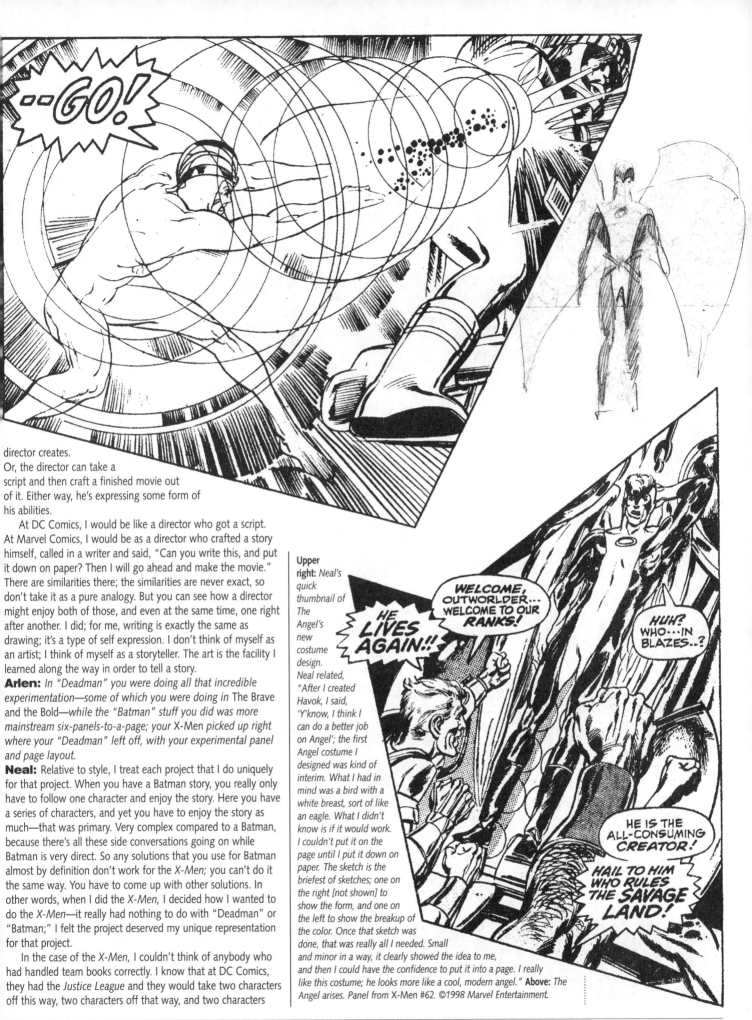

director creates.

Or, the director can take a script and then craft a finished movie out of it. Either way, he's expressing some form of his abilities.

At DC Comics, I would be like a director who got a script. At Marvel Comics, I would be as a director who crafted a story himself, called in a writer and said, "Can you write this, and put it down on paper? Then I will go ahead and make the movie." There are similarities there; the similarities are never exact, so don't take it as a pure analogy. But you can see how a director might enjoy both of those, and even at the same time, one right after another. I did; for me, writing is exactly the same as drawing; it's a type of self expression. I don't think of myself as an artist; I think of myself as a storyteller. The art is the facility I learned along the way in order to tell a story.

Arlen: In "Deadman" you were doing all that incredible experimentation—some of which you were doing in The Brave and the Bold—while the "Batman" stuff you did was more mainstream six-panels-to-a-page; your X-Men picked up right where your "Deadman" left off, with your experimental panel and page layout.

Neal: Relative to style, I treat each project that I do uniquely for that project. When you have a Batman story, you really only have to follow one character and enjoy the story. Here you have a series of characters, and yet you have to enjoy the story as much—that was primary. Very complex compared to a Batman, because there's all these side conversations going on while Batman is very direct. So any solutions that you use for Batman almost by definition don't work for the X-Men; you can't do it the same way. You have to come up with other solutions. In other words, when I did the X-Men, I decided how I wanted to do the X-Men—it really had nothing to do with "Deadman" or "Batman;" I felt the project deserved my unique representation for that project.

In the case of the X-Men, I couldn't think of anybody who had handled team books correctly. I know that at DC Comics, they had the Justice League and they would take two characters off this way, two characters off that way, and two characters

Upper right: *Neal's quick thumbnail of The Angel's new costume design. Neal related, "After I created Havok, I said, 'Y'know, I think I can do a better job on Angel'; the first Angel costume I designed was kind of interim. What I had in mind was a bird with a white breast, sort of like an eagle. What I didn't know is if it would work. I couldn't put it on the page until I put it down on paper. The sketch is the briefest of sketches; one on the right [not shown] to show the form, and one on the left to show the breakup of the color. Once that sketch was done, that was really all I needed. Small and minor in a way, it clearly showed the idea to me, and then I could have the confidence to put it into a page. I really like this costume; he looks more like a cool, modern angel."* **Above:** *The Angel arises. Panel from X-Men #62. ©1998 Marvel Entertainment.*

another way, and they'd come together at the end of the book.

Arlen: *What were they doing in the Marvel team books?*

Neal: They seemed to go in lots of different directions. Except for Jack Kirby, it didn't seem that anybody had a handle on how to do group books; how to interweave the characters so you could get through the book. *The Avengers* was an attempt to do a group book, but again, my impression of it was that it would focus on a single character. It was like the *Justice League* thing: They would focus on one group of people and then focus on another group of people. There didn't seem to be this interweaving that I feel is a good idea—to keep them moving along the same path but interweaving together. Because of that, when I got to do the *X-Men,* I really focused on interweaving

the characters. And to make it clear. You have to do things to make something like that clear.

What I did was make the world of the *X-Men* more complicated; build one thing on top of the other, integrate one thing into the other, so that after a while, you get a whole world populated by these characters, all integrated, so that you started to see a tapestry of characters, all having these different interrelationships. I don't think the *X-Men* ever should have been a story, and then a story, and then a story; it should be this tapestry that goes on.

I think that if a contribution was made it was to tell people, yeah, you can do a group book and not do it the way the *Justice League* was done, and it could be just as satisfying as doing a single character book. You just had to make that extra effort to do it and it would work. I had never really seen it done before so that was intriguing creatively.

Arlen: *In your revamping of the X-Men, you were the first to actually revamp the Marvel characters, since they had all been created rather fresh only a few years before.*

Neal: You'd have to say that nobody really creates anything new; there's very little new under the sun. We did a little analysis here at Continuity on what if Marvel were to only do one book of each of its main characters; how many titles would they have? We figured around 12—almost all created by Jack Kirby. If you go to DC and do the same thing, you'd find they have about 12 titles, all created during the Golden Age by a variety of people, including Jerry Siegel and Joe Shuster and Bob Kane, and nothing since then. If you boil it all down, it's all built on top of two solid foundations: The Golden Age of primitive, "Let's create some super-heroes. What are super-heroes? Well, we'll make it up," and then Jack Kirby creating this whole universe.

My contribution in the midst of that was to bring a bunch of that stuff back to life. I fed off of Jack's stuff and I tried to bring back a lot of the stuff that Jack started. And that's what I did. I don't think I did anything first, but I think that in some ways I did it with such surprise, and it seemed bigger than life, that it made it seem almost new and different. I was re-establishing the characters; I was introducing new characters; I was saying, "Hey, this is a good thing—let's play with it; this is something to do." I didn't like the idea that Marvel was waiting to cancel this comic book. I was trying to make this comic book come alive.

Arlen: *Critics say Jack Kirby created characters and you didn't. But your act of recreating is original in and of itself—like Green Arrow, like Batman, like Deadman. You didn't create Batman, but your recreation of Batman is just as impactful as the original. You recreated the X-Men in such a way as to give them new life.*

Neal: In a way, at DC, Batman was never my character. I kind of turned him into my character, but he was never my character. At Marvel, I felt to a certain extent that, especially with the X-Men, that enough bad had been done to the X-Men, that in a way I could recreate them and

they would become my characters. So to a certain extent, they did become my characters. Especially the new characters became my characters.

Arlen: *Like Havok, who had a revolutionary costume design. He precedes those black figures in the "Batman" story ["The Challenge of the Man-Bat", Detective Comics #400]. This delineation had not been done in comics before— there's a realism to the outfit yet it's also very surreal at the same time. What was your thought process?*

Neal: It was like a mime who moves around—you look at the silhouette of the body; you don't look at the interior of the body. It seemed to me that that would be a great idea for a costume—the idea of doing a silhouette like that and then doing the energy. So if you speculate on the idea, you can say that the costume isn't really a costume; it is a kind of energy container through which you can actually see the energy inside of his body. So many guys draw Havok with this thing on his chest and that's not the idea; you're supposed to be able to see in the middle of his chest the energy no matter where he turns.

Tom Palmer, in order to help me out and delineate the drawing, added highlights to Havok's costume. I explained to him, "Tom, I've drawn the character in such a way that you can tell what he's doing in every silhouette—you don't have to worry about it; remove the highlights." While there are positions you could put such a character in so that you would need highlights, I made it my business when I did Havok not to put the character in those positions. If you limit yourself to certain positions, you would never have a problem; the audience never loses track of it and they get it every time. That was the philosophy behind it.

Havok was certainly not a Jack Kirby-type of character; he was something new and different, and a little hipper.

Arlen: *Let's talk about Tom Palmer's inking. Palmer had just come off of a great run inking Gene Colan on* Dr. Strange *that was beautiful.*

Neal: One of the things about Gene Colan that I have always felt was that Gene never got a good inker; I guess I must have liked what Tom was doing on Gene's pencils. I think Roy offered me Tom Palmer and I must have talked to Tom on the phone. The other thing I liked was it was very clear from looking at the work and also hearing from him, that Tom was a Stan Drake fan and there was very much a Drake influence in his work. I thought, "I'm not seeing enough Stan Drake in comics these days, and if I had a Stan Drake kind of line on top of my stuff, it would definitely give it a different look"—and it did.

There are people who believe that Tom Palmer is my best inker. The thing about Tom's work is it's tremendously sincere and thorough. He never backed-off from anything that I gave him; he always went for it and, if I was vague, he cleaned it up; if I gave him something awfully hard to do, he did his best to finish it. He really, really did the kind of professional job that I respect. For me it was a wonderful job and I think he gave the whole series a classy look.

Arlen: *Even though these took place in the late '60s—you even have a character wearing a medallion and a turtleneck, which might seem dated—because of the quality of the art and the intense realism, it's not dated. The machinery, everything you used in here, still looks very fresh. It doesn't have a dated look, and I think that's just because of the quality of the realistic drawing.*

The guy in the mask! So you were for real, anyway!

More real than you dare imagine, mutant! For, I am not masked... and my name is... Sauron!!

Sauron!! He who was born that fateful day, when a frantic search became a dreaded death-struggle between primordial reptiles ...and a small, frightened boy..!*

For, during the night which followed, that boy discovered both a desperate need...and a terrifying power...in the ability to drain energy from the bodies of living things...!

Still, it was not the need for energy, but the need for wealth that drove the youth over the brink...for nothing but riches could earn the hand of the girl he loved... the girl he had saved!

And so, on this night, Karl Lykos had taken the final step...drained the mutant energy of Scott's brother Alex ...and become a careening, clawing creature of darkness...

...a creature which must have mutant energy...more mutant energy if it is to go on living...

* As dramatically depicted in our previous issue! ...Stan.

Neal: What I find that I enjoy about these books, is everything that I did, to one degree or another, was an experiment. I liked that experience. For example, here I was going to a company that was Jack Kirby-inspired. You had to have roomfuls of machinery. So of course, in my scientific-oriented world, roomfuls of machinery couldn't just be random shapes—as lovely as random shapes are. They have to make sense to me. I had to take what was done before, and make them seem real to me. So here was a wonderful experience to be able to do all that machinery that I wasn't obligated to do over at DC, and somehow make it look realistic and satisfy me that it worked.

Arlen: *One of the most fascinating of your "new" characters was Sauron; what was the genesis of that character?*

Neal: When I was doing Sauron, I thought, what I want to do really is a vampire, but a vampire that's not a vampire, that doesn't suck blood, that's not based on a bat.

Arlen: *Why were you interested in vampires to begin with?*

Neal: I think the idea of sucking something out of somebody else, to make you powerful, is a very good theme. We did it on Havok with the Pharaoh. But as a super-villain, to be tragically dependent on somebody else is a very good theme for a story. I thought, "How far away can I go from a vampire and still keep the same idea?"

So I went all the way back to pterosaurs, and used the idea of some kind of energy that's based in some kind of disease, like a blood disease, to cause this character to have to... not suck blood, which the Comics Code wouldn't have approved at that time, [laughter] but suck energy; mutant energy, to be satisfied.

Presumably, in the years after he left this cave, he absorbed energy, not realizing what would happen to him if he absorbed a lot of energy. In our book, of course, he absorbed that amount of energy which would suddenly turn him into this pterosaur-type character, which is sort of like Dracula absorbing a lot of energy and becoming a giant bat. The similarities are very obvious, though nobody's ever brought it up to me! Apparently I had gone far enough away for the analogy to no longer apply.

Arlen: *What made you bring in Ka-Zar to the strip? Were you a fan of the character?*

Neal: The thing that set me off was the death of Magneto. They had done what I consider to be some terrible things to the X-Men at Marvel; you gotta read the issues that come before this, maybe two year's worth. Magneto was essentially dead (he fell off a cliff or something), not that anybody much cared.

I tried to imagine how Magneto, after falling off that cliff, could somehow survive. Rather than being washed up on shore somewhere, it seemed to me the way he survived was using his magnetic ability to burrow his way into the earth, and drive the earth away from him while he was falling, and slowing himself down. In the end, where would that take him? It might take him into this Ka-Zar land; it's kind of a nice *segue*, and it works.

Also, I had set up a cave with Sauron that led to some prehistoric place, which either has to be explained as some incredible cave that's lost in time, or an incredible cave that leads down to the Savage Land. Well, since the Savage Land has been established, why not have it lead down to there? It'd make it much more logical that this'd be the case.

The elements started to come together, and I realized that's where I wanted Magneto to be: Down there, and since he's down there, why do I want to reveal that it's Magneto right away? Why don't I just hide it? Who would ever suspect? Since

e had never taken his helmet off, no one knew what he looked like. When I finally revealed that e was Magneto, Roy supported it with the line, "Maybe clothes do make the man," which I think as become a classic line in comics.

Arlen: *So you obviously did more than two issues of the X-Men; what happened? Did Stan say, Neal, I like your first two issues. Keep going."?*

Neal: No. They said they were going to cancel it in two issues or thereabouts. It wasn't like it was ecided and, once I started doing it, it seemed pretty much a given we were going to continue.

Arlen: *So the story grew and Roy was inspired. How did this whole thing just keep steamrolling long?*

Neal: It just kept on going, y'know? In the Marvel style, as long as you do your homework and ave respect for the work—you have to have respect for the artists and writers that have gone efore; you can't just take it and throw it out the window and say, "Now I'm gonna show every-ody." With all that, to then take it and put your stamp on it, and go and create a Havok and a auron and bring back the Sentinels if you feel like it, and go into that world of dinosaurs, it was nind-boggling to be able to do that, and I did one a month for, like, ten months, and every single ne took me further and further out. It was a tremendous experience! The *X-Men* was taking omething that practically was ready to go into the garbage can and saying, "Wait a second! Let's ust go crazy with this!"

Arlen: *You brought Professor X back from the dead in your last issue—how did you accomplish hat?*

Neal: Not only was Professor X dead, they took a year to kill him. They made sure that rofessor X was so dead that he would never come back again. It's incredible! No character in omics, that I know of, had been killed so unequivocally. Professor X got sick, got worse, got really ad, and before he died, he lost his powers slowly over a period of time, so Marvel Girl had to elp him out. Then, after a lingering loss of powers, he finally dies. He was unequivocally dead! hey buried him. How do you get out of this?

It was really a hard thing to figure out but I did. First I laid in a clue: I brought the Sentinels ack (I love the Sentinels; they were one of Jack Kirby's greatest creations), unthinking, mindless obots who could beat the sh*t out of anybody and just want to kill mutants; they were such a olid concept. And how do you deal with the Sentinels? The guy who created them was dead so I rought in his son. I thought I have to lay in a clue, so when I bring Professor X back nobody can ver go back and say, "Nah, you're cheating; you just made this up."

So the clue I laid was all these Sentinels had captured all these mutants that have appeared reviously in the *X-Men* and put them in these tubes. And then, when the good guys win and the entinels get sent into the sun, all the mutants are let out of their tubes, except for one. And if you ook at that panel, all the mutants that appeared in the *X-Men* up to that point are there except or one. That one is The Changeling and the reason that he's not there is because he is dead in the lace of Professor X.

The story we did later (which I did with Denny O'Neil's dialogue) was this: Professor X has ound that there is an invasion that is coming from outer space and he has to protect the Earth. Only he can do it by moving the minds of everybody on Earth essentially. He can't do that without raining himself to do it. In order to train, he has to disappear for a year.

While he is pondering his problem, the Changeling visits him and says, "Look, Professor X: I now you think I'm a rat, but I just found out from the doctor that I'm going to die, and I'd really ke to make up for all the sh*t I've done all of my life."

Professor X says, "That's really good but what can I o?" The Changeling says, "Can you think of nything I can do to redeem myself?"

And suddenly Professor X says, "There is omething you can do: You can pose as ne." But The Changeling doesn't have he professor's powers and abilities. "But if Marvel Girl helps you," Prof xplains, "your powers and bilities will seem as though ou're me in decline and dying. I an go away and train to save the arth. She's going to be the only erson who knows this, and terrible s it is that you're going to die, ou will participate in saving the arth." And that's how we rought Professor X back.

YOUR EYES! YOUR EYES...!!

Arlen: *Did you know X-Men #65 would be your last ssue? Why did Denny O'Neil script that issue?*

TOM PALMER: The Art of Inking Neal Adams

Considered by many to be Neal Adams' greatest inker, Tom Palmer was interviewed via telephone by Arlen Schumer on November 12, 1998. Following is a composite statement.

I remember the first time I had seen Neal's work—Roy Thomas had bought a half-page of "Deadman" [*Strange Adventures* #212, pg. 8] and had it framed, and it was quite different from other comic book artwork that I had seen up to that point.

I was young, but I had seen Kirby's stuff, I had seen Buscema's stuff, it was all very good—I mean, just fantastic— but there was something else, there was a maturity to Neal's work that was so much different. He should've been older than all of them to have that maturity; it was natural, almost a gift.

By going to Johnstone & Cushing—that was the spot line-drawing studio of the city—and meeting Lou Fine, and Stan Drake, and all those people, Neal, at a very young age, was brought up the right way, he got the right input, and it served him well. Even without that schooling, he still would've achieved 95% of what he has. It is irrefutable when you see Neal's work, that he is an exception. And he was then.

The first issue of the *X-Men* is what I remember the most vividly. The first three to five pages, with the Sphinx in the background, the rocket car—I would just sit back and marvel at these beautiful renderings. In Neal's second issue with the shot of King Faisal, where he's pointing—you can see Neal used a photo—I was just taken aback by the render-ing of that pencil drawing. It's easy for me to describe from my eyes or my memory of that time, but to sit there and look at that stuff—I don't mean to make this sound too much like a religious experience, but it was whatever would be close to that.

I'm sure other pencils have impressed me over the years when they've come across my drawing board, but maybe because Neal's were the first, they left such an impression that it still lingers today. It's like your first love—you always remember it. It really caught me between the eyes, the way it caught everyone else who saw those books, and it affected me the same way. Neal influenced a whole generation of artists—myself included—just as Milton Caniff did years prior.

Neal's ability—it was not so much the realism as the way he handled the pencil. I saw him penciling once, and he didn't hold it as if you were writing with it, nor did he take the broad side of a pencil, so everything had a broad side. He held it at an angle, he turned it—not in a very mannered way, but as if he were sketching something, so the lines were not stroked as evenly-thick pencil strokes. I remember the line getting thinner and thicker, this pencil line that kind of undulated between the two; it ebbed and flowed as if it was a drawing done as a rendering.

I've seen people try to pencil like Neal, but you could tell immediately it's all bogus, because they never had that line. He was the natural, he was the one they were all trying

continued on the next page

continued from the previous page

to copy. Other guys today try to pencil as if they were going to ink it, or they're trying to set it up for the inker. Neal penciled for penciling; the inking became another art that you brought to it. And I think that's what I was challenged by. He didn't put a line down that you just filled in. You didn't trace it—you had to bring something to it.

As far as inking over Neal, you realized you couldn't do it all in pen, nor could you do it just in brush—you needed both if you wanted to pick up what he was doing when he inked. He would probably render in pen, and then go back with a brush, and hit some of the heavier lines, and also some of the shadowing. You could tell, because it was a real juicy black line; it kind of forced me to match it.

I remember taking a day or more to ink one page—not every page, but certain pages. It wasn't something that you knocked out in a couple of days. Not that I was doing that with *Dr. Strange* with Gene Colan, and that's what I had gained some favor for. Maybe it was because of my youth, or the "golly-gee-whiz" point of my life—but I slowed down and put every ounce of whatever skill I had at that moment. I may have worked too hard on those *X-Men* issues—I may have stiffened up some of the fluid lines that Neal had done.

In a way, I thought that the *Avengers* was my better work. When we got into that series, I think I had matured a little bit, plus I felt a little bit more at ease with Neal's pencils. And I think Neal was more comfortable going in, too. Over the years I've come to realize, working with different people, you can tell when someone is interested or excited about the story. The *Avengers* was something Neal was really looking forward to.

The first pages of that "Fantastic Voyage" issue [#93] just blew me away. Neal just amazed me with what was going on. There were some shots in there, some of the scenes—it was all so original. I remember spending a lot of time on that issue—and coloring it also. I don't know if we traded coloring assignments, but I remember Neal felt confident about that. There was a satisfaction, I think, for both of us—that issue may have been the high point of it all. At least I remember being very proud it.

It's something I've always remembered; I kind of hold it up as the criteria to whatever I'm working on. Not to say no one ever reached that criteria, but in a different way. I've worked with some talented people, and I have respect for anybody in the business. Working with Neal was always fun, I always looked forward to it, and it helped me grow a little bit; each job helped me grow because it challenged me.

And I know it did Roy; Roy was just on a cloud—he just loved it. Whether it was the writer, the colorist, the inker, or even the letterer, working on Neal's stuff brought out the best in anyone.

Tom Palmer

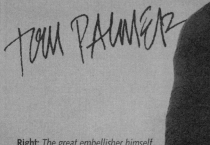

Right: *The great embellisher himself, Tom Palmer. Much thanks to Tom for the last-minute interview and supplying us with this promotional shot by Janis.*

Neal: I was very unhappy with that, and I love Denny O'Neil's stuff, but I did not consider Denny O'Neil to be the dialoguer of the *X-Men*. I knew who the dialoguer was; it was Roy. He didn't dialogue this. It was just handed over to Denny, and Denny did it. It was not a happy situation for me. It was sufficiently unhappy for me to say if Marvel wasn't going to cancel the book, maybe I'd have gone to something else anyway.

I loved Denny O'Neil on *Batman* and *GL/GA*, but Roy and I had established a professional relationship and I didn't find anybody else's work to be as satisfactory. Also, Denny, as talented as he is, was thrown into the middle of this, a story that I had essentially started months before; suddenly, it's thrown into Denny's hands, and he has to come up with dialogue. I didn't think that Denny was the greatest dialoguer in the world for a Marvel book. I thought Roy was, but as far as structuring a story is concerned, I thought Denny was a tremendous story structurer, and he knows how a beginning and a middle and an end work. I don't know that I could look at the qualities of Roy and Denny and pick my favorite, because they're so different from one another.

One of the things Roy did almost better than anybody at Marvel is give the right amount of copy to tell the story and not clutter up the art. It doesn't matter how good the copy is if you're covering too much important art, because then you're hurting the enjoyment of the story. Imagine me coming from DC Comics, where I am designing a page and the placement of the balloons, and at Marvel turning over that job to somebody else and have that person have the same or similar sensibilities—to be able to place the balloons in such a way that they read in order, they tell the story, and they don't get in the way of the art.

Arlen: *Your last issue is also infamous for the blatantly obvious changes to the monster on the cover and interior art; what happened?*

Neal: I had decided, because not too much was going on in the story, that I wanted to have some watchdog in this alien ship. So I created a watchdog that would prowl through this ship, and handed in my pages for dialogue and inking.

I came into Marvel one day, and Marie Severin—one of the nicest people in the world, the salt of the earth, kind to everybody—came running up to me and said something like, "It wasn't me, Neal. Stan made me do it!" I said, "What are you talking about, Marie?" I couldn't figure out what she was talking about until I got up front, and she was all over herself with embarrassment about the whole thing. I couldn't for the life of me understand until I saw the inked pages.

Sure enough, patches had been put in over my spaceship watchdog, who went around on all fours, and it had been turned into a man-like creature walking around on his hands and knees, which seems a little strange for a biped to have to do. But since the ceiling was there, he couldn't stand up.

Arlen: *Palmer inked it, and no records of the earlier pencils exist?*

Neal: None that I know of. And the patches aren't even Palmer's inking. It was one of those decisions that I think Stan made quickly. I have a feeling communications broke down somehow. Maybe Stan made some offhand comment that it shouldn't be a dog-like creature, it should be something else; maybe that's all he said. However it happened, I have no idea. It certainly isn't something anybody would consciously want to do. That was such an atrocious change that I don't think I'll ever forgive Stan for that one. I guess I probably should've found the page and ripped that off and gone into Stan and said, "Stan, this is ridiculous!" [laughter] But I didn't; I must've been tired that day.

Arlen: *Why were so many of your covers at Marvel retouched, unlike your DC's?*

Neal: At Marvel, what would happen was, I'd get a layout or I'd submit a layout which would get rejected, and then I'd get a layout which I would have to pencil to. Then they would be dissatisfied with the pencils, and they'd work on it. It would just become a mishmash.

Every time I tried to hand in something original, it was looked upon as being different and weird, where at DC I was expected to come up with original and fantastic covers.

Stan Lee was always suspicious that I did better covers for DC than I did for Marvel; if he were to say it to my face, I'd have to say, "Gee, Stan, maybe that's because you keep changing my covers." If they left them alone, the covers would be fine. They felt they had a point of view, but almost consistently with Marvel Comics, the insides were better than the covers; where at DC Comics, the covers were better than the insides. [laughs]

Below: *The notorious watchdog sequence from Neal's final issue, X-Men #65. On the left is the thumbnail drawing, possibly the only remaining evidence of Neal's monster design. And, on the right, the final version as redrawn by the Marvel Bullpen under Stan Lee's instruction. ©1998 Marvel Entertainment.*

©1998 Marvel Entertainment.

Center image: *Silent sequence from X-Men #62. Neal says, "This is one of those mime situations here. Nothing about this needed dialogue. This is not to say Stan would have put dialogue in there, but I think probably he would have. [laughter] Roy obviously looked at it and thought, 'Gee, I don't need to do it, and I don't have to do it, and I don't want to do it,' and he made the choice not to do it. What a great choice! A writer is marked by what he doesn't do as well as what he does do. I believe he was right in this case. It flows so well and goes right into the next sequence, it doesn't even occur to you that there was no dialogue there. " ©1998 Marvel Entertainment.*

Above and below: A great Kirby splash page from Thor #160. *Note Neal's take on a seminal Kirby character in the splash page from* Thor #180, *shown below. ©1998 Marvel Entertainment.*

Arlen: *Why do you think that was?*

Neal: At DC Comics, there must've been six or seven editors, and they would discuss and have conversations with the production room, and there was more discussion, and they would discuss the insides as well as the covers.

At Marvel, all there was was one guy, Stan. He had to go and take the stuff to his bosses, so basically he took the covers; I don't think he ever took the insides. There was never a discussion about the insides. Essentially, the books were just pushed through as quickly as possible and printed.

Arlen: *You seem to have had an insider's view of the workings at Marvel; did you do any work in the office?*

Neal: I did spend some time up at Marvel in order to get to know the guys. I'd go and spend the day—maybe once a week. I did a little drawing up there; I'd do a cover. I like to hang out in the office to get to know who the people are, who is there, and what they do. Mostly I would work at home but I spent enough time up there to meet Herb [Trimpe] and all of those guys. John Romita was there. Marie. Frank Giacoia was in and out. They had a very small office. They had cubicles with five people in one! A true bullpen.

Arlen: *Was it a happy place?*

Neal: Oh yeah. They had the thought in mind that they were kicking in DC Comics' butt and it was almost a miracle that this was happening. They almost couldn't believe it that out of this little place, they were kicking butt.

Arlen: *Was there any reaction at DC to the fact you were working for Marvel?*

Neal: They tried to pile more work on me. DC had the good sense not to fight something that was already done, but I was the first to go in and say, "I just want you to know that I've picked up some work at Marvel; it's not going to interfere with my work here." I didn't turn down more work. I've never done anything in my life, to the best of my knowledge, to hurt anybody or hurt a business relationship.

When you come right down to it, I wanted both DC and Marvel to do well, and continue to feel that way.

Arlen: *Why was* X-Men *cancelled?*

Neal: I can't even tell you why it was cancelled in the end. To be perfectly honest, I knew that it didn't have the greatest sales figures in the world, but certainly it was bringing a lot of attention to Marvel.

One of the things I and others observed was that after the *X-Men* was cancelled, almost every new artist and writer that came to Marvel wanted to do the *X-Men* because of those ten issues. And as the book was passed to each in his turn, they all do Sauron, they all do the Sentinels, they all do Havok, they all go into the Savage Land, they all do Magneto.

Arlen: *The impact of this work incubated for x-number of years amongst the Dave Cockrums, Len Weins, John Byrnes, the second wave that came in after you, paying homage to your X-Men. This is the foundation of the new X-Men, which in turn became the foundation of the modern Marvel Comics.*

Neal: It didn't necessarily just stay with comic books; there were movies and television shows and all kinds of stuff.

I don't want to blow my own horn, but the first year of the *X-Men* animated series had an awful lot of our stuff. Although they weren't direct adaptations, they were generally those series of stories—or relating to those series of stories that first year.

Is there a direct link between the *X-Men* and a lot of creation between a lot of people? I think there is, and perhaps it's speaking arrogantly to say this, but I've been told by enough people that the connection is direct. I've spoken to people at conventions; I've spoken to producers and directors and writers who said that series of *X-Men* books opened their eyes to what comic books could do; "You inspired me to do this, to think differently, to expect more. Not to think that this is trash, but that this is an art form."

So I think that those *X-Men*—I'm not saying they're the epitome of what comic books could be, but they certainly, for me, made and continue to make very entertaining comic books to read.

Arlen: *After your run on the* X-Men *ended, you did a couple of issues of* Thor *immediately following Kirby's departure from Marvel; how did that come about?*

Neal: I don't know quite when it was. Stan asked me, "What would you like to do next?" I said, "Y'know, Stan, I would love to work on a *Thor* with you." He said, "Really?" But I don't think Stan trusted me because he had seen my layouts on *X-Men.* He said, "I don't really like those." And I said, "Stan, don't worry. I'll do a Marvel layout. It'll be just fine. In fact, I'll do a 'Marvel Comic Book.'" My intention with these two *Thors* was to do 'Marvel Comic Books,' so Marvel that you couldn't tell if John Buscema or John Romita did it. You'd flip through th ages and go, "Yeah, it's a Marvel comic book."

So then Stan asks, "What do you think you want to do?" I said, "Well, do you have a story?" Stan would go, "What do you think you want to do?" (rather than say no). So I said, "I'd like to change identities between Thor and Loki." He said, "Oh, that's fine. Go ahead and do that." I said, "I'd like to do that for two issues. Is that okay?" He said, "Yeah, sure, sure. Go ahead and do it." So that was pretty much the story conference.

Stan dialogued the first book and after about 20 pages he comes up to me and says, "Y'know, I thought I was going to have a hard time with your stuff, but it was as easy to work on as anything I've ever worked on. I had a great time."

But Stan had a certain attitude about things. For example, I had left a space for copy [pg. 17 of *Thor* #180, second panel] because something had to be told there. So I left a space and wrote "Space for copy." Stan got so upset with me that he called me and said, "Why did you do that? Don't ever do that again! Don't leave space for copy! You don't make decisions where the copy goes!" He got all bent out of shape, but I thought it seemed to need some room for copy that I didn't want to draw all over. "Well, I can take care of that! Don't ever do that again." Awright, Stan! I had forced him to write where I thought he needed to write, and he sure didn't like that.

Arlen: *Roy says you had a different style with him; he says you'd leave blank spaces and leave a note, "Write pretty, Roy."*

Neal: [laughs] Yes. And he would! He never let me down. Maybe that's where I got spoiled.

Arlen: *So Thor #180 and 181 was as long as your collaboration with Stan lasted?*

Neal: I got my chance to work with Stan and do a couple of Marvel comic books. I was a happy puppy; I got to work with Stan, ya know.

Arlen: *I believe whenever you tackled specifically Kirby's characters, your realistic style was at odds with them—which, in the case of Thor, made him look like a hippy with a helmet on.*

Neal: I didn't think I was trying to do Kirby, but Buscema! Doing Thor was like me getting to be John Buscema for a book. This is the Thor of Buscema, Romita, and everybody else—sometimes Kirby. I didn't think of myself as able to do Kirby; all I cared about was doing Marvel. *Thor* was me doing a Marvel comic, not a Jack Kirby comic because I never tried to do a Jack Kirby comic—and I don't think anybody can.

Is it a success? I think I successfully put together a book in the Marvel Style. I think this looks as much like a Marvel comic as any one either done by Kirby, Buscema, or Romita with Sinnott's inking over it. Does it look like a Marvel comic? It certainly doesn't look like a Neal Adams comic. It looks like my pencils, but in an awful lot of panels it really just looks like Sinnott. And wasn't, in a way, Sinnott indicative of Marvel, and wasn't this perfect to give to Sinnott?

Arlen: *Did you ask for him?*

Neal: Oh yeah, absolutely. I didn't want to do it unless I got Sinnott's inking. I love Sinnott's inks! On anybody!

Arlen: *After your stint on* Thor, *you followed in the departing steps of Kirby again when you took over the 10-page "Inhumans" strip running in* Amazing Adventures *with issue #5; how did that come about?*

Neal: Roy was pretty much the person who would suck me into whatever was going on; he gave me a call and said, "So what are you going to do next?" Well, whaddaya got? "How would you feel about doing the Inhumans for a while?" I had made an agreement with Stan to do the *Avengers,* but I didn't mind doing "The Inhumans." I liked the Inhumans and said, "Sure, why not?"

It seemed to me the Inhumans were right on, whereas the X-Men deserved to be remade. I didn't think that the Inhumans deserved to be remade; Jack had done them so well.

Arlen: *Again, as in Thor, your realistic style clashed with Kirby's—your Black Bolt lacked Kirby's majestic, godlike feeling—it's a guy in a slick black outfit with black boots. While your style worked for realistic characters, I don't know if it necessarily worked for these godlike characters.*

Neal: I knew my style wasn't Jack Kirby's style but I felt the group wasn't a Jack Kirby series as much as it was just a big group of people—so I tried to do the best "Jack Kirby Inhumans" in my style that I could. I tried to do a more realistic version of the Inhumans, but they are so incredible, so fantastic, there's so many of them, they all have super-powers; in a way it was too much for a realistic artist. I think I would have to dedicate a chunk of my life to do it right, and I wasn't going to do that.

I think I did a good job on "The Inhumans," a professional job. In the end, I felt if I had full books to do, I could have paid more attention to it. I thought maybe I could make a contribution, to in effect reenter the Inhumans back into the Marvel Universe, where they were missing from. People didn't really make much of these stories; I liked them more than other people did. I added more of a melodramatic spiel to it—it wasn't as big

Left: Two great comic artists give us similar interpretations of the ruler of the Inhumans, Black Bolt. Top is Jack Kirby's version from the cover of Marvelmania Magazine #1, and bottom is Neal and Tom's splash page image from Amazing Adventures #5. ©1998 Marvel Entertainment.

a story as Jack would do. I also had been forced now to plant them in my psyche.

Arlen: *Did you feel like you told the story you wanted to tell with "The Inhumans"?*

Neal: I started to, but in a particular issue, Roy gave the dialoguing over to Gerry Conway. I was already a little upset with Roy at that time for not having dialogued the last issue of *X-Men*. I really agreed only to do this if Roy was going to dialogue it. Suddenly I had a writer who I didn't agree to work with. I didn't feel his writing matched in tone my artwork; I don't think that our styles matched. That's not even a criticism of Gerry; I just didn't like the idea that another writer entered into this without my agreement.

It's odd; it shows you the difference between the companies. At DC Comics, the script, whether I did it or someone else did it, becomes established. You know who the writer is ahead of time, and generally you know who the inker is. There's no opportunity for any kind of change, because the script is done already. So you're pretty secure. It was very odd for me at Marvel, to feel secure in that I knew who my dialoguer was, and then it just got pulled out from under me.

Some people might think, after these two experiences with Denny O'Neil [on *X-Men*] and Gerry Conway on "The Inhumans," that if I was smart I would've seen the writing on the wall, and seen that this perhaps was going to turn into a disaster. I guess I didn't see it; I guess I thought these were anomalies and this wasn't going to continue.

But certain things happened to make me think that, for whatever reason, however it worked out, I really wasn't going to end up completing much of the projects I began at Marvel. I was going to start them, but I wasn't going to get to finish them. That's sort of the way it worked out. You can see that the forces were marshalling. Somehow this wasn't turning out to be the wonderful experience I hoped it would be at the beginning.

Arlen: *Your first inker was Palmer. Did he get yanked off the book?*

Neal: I don't know what he was doing. He was certainly busy.

Arlen: *How did John Verpoorten come to ink you next?*

Neal: I was asked if I minded having John Verpoorten ink my stuff. It's funny; there were people who said, "You really don't

want John Verpoorten." At one point, I thought, "Y'know, I really want that Marvel kind of thing."

Arlen: *What is the "Marvel kind of thing"?*

Neal: That big, thick line; very little sensitivity but lots of brushstrokes.

Arlen: *That sounds so contradictory to wanting a good artistic product.*

Neal: For "The Inhumans," I felt I'd like to see that heavy brushstyle. I felt this was good for this strip. I had a very strong feeling about Marvel and, in some ways, John was the heart of what was going on at Marvel at the time, and it really pleased me to have him work on my stuff and do what he considered to be a sincere job. I had personal conversations with John, in which he told me how much he enjoyed inking my work. That pleased me.

Arlen: *But what did you think of his inking?*

Neal: He tried to do a good job. I realized he wasn't Tom Palmer, but Tom was Tom and John was John. There were other people who inked better than John, like Frank Giacoia (who inked better than a lot of guys), but Frank has a certain coldness; I wouldn't have used him on something like the Inhumans because it was very melodramatic. It wasn't tragic, so it needed to have a little bit of warmth. No matter what you say about John Verpoorten's work, a certain warmth came through—I can feel it. There was a caring and I liked that.

I felt very good about what was going on. I had been inked by a lot of people, and I had my choices. When I did the *GL/GA* stories, I invited different artists to ink the stuff, including Giacoia, Bernie Wrightson, Dan Adkins, people with very different styles from one another, to see how they would look on my stuff. Some would disappoint me, some would surprise me. If I took a negative attitude about anybody I invited to work on my stuff, I think it probably would've shown in my pencils. I didn't ever want my pencils to be the thing people were criticizing, so penciled the same quality for each inker, in the hopes it would bring something out of him that he hadn't experienced before. What you look for in an inker is a good percentage; you don't look for what you would call perfection. You look for a sufficient number of areas where you agree, to make the work strong.

Arlen: *Who was your favorite inker?*

Neal: People are constantly asking me that. Of course, sitting in the middle, I would have to say my favorite inker is me, because that's the way I would do it. If I'm inking my own story, I consider it a discipline. If other people ink my story, I consider it an experiment. I like to experiment and I enjoy myself when I do it. I am always interested in change and in doing something new, something challenging, something different, and (to a small extent) something unexpected.

Arlen: *After your four-issue "Inhumans" stint, you finally went on to* The Avengers. *Because it came right on the heels of you finishing "The Inhumans," was this a case of, "Okay, I'm done with 'The Inhumans'; whaddaya got?" Or does it go back to the deal you made with Stan that you would do* The Avengers *after the X-Men?*

Neal: I don't know what happened, to be perfectly honest. I don't remember the conversation, but I wouldn't be surprised if Roy didn't come to me one day and say, "Remember what you told Stan; you said you'd do it." So many elements were mixed into this thing; my relationship with Roy was mixed in.

When Roy had Gerry Conway dialogue the second-to-last episode of "The Inhumans," I did not perceive that as a good experience; I was not happy with it. So I told Roy I would do *The Avengers* only if he dialogued it; I didn't want anybody else working on them. My deal at Marvel was I got to work with Roy; I was much more comfortable with that.

Arlen: *Was Thomas writing and planting the seeds for the Kree-Skrull War before you came along?.*

Neal: My memory—and I'm sure it's different from Roy's—says Roy had wanted to do this "Kree-Skrull War," and in the issues he'd done—I think it was two issues before mine—the Kree and the Skrulls ended up going to war in some far-off galaxy, but he didn't know for sure if wanted to continue on that plotline, or go on to something else. He asked me how I felt about it. I thought, gee, a war, I'd love to do that. So once again, it was one of those "Where do you want to start?" things; I said, "Let me go and think about it."

Here we had these Kree and these Skrulls off in this intergalactic battle, and here we were on Earth, and there were no Skrulls... wait... no, there were these cows. Mr. Fantastic had somehow convinced these Skrulls that they were cows. I thought, at some point they've got to come out of this. They're cows! They're eating grass, y'know? I think they'll probably come out of it just before they get to the slaughterhouse, [laughter] where they stick that trip hammer to their heads. It's got to occur to them they're smarter than cows, and maybe they don't want to go in there. But given all that, I thought, "I like those cows; that's a great image. We ought to use that. We ought to have the cows do something." That was the basis of the way I wanted to start reintroducing the subject. I indicated that I'd like the first story

Above: *Note Neal's suggestion for story title in the bottom margin of this, the pencils from the splash page to Avengers #93. Neal says, "The first title that I designed was 'Three Cows Shot Me Down,' and Roy changed the title to 'This Beachhead Earth,' which I feel is an inferior title, and I argued with Roy about it. But there wasn't a moment that Roy didn't get the inference of 'Three Cows Shot Me Down.' He asked me about my title, I said, 'Roy, maybe you don't remember…' Roy said, 'You mean the three cows in Fantastic Four, right? The Skrulls?' He got it right away! He didn't miss a beat but he decided to do the other title. I think 'Three Cows Shot Me Down' would've been the greatest title… maybe the best title in comics outside of "But Bork Can Hurt You." [laughter] I'm sure that Roy wrote that title for Stan; it was definitely a Stan Lee title." ©1998 Marvel Entertainment.*

title to be "Three Cows Shot Me Down." Heh.

The concept of the War had to be left in the background, because there was no rationale. We were talking about having a Kree-Skrull War, but how this would affect the Earth, and what would be the significance, sort of got left in the gray area later

concepts, design work, all kinds of stuff. This was going to be a big deal to me, a very big deal. And it would include the Inhumans. I would make it, I thought, a validation of… well… never mind.

The first issue was 34 pages, a big issue. Normal stories were about 22 pages in those days; that's another half a book. I must admit, the idea of doing that many pages was daunting. But I was ready to do it, prepared to do it, and doing it.

Arlen: *Then how did the John Buscema chapter insert in your second issue come about?*

Neal: It came as a surprise to me; I did not ask for it and I did not feel that it was necessary. I thought, well, we're off to a shaky situation here, but maybe if Roy's concerned about the amount of pages I can get out, I'll just make sure the next one is in quicker, so I did it.

I talked to Roy about the story as it progressed, and we were collaborating more on the individual book storylines at that point, but only I knew where it was going. I suggested to Roy

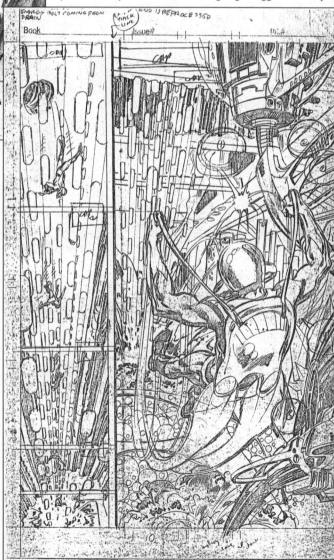

into the progress. I realized at some point I wanted to bring Rick Jones into it for a very significant reason, and I didn't quite know how, and I wanted to go into this other dimension where Annihilus is, and somehow utilize that to create the introduction of Earth into the War.

Arlen: *Your first* Avengers *is memorable especially for the opening sequence, in which Ant-Man travels microscopically within the Vision's body; were you influenced by the comparable 1967 sci-fi movie* Fantastic Voyage?

Neal: I saw it later actually, but I knew what it was about. I had a lot of characters to deal with, and I thought, well, let's start off small—we started off incredibly small, inside the Vision's body—and grow out from there. What a nice thing to do, to go all the way down, and start to move outward and outward into the universe.

I decided I was gonna kick ass on this thing. I was going to dedicate myself to this Kree-Skrull War with these Marvel heroes, and just really go crazy with it. My view of the War was very expansive—I was headed toward a 10- to 30-issue miniseries of an intergalactic war between the Kree and the Skrulls using the Earth as a battlefield. I thought, this is gonna be one hell of a series. Inside my head, I was going to do the best series I had ever done. I was determined to do that; throw in new ideas and

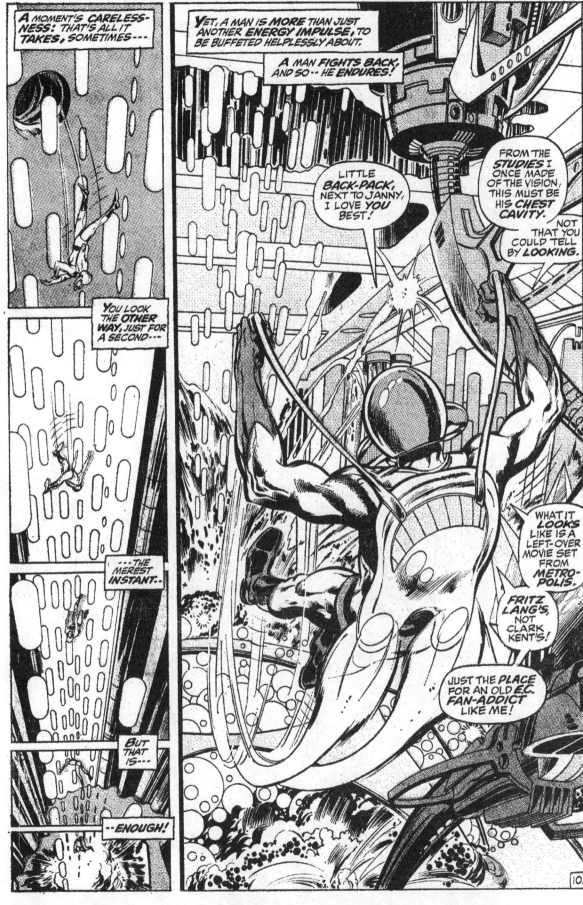

e idea of doing the next
story from the point of view of
classroom in the future,
elling the story of how the
ree-Skrull War got to Earth.
oy kind of questioned that;
e thought it really sort of says
at we survived. I thought it
eally wasn't that important at
at point; we know we're
onna survive. I thought it
ould be an interesting way
 do the story; he didn't like
 very much. I said I thought I
ould make it work; he said
kay, go ahead.

I went home thinking, "Let
e think about this. Let me try
ut some different ideas."
fter a few days I realized it
ally wasn't going to work, so
 probably wasn't such a great
ea. Not only that, Roy didn't
e it that much. So I just
ent back to straight
arrative. I had some other
ork I had to get done at the
me, and it took me a good
eek to get back to it. When I
ot back to it, I was fine. I had
ages, I brought them in.

Well, apparently Roy had
ecided he was going to go
ith a different way to tell the
ory, and he had sent the
ory to John Buscema! It
rew me for a loop. As much
 I had been surprised by
me of his decisions in the
ast, this one just got me, and
thought, "This is not good." I
was just taken aback by the
hole thing. There was
owhere for me to go, so I
asically bowed out. I knew it
as not going to be what I
anted it to be, go where I
anted it to go, or be as big
 I wanted it to be.

I really had the sense that I
ould do something bigger,
mething really, really big
ith Marvel's key characters. If
ou look at the four issues of
e *Avengers* and see all the
uff that's in there, you really
t the sense of a tremendous
amework building in a short
ount of time; it's an awful
t of work. Consider the work
at went into the layout of every page; look at the detail in
ese pages. I turned out an awful lot of pages for this with a
emendous amount of sincerity, and I felt it was going to turn
 to something. I was building a kind of Marvel *New Gods*.

I felt I was embarked on an epic and I discovered the
support for doing an epic wasn't there, in general. The Marvel
"machine" was not prepared to get behind something as big as
this, for whatever reason. It just didn't feel to me that the team

THE ANDROMEDA SWARM!

Right: *Main image of Triton from the splash page of Avengers # 95. Neal says, "I'm totally taken by how many people think this is one of the best panels in comics. They're constantly bringing it up to me; they think that it has an influence on The Savage Dragon."*

was operating as a team; I didn't feel it was together. When something isn't working, it starts to unwind. If you have a certain dedication to something, it gets worn away and there's no use or reason to try to save it.

Arlen: *Did you ever have the desire to finish the War your way?*

Neal: Not really… Marvel folks have asked, but not in a way that seemed workable. It would be very nice to finish it, but I don't think I'll ever get to finish it—and I don't necessarily think that anybody could finish it as well as I could (sort of how I feel about "Deadman").

Arlen: *How is it that you came to do "The War of the Worlds" [Amazing Adventures #16] in 1973, a year after your Avengers run was over? Were you a fan of the movie?*

Neal: I didn't even like it; it was just a good idea. There was potentially a better story.

This character—later named Killraven—was travelling through his world, collecting things. And he would trade things in order to create and put together technology to fight the aliens. He carried his backpack all of the time and everywhere he went, he would trade off bits of technology for other bits until he could bring the world together, by putting the pieces back together again, to fight the aliens because civilization was being destroyed.

I was putting together a science-fiction concept. This guy, in effect, was the son of Doc Savage—not *the* Doc Savage, but a Doc Savage-like character—his genes are imprinted with the desire to put the world back together again. It can only be done genetically; nobody can naturally do that. That is the advantage of this character. This guy is motivated by instincts he doesn't even understand; he's doing these things, but he doesn't know why he's doing

them—he's very good at doing them because he's the son of Doc Savage and he's a wonderful genetically-created person.

And he has a twin brother—only he's working for the aliens. To me, that's a set-up for a really good series.

That concept got lost and, in place of it, was an adventure that didn't actually have progression. My tendency is to move things from point one to point two and on, and when that's not happening, then people jump in and out. It was like what was happening with "Deadman"; they would have writers come in and do a story that would have nothing to do with the last story or anything to do with the next story, so there was no progression. Here, this story was started by Roy and I, and midpoint into it, it was turned over to Gerry Conway again, so I backed out of it. This sounds like a criticism of Gerry again, but it's really not. It has to do with working with the people and having a relationship, and trusting that it's going to go forward and be positive, and it just seemed to crumble. I felt betrayed.

Arlen: *Then you went on to do* Conan, *in issue #37, in 1974.*

Neal: I started a *Conan* and they told me it was going to be a 32-page story—it was going to be a big book. I had decided to ink it, especially because I knew it was going to be a large book.

I had done the first three pages and then was told that this was going to be a 19-page book! I couldn't go back and redo those three pages, but I had to grab the remaining story and [straining groan] compress it to remaining 16 pages. It was in fact a 34-page book jammed down into 19 pages. I refused in my own mind to limit the events of the book to shorten the story.

For that reason, the book to a certain degree suffers because of the smallness of the size. There are a lot of little drawings in there; they're like Sunday pages—13 panels to a page! So if you

Right: *Thumbnail to a page from Conan #37. Neal says, "A very interesting thing is the musculature of Conan compared to Juma; Conan looks like he was put together like bricks and Juma looks rounded and bulgy; to me, doing the two kinds of musculatures next to one another was a fun way to show different kinds of anatomy."*

Below: *Conan pencil drawing that first appeared in Doug Murray's The Art of Neal Adams with the word balloon, "Back to work, Adams!" Conan ©1998 Conan Properties.*

read that book, you almost have to mentally enlarge the pages to get the impact of the story, and there are pages that have a tremendous amount of lettering on them, simply because that much story had to be told.

A publisher in France loved the book so much, they gave me the opportunity to re-layout the same

pages, allowed me to make diagrams of new layouts, and expanded the book to something near a 34-page book again, so you got to see some of these panels reproduced bigger.

Arlen: *What was your general artistic approach to Conan?*

Neal: I was first struck by Frazetta's Conan, who was put together like bricks, and I relate to that character to a certain extent. I'm one of the few people who really relate to John Buscema's Conan. Ideally, I see this character in my head very much the way I think Robert E. Howard saw him, certainly the way Frazetta saw him, maybe a little taller.

Arlen: *What happened with* Savage Sword of Conan #14, *"Shadows of Zamboula"? Though credited as "Art by Neal Adams and the Tribe," the pages begin with what looks like your tight pencils inked by you first, then the Tribe, but by the end, only your basic layouts are detectable.*

Neal: After I had done the first Conan story, I told Roy I need to be able to have the time to do this. We agreed it wasn't going to be put on the schedule until I finished the whole job (for the first time in my career). I laid out a book completely, so that I would be satisfied with the whole project. These layouts were done so tight that you could almost ink them.

How this unsched-

uled book got put on the schedule, and what happened subsequently to that book, is something that I don't really know or understand and consider a real tragedy in my professional life. Roy suddenly sent copies of my layouts to the Philippines, where they were finished up by Filipino artists who obviously didn't understand them.

To make matters worse, I had been drawn voluntarily into a battle to find some justice for Jerry Siegel and Joe Shuster (the creators of Superman), and it absorbed much of my time. While I was out of the studio, someone from Marvel came to the studio and asked for the pages and in a spirit of cooperation they were handed over. When I returned to the studio, I was dumb-founded, but I was too involved with "The Boys" to respond to this unfortunate event. The rest is… as they say….

There are a certain number of pages here that I carried through exactly the way I wanted to see them done. In the panels that I inked, you can clearly see the sincerity of what I was doing. To have this thing treated this way was just so very, very disheartening. To have layouts taken away and done by other people is not something that should be done to anybody, for any reason. I really wanted to finish this story; I felt this would be my definitive Conan story. The thumbnails alone show the potential of that story. You can see the devotion I gave to these.

That was pretty much the last positive project I did for Marvel at that time.

Arlen: *Why was that?*

Neal: My association with Marvel Comics had always been good, but in this time frame, with *Conan, The Avengers*, it was happening again and again and again. There was never a point—even though they were doing these things and making me crazy—where they would approach me with something and I would say, "No, I won't do it. I'm pissed off at you guys." I just couldn't find it in myself to be mad at a company because things weren't going my way.

But when individual projects would go sour on me, it's tough to drop them. It's tough to drop a project like the Kree-Skrull War; it's tough to back away from Conan when I thought I was doing the best Conan around; it's tough to leave "War of the Worlds"—jeez, I was off to a run on that baby!

So my contribution to Marvel was done in spite of the fact the logs were rotting under my feet.

Arlen: *At about the same time your color comics work for Marvel waned, the black-&-white magazine line was starting up, and you painted most of their debut covers.*

Neal: For whatever reason, they felt I had the drawing power to launch these magazines, and I never said no to them when they asked. I painted covers for them and never backed away from them. Not only did these paintings allow me to flex my muscles a little bit, but they also represented no pressure. I was doing an awful lot of *Deadly Hands of Kung Fu* covers, but as they went on,

Right: Two of the same panel from Neal's pencils to "Shadows Over Zamboula." Apparently Neal was working on the job, simultaneously inking it while members of "The Tribe" (Tony DeZuniga's Filipino crew) were also inking from photocopies of Neal's layouts under instructions from Marvel—unbeknownst to Neal. The top panel is as inked by Neal and below by the Tribe. This represents the last major job Neal did for the House of Ideas and appeared in Savage Sword of Conan #14. ©1998 Marvel. Conan ©1998 Conan Properties.

SNAP SNAP

YOU KILLED HER, YOU STINKING SCUM! YOU KILLED HER!

NO! -- SHE FELL -- I HAD **NOTHING** TO DO --

GUARD! STOP HIM -- SLAY HIM, QUICKLY

YOUR **GUARDS** WILL NOT STOP ME, DAMNED ONE!

NO -- ALL THEY GIVE ARE **MORE TARGETS** TO VENT MY RAGE -- TO LET MY HATE FOR YOU GROW --

-- STRONGER ... MORE POWERFUL ...

-- UNTIL I CAN GET TO YOU --

AND THEN NOTHING -- NOTHING SHALL STOP ME FROM KILLING YOU --

GET BACK -- YOU'RE MAD -- MAD!!

they got to be more like drawings that were colored rather than paintings.

What's interesting is that Marvel had a sister company that hired illustrators all the time, but they never seemed to go to these artists to do these illustrations.

Arlen: *The one interior black-&-white illustration job you did do was a beauty, Dracula Lives #2.*

Neal: One of the reasons I was so happy with this Dracula story was because I got Marv Wolfman, and I got to do this

really nice black-&-white Dracula. I think I got a full script for it and, if I didn't, I got a full outline from Wolfman—it's his story.

Arlen: *Did you want to do more Dracula stories—or more black-&-white stories of any genre?*

Neal: Not really. The truth is, for me to a job like this and to do it in wash, and to finish and ink it, was a loss. I don't know what I was paid for these pages but it couldn't have been much. And for me to sit down, lay it out, pencil it, have it lettered and brought back to me, ink it, and then to lay washes on it, is an awful lot of work. Normally, you'd give this to an inker and you take your check and go away. This is a lot of work for one guy to do, so I really did it for Marv and to do a Marvel Dracula story, and once done I'd better get back to doing easier-to-do stories so I can make a living.

Arlen: *It's as if you never said no to anything they asked you, at DC and Marvel.*

Neal: I never did.

Arlen: *You took on as much work as you could do without saying no, satisfying everybody.*

Neal: I did it to the best of my ability every time.

Arlen: *Around this time you developed the inking crew, "The Crusty Bunkers." How did they originate?*

Neal: When artists used to come in the field, they came directly to either my room or the coffee room at DC Comics. There was hardly any way to get up to Marvel (except through Herb Trimpe and some nice people up there), but at DC they came through me or the coffee room. Guys would hang out late at night bullsh*tting, and I'd say, "I just pulled in this Howie Chaykin job from the editor but can't do it all, so everybody else is going to have to do some of it; so start inking!"

The money was split up by me; it was my decision. It was sort of like the guy who splits up the money when you get the check after dinner; usually the guy who's in charge of it loses the most. [laughter] "There's got to be a tip, right? Am I paying for everything?" You don't want to be that guy; you want to be the

...uy who throws in 10 bucks.

Arlen: *Your work at Marvel, like your DC work, petered out at the same time as you formed Continuity Associates and did more advertising work; is that an accurate assessment?*

Neal: I don't even know how this evolutionary process took place, but you have to remember that at both Marvel and DC, a tremendous amount of my time was reluctantly spent making changes in the field. I helped to change the code. I helped to satisfy and settle disputes between the two publishers. There was a certain part of me that said,

"There's more to do," and another part that said, "I think I can affect more change from the outside than the inside." I just simply didn't accept work that I had no time to do.

Everybody was getting confident that the comic book business was really good, and getting better. When enough people got in and DC and Marvel welcomed new people, we opened Continuity on 49th Street. Then people came up to Continuity, and that became the new meeting place to get together and hang out.

It was time for me to back away and make my own way,

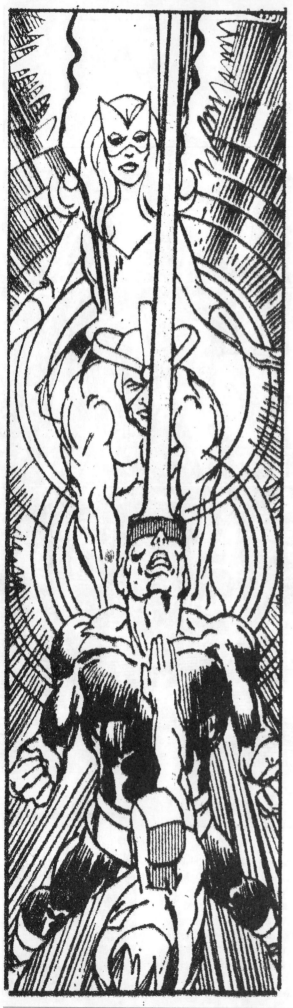

and to be a little less dependent on DC and Marvel. But there was never a moment when I ever said to DC or Marvel, "I'm going to say no to you. If you have a job and want me to do it (and I'm in a position to do it and handle the deadlines), I will do it." But as time went by, I could handle the deadlines less and less because I had more work on the outside.

It was time for a change and I was moving on.

Arlen: *If there's a legacy to the Marvel years, I would say that, like Steranko's, yours was a small body of work that had tremendous impact. Your* X-Men *and* Avengers, *in particular, seem to have had an enormous influence on artists and writers years later. Your stories—and of cours your artwork— have stood the test of time.*

Neal: Think of what Marvel is: Jack Kirby and the generation that followed. I jumped into the X-Men and jumped into the *Avengers*; the X-Men have had the longest and most powerful impact.

When Marvel Comics wanted to go into black-&-white magazines with color covers, I started that off.

With Barry Smith, I was given a shot at doing Conan; I don't know how much impact my Conan has had, but I did a really, really nice Conan.

The other work I did for Marvel was more spotted: The Dracula story, these other stories, but they all added a kind of sparkle to each area. Whether it was covers or *Crazy* magazine, all those things served to be a positive experience… or maybe it's just me.

On a personal level, I liked everybody at Marvel, I liked the people who ran Marvel. I never had a difficult time with Marvel; my relationships were always good. People were loving the wor that was happening, and were just as disappointed as I was when things didn't continue.

When the work was good, it was great, and the work changed the face of Marvel to that extent—look at the X-Men. It was in the X-Men that the impact was felt because it was a continuity that lasted a good ten issues, and you can look at the run of it and say, this is what the X-Men can become.

The Avengers was a small, bright star that dimmed and went away; it's too bad. I can't have a conversation with Marvel fans without the subject of finishing the Kree-Skrull War coming up. Why didn't I finish it… or will I ever finish it? It rankles me, because I know it would've been great, and I know they were disappointed, and I feel like I let them down. If I had finished that War, there's a suspicion that *The Avengers* could have been as strong and as powerful as the X-Men. I know it could have and would have been.

I feel in some ways that my work with Marvel is sort of an unfinished symphony that everybody would have enjoyed had we finished it.

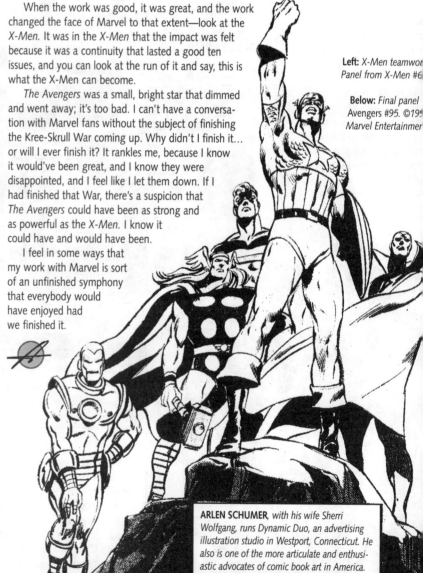

Left: *X-Men teamwor Panel from X-Men #6*

Below: *Final panel Avengers #95. ©19 Marvel Entertainmer*

ARLEN SCHUMER, *with his wife Sherri Wolfgang, runs Dynamic Duo, an advertising illustration studio in Westport, Connecticut. He also is one of the more articulate and enthusiastic advocates of comic book art in America.*

Neal Adams' Marvel Work: A Checklist

by David Berkebile

This checklist was initially based on the work of David Berkebile and augmented with reference to Doug Murray's *The Neal Adams Index* (1974), Greg Theakston's *The Neal Adams Treasury* (1976), research by Rick Norwood, Alex G. Malloy's *Comic Book Artists* (1993), and Bob Overstreet's *Comic Book Price Guide* (1997). Much thanks to Richard Martines, Roy Thomas, Albert Moy, Steve Alhquist and Atomic Comics, and (of course) Neal Adams and Continuity Associates for their assistance. (Heaven forbid there are any mistakes, but just in case: Any additions and/or corrections are welcome. Please write in care of the editor.)

MAGAZINE	ISSUE #/DATE		SERIES	STORY TITLE	PAGES	INKER/COMMENTS
Amazing Adventures	#5	Mar 1971	Inhumans	"My Brother's Keeper"	10 pgs.	Tom Palmer
	#6	May 1971	Inhumans	"Hell on Earth" + cover (Tom Palmer inks)	10 pgs.	John Verpoorten
	#7	July 1971	Inhumans	"An Evening's Wait for Death" + cover	10 pgs.	John Verpoorten
	#8	Sept 1971	Inhumans	"An Hour of Thunder" + cover	10 pgs.	John Verpoorten
	#18	May 1973	War of the Worlds	"The War of the Worlds"[1]	10 pgs.	Frank Chiaramonte
Astonishing Tales	#12	Jun 1972	Ka-Zar	"The Man-Thing"[2]	7 pgs.	pencils only [with John Romita Sr. modifications]
Avengers	#92	Oct 1971		Cover		
	#93	Nov 1971		"This Beachhead Earth" + cover	34 pgs.	Tom Palmer [with John Romita Sr. modifications]
	#94	Dec 1971		"More Than Inhuman" + cover	13 pgs.	Tom Palmer
	#95	Jan 1972		"Something Inhuman This Way Comes"	21 pgs.	Tom Palmer
	#96	Feb 1972		"The Andromeda Swarm" + cover	21 pgs.	Tom Palmer
Bizarre Adventures	#28	Oct 1981	Shadowhunter	"Shadowhunter"	20 pgs.	Penciled w/Larry Hama[3]
Conan the Barbarian	#37	Apr 1974		"The Curse of the Golden Skull" + cover	19 pgs.	Neal Adams
	#44	Nov 1974		"Of Flame and the Fiend" (JB)	18 pgs.	Inks only w/ Crusty Bunkers
	#45	Dec 1974		"The Last Ballad of Laza-Lanti" (JB)	18 pgs.	Inks only w/ Crusty Bunkers. Cover inks (GK).
	#116	Nov 1980		"Crawler in the Mist" (JB)	22 pgs.	Inks only
Conan Annual	#3	1977	King Kull	(r) "Beast from the Abyss" (HC)	9 pgs.	Inks only w/Crusty Bunkers
Conan Saga	#8	Dec 1987		(r) "Curse of the Golden Skull" (CTB #37)	19 pgs.	Neal Adams
	#10	Feb 1988		(r) "Night of the Dark God" (GK) (ST #4)	21 pgs.	Inks only w/ "Diverse Hands"
	#17	Sept 1988		(r) "Shadows in Zamboula" (SSOC #14)	39 pgs.	"The Tribe" (DeZuniga & Co.)
	#31	Nov 1989	Red Sonja	(r) "Red Sonja" (EM) (SSOC #1)	10 pgs.	Inks only w/ Chua (Chan)
Crazy	#1	Dec 1972		"The Great American Dream" (as model)	3 pgs.	Appears in photo fumetti story

Crazy (cont.)	#2	Feb 1973		"McClown"	5 pgs.	Neal Adams
				"Live and Let Spy" (JB)	8 pgs.	Inks only w/Crusty Bunkers
	#61	?		(r)?		
	#94	?		(r)?		
Crazy Super Special	#1	?		(r)?		
Deadly Hands of Kung Fu	#1	Apr 1974	Bruce Lee	Cover		
			Sons of the Tiger	"The Sons of the Tiger" (DG)	15 pgs.	Inks only w/Dick Giordano
	#2	Jun 1974	Shang-Chi	Cover		
	#3	Aug 1974	Bruce Lee	Cover		
	#4	Sep 1974		Cover		
	#11	Apr 1975		Cover		
	#12	May 1975	Roger Moore	Cover		
	#14	Jul 1975	Bruce Lee	Cover		
	#17	Oct 1976	Bruce Lee	Cover		
Deadly Hands of Kung Fu Special Album	#1	Sum1974	Iron Fist	"Master Plan of Fu Manchu" Chap. 1 (FM)	10 pgs.	Inks only w/Crusty Bunkers
Dracula Lives	#2	1973	Dracula	"That Dracula May Live Again"	13 pgs.	Neal Adams
	#3	Oct 1973	Solomon Kane	"Castle of the Undead" (AW)	12 pgs.	Inks only w/Crusty Bunkers
	#10	Jan 1975	Lilith	"The Blood Book" (BB)	16 pgs.	Inks only w/Crusty Bunkers
Dracula Lives Annual	#1		Dracula	(r)"That Dracula May Live Again" (DL#2)	13 pgs.	Neal Adams
			Solomon Kane	(r)"Castle of the Undead" (AW) (DL#3)	12 pgs.	Inks only w/Crusty Bunkers
Epic Illustrated	#6	Jun 1981		Cover		
	#7	Aug 1981		"Holocaust"[4]	16 pgs.	
Fear	#11	Dec 1972	Man-Thing	Cover		
Giant-Size X-Men	#2	Nov 1975		(r)"The Sentinels Live" + cover (XM #57)	15 pgs.	Tom Palmer
				(r) "Mission Murder" (XM #58)	20 pgs.	Tom Palmer
Haunt of Horror	#4	Nov 1974	Devil-Hunter	Pin-up	2 pgs.	Pencils only
Iron Man	#72	Jan 1975		"Convention of Fear"[5] (GT)	17 pgs.	partial inks on 2 panels, pg. 14
Journey Into Mystery	#2	Dec 1972		"Yours Truly, Jack the Ripper" (GK)	10 pgs.	Inks only w/Ralph Reese
The Kree/Skrull War Starring The Avengers	#1	Sep 1983		(r) "This Beachhead Earth" (A #93) + cov (r)	34 pgs.	Tom Palmer
				(r) "More Than Inhuman" (A #94) + cov (r)	13 pgs.	Tom Palmer
	#2	Oct 1983		(r) "Something Inhuman…" (A #95)	21 pgs.	Tom Palmer
				(r) "The Andromeda Swarm" (A #96) +cov(r)	21 pgs.	Tom Palmer
Kull and the Barbarians	#1	May 1975		Four illustrations	2 pgs.	Pencils only
	#2	Jul 1975	Solomon Kane	"The Hills of the Dead" (AW)	10 pgs.	Inks only w/Terry Austin
	#3	Sep 1975	Solomon Kane	"Into the Silent City" (AW)	13 pgs.	Inks only w/Pablo Marcos
Legion of Monsters	#1	Sep 1975		Cover		
Marvel Feature	#1	Nov 1975	Red Sonja	(r) "Red Sonja" (EM) (SSOC #1)	10 pgs.	Inks only w/,Chua (Chan)
Marvel Premiere	#10	Sep 1973	Dr. Strange	"Finally, Shuma-Gorath" (FB)	19 pgs.	Inks only w/Crusty Bunkers
	#12	Nov 1973	Dr. Strange	"Portal to the Past" (FB)	19 pgs.	Inks only w/Crusty Bunkers
	#13	Jan 1974	Dr. Strange	"Time Doom" (FB)	19 pgs.	Inks only w/Crusty Bunkers
Marvel Preview	#1	1975	Man-Gods	Cover		
				"Good Lord" (DC)	10 pgs.	Inks only w/Crusty Bunkers
	#20	Win 1980	Bizarre Adventures	(r) "Good Lord" (DC) (Marvel Preview #1)	10 pgs.	Inks only w/Crusty Bunkers
Marvel Spotlight	#1	Nov 1971	Red Wolf	Cover		
	#2	Feb 1972	Werewolf by Night	Cover[6]		
Marvel Treasury	#6	1975	Dr. Strange	(r) "Finally, Shuma-Gorath" (FB)	19 pgs.	Inks only w/Crusty Bunkers
	#15	1977	Conan	(r) "Night of the Dark God" (GK) (ST #4)	21 pgs.	Inks only w/Marcos & Colletta(?)
Masters of Terror	#1	Jul 1975		(r) "One Hungers" (TOS #2)	7 pgs.	Dan Adkins
Monsters Unleashed	#3	Nov 1973	Man-Thing	Cover		
				"Birthright" (GK)	13 pgs.	Inks only w/Crusty Bunkers
	#8	Aug 1974		(r) "One Hungers" (TOS #2)	7 pgs.	Dan Adkins
Power Man	#31	May 1976		"Over the Years They Murdered the Stars"	17 pgs.	Inks only w/Crusty Bunkers

Title	Issue	Date	Character	Story	Pages	Credits
Savage Sword of Conan	#1	Aug 1974	Red Sonja	"Red Sonja" (EM)	10 pgs.	Inks only w/Chua (Chan)
	#2	Oct 1974	Blackmark	? + cover	10 pgs.	Inks only
	#3	Dec 1974	King Kull	"Beast from the Abyss" (HC)	9 pgs.	Inks only w/Crusty Bunkers
			Blackmark	? (GK)	? pgs.	Inks only
	#4	Feb 1975	Blackmark	? (GK)	? pgs.	Inks only
	#14	Sep 1976	Conan	"Shadows in Zamboula"	39 pgs.	"The Tribe" (DeZuniga & Co.)
	#60	Jan 1981		Storyboards	20 pgs.	Pencils only
	#83	Dec 1982	Red Sonja	(r) "Red Sonja" (EM) (SSOC #1)	10 pgs.	Inks only w/ Chua (Chan)
Savage Tales	#4	May 1974	Conan	"Night of the Dark God" (GK) + cover	21 pgs.	Inks only w/"Diverse Hands"
	#5	Jul 1974	Conan/Ka-Zar	Cover		
	#6	Sept 1974	Ka-Zar	Cover		
	#7	Nov 1974	Ka-Zar	"The Dream Temple of Candu Ra" (JB)	16 pgs.	Inks only w/Crusty Bunkers
	#10	May 1975	Ka-Zar	"Requiem for a Haunted Man" (RH)	20 pgs.	Inks only w/Crusty Bunkers
Thor	#179	Aug 1970		Cover (heavily altered by Bullpen)		
	#180	Sept 1970		"When Gods Go Mad"	20 pgs.	Joe Sinnott
	#181	Oct 1970		"One God Must Fall"	20 pgs.	Joe Sinnott
Tomb of Dracula	#1	Apr 1972		Cover		
	#4	Sep 1972		Cover[7]		
	#6	Jan 1973		Cover		
Tower of Shadows	#2	Nov 1969		"One Hungers"	7 pgs.	Dan Adkins
Unknown Worlds of Science Fiction	#1	Jan 1975		(r) "A View from Without"[8]	8 pgs.	Neal Adams
Werewolf by Night(?)	#?	1998		Cover (see pg. 3 of this issue of CBA)		
X-Men	#56	May 1969		"What Is the Power?" + cover	15 pgs.	Tom Palmer
	#57	June 1969		"The Sentinels Live" + cover	15 pgs.	Tom Palmer
	#58	Jul 1969		"Mission Murder" + cover	20 pgs.	Tom Palmer
	#59	Aug 1969		"Do or Die, Baby" + cover	20 pgs.	Tom Palmer
	#60	Sep 1969		"In the Shadow of Sauron" + cover	20 pgs.	Tom Palmer
	#61	Oct 1969		"Monsters Also Weep" + cover	20 pgs.	Tom Palmer
	#62[9]	Nov 1969		"Strangers in a Savage Land" + cover	20 pgs.	Tom Palmer
	#63	Dec 1969		"War in the World Below" + cover	20 pgs.	Tom Palmer
	#65	Feb 1970		"Before I'd be Slave"[10]	20 pgs.	Tom Palmer
X-Men Classics	#1	Dec 1983		(r) "The Sentinels Live" (XM #57)	15 pgs.	Tom Palmer
				(r) "Mission Murder" (XM #58)	20 pgs.	Tom Palmer
				(r) "Do or Die, Baby" (XM #59 partial)	9 pgs.	Tom Palmer
	#2	Jan 1984		(r) "Do or Die, Baby" (XM #59 partial)	11 pgs.	Tom Palmer
				(r) "In the Shadow of Sauron" (XM #60)	20 pgs.	Tom Palmer
				(r) "Monsters Also Weep" (XM #61 partial)	14 pgs.	Tom Palmer
	#3	Feb 1984		(r) "Monsters Also Weep" (XM #61 partial)	6 pgs.	Tom Palmer
				(r) "Strangers in a Savage Land" (XM #62)	20 pgs.	Tom Palmer
				(r) "War in the World Below" (XM #63)	20 pgs.	Tom Palmer
X-Men Visionaries 2 The Neal Adams Collection		1996		Cover[11]		
				(r) "What Is the Power?" (XM #56)	15 pgs.	Tom Palmer
				(r) "The Sentinels Live" (XM #57)	15 pgs.	Tom Palmer
				(r) "Mission Murder" (XM #58)	20 pgs.	Tom Palmer
				(r) "Do or Die, Baby" (XM #59)	20 pgs.	Tom Palmer
				(r) "In the Shadow of Sauron" (XM #60)	20 pgs.	Tom Palmer
				(r) "Monsters Also Weep" (XM #61)	20 pgs.	Tom Palmer
				(r) "Strangers in a Savage Land" (XM #62)	20 pgs.	Tom Palmer
				(r) "War in the World Below" (XM #63)	20 pgs.	Tom Palmer
				(r) "Before I'd be Slave" (XM #65)	20 pgs.	Tom Palmer
X-Men/WildC.A.T.S.: The Silver Age		1997		Cover		

FOOTNOTES:
[1] Adams penciled pages 1-9 and 11; other pages are said by Adams to have been completed
[2] Originally intended for publication in the cancelled *Savage Tales* #2, penciled piece with some faces erased and redrawn by Marvel Bullpen
[3] Inks by Adams, Dick Giordano, Terry Austin, and Dennis Francis
[4] Originally conceived as a record cover project with Eric Burden (formerly of The Animals)
[5] Otherwise inked by Vince Colletta, Adams partially inked two panels—only the face of a character he identified as Continuity associate Steve Mitchell
[6] Heavily reworked by Bullpen; Adams said the only thing of his remaining is werewolf vignette
[7] Heavily reworked by Bullpen; Adams said only figures of his remaining are the victim couple
[8] Reprinted from *Phase* #1
[9] Watchdog character redrawn by Marie Severin as humanoid
[10] Facsimile edition published in the early '90s
[11] Cover art drastically changed from submitted piece; see cover to *CBA* #3 and pg. 2 for details

KEY:	
AW Alan Weiss	FM Frank McLaughlin
BB Bob Brown	GK Gil Kane
DC Dave Cockrum	GT George Tuska
DG Dick Giordano	HC Howard Chaykin
EM Esteban Morato	JB John Buscema
FB Frank Brunner	RH Russ Heath

AH SOME CLEAR SPACE

NOW --NOW I STAND AND FIGHT

①

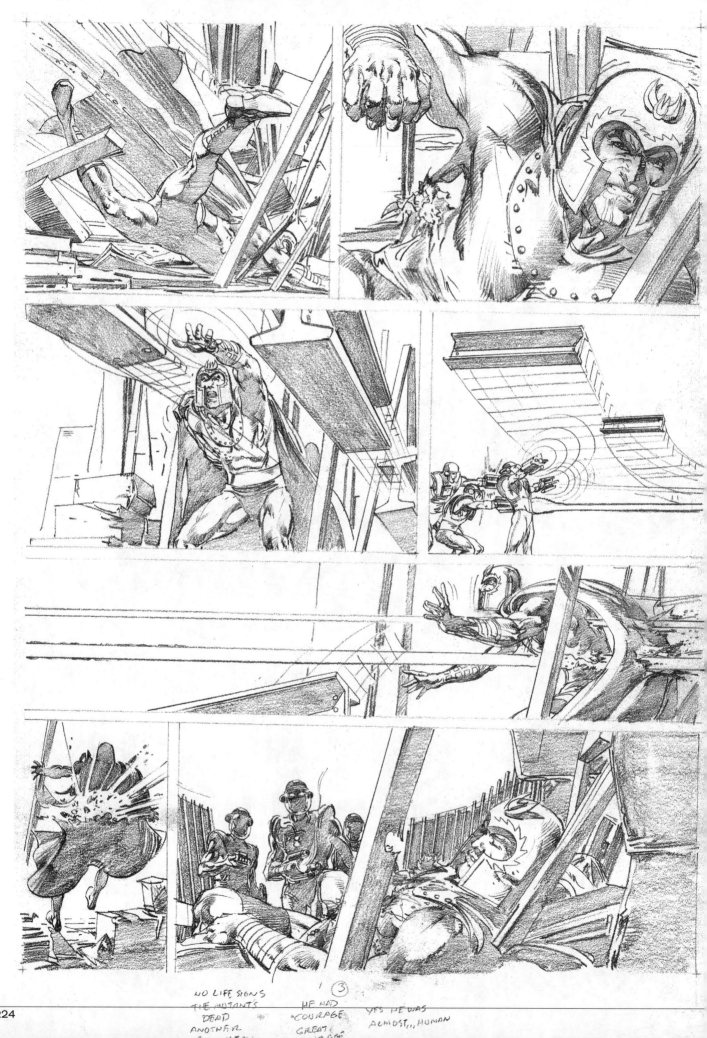

NO LIFE SIGNS
THE MUTANTS
DEAD
ANOTHER

HE HAD
*COURAGE
GREAT

YES HE WAS
ALMOST... HUMAN

③

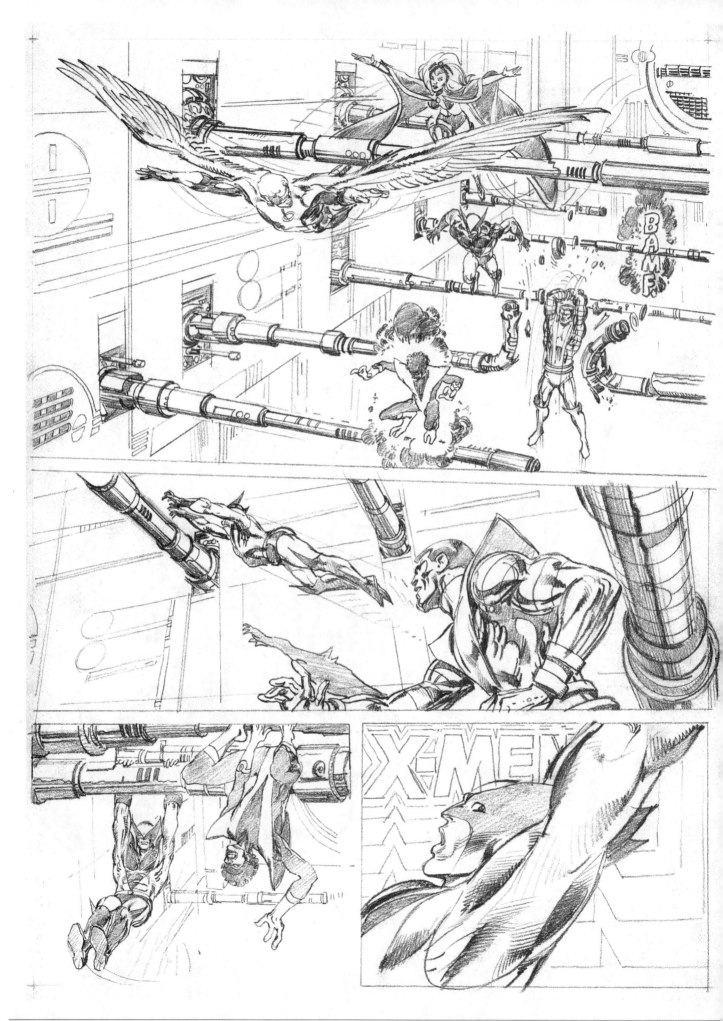